CONSUMER GENETIC TECHNOLOGIES

For the average person, genetic testing has two very different faces. The rise of genetic testing is often promoted as the democratization of genetics by enabling individuals to gain insights into their unique makeup. At the same time, many have raised concerns that genetic testing and sequencing reveal intensely personal and private information. As these technologies become increasingly available as consumer products, the ethical, legal, and regulatory challenges presented by genomics are ever looming. Assembling multidisciplinary experts, this volume evaluates the different models used to deliver consumer genetics and considers a number of key questions: How should we mediate privacy and other ethical concerns around genetic databases? Does aggregating data from genetic testing turn people into products by commercializing their data? How might this data reduce or exacerbate existing healthcare disparities? Contributing authors also provide guidance on protecting consumer privacy and safety while promoting innovation.

I. Glenn Cohen is the James A. Attwood and Leslie Williams Professor of Law at Harvard Law School. He is one of the world's leading experts on the intersection of bioethics and the law, as well as health law. He is the author of more than 150 articles in venues like the *New England Journal of Medicine*, *JAMA*, *Science* and the *Harvard Law Review*, and the author, editor, or co-editor of 15 books. He has appeared on or been covered by media outlets such as PBS, NPR, ABC, CNN, MSNBC, the *New York Times*, and the *Boston Globe*. Professor Cohen has also been a Radcliffe Institute and Hastings Center Fellow.

Nita A. Farahany is Distinguished Professor of Law and Philosophy at Duke University. She is a widely published scholar on the ethical, legal, and social implications of the biosciences and emerging technologies, and a frequent commentator at international conferences including the Aspen Ideas Festival, TED, and the World Economic Forum.

Henry T. Greely is the Deane F. and Kate Edelman Johnson Professor of Law at Stanford University where he specializes in ethical, legal, and social issues arising from the biosciences. He is the author of *The End of Sex and the Future of Human Reproduction* (2016) and *CRISPR People: The Science and Ethics of Editing Humans* (2021).

Carmel Shachar is the Executive Director of the Petrie-Flom Center at Harvard Law School. Her work focuses on access to care and digital health. She is the co-editor of several other volumes including *Transparency in Health Care* and *Disability, Law, Health, and Bioethics*.

Consumer Genetic Technologies

ETHICAL AND LEGAL CONSIDERATIONS

Edited by

I. GLENN COHEN

Harvard Law School

NITA A. FARAHANY

Duke University School of Law

HENRY T. GREELY

Stanford Law School

CARMEL SHACHAR

Harvard Law School

CAMBRIDGE
UNIVERSITY PRESS

CAMBRIDGE
UNIVERSITY PRESS

University Printing House, Cambridge CB2 8BS, United Kingdom

One Liberty Plaza, 20th Floor, New York, NY 10006, USA

477 Williamstown Road, Port Melbourne, VIC 3207, Australia

314–321, 3rd Floor, Plot 3, Splendor Forum, Jasola District Centre, New Delhi – 110025, India

103 Penang Road, #05–06/07, Visioncrest Commercial, Singapore 238467

Cambridge University Press is part of the University of Cambridge.

It furthers the University's mission by disseminating knowledge in the pursuit of education, learning, and research at the highest international levels of excellence.

www.cambridge.org
Information on this title: www.cambridge.org/9781108836616
DOI: 10.1017/9781108874106

First published 2021

A catalogue record for this publication is available from the British Library.

ISBN 978-1-108-83661-6 Hardback
ISBN 978-1-108-81267-2 Paperback

Contents

Contributors

Kif Augustine-Adams, Brigham Young University Law School

Mark Barnes, Ropes & Gray LLP

Benjamin E. Berkman, Department of Bioethics, National Institutes of Health

Ellen W. Clayton, Vanderbilt University Medical Center and University

I. Glenn Cohen, Harvard Law School

Ronald A. Conlon, Case Western Reserve University School of Medicine

Jorge L. Contreras, S. J. Quinney College of Law, University of Utah

Bryan Cosca, Veritas Genetics

Ryan Durigan, Veritas Genetics

Barbara J. Evans, Colleges of Law and Engineering, University of Florida

Nita A. Farahany, Duke University School of Law

Doug Flood, Veritas Genetics

Birgit Funke, Veritas Genetics

Henry T. Greely, Stanford Law School

Christi J. Guerrini, Baylor College of Medicine

James W. Hazel, Vanderbilt University Medical Center

Yaniv Heled, Georgia State University College of Law

Rebecca Hodges, Veritas Genetics

Leila Jamal, Department of Bioethics, National Institutes of Health

Jonathan Kahn, Northeastern University School of Law; Department of Biology in the College of Science, Northeastern University

Emily Largent, Perelman School of Medicine, University of Pennsylvania; Penn Law

Magalie Leduc, Veritas Genetics

Gary E. Marchant, Sandra Day O'Connor College of Law, Arizona State University

Laurie McCright, Veritas Genetics

Maxwell Mehlman, Case Western Reserve University School of Law; Case Western Reserve University School of Medicine

Seema Mohapatra, Indiana University Robert H. McKinney School of Law

Kenneth Offit, Memorial Sloan Kettering Cancer Center

Anya E. R. Prince, University of Iowa College of Law

Emily Qian, Veritas Genetics

Natalie Ram, Francis King Carey School of Law, University of Maryland

Vardit Ravitsky, School of Public Health, University of Montreal

Jessica L. Roberts, University of Houston Law Center

Will Schupmann, Department of Bioethics, National Institutes of Health

Scott J. Schweikart, American Medical Association

Carmel Shachar, Harvard Law School

Catherine M. Sharkey, New York University School of Law

Jacob S. Sherkow, University of Illinois College of Law

Kayte Spector-Bagdady, University of Michigan Medical School

Melissa Uveges, Harvard Medical School

Liza Vertinsky, Emory University School of Law

Michael F. Walsh, Memorial Sloan Kettering Cancer Center

Susan M. Wolf, University of Minnesota Law School and Medical School

Xiaohan Wu, University of California, Berkeley, School of Law

Patricia J. Zettler, The Ohio State University Moritz College of Law

Acknowledgments

A book like this is the result of the hard work of many. We thank our student line editors, Margaret Mattes, Matt Morris, MacKenzie Arnold, Taylor Custer, and Sunnie Yi Ning, for their meticulous work. We are also grateful to Cristine Hutchison-Jones for her administrative support in putting on the conference that gave rise to this book as well as her and Laura Chong's hard work shepherding all the many pieces of this manuscript. We gratefully acknowledge the Petrie-Flom Center for Health Law Policy, Biotechnology, and Bioethics at Harvard Law School, with support from the Oswald DeN. Cammann Fund, for conference sponsorship. We also thank the American Academy of Arts and Sciences for hosting a pre-conference dinner for all our contributors, facilitating discussion and collaboration between our authors. Finally, of course, we thank the contributors for their thoughtful and important scholarly contributions.

Introduction

Carmel Shachar, I. Glenn Cohen, Nita A. Farahany, and Henry T. Greely

For the average person genetic testing has two very different faces: the rise of genetic testing is promoted as the democratization of genetics by enabling individuals to gain new insights into their unique makeup. At the same time, many regard genetic testing and sequencing as revealing something intensely personal and private about themselves. Genetic testing raises legal and ethical questions that loom ever larger, especially as genetic testing is becoming more commonplace, affordable, and comprehensive. Already in 2018 the global genetic testing and consumer/wellness genomics market was valued at $3.4 billion, with market analysts in 2019 predicting that it will double in value by 2025.[1]

Direct-to-Consumer (DTC) genetic testing kits have become an essential part of this global industry. Because DTC bypasses traditional trusted health care intermediaries, DTC genomics also raises the legal and ethical stakes. For example, what standards should the regulators like the Food and Drug Administration apply in determining which tests are available to consumers? How should we mediate privacy and other ethical concerns around genetic databases, especially considering that genetic information is at once both individualistic and communal? In an age where serial killers are caught because their relatives chose to submit DNA to a consumer genealogy database, is genetic privacy for individuals really possible?

This volume will consider the ethical, legal, and regulatory challenges presented as genomics become commonplace, easily available consumer products. The most significant focus of the volume is to articulate regulatory solutions to protecting consumer safety and privacy while still promoting innovation. Throughout the volume, our authors evaluate the myriad of models used to deliver consumer genetics, including the traditional health care setting, life insurance, Do-It-Yourself (DIY) Bio, and, most notably, DTC. The DTC delivery model, in particular, requires us to reopen questions that have already been answered for more traditional health care delivery models. The book's goal is to provide guidance for

[1] Grand View Research, Predictive Genetic Testing and Consumer Genomics Market Size, Share & Trends Analysis Report by Test Type (Population Screening, Susceptibility), by Application, by Setting Type, and Segment Forecasts, 2019–2025 (June 2019).

medical providers, patients, policymakers, and other stakeholders interested in this field.

The book is divided into five parts. Part I, *Consumer Genetic Technologies: Rights, Liabilities, and Other Obligations*, introduced by I. Glenn Cohen, orients the reader both to the structure for delivering genetic technologies to consumers and also to the ethical questions raised by the widespread availability of these products. These chapters show how the chimeric nature of consumer genetic technologies make them challenging to regulate and how the diversity in their structure and delivery defeats any attempt at one-size-fits-all regulatory design.

Gary Marchant, Mark Barnes, Ellen Clayton, and Susan Wolf, in their chapter, *Liability Implications of Direct-to-Consumer Testing*, introduce the reader to direct-to-consumer genetic testing, one of the most common delivery models for genetic technologies. Marchant et al. explore the liability questions raised when genetic tests produce erroneous results. This chapter illustrates the tension between the health care system and the DTC model. When patients give their physicians DTC genetic data, they struggle with whether to use and rely upon this information or to disregard it. By examining the challenges that health care providers face when incorporating DTC products into their work, Marchant et al. help the reader to begin to understand how different DTC genetic technologies can come from genomics delivered more traditionally within the health care system. This chapter is part of a central dialogue of the book – how to choose between self-regulation, increased traditional regulation, or other solutions to governing this space.

Anya Prince, in her chapter, *Consuming Genetics as a Life Insurance Consumer*, considers a very different delivery model. Prince focuses on the development of life insurers as genetic consumers, initiating testing for potential enrollees. While Marchant et al. are concerned with the impact that consumer-initiated testing will have on medical professionals, Prince wrestles with the opposite scenario: How can individuals be properly protected when they are *compelled* to undergo genetic testing by a third party?

Jessica Roberts argues for personal property rights as a necessary protection for consumers in her chapter, *In Favor of an Action for Genetic Conversion*. She notes that consumers who use DTC genetic tests rarely enter into the kind of fiduciary or research relationships with the DTC companies that would provide consumers with protections against breach of fiduciary duty, lack of informed consent, invasion of privacy, or unjust enrichment. Therefore, genetic conversation claims, although historically disfavored by courts, could be a useful tool to protect the rights of consumers.

The next chapter, Jorge Contreras's *Direct to Consumer Genetics and Personal Health Data*, offers a very different answer to the same question for consumer genetic technologies, such as "who owns this data?" He recognizes that many consumers expect some sort of personal property rights in their genetic data, and that many DTC-GT companies imply such a right in their advertisements.

Nevertheless, a personal property right in genetic data would be a significant departure from current US law and would cause significant barriers in using genetic data for biomedical research and public health purposes. Therefore, he argues, protecting consumers' privacy interests can be better accomplished through contractual arrangements. This demands more focus and regulation of DTC providers' privacy policies and practices, along with regulatory oversight of data governance. (A chapter in the last section of this book, by James Hazel, complements Roberts and Contreras' work by providing a deep-dive into the current privacy policies of DTC companies.)

Scott Schweikart closes Part I with his chapter, *Governance in the Era of CRISPR and DIY-Bio: Regulatory Guidance of Human Genome Editing at the National and Global Levels*.

Schweikart reminds the reader of the diversity of delivery models for these technologies by comparing the regulation of consumer genetic technologies via "Big-Bio" and "DIY-Bio." He argues that the traditional top-down regulatory model, used to regulate pharmaceutical safety for example, can be successfully applied to consumer genetic products offered by Big-Bio. By contrast, DIY-Bio consumer genetic offerings will require a more creative bottom-up approach to successfully protect consumers, such as incentives to build proper ethical and regulatory consensus among DIY-Bio groups. Schweikart sets the stage for several later chapters, which make the argument that new delivery models compel novel approaches to regulation.

Part II of this volume, *Privacy in the Age of Consumer Genetics*, introduced by Nita A. Farahany, explores the ethical challenges brought about by increased genetic testing. The first two chapters consider how additional information will affect relationships between biological parents and potential children, introducing readers to another significant theme of the volume: that genetic information is at once intensely personal but also communal, shared between people who may otherwise be strangers to each other. This duality makes it challenging to regulate from a data privacy perspective.

In the first chapter of this Part, *Non-Invasive Prenatal Whole Genome Sequencing: Ethical and Policy Post-Birth Implications*, Vardit Ravitsky considers questions of privacy and right to access information at the start of life. Ravitsky explores the implications of Non-Invasive Prenatal Testing (NIPT), which is increasingly popular among potential parents. Many ethicists are uncomfortable with parent-initiated genetic testing of children, unless there is an immediate health need, in order to preserve that individual's ability to choose whether or not to undergoing testing once they reach adulthood. On the one hand, this logic applies to NIPT, preventing potential parents from sequencing a fetus's whole genome. On the other hand, unlike a child, many would argue that a fetus does not have a right to privacy. Ravitsky considers both perspectives, concluding that the wishes of the parent should govern, especially if we are to respect the reproductive autonomy of the pregnant person. Ravitsky evaluates possible mechanisms to balance the reproductive autonomy of pregnant consumers with the interests of their prospective children.

Seema Mohaptara, in her chapter, *The Myth of "Anonymous" Gamete Donation in the Age of Direct-to-Consumer Genetic Testing*, likewise focuses on privacy in the context of reproduction, this time in the context of anonymous gamete donation. Mohapatra notes that the widespread use of DTC-GT has undermined the ability of gamete donors to be anonymous, despite any legal or regulatory promises. She rightfully argues that a façade of anonymity presents significant legal and ethical quandaries. Mohapatra concludes that the lack of anonymity is a reality that must be disclosed to potential donors, even if it ultimately may deter gamete donation. Privacy as anonymity may be unattainable in gamete donation, so the best we might hope for is informed decision-making by potential donors. Mohapatra's chapter demonstrates to the reader a unique tension in genetic data privacy, that is, that our genetic material is shared with relatives and our individual privacy can be undermined by the choices of others. This tension is reflected in other chapters, most significantly in Kif Augustine-Adams' very personal reflection on the topic in Part IV.

Kayte Spector-Bagdady, in her chapter, *Improving Commercial Genetic Data Sharing Policy*, demonstrates that there is a clear gap between the professional privacy standards for DTC consumer genetic testing and the privacy needs of consumers using these tests. Spector-Bagdady argues that the lack of clarity and transparency in the commercial genetic data research industry prevents individuals from making informed choices about using DTC tests and contributing their data to these databases. Spector-Bagdady flags two areas that need improvement in order to achieve "privacy best practices" for the DTC consumer genetics industry: (1) transparency in sharing deidentified health data; and (2) specific consent (as opposed to broad consent). Spector-Bagdady's concerns, that our consumer genetic privacy standards and frameworks are inadequate, is a pervasive theme in this volume. She is one of many contributors, such as Jessica Roberts in Part I, grappling with the sense that genetic information requires heightened protections and that our delivery models for consumer genetic testing fail to meet these needs.

Yaniv Heled and Liza Vertinsky bring our privacy exploration into the near future with their warning regarding potential genetic paparazzi in their chapter, *Genetic Paparazzi*. They anticipate a future in which the genetic information of public figures will become a subject of fascination and media interest. Will the paparazzi bring swabs and sterile tools along with cameras as they follow celebrities and politicians? If so, Heled and Vertinsky note that the right to privacy exercised by these notable figures will conflict with the right of the public to share newsworthy information. Unfortunately for these celebrities, they argue, the current legal framework does not adequately guard against nonconsensual testing, sequencing, analysis, and publication of genetic material and information. While most of us are not famous enough to need to worry about the genetic paparazzi, Heled and Vertinsky explore hypotheticals in this chapter that help sharpen our sense of how genetic testing and knowledge should be disseminated or protected in more prosaic situations, for the rest of us.

Part III, *Tinkering with Ourselves: The Law and Ethics of DIY Genomics*, introduced by Henry T. (Hank) Greely, turns the focus of our volume from using consumer genetic technologies to the production and delivery of genomics. Called by a variety of names, including DIY gene editing, DIY-Bio, Community Bio, genetic biohacking, or nontraditional gene editing, this community moves genomics from more traditional settings and into people's private homes. Aided by knowledge sharing communities online, the DIY community is a major player in how genetic technologies are delivered. As Schweikart argued in Part I earlier, this nontraditional system will require innovative approaches to regulation. Otherwise, we run the risk of smothering this novel delivery model and losing a valuable source of innovation in genetic technologies. The chapters in Part III all attempt to address the question: How do the regulatory and ethical questions and answers change when we move away from traditional delivery models into DIY genomics?

Barbara Evans, in her chapter, *Programming Our Genomes, Programming Ourselves: The Moral and Regulatory Challenge of Regulating Do-It-Yourself Gene Editing*, provides the reader with a solid overview of the difficulties of applying traditional regulations to a decidedly nontraditional scientific ecosystem. Evans documents the "Coordinated Framework," a compilation of statutes and regulations that are intended to govern DIY gene editing and highlights both the micro-problems and the macro-issue that a DIY community structure does not naturally lend itself to regulation. Evans then challenges the reader to consider whether regulation of DIY gene editing is necessary or justified.

Max Mehlman and Ronald Conlon also consider an appropriate approach to the regulation of DIY gene editing in their chapter, *Governing Non-Traditional Gene Editing*. The reader will likely be surprised to learn that ham radio, sport rocketry, home brewing, and computer hacking are all useful historic analogies to DIY gene editing analogies that can help inform an appropriate regulatory response. Mehlman and Conlon argue that most of these activities rely heavily on self-regulation, facilitated by organizations that represent amateur's interests, and include expectations of self-monitoring. They do note that traditional regulation of these types of activities can become appropriate as the community experiences significant growth and activities become riskier. Therefore, they suggest that self-regulation may be appropriate for DIY gene editing at the moment, but external regulation may become the better choice once DIY gene capabilities expand.

Patti Zettler, Christi Guerini, and Jake Sherkow close Part III with a very human focus on the people active in the DIY gene editing community in their chapter, *Finding a Regulatory Balance for Genetic Biohacking*. Their focus is still on articulating the appropriate regulatory mechanisms for DIY gene editing, but the authors add qualitative interviews with members of the DIY gene editing community.

Zettler, Guerini, and Sherkow argue for a range of regulatory approaches, moving beyond relying on FDA enforcement actions to include educational and engagement activities by other agencies such as the National Science Advisory Board for Biosecurity. They, along with Mehlman, Conlon, and Evans, recognize the valuable innovation that the DIY gene editing community contributes to public health and science, and argue that any regulatory approach should attempt to preserve that perspective.

Part IV, *Consumer Genetics and Identity*, introduced by Carmel Shachar, focuses on the very personal impact that consumer genetic technologies can have on users. The appeal of genetic testing is that we learn more information about ourselves, but that information is a double-edged sword. Genetic testing can be problematically conflated with race, as Jonathan Kahn describes, or predict an unhappy medical future as Emily Largent discusses. Genetic information is also closely tied to family as demonstrated from very different perspectives in the chapters Kif Augustine-Adams and Natalie Ram. It is becoming increasingly difficult to avoid being affected by genetic testing because it is becoming very likely that at least one of one's genetic relatives will test, revealing communal genetic information.

Kif Augustine-Adams open Part IV with a powerful personal narrative, *Generational Failures of Law and Ethics: Rape, Mormon Orthodoxy, and the Revelatory Power of Ancestry DNA*. Augustine-Adams tells the story of her mother, a sexual assault survivor who gave birth in secrecy, pursued a closed adoption, and hoped to keep that chapter of her life secret from her subsequent children. Augustine-Adams also tells her own story, that of a woman discovering a sibling through a third relative's use of DTC-GT. Augustine-Adams and her mother's stories collide as Augustine-Adams shares her knowledge with her mother, to her mother's great distress. Augustine-Adams understands that genetic testing has stolen her mother's ability to control the narrative of her own life. This chapter focuses the reader on a central problem in the area: How can we preserve individual autonomy and privacy when biological relatives can make choices about our shared genetic information that undermine our personal preferences?

Jonathan Kahn takes us one step broader, away from the family and into questions of race and ethnicity in his chapter, *Precision Medicine and the Resurgence of Race in Genomic Medicine*. Kahn documents the desire of biomedical researchers over the past decade to explore the complexities of gene environment interactions as to racial groups and the unfortunate tendency to forget the environmental contributions in favor of drawing relationships between genes and race. Kahn notes that race is a useful and convenient category for use in biomedical and genetic projects, acting as a proxy not only for genetic/geographic ancestry but also for social circumstances, such as environment and class. Kahn warns the reader that diversity as a goal in genomics initiatives can introduce a potentially problematic focus on race. This chapter causes the reader to reflect both on the role of genetics and environment in shaping people, and on how we import our own identifies and understanding into genomics.

Emily Largent, in her chapter *Losing Our Minds? Direct-to-Consumer Genetic Testing and Alzheimer's Disease*, considers the age-old question "is it always better to know or can ignorance be bliss?" in the context of genetic testing. She focuses on a test for a marker of Alzheimer's Disease, a devastating condition with no treatment or cure, and considers whether the DTC setting is an appropriate one for delivering such significant information. Largent suggests that consumers largely are not harmed by this knowledge and that it is indeed better to know, so that appropriate preparations can be made. Like the other chapters in this Part, Largent focuses on how an individual's identity may be affected and reshaped by genetic information.

Finally, in her chapter *Investigative Genetic Genealogy and the Problem of Familial Forensic Identification*, Natalie Ram returns the reader to the privacy challenges raised by shared genetic information. Ram considers recent high-profile arrests made on the basis of genetic genealogy, often using distant genetic relatives to identify suspects. Ram notes that genetic relatives share genetic data in ways that are immutable and involuntary. She is concerned with both the broad reach of genetic genealogy, which can be used to identify a majority of Americans of European descent already, and the lack of voluntariness, that is, that individuals are not actively choosing to participate in the databases used by law enforcement. By raising the ethical and legal concerns with the use of genetic genealogy to solve crimes, Ram complicates the media narrative presentation of law enforcement triumphs and reminds the reader that not all applications of technology should be allowed.

Melissa Uveges introduces Part V, *The Impact of Genetic Information*. In some ways this Part is a continuation of Part IV, as both focus on the implications of genetic testing for individuals and families. While Part IV concerns how genetic information informs identity, Part V explores the effects that individuals, families, and health care providers must grapple with as they engage in consumer genetic technologies. Part V introduces genetic counselors as important players in the exercise of consumer genetic technologies, with contributions both about and by genetic counselors. Part V then continues our exploration of the appropriate regulatory approaches to a technology that is often delivered outside of the hospital or clinic, with two chapters that consider the role of traditional regulatory action and self-regulation. By returning to this central theme, Part V invites the reader to consider which regulatory tools they find most likely to strike the right balance between protecting patient safety and privacy while harnessing the innovation and potential of genomics.

Leila Jamal, Will Schupmann, and Benjamin Berkman open this Part with their chapter, *An Ethical Framework for Genetic Counseling in the Genomic Era* by considering the standard of clinical care for genetic counselors and articulating a set of ethical principles that should be used to guide genetic counseling practice.

Many previous chapters have discussed self-regulation from the perspective of those developing and delivering consumer genetic products, but Jamal and her colleagues apply self-regulation to the relatively new profession of genetic counseling. The authors urge genetic counselors to de-emphasize non-directiveness in genetic counseling, arguing that it overprivileges patient autonomy to the detriment of other important ethical values. Genetic counselors should instead be guided by principles of individual and familial beneficence and nonmaleficence, they argue, incorporating factors such as: whether counseling occurs before or after testing, the information burden of testing, the magnitude and risk of the conditions tested for, relational considerations, role-based considerations, and familial considerations.

Emily Qian, Magalie Leduc, Rebecca Hodges, Bryan Cosca, Ryan Durigan, Laurie McCright, Doug Flood, and Birgit Funke continue the exploration of the role of genetic professionals in their chapter, *Physician-Mediated Elective Whole Genome Sequencing Tests: Impacts on Informed Consent*. Qian and her colleagues explore how genetic testing increasingly utilizes a physician-mediated consumer-driven model, in which consumers initiate a request for genetic testing that is then approved by a physician. They then consider the demographics of the providers participating in this model, noting that genetic professionals are rarely included in the initial ordering process and that primary care providers provide the majority of genetic test authorizations. This raises concerns that primary care providers may not be best equipped to counsel patients on their genetic test results and that genetic professionals should enter earlier in the process to ensure informed consent from patients.

Catherine Sharkey and Kenneth Offit then return us to the central question of the best tools to regulate DTC-GT with their chapter, *Regulatory and Medical Aspects of DTC Genetic Testing*. Sharkey and Offit flag the FDA's recent marketing authorizations for testing for mutations associated with hereditary breast and colon cancer and pharmacogenetic susceptibilities to provide an opportunity to reconsider the regulatory framework for DTC-GT. Tracing the history of DTC-GT and its incorporation into precision/personalized medicine, they explore the FDA's role as safety regulator and protector of patient privacy. Sharkey and Offit end with an interesting exploration of the FDA's potential to regulate the big genetic databases potentially amassed by DTC-GT companies. While many previous chapters argued for an emphasis on self-regulation, Sharkey and Offit provide a counterpoint and argue that the FDA has an important role to play in the regulation of some DTC genetic tests.

In the book's last chapter, *Privacy Best Practices for Direct-to-Consumer Genetic Testing Services: Are Industry Efforts at Self-Regulation Sufficient?*, James Hazel revisits the question of self-regulation. He evaluates the Future of Privacy Forum's "Best Practices for Consumer Genetic Testing Services," and considers the extent to which industry leaders have implemented these nonbinding guidelines. Of the eight DTC-GT companies involved with the Best Practices for Consumer Genetic

Testing Services, not one, he notes, had privacy documents that appeared to comply with all aspects of these voluntary guidelines. Hazel's work is again a counterpoint to many of the calls for self-regulation found throughout this volume.

Instead, he argues for the Federal Trade Commission to play a greater role in protecting consumer privacy.

CONCLUSIONS

Consumer genetic technologies are relatively new and still in a period of innovation and uncertainty. As would be expected in such a nascent field, many delivery models are used to allow access to genetic testing technologies, including incorporation into the traditional medical system, DTC delivery of products, and DIY genetic testing. Our volume explores the many different regulatory schemes that could be used to protect consumer privacy and safety. Some of our contributors are concerned that traditional regulation will stifle innovation or be inappropriate for DTC or DIY genetic testing and argue for thoughtful self-regulation. Other contributors worry that self-regulation will be insufficient and that regulatory agencies must think creatively about how to achieve privacy and safety goals in this field. Finding appropriate regulatory tools is an important task for all stakeholders because of the substantial impact that consumer genetic technologies can have on our identities, families, and personal choices.

PART I

Consumer Genetic Technologies: Rights, Liabilities, and Other Obligations

Introduction to Part I

I. Glenn Cohen

In Greek mythology, as part of his quest, Oedipus must answer a riddle posed by the Sphinx: What goes on four legs in the morning, two legs at noon, and three legs in the evening? The answer is humans – a baby, an adult, and then in old age supported by a cane. The chapters in this Part similarly show how protean many of the concepts and constructs used in arguments about genetic privacy and genetic testing are, and how challenging that makes it for one-size-fits-all regulatory structures.

Jorge L. Contreras's *Direct to Consumer Genomics and Personal Health Data* and Jessica Roberts' *In Favor of an Action for Genetic Conversion* are directly in dialogue, taking opposite perspectives on the question of whether human genetic material or information should be treated as personal property and thus give rise to something like the tort of conversion – Roberts argues no, Contreras argues yes. Of course, as property theorists have reminded us for decades, property is a "bundle of sticks" and affording one stick to one person (say a right to exclude) does not necessarily require including another stick (for example a right to sell). Recognizing this raises the question whether "propertization" is the best construct to use in debating this issue. One is reminded by the Tennessee Supreme Court's admonition in *Davis v. Davis* that fertilized embryos yet to be implanted "are not, strictly speaking, either 'persons' or 'property,' but occupy an interim category that entitles them to special respect because of their potential for human life."[1] Like many, I have sometimes chafed at this language as a cop-out, but reading these chapters made me more sympathetic to attempts to resist the all-or-nothing nature of some legal categories in this adjacent area.

Like the aging human in the Sphinx's riddle, Anya E. R. Prince's *Consuming Genetics as a Life Insurance Consumer* and Gary E. Marchant, Mark Barnes, Ellen W. Clayton, and Susan M. Wolf's *Liability Implications of Direct-to-Consumer Genetic Testing* examines the impact of genetic testing along different points in the lifecycle. Prince is interested in testing that is insurer- initiated and how "[u]nlike

[1] Davis v. Davis, 842 S.W.2d 588, 596 (Tenn. 1992).

DTC-GT companies that primarily interface with individuals, these new companies are seeking to carve out a share of the marketspace by inviting life insurers to become genetics co-consumers." Doing so requires, among other things, untangling clashing conceptions of what life insurance is "for" and tradeoffs between solidarity and actuarial fairness in whether and what way to consider genetic luck. In the case of Marchant et al., the consumer is not only the object of direct-to-consumer (DTC) genetic testing but the subject who is initiating it. While such testing may sometimes yield insights, the authors also show how both false negatives and false positives may put patients at risk and how companies creating and marketing such tests like 23andMe have powerful liability shields: disclaimers buried in the terms of service indicating that the tests should not be relied upon in making medical decision-making and mandatory arbitration clauses. By contrast, patient use of DTC testing may impose significant liability on physicians – who may face liability if they ignore a DTC test result the patient brings to their attention and also face liability if they rely on a DTC test results – especially when a patient's insurance will not pay for a confirmatory test. Here again the protean nature of DTC-GT – medical in the minds of some consumers and arguably in their advertising, but not medical *enough* for physician reliance – becomes manifest.

Finally, Scott J. Schweikart's, *Governance in the Era of CRISPR and DIY-Bio: Regulatory Guidance of Human Genome Editing at the National and Global Levels*, offers still another slice (or perhaps splice) of the Sphinx's riddle: an examination of how ethical and regulatory issues relating to gene editing look different when the community of interest is the old guard – in the form of the "large corporations and academic institutions that produce biotechnology" that he calls "Big-Bio" – as opposed to the young upstarts of "do-it-yourself biology" (DIY-Bio for short) that conduct gene editing outside of professional laboratories, universities, and large corporations. For the latter, he argues that jurisdictions should focus on "bottom-up" style regulatory approaches like incentives towards regulatory and ethical self-governance as well as considering criminal law or trade restrictions to police the outer edges of what might be acceptable.

Collectively, these chapters show why its protean nature makes regulating DTC-GT so tricky. What works for Big Bio and its iterated relations with FDA and other agencies will not work for individual innovators working in makeshift laboratories; traditional property concepts like the right to exclude may be sufficient when thinking about genetic information as a valuable commodity, but less so when thinking about its ability to reveal information about those related to the source; genetic testing is often sold to consumers as a tool to empower and promote wellness, but it may expose physicians to liability when something goes wrong and information and may expose individuals to adverse pricing or coverage in the life insurance market. All this suggests that any attempt to regulate "DTC genetic testing" as a category is likely to fail, instead the reality is a need for many different types of regulations for its many facets.

1

Liability Implications of Direct-to-Consumer Genetic Testing

Gary E. Marchant, Mark Barnes, Ellen W. Clayton, and Susan M. Wolf[*]

I INTRODUCTION

Direct-to-consumer (DTC) genetic testing differs in significant ways from the traditional clinical model in which most health-based genetic testing is conducted. The DTC model also creates distinctive liability risks. In the clinical context, a physician (either a primary care physician or a specialist) will generally order genetic testing by a test laboratory for a specific patient in order to address a medical question relating to that patient's care. In this context, the physician (and sometimes the testing lab and other professionals involved such as genetic counselors) may be subject to medical malpractice liability for failing to recommend appropriate genetic testing, misinterpreting the test results, or otherwise being negligent in addressing the patient's genetic risks and results.[1]

DTC-GT presents a very different configuration. Here, the patient, or perhaps more accurately the consumer, initiates the genetic testing process, often in response to an online advertisement, offer, or marketing campaign initiated by a DTC company. The consumer orders the test kit from the DTC company, collects and sends in a blood or saliva sample, and then waits for the results to be returned, typically online. The test results (depending on the DTC vendor) may include an explanation of the genetic test results, and these explanations have varying levels of detail and accuracy. Many consumers may take their results to their personal physicians for follow-up, which creates dilemmas for the physicians (discussed in more detail in Section III of this chapter) who may not have the

* Preparation of this chapter was funded by National Human Genome Research Institute (NHGRI) and National Cancer Institute (NCI) grant #1R01HG008605 (Wolf, Clayton, Lawrenz, PIs), as part of a project on "LawSeq[SM]: Building a Sound Legal Foundation for Translating Genomics into Clinical Application." The views expressed in this article are those of the authors and not necessarily those of the funders.

1 See Gary E. Marchant & Rachel Lindor, Genetic Malpractice: An Emerging Tide or Gentle Ripple?, 73 Food & Drug L.J. 1 (2018) (reviewing empirical evidence on liability lawsuits for "genomic malpractice").

expertise, time, or reimbursement incentive to explain the test results to the patients.[2]

Providing genetic results through DTC companies raises many controversial policy and ethical concerns.[3] But DTC-GT can also raise liability issues, possibly for the DTC companies themselves, but more likely for the health care providers whose patients have obtained DTC-GT and have offered the results to their providers. This chapter addresses liability issues presented by DTC-GT, focusing primarily on potential liability issues for health care providers who may face troubling legal and ethical dilemmas when their patients bring them DTC genetic test results for advice and consultation.

II LIABILITY RISKS FOR DTC COMPANIES

DTC companies offer to provide many different types of genetic information. At least ninety commercial entities currently offer some type of DTC-GT in the United States.[4] Most of these tests are for ancestry or lifestyle information, neither of which is likely to generate injuries and claims that can result in liability, but for liability purposes, the most important DTC genetic tests are health related. To date, only 23andMe has been approved by FDA to offer health-related genetic tests directly to consumers. 23andMe currently offers a suite of tests that includes ten health predisposition reports including tests for variants in the *BRCA1/BRCA2* genes that increase risks for breast and ovarian cancer, variants that increase the risk of late-onset Alzheimer's, and variants increasing the risk for Parkinson's disease. The same testing also assays carrier status for over forty recessive genetic diseases. 23andMe has recently been approved by the FDA to offer pharmacogenetic testing for drug susceptibility, as well as testing for specific gene variants that increase the risk of colon cancer and diabetes.

In some individual cases, DTC testing has provided useful information to consumers, whether it be by satisfying curiosity about a genetic trait, identifying carrier mutations such as a cystic fibrosis (CF) variant that may affect future parenting decisions, or identifying disease susceptibility risks that may be actionable. In one anecdotal report, for example, Lara Diamond of Oakland, California took 23andMe's DTC test while seeking ancestry information that could be used to

2 See Kyle B. Brothers & Esther E. Knapp, How Should Primary Care Physicians Respond to Direct-to-Consumer Genetic Test Results?, 20 AMA J. Ethics E812 (2018).

3 See, e.g., Am. Coll. of Med. Genetics and Genomics, Direct-to-Consumer Genetic Testing: A Revised Position Statement of the American College of Medical Genetics and Genomics, 18 Genetics in Med. 207, 207–08 (2016); American Soc'y of Clinical Oncology, American Society of Clinical Oncology Policy Statement Update: Genetic and Genomic Testing for Cancer Susceptibility, 28 J. Clinical Oncology 893 (2010).

4 See James W. Hazel & Christopher Slobogin, Who Knows What, and When?: A Survey of the Privacy Policies Proffered by U.S. Direct-to-Consumer Genetic Testing Companies, 28 Cornell J.L. & Pub. Pol'y 35, 47 (2018).

complete her family tree, but also found to her surprise that she carried a pathogenic *BRCA2* mutation.[5] She followed up that result with an MRI and discovered she had a Stage 1 breast tumor, which she was able to treat successfully with surgery.[6] She credits the 23andMe test with helping her detect and treat her cancer early before it became more serious.[7] DTC testing may also be useful to the large number of US women who carry a pathogenic *BRCA1/BRCA2* variant but do not qualify for genetic screening based on family history and other factors under current reimbursement guidelines.[8] For people of Ashkenazi Jewish ancestry, DTC testing provides a relatively low-cost and fast way to screen for the three variants in *BRCA1/BRCA2* found most commonly in that population.

However, DTC genetic results could mislead or even cause harm to some individuals. For example, a woman with a family history of breast or ovarian cancer may get tested for *BRCA1/2* on a DTC platform such as 23andMe, which as noted tests for just three major pathogenic variants in these susceptibility genes. If the woman tests negative for these three variants, she may (incorrectly) conclude that she is not at increased genetic risk for breast cancer due to *BRCA1/2*, even though there are over 2000 other less common pathogenic variants for each of the *BRCA1* and *BRCA2* genes that are not included in the 23andMe test.[9] A recent analysis found that the 23andMe three-variant test misses almost ninety percent of *BRCA* mutation carriers.[10] In one case, an unnamed DTC company misleadingly classified a customer with a family history of breast cancer as being of "typical risk" based on testing only three *BRCA* variants.[11] 23andMe does prominently inform customers that a negative result for the three variants it tests does not rule out another pathogenic *BRCA* variant.[12] Nevertheless, the psychological effect of the DTC result showing the absence of these three common variants may cause some women to

5 See Angelica LaVito, 23andMe's Test for a Breast-Cancer Gene Can Reveal Life-Changing Information, But Can Also Lead Down an Expensive and Complicated Path, CNBC (June 22, 2018), www.cnbc.com/2018/06/22/23andmes-test-results-for-cancer-risk-can-be-costly-to-confirm.html.

6 See id.

7 Id. ("I was very fortunate. If it was just a little bit bigger, I would've needed chemo. 23andMe saved me from chemo.")

8 See U.S. Preventive Services Task Force, Risk Assessment, Genetic Counseling, and Genetic Testing for BRCA-Related Cancer, 322 JAMA 652–65 (2019); Eli Marie Grindedal et al., Current Guidelines for BCRA Testing of Breast Cancer Patients Are Insufficient to Detect All Mutation Carriers, 17 BMC Cancer 438 (2017).

9 BRCA Exchange, Variants, https://brcaexchange.org/variants?filter%5B%5D=Pathogenicity_expert&filter%5B%5D=Gene_Symbol&filterValue%5B%5D=Pathogenic&filterValue%5B%5D=BRCA1 (last visited Sept. 9, 2019).

10 Julia Karow, 23andMe DTC Breast and Ovarian Cancer Risk Test Misses Almost 90 Percent of BRCA Mutation Carriers, GenomeWeb (Apr. 5, 2019), www.genomeweb.com/cancer/23andme-dtc-breast-ovarian-cancer-risk-test-misses-almost-90-percent-brca-mutation-carriers#.XkyrUWhKg2w.

11 C. A. Brownstein, D. M. Margulies & S. F. Manzi, Misinterpretation of TMPT by a DTC Genetic Testing Company, 95 Clinical Pharmacology & Therapeutics 598, 599 (2014).

12 See Steven Salzberg, NY Times, Why Are You So Worried About 23andMe's Genetic Tests?, Forbes (Feb. 4, 2019), www.forbes.com/sites/stevensalzberg/2019/02/04/ny-times-why-are-you-so-worried-about-23andmes-genetic-tests/#1d1af5029179 (noting that 23andMe provides the following message to

forgo additional genetic testing, in some cases to their detriment when they do carry a different pathogenic variant.[13] There are news stories about specific women who experienced exactly this "false negative" situation.[14]

DTC companies may also cause harm if they provide consumers with erroneous results. For example, one patient received an incorrect report from a DTC company indicating a mutation in the *TPMT* gene and thus "an increased risk of toxicity when treated with thiopurine drugs at standard doses."[15] Patients with such mutations should be given a 90 percent lower dose when treated with a thiopurine for leukemia.[16] If the patient did not actually have the *TPMT* mutation reported by the DTC test, such a reduced dose would result in a less effective treatment and likely disease progression.[17] While most physicians would likely not reduce the dose based on a DTC genetic test result alone, and the FDA has expressly warned physicians against such reliance without test validation,[18] it is possible that some providers might rely on such DTC results if they lack the time, resources, and expertise to order confirmatory testing.[19]

If DTC results provide a false positive indicating a consumer may have a medically actionable and high-risk variant, it could result in the patient and the patient's physician deciding on a risky course of action.[20] This highlights the

customers who test negative for the three variants included in the company's testing panel: "You do not have the three variants we tested. However, more than 1,000 variants in the BRCA1 and BRCA2 genes are known to increase cancer risk, so you could still have a variant not included in this test").

13 See Turna Ray, 23andMe Health Report Concerns Linger Amid Incremental Acceptance of DTC Testing Model, GenomeWeb (Mar. 7, 2019), www.genomeweb.com/cancer/23andme-health-report-concerns-linger-amid-incremental-acceptance-dtc-testing-model#.XkytYGhKg2w (quoting a UCLA medical expert who stated: "There probably are some people who are very high risk [based on personal and family history of cancer] . . . who shouldn't be so happy when they get a negative result").

14 See, e.g., Catherine Harrop, Online Genetic Test Gives Woman False Hope of Cancer-Free Life, CBC News (June 20, 2018), www.cbc.ca/news/canada/new-brunswick/online-genetic-testing-breast-cancer-gene-23andme-iwk-1.4711047 (describing a woman with family history of breast cancer who did not meet criteria for BRCA testing and completed 23andMe DTC testing and tested negative; she was relieved and did not plan any more follow-up until she was admitted into a previously applied-for testing program, which revealed she had a pathogenic BRCA variant).

15 Brownstein et al., supra note 11, at 598.

16 Id. at 599.

17 Id.

18 Press Release, FDA, The FDA Warns Against the Use of Many Genetic Tests with Unapproved Claims to Predict Patient Response to Specific Medications: FDA Safety Communication (Oct. 31, 2018), www.fda.gov/medical-devices/safety-communications/fda-warns-against-use-many-genetic-tests-unapproved-claims-predict-patient-response-specific#actions.

19 See Brownstein et al., supra note 11, at 599.

20 See, e.g., Ellen Matloff, I Had Lynch Syndrome for 30 Hours, Forbes (Feb. 12, 2019), www.forbes.com/sites/ellenmatloff/2019/02/12/i-had-lynch-syndrome-for-30-hours-2/#619470462567 (describing an experienced genetic counselor's confusion and concern because of an erroneous DTC finding that she has Lynch syndrome).

importance of confirmatory testing. Indeed, one recent study of forty-nine DTC customers referred for follow-up confirmatory testing found a 40 percent false positive rate for clinically relevant genes in the raw genotyping data provided to customers by DTC companies.[21] Many patients who receive results indicating a serious genetic risk are likely to follow up with their physicians. Although some labs now offer low-cost confirmatory testing of DTC genetic results,[22] some patients may forgo confirmatory testing due to cost, lack of insurance coverage for such retesting, or because their physicians do not recommend it. These false positive results could impose unnecessary stress and anxiety on the consumer,[23] and if not corrected by a competent physician, could lead to unwarranted and possibly harmful medical interventions.

A DTC-GT company may potentially be held liable if it reports inaccurate results, that error is determined to be negligent, and those erroneous results cause the consumer to take action (including forgoing medical procedures or counseling) that results in injury. For example, the patient may undertake further medical procedures in reliance on the (faulty) DTC test results, such as additional and perhaps more invasive testing, changes in medication regimes, or even surgical interventions. It is possible that some of these follow-on medical procedures could result in physical or psychological harms. A consumer may also be harmed if the DTC company provides accurate test results but misleads the consumer about the implications of those results. For example, a consumer may be falsely assured if a DTC company offers genetic testing for a condition such as breast cancer, and after testing for only a small subset of breast cancer susceptibility genetic variants, states or implies to the customer that they are not at a higher-than-average risk of breast cancer based on the test results.[24] In that situation, the consumer, who may have a family history of breast cancer, may be improperly reassured that she is not at higher risk and forgo further testing and surveillance, thereby forgoing earlier detection or prevention strategies.

A DTC company could be sued for providing erroneous or misleading test results, and DTC companies can, and so far have, taken actions to minimize their liability exposure. A DTC company can limit its liability by clearly notifying its customers

[21] S. Tandy-Connor et al., False-Positive Results Released by Direct-to-Consumer Genetic Tests Highlight the Importance of Clinical Confirmation Testing for Appropriate Patient Care, 20 Genetics in Med. 1515 (2018). But see Shirley Wu et al., Addressing the Accuracy of Direct-to-Consumer Genetic Testing, 21 Genetics in Med. 758–59 (2019) (discussing accuracy of results from 23andMe).

[22] See, e.g., Jonah Comstock, My Gene Counsel, Ambry Genetics Team Up to Offer Re-Testing for Certain D2 C Genetic Test Users, MobiHealth News (Mar. 27, 2019), mobihealthnews.com/content/my-gene-counsel-ambry- genetics-team-offer-re-testing-certain-d2 c-genetic-test-users.

[23] See Matloff, supra note 20, at 2 (referring to some patients who are "very alarmed" by their DTC results); Tandy-Connor et al., supra note 21, at 1516.

[24] See, e.g., Jennifer Schleit, Lorraine V. Naylor & Fuki M. Hisama, First, Do No Harm: Direct-to-Consumer Genetic Testing, 21 Genetics in Med. 510 (2019) (discussing the potential for harm caused by a false negative BRCA result following limited BRCA testing, such as that performed by 23andMe).

that the results it is providing are preliminary only and should be validated through the consumer's physician before taking any medical action and should not be used to make medical decisions. 23andMe, for example, provides such a disclaimer in its terms and conditions that provides, in relevant part: "You understand that information you learn from 23andMe is not designed to independently diagnose, prevent, or treat any condition or disease or to ascertain the state of your health in the absence of medical and clinical information" and "while 23andMe information might point to a diagnosis or to a possible treatment, it should always be confirmed and supplemented by additional medical and clinical testing and information."[25] The terms further specify that:

> [W]ithin the limits allowed by applicable laws, you expressly acknowledge and agree that 23andMe shall not be liable for any direct, indirect, incidental, special, consequential, or exemplary damages, including but not limited to, damages for loss of profits, goodwill, use, data or other intangible losses (even if 23andMe has been advised of the possibility of such damages), resulting from: (a) the use or the inability to use the services.[26]

In the past, when a company unilaterally imposed such one-sided limitations on the rights of its customers by such a disclaimer, courts would have considered holding the waiver unenforceable, but in today's legal environment, such disclaimers are generally enforced by the courts.[27] This is, of course, remarkable when one considers that health care providers themselves are generally forbidden from contracting out of professional standards of care by offering such contracts of adhesion to patients.

Another procedural protection DTC companies use is inserting clauses in their terms of service requiring any disputes to be resolved by arbitration rather than by litigation. In a 2016 decision, the United States Court of Appeals for the Ninth Circuit upheld the 23andMe arbitration requirement as not unconscionable.[28] In that case, consumers sued 23andMe asserting claims for unfair business practices, breach of warranty, and misrepresentations about the health benefits of the provider's services. Citing California law, the court upheld 23andMe's terms, which required any disputes to be resolved by arbitration in San Francisco, provided a one-year statute of limitations to bring such claims, and required the losing party to pay for the arbitration costs and attorney's fees of the prevailing party.[29] The combination of the liability disclaimer and the arbitration requirement is likely to provide an effective barrier to tort liability for DTC companies, and they are unlikely to be

25 Terms of Service, § 6(a) User Representations, 23andMe, www.23andme.com/about/tos/ (last visited Sept. 9, 2019).

26 Id. at § 24, Limitation of Liability.

27 See Ryan Martins, Shannon Price & John Fabian Witt, Contract's Revenge: The Waiver Society and the Death of Tort, 41 Cardozo L. Rev. 1265 (2020).

28 Tompkins v. 23andMe, 840 F.3d 1016, 1020 (9th Cir. 2016).

29 Id. at 1021.

held responsible through litigation for any erroneous or misleading results they communicate.

III LIABILITY RISKS FOR PHYSICIANS OF DTC CUSTOMERS

Such insulation from liability is not, however, available to physicians in this context.

Many patients who receive DTC genetic test results print out their results and bring them to their primary care physicians for interpretation.[30] This puts physicians in a potentially precarious dilemma. Most physicians lack the expertise, resources, and reimbursement needed to evaluate genetic test results properly.[31] At the same time, hospitals and freestanding clinics typically lack genetic specialists, leaving the primary care physician as the sole professional during the patient's visit to help the patient understand their DTC results.[32] Even a trained genomics medicine expert may need significant time to understand and communicate results of comprehensive genetic testing. In light of these challenges, a physician who tries to interpret a patient's DTC test results risks incurring major burdens and providing inaccurate information.

The physician presented with DTC test results risks new types of liability exposure. For example, a patient's DTC genetic test results may indicate a pharmacogenetic variant that affects drug metabolism and thus enhances the risks associated with a prescription drug such as warfarin. Some fairly common genetic variants indicate that an individual may metabolize warfarin more slowly than do other patients; as indicated on the FDA-approved warfarin drug label, such an individual should be given a lower starting dose.[33] If the physician ignores the DTC genetic results indicating a lower starting dose, but nevertheless orders the standard starting dose, and the patient subsequently experiences a serious bleeding event, the physician may face a liability claim. Even though the current standard of care does not require ordering genetic testing before prescribing the drug,[34] if the physician already has the relevant genetic information available before prescribing the drug, there is a much stronger argument that the physician should consider and reconfirm that information in determining the starting dose consistent with the FDA label.[35] If a patient has received test results from a DTC company such as 23andMe, the patient may very well

30 Brothers & Knapp, supra note 2, at E813 ("In recent years, primary care physicians have faced increasing demands from patients for this kind of assistance.").

31 See id. at E814; Karen P.Powell et al., Educational Needs of Primary Care Physicians Regarding Direct-to- Consumer Genetic Testing, 21 J. Genetic Couns. 469, 472 (2012).

32 Brothers & Knapp, supra note 2, at E814.

33 FDA, Coumadin (warfarin sodium) Tablets Label, at 6, available at www.accessdata.fda.gov/drugsatfda_docs/label/2011/009218s107lbl.pdf.

34 See Munir Pirmohamed, Warfarin: The End or the End of One Size Fits All Therapy?, 8 J. Personalized Med. 22 (2018); see also Dan M. Roden et al., Benefit of Preemptive Pharmacogenetic Information On Clinical Outcome, 103 Clinical Pharmacology & Therapeutics 787 (2018).

35 Gary E. Marchant, Kathryn Scheckel & Doug Campos-Outcalt , Contrasting Medical and Legal Standards of Evidence: A Precision Medicine Case Study, 44 J. L. Med. & Ethics 194, 200 (2016).

have their warfarin pharmacogenetic information available. In approving 23andMe's pharmacogenetic testing for susceptibility to warfarin and other drugs, the FDA stated that patients should not rely on those test results without confirming their validity in a clinical test.[36] However, health insurers are currently not paying for clinical testing of genetic susceptibility to warfarin, and physicians predictably will often want to start warfarin treatment immediately, without waiting several days for the genetic results to be returned – assuming that the patient is willing to pay for such testing out of pocket.

The physician may consequently face a "damned if you do, damned if you don't" dilemma. Suppose a doctor decides to put a patient at serious risk of stroke on warfarin. The patient shows the doctor her 23andMe results showing a sensitivity to warfarin, which according to the FDA label would suggest a much lower starting dose than would usually be prescribed for that patient. The patient also cannot afford to spend several hundred dollars for an additional clinical test to validate the 23andMe results, and the doctor thinks the patient needs to start warfarin immediately in any event and cannot wait for the clinical validation results even if the patient is willing to pay for the additional test. If the doctor relies on the 23andMe results and starts the patient at a much lower warfarin dose than would normally be prescribed, the patient may be under-protected and suffer a stroke if the 23andMe result is erroneous. On the other hand, if the doctor ignores the 23andMe result and starts the patient on a normal warfarin dose, the patient may have a serious or even fatal bleeding event because her dose is too high. If either unfortunate outcome occurs, the doctor could be sued and found liable for the patient's injury.

A similar dilemma may be presented if a patient's DTC results identify a significant and actionable genetic disease risk, such as a pathogenic *BRCA* variant. This genetic result may indicate that follow-up testing or even surgical intervention is appropriate. Such follow-up procedures may impose their own risks. The recommended practice is for the physician to validate the DTC result in a clinical lab before acting on the result. But again, what if the patient lacks the resources or insurance coverage to pay for the validation test?[37] In that situation, the physician may face liability for ignoring the DTC result. On the other hand, a physician who recommends a course of action or medical intervention based on an unverified DTC test result that turns out to be erroneous could be held liable for any adverse consequences resulting from the follow-up procedures. While such situations are

36 Press Release, FDA, FDA Authorizes First Direct-To-Consumer Test For Detecting Genetic Variants That May Be Associated With Medication Metabolism (Oct. 31, 2018), www.fda.gov/news-events/press-announcements/fda-authorizes-first-direct-consumer-test-detecting-genetic-variants-may-be-associated-medication.

37 A few insurers have recently adopted new policies to pay for confirmatory testing for DTC genetic test customers who test positive for a BRCA mutation. See Turna Ray, Confirmatory Testing, Insurance Coverage Growing Alongside DTC Genetic Testing, GenomeWeb (Mar. 22, 2019), www.genomeweb.com/molecular-diagnostics/confirmatory-testing-insurance-coverage-growing-alongside-dtc-genetic-testing#.Xky-y2hKg2w. However, other payers, such as Medicare and Medicaid, do not currently cover such confirmatory testing.

likely to be rare, there are examples in medical history where ill-advised testing resulted in unnecessary and sometimes harmful surgical interventions.[38]

Given the known error rate of DTC results, it would be inappropriate and legally risky for a physician to recommend a specific course of treatment without first confirming a genetic test result. Yet, as the examples discussed above illustrate, this approach may be problematic if the patient's insurer is not willing to pay for the follow-up testing (which may especially occur when genetic testing was not indicated initially) and if the patient is not willing or able to pay for that testing out of pocket.[39] The lack of reimbursement for confirmatory testing does not absolve the physician of the duty to exercise due care, and a physician could be held liable for recommending prophylactic surgery, pharmaceutical treatment, or some other unnecessary and possibly risky treatment without confirming the DTC genetic results.[40] In this situation, the prudent physician would explain the dilemma to the patient and ask the patient to make the decision, perhaps thus invoking an assumption of risk defense if a bad outcome and litigation ensues. Yet courts and juries may refuse to allow physicians to avoid their professional obligations by shifting this burden to the patient.[41]

Given the limitations and questionable reliability of DTC genetic test data and the limited resources, expertise, and time of busy physicians, some physicians may be tempted simply to refuse to consider DTC genetic test results. While the ethics of such a practice may be questioned, in many cases such refusal by a physician to consider DTC results may result in no harm to the patient. But in some cases, the patient may have received clinically significant and actionable results from DTC testing, and the physician's refusal to consider such information may prejudice the patient's health. For example, a patient may obtain a result showing she has a pathogenic *BRCA* variant and may not fully understand the clinical significance of that result. If she tries to consult her physician about this worrisome result, but the physician refuses to look at the result and the patient is unable to obtain further advice and goes on to develop breast or ovarian cancer several years later, there may be a plausible liability claim against the physician for refusing to consider such data.

38 For example, Japan terminated population screening for neuroblastoma after finding that such testing resulted in unnecessary surgeries to remove renal masses in infants. See Brothers & Knapp, supra note 2, at E816 (citing Y. Tsubono & S. Hisamichi, A Halt to Neuroblastoma Screening in Japan, 350 New Eng. J. Med. 2010 (2004)).

39 See, e.g., LaVito, supra note 5(describing how health insurers would not pay for confirmatory testing for a customer who tested positive for BRCA mutation in 23andMe test, because she had no family history of breast cancer).

40 Clinician reliance on DTC testing has sparked substantial discussion and commentary. See, e.g., Tandy-Connor et al., supra note 21; Schleit et al., supra note 24.

41 See, e.g., Tracy Dobson, Achieving Better Medical Outcomes and Reducing Malpractice Litigation Through the Healthcare Consumer's Right to Make Decisions, 15 J. Contemp. L. 175, 186 (1989) ("Court holdings in malpractice cases make it almost impossible for patients to assume the risk of their own decisions when they are permitted to make them. As a result, even though the patient is competent and well-informed, the physician remains liable in the event of an undesirable outcome.").

There are potentially applicable legal precedents where patients have taken legal action against physicians because the physicians failed to consider relevant information in treating the patients.[42] However, in such cases, that disregarded information is usually some type of clinical data that a typical physician operating within the standard of care should have considered in treating a similarly situated patient. There is no current standard of care related to, and there are no practice guidelines addressing, consideration of DTC genetic information. A physician might therefore try to defend a decision to disregard the DTC results by arguing that a reasonable physician has no duty to examine DTC results. Resolution of this issue would come down to whether a reasonable physician in a similar situation would consider the DTC evidence in treating the patient, which could turn in significant part on how relevant the DTC evidence was. If the plaintiff's expert could show that the DTC test result revealing a pathogenic *BRCA* mutation was a valid and relevant risk factor, the physician may be vulnerable to liability for failing to consider that data.

IV CONCLUSION

DTC-GT raises unique liability issues. The DTC companies themselves are likely to be largely immunized from liability by imposing disclaimers in their terms of service that their test results should not be relied on to make medical decisions. While it is possible that a jury could determine that such disclaimers should not be enforced when the DTC companies test for genetic variants that clearly affect health such as *BRCA* mutations, it is unlikely that a jury will get to decide any such case because of mandatory arbitration clauses in the DTC companies' terms and conditions. This one-two punch of liability disclaimer and mandatory arbitration, both of which tend to be strictly enforced in today's legal climate, suggests that DTC testing companies are unlikely to face tort liability even if and when their results are erroneous and harm customers.

Health care providers may be put at liability risk, however, although the litigation outcomes will likely depend on the specific facts, jurisdiction, lawyers, experts, judge, and jury involved. Because DTC companies such as 23andMe do not provide genetic counseling, they are shifting the burden of explaining the test results to their customers' private physicians. This practice can impose significant burdens on physicians, because they lack the expertise, time, resources, and reimbursement needed to advise patients fully and accurately on the significance of DTC genetic test results. However, DTC testing imposes not only a burden on physicians, but also a potential liability risk. A physician who declines to review the DTC results of

42 In Houser v. Kaufman,972 N.E.2d 927 (Ind. Ct. App. 2012), the doctor allegedly failed to consider the results of a newborn genetic test in treating the newborn, and in Breen v. Upper Chesapeake Health System, Inc., No. 1:08-CV- 02970 (D. Md. Feb. 25, 2010) the doctor allegedly failed to take into account or communicate clear abnormalities in an ultrasound that should have indicated health problems with a fetus.

a patient risks potential liability if the results show a significant health risk that may be actionable, such as a pathogenic *BRCA* variant. On the other hand, if the physician does try to address a patient's DTC report, the FDA, professional society guidelines, and the DTC companies themselves suggest that the DTC results should be validated in a clinical laboratory before they are relied on for medical advice and care. The problem arises when the patient's insurer will not pay for such validation, and the patient is unable or unwilling to pay for the validation testing out of pocket. In such a situation, the physician could be found liable in a lawsuit for relying on any erroneous DTC results, or for disregarding the DTC results if they are accurate. And yet if validation testing is not done, physicians cannot know if the DTC results are accurate. Physicians are, and should be, displeased about being put in this ethical and legal predicament.

2

Consuming Genetics As a Life Insurance Consumer

Anya E. R. Prince[*]

I INTRODUCTION

The image evoked when one hears of direct-to-consumer (DTC) genetic testing is that of a company selling directly to an individual. However, individuals are not the only potential customers. Recently several "insurtech"[1] companies have begun marketing to life insurers, who have been described as "the next larger consumer of genomic products."[2] Unlike DTC-GT companies that primarily interface with individuals, these new companies are seeking to carve out a share of the marketspace by inviting life insurers to become genetics co-consumers.

Take, for example, two recently launched genomic-based insurtech companies affiliated with the life insurance industry. In 2017 LifeEpigenetics began partnering with life insurers to provide an epigenetic test that measures how one's chronological age differs from one's biological age. The goal is to incorporate epigenetic lifespan information into life insurance underwriting as a potential way to more accurately assess risk.[3] In the same year, Wamberg Genomic Advisors launched to advise employers and life insurers about incorporating genetic testing into wellness

* Thank you to the Petrie-Flom Center for developing the Consuming Genetics conference and book. Thank you to the participants of RIBs 2019 and I. Glenn Cohen for feedback on the manuscript. This research was supported by the National Human Genome Research Institute of the National Institutes of Health under Award Number R00HG008819. The content is solely the responsibility of the author and does not necessarily represent the official views of the NIH.

1 Insurtech is a subset of the growing fintech sector and is described as "the innovative use of technology in insurance." Insurtech companies alter existing business models of insurance through implementation of new technology. National Association of Insurance Commissioners, Insurtech, www.naic.org/cipr_topics/topic_insurtech.htm (last updated Feb. 19, 2020).

2 Molika Ashford, *Seeing Growing Interest*, Consultants Seek to Link Genomics with Insurance, Other Benefits, GenomeWeb (Aug. 31, 2017), www.genomeweb.com/business-news/seeing-growing-interest-consultants-seek-link-genomics-insurance-other-benefits#.XR4F6S2ZPOR.

3 See Brian Anderson, Saliva Tests as Longevity Predictor Inch Closer to Becoming a True Disruptor for Life Insurers, Insurance Forums (Oct. 10, 2017), https://insurance-forums.com/life-insurance/saliva-tests-longevity-predictor-inch-closer-becoming-true-disruptor-life-insurers/.

programs.[4] The company advocates for life insurers to offer various genetic tests to their existing policyholders in order to maintain a healthy insurance pool.

These examples highlight two potential purposes for life insurer-initiated genetic testing. First, testing serves a gatekeeping role by providing life insurers with information to incorporate into ratemaking, marketing, or underwriting decisions. Second, offering testing serves a maintenance role, where life insurers provide existing policyholders with access to predictive genetic information, thereby facilitating prevention and, theoretically, a healthier insurance pool.

Expanding consumer access to genetic information could magnify the societal benefits of genomic testing. Yet, ultimately, the individual applicant or policyholder remains the underlying consumer who is being tested, even if the insurer pays for the service. Questions abound as to who has access to data and how it is used. For example, depending on the design, the individual's data may accrue to both the DTC company and the insurer. Through this model, all three actors – life insurers, DTC companies, and individuals – may benefit from the data generated, yet it is the individual who bears the risks, such as pressure to test, loss of privacy, and threat of discrimination. This chapter highlights a range of potential regulations that could be implemented to address concerns raised by genetic testing initiated by a life insurance company and discusses why they may or may not be desired.

II GATEKEEPING VERSUS MAINTENANCE TESTING

Two types of insurer-initiated DTC testing are emerging: gatekeeping testing and maintenance testing. Each type of testing arises from distinct populations – one focuses on potential future customers and the other on existing customers. In reality, the two categories are likely to merge as data from testing in one realm may be incorporated into decisions in the other realm.

A *Gatekeeping*

Insurers attract and select customers through three primary gatekeeping functions – ratemaking, underwriting, and marketing. Life insurers could undertake genetic testing prior to forming the insurer/policyholder relationship. Here, data stemming from the testing is collected to decide whether to insure the applicant (underwriting), at what premium level (rating), and which products to promote (marketing). Life insurers have long used existing genetic information to assist with gatekeeping decisions. Some uses, such as the collection of family medical history, have garnered little controversy. Other uses, such as considering existing genetic test results in

[4] See Ashford, supra note 2.

medical records or disclosed on applications, have engendered a great deal of debate across the globe.[5] Within these current practices the insurer is not acting as a genetics consumer, but rather is using existing medical information. Insurtech companies, however, are encouraging insurers to initiate testing themselves.

An initial question is why have life insurers not initiated such testing before? Overall, life insurers gather medical information that helps to predict an applicant's risk of death. However, not all types of data are collected and incorporated into models. Instead insurers weigh various considerations to determine what factors to employ, such as how to assess risk in the most cost-efficient manner and the potential for reputational harm.[6] Therefore, there are times life insurers may settle for less accurate, but cheaper or more verifiable information, in lieu of either expensive information or controversial data with greater accuracy.[7]

The balance between information gathering and cost, both monetary and reputational, translates well into the genomics context. While some genetic tests provide medically relevant information, insurers may not be willing to pay extra to collect this data. Oftentimes insurers can gather genetic risk data through family history or manifested symptoms found in medical records. Therefore, there are relatively limited times when an insurer would be unable to at least roughly assess genetic risk through sources besides genetic tests.[8]

Despite this reality, one could assume that simply having more data could be beneficial to insurers. Sure, family history alone could potentially flag much genetic risk, but wouldn't consideration of both genetic information and family history be beneficial? One potential reason for not actively collecting genetic information is cost. But as the cost of genetic testing goes down, another potential reason is reputation. Insurers will avoid use of a trait for underwriting if doing so is seen as

5 See, e.g., Bartha Maria Knoppers et al., A Comparative International Overview, in Genetics and Life Insurance: Medical Underwriting and Social Policy 175 (Mark A. Rothstein ed. 2004); Robert C. Green et al., GINA, Genetic Discrimination, and Genomic Medicine, 372 New Eng. J. Med. 397, 399 (2015) (stating that "[i]n defending the right to such discriminatory underwriting, insurers have claimed that if applicants have relevant information that isn't available to insurers, such as robust genetic risk information, low-risk consumers will drop out of the mix and higher-risk consumers will disproportionately purchase coverage, forcing companies to raise prices and causing a 'death spiral' of adverse selection"); Yann Joly et al., Genetic Discrimination in Private Insurance: Global Perspectives, 29 New Genetics & Soc'y 351, 354–55 (2010); Anya E. R. Prince, Comparative Perspectives: Regulating Insurer Use of Genetic Information, 27 Eur. J. Hum. Genetics 340, 346–47 (2019).

6 See Anya E. R. Prince, Insurance Risk Classification in an Era of Genomics: Is a Rational Discrimination Policy Rational?, 96 Neb. L. Rev. 624, 661–63 (2017).

7 See id. at 651–52; Kenneth S. Abraham, Distributing Risk: Insurance, Legal Theory, and Public Policy 85 (1986); Comm. On Risk Classification, Am. Acad. Of Actuaries, Risk Classification Statement of Principles 13 (2014), http://www.actuarialstandardsboard.org/wp-content/uploads/2014/07/riskclassificationSOP.pdf.

8 Angus MacDonald & Fei Yu, The Impact of Genetic Information on the Insurance Industry: Conclusions from the 'Bottom-Up' Modelling Programme, 41 Astin Bulletin 343, 345–46 (2011) (highlighting that most genetic conditions will have a limited marginal benefit due to onset, symptoms, treatment options, and predictive value).

socially unacceptable.[9] Life insurers generally do not include a direct question about genetic testing on insurance applications – at present they mostly gain knowledge about genetic risk from family history, medical records, or follow-up questions.[10] This is likely in part due to the fact that insurer use of genetic test results is highly controversial.[11]

As costs drop and more genetic tests, such as polygenic risk scores and epigenetics, potentially become relevant for assessing risk, insurers themselves could conceivably commence genetic testing on applicants, thus taking the role of co-consumer.[12] Adding genetic testing to these collection efforts is entirely plausible, albeit undoubtedly controversial. For example, there is likely a reason why one of the first companies to publicly market testing for life insurer underwriting, Life Epigenetics, tests for epigenetic markers; insurers may believe that there is something qualitatively different between epigenetic and genetic testing since epigenetics can change based on individual action. Thus, epigenetic testing could be seen as less of a reputational harm than traditional genetic testing, although whether the public agrees with this conceptualization remains to be seen.

B *Maintenance Testing*

Traditionally life insurers have had a fairly hands-off relationship with their policyholders once underwriting is complete; premiums are paid, renewal notices sent, but there is little ongoing relationship. However, several prominent insurance companies have begun to experiment with building wellness programs into existing insurer/policyholder relationships. For example, life insurers have begun to offer incentives, such as Fitbits or AppleWatches, to policyholders, in some cases offering discounts on premiums for those who meet health goals.[13]

In maintenance testing, insurers could offer genetic testing as part of a wellness program. Here, testing at first blush serves several potential maintenance goals; however, some of these goals are potentially masking alternative underlying motivations.

9 See Comm. On Risk, Am. Acad. Of Actuaries, supra note 7, at 1, 13–14.

10 See Prince, supra note 6, at 661.

11 See, e.g., Mark A. Rothstein, Time to End the Use of Genetic Test Results in Life Insurance Underwriting, 46 J.L. Med. & Ethics 794, 797 (2018) ("Numerous countries explicitly prohibit the use of genetic test results by life insurers, including Argentina, Belgium, Bulgaria, Denmark, Estonia, France, Germany, Iceland, Ireland, Israel, Lithuania, Luxembourg, the Netherlands, Portugal, Sweden, and Switzerland. Other European countries prohibit genetic discrimination in insurance through general antidiscrimination laws." (citations omitted)).

12 See, e.g., id. at 795.

13 See, e.g., Vitality, John Hancock, www.johnhancockinsurance.com/vitality-program.html; Aaron Pressman, How You Might Be Eligible for a Free Apple Watch from Your Health Insurer, Fortune (Nov. 8, 2017), http://fortune.com/2017/11/08/free-apple-watch-aetna; Wearables, Nat'l Ass'n of Ins. Comm'rs (Jan. 3, 2019), www.naic.org/cipr_topics/topic_wearables.htm.

1 Outward Facing Goals of Wellness Programs

The insurer wellness programs mirror counterparts in the employment setting, where many employers seek to improve the health of employees through incentives or health education. The model envisions a win-win prospect – employees obtain better health, and employers benefit from having a healthier workforce that has less absenteeism and is less costly to insure.

In recent years, genetic testing has been added to several employer-sponsored wellness programs under a similar win-win theory.[14] Some genetic information has the potential to improve public health by providing individuals with risk information prior to their developing a genetic condition. When preventive measures are available, such as screening and surgeries for those with predispositions to breast or colon cancer, early knowledge and action could save lives.[15] The preventive potential of early knowledge makes genetic testing an alluring fit for wellness programs. Employees can learn about their previously unknown genetic risks and prevent disease, and employers – at least theoretically – can develop a healthier workforce.

It is foreseeable that, as life insurance wellness programs grow, they may incorporate genetic screening just as their employer counterparts have done. Life insurers have an interest in encouraging their policyholders to learn of preventable risk, because the longer their customers live, the longer the insurers collect premiums and avoid paying out claims. To date, at least one genetic testing company is marketing such a program to insurance companies, and at least one insurance company is offering genetic testing, albeit at this time it appears just to its employees.[16]

There is much debate, however, over whether wellness programs will actually be successful in improving health. Indeed, empirical evidence finds that wellness programs are generally bad at improving employee health, but are good at shifting health care costs from employers to employees.[17] For example, a recent randomized trial on the effects of employer wellness programs found that, although worksites

14 Gregory M. B. Steinberg et al., Reducing Metabolic Syndrome Risk Using a Personalized Wellness Program, 57 J. Occupational Envtl. Med. 1269, 1272–73 (2015) (discussing an AETNA workplace wellness pilot program involving genetics); James McGivern, The Evolution of Corporate Wellness to Corporate Genetics Programs, AGS Health (Nov. 9, 2017), www.ags-health.com/blog/the-evolution-of-corporate-wellness-programs-to-corporate-genetics-programs (same).

15 See James P. Evans, We Screen Newborns, Don't We?: Realizing the Promise of Public Health Genomics, 15 Genetics Med. 332, 332–33 (2013).

16 Press Release, Wamberg Genomic Advisors, Wamberg Genomic Advisors Inks Partnership with National Benefit Partners to Distribute Cancer Guardian, a Comprehensive Cancer Support Program, to Employers as a New Employee Benefit (Sept. 18, 2018), www.prnewswire.com/news-releases/wamberg-genomic-advisors-inks-partnership-with-national-benefit-partners-to-distribute-cancer-guardian- a-comprehensive-cancer-support-program-to-employers-as-a-new-employee-benefit-300714198.html (announcing partnership between Wamberg and NBP to distribute genetic testing tied to insurance).

17 See, e.g., Samuel R. Bagenstos, The EEOC, the ADA, and Workplace Wellness Programs, 27 Health Matrix 81, 82 (2017); Jill R. Horwitz et al., Wellness Incentives in the Workplace: Cost Savings Through Cost Shifting to Unhealthy Workers, 32 Health Aff. 468, 471–72 (2013).

with wellness programs had greater reports of employees regularly exercising and actively managing weight, there were no differences in clinical health markers, health care spending, or employment metrics like absenteeism, length of employment, or job performance.[18]

Similarly, it is unclear whether providing individuals with information about genetic risk will improve public health or sufficiently encourage individuals to make necessary behavioral changes.[19] There are many reasons why an individual's health may not improve following an actionable genetic test, including lack of behavioral change,[20] complexity of genetic conditions,[21] or inability to pay for preventive measures.[22] Thus, it is unclear whether integration of genetic testing into life insurance will vastly alter health or mortality.[23] It may identify important preventable conditions in a small segment of the population, but it remains to be seen whether genetic testing in wellness programs will have a significant impact on health.

2 Potential Goals of Wellness Programs

If the health impact of wellness programs is dubious, why might an insurer be interested in offering genetic screening for existing policyholders? There are at least three potential, and not mutually exclusive, reasons a life insurer may desire to become a co-consumer of genetic tests. First, an insurer may be interested in developing relationships with its policyholders. By maintaining a more hands-on relationship between company and policyholder, the life insurer has a greater potential to be able to maintain good customers, know about life event changes that could trigger the need for greater coverage, or potentially upsell different products to customers. Providing benefits that are marketed as improving the health and wellbeing of customers could also help the public image of the company. Indeed, policyholders may see it as a positive that their life insurer cares about

18 Zirui Song & Katherine Baicker, Effect of a Workplace Wellness Program on Employee Health and Economic Outcomes: A Randomized Clinical Trial, 321 JAMA 1491, 1500 (2019).

19 See Gareth J. Hollands et al., The Impact of Communicating Genetic Risks of Disease on Risk-Reducing Health Behaviour: Systematic Review with Meta-Analysis, 352 The BMJ 1102, 8–9 (2016); Muin J. Khoury & Sandro Galea, Will Precision Medicine Improve Population Health?, 316 JAMA 1357, 1357 (2016).

20 Hollands et al., supra note 19.

21 Khoury & Galea, supra note 19.

22 Anya E. R. Prince, Prevention for Those Who Can Pay: Insurance Reimbursement of Genetic-Based Preventive Interventions in the Liminal State between Health and Disease, 2 J.L. & Biosciences 365, 374 (2015).

23 See Hannover Re, Personal Genomic Testing (PGT), the Consumer and the Life Insurance Industry, 2–4 (2017), www.hannover-re.com/1158855/recent-medical-news-personal-genomic-testing-pgt-the-consumer-and-the-life-insurance-industry-2017.pdf. But see Swiss Re, Can Life Insurance Pass the Genetic Test? 10 (2019), www.swissre.com/dam/jcr:4d7cf5dd-44a1-44ec-9245-636304418c5c/Genetic_testing_publication.pdf.

their health and offers testing perks. Thus, implementing wellness testing could be beneficial for company reputation.

Second, the life insurer may believe that it can motivate individuals to alter behavior and seek preventive care. After all, insurers have the potential to not just nudge policyholders toward improved health, but to provide a stick if this behavior is not achieved. For example, auto insurers place telematic devices in the cars of policyholders to measure risky driver behaviors and alter premiums based on the results.[24] If life insurers similarly altered premiums based on preventive measures, this could potentially better motivate behavioral change than can genetic knowledge alone.[25] If policyholders do get healthier, this would be economically beneficial for the company.

Third, the life insurer may be attempting to use the data gathered from existing policyholders to reincorporate back into marketing or underwriting decisions. Employer-sponsored wellness programs have been similarly critiqued as vehicles for subsequent discrimination against those employees found to have disabilities or indicators of health risks. This problem also exists in the insurance context. Data from a wellness program could be incorporated into future underwriting, aggregate rate setting, or marketing.

For example, at the end of a term policy, a life insurer has a general interest in keeping the policyholder as a customer. Therefore, the company will send renewal notices to remind the policyholder that their existing policy is ending. The insurer may also use this opportunity to try to upsell by encouraging their customer to upgrade their policy – and thus their premium – amount in the next term. However, if a wellness program result shows that a current policyholder is at risk of developing a genetic condition, the company has an incentive to remove the individual from the insurance pool. Conversely, they will want to retain those with good risks. Therefore, the company could change their marketing and renewal notice strategies depending on the risk information gathered through the wellness programs.

III REGULATION OF INSURER-INITIATED GENETIC TESTING

For the most part, life insurer use of genetic information is not regulated. Although health insurers are generally barred from collecting and considering genetic information under the Genetic Information Nondiscrimination Act (GINA),[26] life insurers have much greater leeway to incorporate genetic testing into their business models. There were several motivations for passing GINA in the context of health

24 Dimitris Karapiperis et al., Nat'l Ass'n of Ins. Comm'rs, Usage-Based Insurance and Vehicle Telematics: Insurance Market and Regulatory Implications 2 (2015).

25 But see Jessica L. Roberts, Nudge-Proof: Distributive Justice and the Ethics of Nudging, 116 Mich. L. Rev. 1045 (2017) (arguing that not all individuals are "nudgeable" if they do not have the ability to make a choice).

26 Genetic Information Nondiscrimination Act (GINA) of 2008, Pub. L. No. 110–233, 122 Stat. 881 (codified as amended in scattered sections of 26, 29, and 42 U.S.C.).

insurance. First, there was a concern that fear of genetic discrimination was causing individuals to refuse medically recommended genetic testing or to avoid participation in genetic research.[27] Second, it was seen as unfair for an individual to lose access to health insurance simply because of brute luck.[28] Since one cannot control one's genetic lot in life, it is seen as less acceptable to use in underwriting for health insurance.

There has been much debate about whether the antidiscrimination protections that apply in health insurance should be extended to life insurance. On the one hand, there is evidence that fear of genetic discrimination continues to be a concern despite the protections of GINA.[29] On the other hand, genetic information helps insurers stratify applicants by risk levels and therefore leads to premium levels that are arguably more fair to those at lower risk.[30] Since life insurance is generally seen as an economic tool, not a necessary social good akin to health insurance, there is less of an argument for ensuring access despite one's fate in the genetic lottery.[31]

Additionally, the perennial question of whether genetic information should be treated as exceptional applies. Life insurers freely underwrite on the basis of a host of medical and social factors, from one's cholesterol levels to family history to, more recently, social media posts.[32] There is continued debate in many areas over whether genetic information should be treated legally differently than other medical information.[33] Despite this divergence in views, several states have opted to limit the ways in which life insurers can use genetic information. This is a trend that could grow. For example, in 2019, four state legislatures introduced bills that would bar life insurers from using genetic information in underwriting.[34] In 2020, the Florida legislature passed such a bill that went into effect January 2021.[35]

As the debate over life insurer use of genetic information persists, it is an opportune time to consider how the growth of insurer-initiated testing fits into the

27 Id. at pmbl.

28 See Shlomi Segall, Health, Luck, and Justice 109 (2009).

29 See, e.g., Dawn C. Allain et al., Consumer Awareness and Attitudes About Insurance Discrimination Post Enactment of the Genetic Information Nondiscrimination Act, 11 Familial Cancer 637, 641 (2012); Annet Wauters & Ine Van Hoyweghen, Global Trends on Fears and Concerns of Genetic Discrimination: A Systematic Literature Review, 61 J. Hum. Genetics 275, 280 (2016).

30 See, e.g., Leah Wortham, Insurance Classification: Too Important to Be Left to the Actuaries, 19 U. Mich. J.L. Reform 349, 361 (1985).

31 Anya E. R. Prince, Tantamount to Fraud: Exploring Non-Disclosure of Genetic Information in Life Insurance Applications as Grounds for Policy Rescission, 26 Health Matrix 255, 262–66 (2016).

32 See, e.g., N.Y. Dept. Fin. Servs., Circular Letter No. 1, Use of External Consumer Data and Information Sources in Underwriting for Life Insurance (2019), https://dfs.ny.gov/industry_guidance/circular_letters/cl2019_01.

33 Mark A. Rothstein, Genetic Exceptionalism and Legislative Pragmatism, 35 J.L. Med. & Ethics 59 (2007).

34 Delaware (S.B. 17, 150th Gen. Assemb., Reg. Sess. (Del. 2019)); Illinois (H.B. 2189, 101st Gen. Assemb., Reg. Sess. (Ill. 2019)); Maine (H.P. 949, 2019 Leg., 129th Sess. (Me. 2019)); Florida (S.B. 258, 2019 Leg., 121st Sess. (Fla. 2019)).

35 Genetic Information for Insurance Purposes, H.B. 1189, 2020 Leg., 122nd Reg. Sess. (Fla. 2020) (enrolled March 12, 2020).

regulatory landscape. With insurer-initiated genetic testing, data accrues to both the underlying DTC company doing the testing and the insurer, thus exposing individuals to potential privacy concerns.[36] While this result may also occur if individuals initiate DTC testing and the results are subsequently provided to insurers, insurer-initiated genetic testing risks the loss of individual autonomy to make the choice whether to test, in what setting, and with which company. This Section explores the current regulatory landscape of life-insurer-initiated genetic testing. It then looks at a range of policy options available to regulators in the space of gatekeeping and maintenance testing.

A *Current Regulation of Insurer-Initiated Genetic Testing*

The laws surrounding whether life insurers can incorporate genetic information into underwriting practices are fairly clear-cut – although part of a complex patchwork of laws developed state-by-state.[37] What is less clear is how current regulation applies to or should address insurer-initiated genetic testing in the maintenance context.

The use of genetic information by insurance companies that are not health insurers is regulated at the state level. While a handful of states regulate the use of genetic information in ratemaking and underwriting, few fully ban the use of genetic information in insurance as a whole.[38] For example, Maryland only allows life insurers to utilize genetic information that is related to risk and specifically excludes consideration of carrier status for genetic traits such as Tay-Sachs or sickle cell anemia, unless there is actuarial justification.[39] Vermont law prohibits life insurers from considering the genetic test results of an applicant's family members.[40] Massachusetts and Vermont allow life insurers to consider existing genetic test results, but do not allow insurers to require an applicant to undertake genetic testing.[41]

Unlike genetic testing in underwriting, integration of genetic testing into existing life insurer/policyholder relationships raises novel legal questions. There are no laws that directly regulate genetic testing in the context of wellness programs. While several state insurance and antidiscrimination laws could conceivably apply, this chapter does not seek to adjudicate these open legal questions. Instead, the takeaway

36 See, e.g., Kayte Spector-Bagdady, "The Google of Healthcare": Enabling the Privatization of Genetic Bio/Databanking, 26 Annals of Epidemiology 515, 515–16 (2016) (highlighting how DTC companies are able to offer genetic testing at relatively low cost because their business model is to then monetize the resulting data by selling it to pharmaceutical companies and researchers).

37 Leslie E. Wolf et al., The Web of Legal Protections for Participants in Genomic Research, 29 Health Matrix 1, 56–60 (2019).

38 Id.

39 Md. Code Ann., Ins. § 27–208(a)(3) (2020).

40 18 V.S.A. § 9334(a)(2) (2019).

41 18 V.S.A. § 9334(a)(1); Mass. Gen. Laws Ann. ch. 175, § 120E (West 2020).

is that overall the legal landscape for life-insurer-initiated genetic testing as part of a wellness program is hazy.

B *Existing versus Insurer-Initiated Genetic Testing in Gatekeeping*

Traditionally, life insurers sought to learn as much about an applicant's risk as the applicant knew. If the applicant knows more about her risk than does the insurer, there is the potential for adverse selection, where insurers do not properly price risk and lose money due to unexpected claims payouts.[42] With insurer-initiated genetic testing, the paradigm is shifted and the insurer is gathering information the applicant does not know, and in some cases may not want to know.[43]

The biological age epigenetic testing product marketed by LifeEpigenetics provides an apt example of these conundrums. Imagine an insurer that genetically tests an applicant, discovers that the applicant's mortality is lower than previously thought due to age acceleration, and subsequently denies the individual life insurance. Explaining the reason for denial may be quite shocking to the applicant and perhaps information that he or she did not wish to know.

There are several policies that could address these concerns. First, some states' laws specifically require life insurers to obtain informed consent prior to genetic testing.[44] This requirement helps to ensure that the applicant understands that testing is being done and that they could opt out of testing if they so desire. Of course, opting out of testing may prevent the applicant from getting insurance from that company, but it at least preserves some applicant choice if they have a strong desire not to know the results of such testing. Second, applicants could be given the option of whether or not to receive the genetic test results initiated by the insurer. This approach, however, may be difficult to implement in practice if a seemingly healthy applicant is denied insurance and wishes to understand the reason why.

A third option is to prohibit life insurers from initiating genetic testing. Generating information beyond the existing applicant knowledge base is no longer about addressing potential concerns of information asymmetry and adverse selection. Instead, insurers are attempting to parse risk as best as possible, or at least better than their market competition. Without major concerns of adverse selection, there are fewer reasons that consumer privacy should be the price paid for increased

42 See Ronen Avraham, The Economics of Insurance Law – A Primer, 19 Conn. Ins. L.J. 29, 45 (2012); Tom Baker, Containing the Promise of Insurance: Adverse Selection and Risk Classification, 9 Conn. Ins. L.J. 371 (2002).

43 Gabriel Lázaro-Muñoz et al., Looking for Trouble: Preventive Genomic Sequencing in the General Population and the Role of Patient Choice, 15 Am. J. Bioethics 3, 10 (2015) (laying out the debate of right not to know in genomics and ultimately calling for increased individual choice in genetic testing); cf. Benjamin E. Berkman, Refuting the Right Not to Know, 19 J. Health Care L. & Pol'y 1 (2016).

44 Wolf et al., supra note 37.

economic competition amongst insurers. Therefore, there is the question of whether insurers should be allowed to undertake this type of information gathering.

Insurers create new risk information about applicants all the time, whether it is requiring an HIV test or merging data from a variety of sources to understand the risk profile of an applicant in a way that perhaps even the applicant does not understand. However, some policies prohibit this in the context of genetics. It is a relatively common policy solution to prohibit insurers from conducting genetic testing, even when they are allowed to consider existing genetic test results. In addition to Massachusetts and Vermont discussed above, several insurance industry codes across the globe have adopted this solution. Thus, the insurance industry itself sees the practice of refraining from initiating genetic testing as a way to address potential distrust of the industry and as a compromise short of barring use of all genetic results.[45]

This range of policy options – from requiring informed consent to barring insurer-initiated genetic testing for gatekeeping – is available for policymakers to promote individual autonomy and avoid concerns of individuals learning genetic information they do not wish to know.

C *Data Flow and Maintenance Testing*

As discussed above, there are three potential goals of maintenance testing: improving policyholder relations, maintaining the health of the risk pool, and reincorporating information into gatekeeping. Both insurers and policyholders benefit if wellness programs lead to increased genetic knowledge, risk prevention, and longer lives. They likely also both benefit from improved relations. However, both of these benefits can accrue whether or not the insurer gets access to the genetic data.

However, life insurers do need access to data stemming from wellness programs to meet the third goal of reincorporating data into gatekeeping. Reincorporation of genetic data raises similar underlying policy arguments as the use of existing genetic data. For some policyholders, such a practice may actually be beneficial – if testing reveals that a policyholder is at lower risk, the insurer may market good products to them or charge them a lower premium. However, for others it may lead to loss of a future insurance policy. Given the lack of regulatory clarity in maintenance testing as compared to gatekeeping testing, life insurers may be able to implement insurer-initiated genetic testing amongst policyholders even when they would not have been able to do this in the underwriting context.

There are several regulatory options that could be implemented to address concerns of misuse of data in the maintenance context. One option is to ban the

45 Anya E. R. Prince, Political Economy, Stakeholder Voices, and Saliency: Lessons from International Policies Regulating Insurer Use of Genetic Information, 5 J.L. & Biosciences 461, 471 (2019).

use in this context. However, in the wellness context one purpose is to return the information in the hopes that it will lead to overall health improvement. Therefore, regulators may want to allow genetic testing in the wellness context, even while prohibiting its use in underwriting.

Another option is to allow genetic testing of current policyholders, but to ensure individuals understand the potentiality of data being reincorporated into gatekeeping when signing up for the wellness program. If information about the testing does not indicate what data flows back to the insurers and how the company can use the data, policyholders may not understand the trade-offs for participation in the program.

A third category of regulations could govern the types of data that insurers can access. In order to maximize the benefits of insurer wellness programs and minimize the harms such as loss of privacy and potential for discrimination, regulation could bar insurers from gaining access to the data from the genetic testing. This would allow for improved policyholder relations and the potential for improved health without the risk of harming some policyholders by reincorporating into underwriting. If a state decides on policy grounds to prioritize solidarity and bar insurers from underwriting on the basis of genetic information, it would be perverse for insurers to be able to skirt the legislation through the guise of wellness programs. Thus, the states introducing legislation barring life insurer use of genetic information should consider adding this regulation.

However, if insurers can access data from the wellness program, it may help them and society at large to better understand links between genetic information and risk, as well as what motivates behavioral change. Therefore regulators may want to allow insurers some access to the genetic information of policyholders. As a middle ground, regulation could restrict life insurers to only access aggregate results of wellness program genetic testing. This is the legal landscape for employer-initiated genetic testing. GINA prohibits employers from collecting and analyzing employee genetic information, but has an exception for voluntary wellness programs.[46] However, employers can only receive aggregate genetic information, not individual-level data.

Under this regulation policyholders would still be exposed to the general privacy concerns of DTC testing at large, but would be insulated from discrimination within the insurance industry itself.

IV CONCLUSION

Consuming genetics as an insurance consumer is complex – although there are some potential benefits of insurer-initiated genetic testing, especially in a maintenance context, there are privacy and antidiscrimination concerns. Current

[46] 42 U.S.C. § 2000ff-1(b) (2012).

laws and regulations do not adequately address the potential for life insurers to become genetic co-consumers. Further research and study of this nascent field is needed to fully understand the potential benefits and harms of insurer-initiated genetic testing. In the meantime, this chapter highlights a variety of policy options available for regulators to begin to address the potential for insurer-initiated genetic testing.

3

In Favor of an Action for Genetic Conversion

Jessica L. Roberts[*]

I INTRODUCTION

When someone tests my genetic material or shares my genetic data without my consent, should I be able to sue? The tort of conversion allows plaintiffs to recover when a third party wrongfully uses their property. It is the civil equivalent of theft. However, until recently, courts have regarded claims for the conversion of both genetic material and genetic data with some skepticism. This chapter considers the potential benefits of genetic conversion claims.

With the rise of consumer genetic technologies, conflicts over genetic ownership will only increase in number. The current legal protections that people enjoy with respect to their genetic data focus primarily on clinical care and research, leaving customers of consumer genetic tests largely unprotected. This chapter offers actions for genetic conversion as a possible solution. I argue that cognizable genetic conversion claims could offer an appropriate remedy for the unauthorized testing of genetic material or the unauthorized use of genetic information and are thus an important legal innovation for the future of consumer genetics.

II REJECTING GENETIC CONVERSION

An action for conversion requires an underlying property right. Although the United States Supreme Court has not addressed property rights in genetic material explicitly, two significant cases found that individuals have no ongoing property interests in their tissue once it has been removed from their bodies. These far-reaching decisions have more or less gutted claims for genetic conversion since the early 1990s.

* This research was made possible by a generous grant from the Greenwall Foundation. Thanks to Emily Lawson, Elaine Fiala, Dave Fagundes, D. Theodore Rave, Jake Sherkow, Brittainie Zinsmeyer, and the participants of the 2019 Petrie Flom Annual Conference: Consuming Genetics: Ethical and Legal Considerations of New Technologies, especially Glenn Cohen and Jorge Contreras and the 2019 UCLA Health Law Workshop.

A *Law*

I begin with an introduction to the basic law of conversion and then consider how early claims for the conversion of genetic material and of genetic information have played out.

1 Conversion

Conversion is an intentional property tort. It has three basic elements. The plaintiff must demonstrate that she owns the converted property, that the defendant violated her ownership rights, and the value of the property.[1] Claims of conversion require that "the defendant wrongfully exercised dominion or control over the plaintiff's property to the exclusion of, or inconsistent with, the plaintiff's rights."[2] A legally recognized property right is, therefore, a precondition to a successful conversion claim. Actions for conversion typically – although not always – deal with tangible personal property.[3] Conversion also requires that the interference with ownership be sufficiently substantial. The Restatement describes conversion as a "forced sale."[4] Establishing that the original owner either abandoned the property or consented to its transfer are therefore both defenses to claims of conversion.

It is worth taking a moment to dig more deeply into the legal meaning of abandonment, because it has special significance in the context of DNA. We arguably abandon our DNA constantly. We shed our hair and skin cells, leave our saliva on drinking glasses, and drip our sweat on the sidewalk. These acts constitute abandonment for Fourth Amendment purposes.[5] However, from a property law perspective, abandonment requires the actual intent to abandon, usually expressed through an overt action.[6] This chapter, therefore, adopts a robust, property-based notion of what it means to abandon property, genetic or otherwise.

Finally, conversion carries with it specific remedies. Plaintiffs whose claims for conversion prevail are entitled to either damages in the amount of the property's value or the return of the property itself.[7] Punitive damages are available in extreme cases where the converter acted recklessly or maliciously.[8]

1 7 Stuart M. Speiser et al., American Law of Torts § 24:1 (2018).
2 Id.
3 Dan B. Dobbs, Paul T. Hayden & Ellen M. Bublick, The Law of Torts §§ 61, 63 (2d ed. 2018); Speiser et al., supra note 1, at § 24:3.
4 Restatement (Second) of Torts §§ 222A, 227 (Am. Law Inst. 2018).
5 But see Elizabeth Joh, Reclaiming "Abandoned" DNA: The Fourth Amendment and Genetic Privacy, 100 Nw. L. Rev. 857, 860 (2006). Note, however, the subtle distinctions between abandonment for purposes of the Fourth Amendment and abandonment in property law. See, e.g., United States v. Lewis, 921 F.2d 1294, 1302 (D.C. Cir. 1990) ("Abandonment for purposes of the Fourth Amendment differs from abandonment in property law; [under the Fourth Amendment], the analysis examines the individual's reasonable expectation of privacy, not his property interest in the item.").
6 Eduardo M. Peñalver, The Illusory Right to Abandon, 109 Mich. L. Rev. 191, 196 (2010).
7 Dobbs et al., supra note 3, at §§ 61,73; Speiser et al., supra note 1, § 24:13.
8 Dobbs et al., supra note 3, at § 73.

2 Traditional Cases

Courts have historically been reluctant to recognize property rights in the body. With no legally recognized ownership interest, there can be no action for conversion.

Moore v. Regents of the University of California was the leading genetic conversion case for almost thirty years.[9] After performing a splenectomy on Moore, Moore's physician collected and subsequently commercialized his tissue without his knowledge or consent. Moore then filed a lengthy complaint alleging thirteen causes of action, including claims for breach of fiduciary duty, lack of informed consent, and – of course – conversion.[10] While the fiduciary duty and informed consent claims proceeded, the California Supreme Court dismissed the conversion claim, holding that Moore had no ongoing property interest in his tissue after it left his body.

According to the court, the other two causes of action gave Moore adequate protection. Thus, the majority in *Moore* reasoned that Moore's conversion action was not just messy, it was needless. Despite being a California case, *Moore* has widely stood for the proposition that people have no property rights in their excised cells. *Moore* has thus undermined claims for the conversion of genetic material in a variety of jurisdictions.

Over a decade later, a federal district court in Florida looked to *Moore* for guidance in another leading genetic conversion case, *Greenberg v. Miami Children's Hospital Research Institute*. *Greenberg* is a sad story of "a successful research collaboration gone sour."[11] Families of children with Canavan's disease provided a researcher with tissue samples and pedigrees to help him study the condition. When he successfully identified the gene, his institution patented the research.

The families decided to sue after learning that the hospital, which held the patent, planned to enforce it restrictively. Like Moore, they alleged several causes of action. In addition to conversion, their six claims included lack of informed consent, breach of fiduciary duty, and unjust enrichment. The court dismissed the conversion claim, finding that both the tissue and the genetic information it contained were donations to research. Citing *Moore*, the court explained that donors maintain no property interest in their samples after donating them for research.[12] The court also declined to apply a Florida statute designating genetic test results as "the exclusive property of the person tested," noting that no case had ever found that the provision created a genetic property interest sufficient for establishing a conversion action.[13] Thus, the

[9] Moore v. Regents of Univ. of Cal., 793 P.2d 479, 489–90 (Cal. 1990).

[10] Id. at 482 & n.4.

[11] Greenberg v. Miami Children's Hosp. Research Inst., Inc., 264 F. Supp. 2d 1064, 1066 (S.D. Fla. 2003).

[12] Id. at 1074.

[13] Id. at 1075–76.

Greenberg court rejected the conversion claims for both genetic material and genetic data.

With respect to lack of informed consent and breach of fiduciary duty, the district court in *Greenberg* emphasized that unlike Moore, who was the defendant's patient, the plaintiffs were donors participating in research. It explained that the research relationship does not carry with it the same duties of care as the treatment relationship does.[14] The court did, however, allow the claim for unjust enrichment to move forward.

Although not related directly to conversion, another case, *Washington University v. Catalona*, also rejected a claim that individuals owned their genetic material. When a physician-researcher decided to accept a new academic appointment, he sent a letter asking donors from his original university to transfer their specimens to his new institution. The university sought a declaratory judgment that it owned the specimens in the biorepository and won.[15]

B *Objections to Genetic Property Rights*

Academics and judges have argued against genetic property rights generally for a variety of reasons.

To start, some scholars have asserted that genetic property rights lack a sound theoretical basis. For example, I. Glenn Cohen has rejected the notion of genetic ownership in the context of unconsented parenthood on desert, Lockean, Kantian, and personhood theories.[16] We do not work for our genetic material or data, so we do not deserve it. We regularly discard it, so even if we own our bodies, we may not own our tissue after its extraction. Moreover, when someone else uses our DNA, it is not clear that person is using "us" as a means to an end. And finally, our biospecimens or genetics may not be clearly tied to our identities. Cohen notes that the problems that he identifies "may not be insurmountable" with respect to establishing a legal entitlement to genetic material. Rather, he explains that these property theories do not provide an adequate foundation for a right not to become a genetic parent.

Jorge Contreras has argued that health-related information, which includes genetic data, is not a good candidate for the common law property framework, since it is hard to define, not readily subject to exclusive possession or control, and the putative owner lacks a legitimate claim to exclusivity.[17]

Moral criticisms allege that acknowledging property rights in DNA could degrade and disaggregate the self. Sonia Suter argues that "because of the importance of genetic information to the self, identity, and formation of relationships of trust and

[14] Id. at 1072.
[15] Wash. Univ. v. Catalona, 490 F.3d 667 (8th Cir. 2007).
[16] I. Glenn Cohen, The Right Not to Be a Genetic Parent?, 81 S. Cal. L. Rev. 1115, 1151 (2008).
[17] See generally Jorge L. Contreras, The False Promise of Health Data Ownership, 94 N.Y.U. L. Rev. 624 (2019).

intimacy, it diminishes the personal value of our genetic information to describe it as a commodity."[18] Justice Arabian's concurrence in *Moore* equated Moore's conversion claim with a request "to regard the human vessel – the single most venerated and protected subject in any civilized society – as equal with the basest commercial commodity."[19] According to Arabian, permitting genetic conversion would "commingle the sacred with the profane."[20]

From a law and economics perspective, critics fear that genetic property rights will lead to inefficiency.[21] Scholars have voiced their concern that too much genetic ownership would lead to gridlock and, as a result, underuse and the potential for hold outs. Genetic ownership may also create opportunities for collective action problems, since research often requires large repositories of tissue and data. Finally, genetic property rights could create perverse incentives to use one's DNA to extract the most individual value, as opposed to furthering the social good through research and innovation.

Both the *Moore* and *Greenberg* courts expressed similar anxieties. The California Supreme Court opined that "[t]he extension of conversion law into this area will hinder research by restricting access to the necessary raw materials."[22] The federal district court in *Greenberg* raised similar issues, stating that "[i]f adopted, the expansive theory championed by the Plaintiffs would cripple medical research as it would bestow a continuing right for donors to possess the results of any research conducted by the hospital."[23] Thus, critics of genetic conversion claims fear that allowing individuals to enforce property rights in their DNA would negatively impact research and, as a result, impede the progress of science.

Some opponents of genetic conversion claims favor other causes of action for giving relief to aggrieved plaintiffs. In the following chapter, Contreras argues that contract law, regulatory oversight, and existing statutes provide adequate protections for customers who purchase direct-to-consumer genetic tests.[24] Suter supports legal recourse via genetic privacy rights in lieu of genetic property.[25] The court in *Moore* took a similar perspective, stating that it was not necessary "to force the round pegs of 'privacy' and 'dignity' into the square hole of 'property' in order to protect the patient, since the fiduciary-duty and informed-consent theories protect these interests

18 Sonia M. Suter, Disentangling Privacy from Property: Toward a Deeper Understanding of Genetic Privacy, 72 Geo. Wash. L. Rev. 737, 799–800 (2004).

19 Moore v. Regents of Univ. of Cal., 793 P.2d 479, 497 (Cal. 1990) (Arabian, J., concurring).

20 Id.

21 Jessica L. Roberts, Progressive Genetic Ownership, 93 Notre Dame L. Rev. 1105, 1138–44 (2018).

22 Moore, 793 P.2d at 494.

23 Greenberg v. Miami Children's Hosp. Research Inst., Inc., 264 F. Supp. 2d 1064, 1076 (S.D. Fla. 2003).

24 See generally Jorge L. Contreras, Direct to Consumer Genetics and Personal Health Data, in Consuming Genetics (I. Glenn Cohen et al. eds. 2020).

25 Suter, supra note 18, at 803–13.

directly by requiring full disclosure."[26] The position seems to be that actions for genetic conversion are both unnecessary and potentially destructive.

III CONSIDERING GENETIC CONVERSION

Despite the highly restrictive precedents of *Moore* and *Greenberg*, two recent cases demonstrate a newfound willingness on the part of courts to consider genetic conversion claims. This recent openness could offer much-needed legal protection to people who purchase direct-to-consumer genetic tests.

A *Law*

At least two recent court decisions have taken on genetic property rights, albeit one more directly than the other. The first relevant case addresses genetic conversion head on. *Peerenboom v. Perlmutter* reads like the plot of a soap opera. Two high-profile businessmen, Harold Peerenboom and Ike Perlmutter, got into a dispute regarding who would run the tennis court at a posh Florida beachfront property where they each had residences. At about the same time, Peerenboom – as well as his friends and business associates – started receiving reams of vitriolic hate mail. Believing the Perlmutters to be responsible for the numerous and highly offensive missives, Peerenboom crafted a plan. He requested that the Perlmutters be deposed related to another lawsuit. At Peerenboom's direction, an employee from a private forensic testing company then went to that deposition and collected the Perlmutters' genetic material from a special kind of paper and a discarded water bottle and cap.

While the testing ultimately appeared to exonerate the Perlmutters, they nonetheless filed suit in Florida state court. Among their allegations was a claim of genetic conversion. In their complaint, they asserted that they "have an exclusive right of possession and ownership of the genetic information encoded in their genetic material" and that "[b]y collecting, analyzing, and testing their genetic material to obtain the Perlmutters' confidential genetic information, Conspirators exercised an act of dominion and authority that deprived the Perlmutters of their rights of ownership, possession, control, and privacy." In denying the defendants' motion to dismiss, the judge found that "[t]he Perlmutters plainly retain important intangible rights to their genetic information" and that "the extension of conversion's definition of property to one's intangible rights in his or her genetic information is therefore appropriate."[27] The judge supported her decision by pointing to the privacy rights that people enjoy in their genetic information, as well as the very same Florida genetic property statute that the *Greenberg* court had read so narrowly.

[26] Moore, 793 P.2d at 491.

[27] Order granting in part the counterdefendant's motions to dismiss the counterclaim and dismissing the counterclaim in part, Peerenboom v. Perlmutter, No. 2013-CA-015257, at 10 (Fla. Cir. Ct. Jan. 23, 2017).

Property rights generally can protect important deontological values, such as privacy.[28] Perhaps then the right not to be identified against one's wishes might be a right within a person's genetic property bundle.[29] *Peerenboom* thus acknowledges the often underappreciated connection between privacy and property.

The *Peerenboom* court distinguished the conversion in that case from the conversion claims in *Moore* and *Greenberg*. It explained that both prior cases focused on the appropriation of genetic material, whereas *Peerenboom* dealt with genetic information.[30] The order went on to note that the alleged conversion in *Greenberg* related to the commercialization of voluntary donations through research.[31] Peerenboom, in contrast, obtained the Perlmutters' genetic material and their genetic data without their consent.

Cole v. Gene by Gene also recognized a genetic property right that could be the basis for a conversion action, although somewhat more opaquely. FamilyTree DNA offers its customers the opportunity to participate in third party-run projects. When Michael Cole took a DNA ancestry test, he signed up for nine such projects. Cole then began to receive large amounts of spam. Frustrated by the intrusion, he searched for his email on the Internet and found it on a website. In so doing, he also discovered that his genetic test results were publicly available.

Cole then sued Gene by Gene – the entity that runs FamilyTree DNA – for violating the Alaska Genetic Privacy Act.[32] He sought class certification, a declaration that Gene by Gene violated the Alaska statute, damages, and an injunction barring the company from disclosing its customers genetic test results. The company responded with a motion to dismiss, alleging that Cole lacked the requisite standing. Specifically, Gene by Gene asserted that Cole had not experienced any actual injury.

The trial court denied the motion based on the Alaska law. The Genetic Privacy Act requires informed consent to collect and analyze a DNA sample or to disclose the results of a genetic test.[33] The legislation also includes a private right of action to enforce its protections.[34] According to the court, "[t]hese statutory entitlements bear a close relationship to the common law torts of conversion of property and invasion of privacy, which have each historically provided a basis for a lawsuit in American courts."[35] By linking the statutory genetic property right to conversion, the court seemed to acknowledge the possibility of an action for genetic conversion.

28 See Roberts, supra note 21, at 1111; see also Gregory S. Alexander et al., A Statement of Progressive Property, 94 Cornell L. Rev. 743, 744 (2009).

29 See I. Glenn Cohen, Is There a Duty to Share Health Data?, in Oversight of Big Data Health Research 209–22 (I. Glenn Cohen et al. eds., 2018) (identifying the difference between traditional autonomy based claims associated with property and privacy based claims associated with reidentification).

30 Peerenboom, No. 2013-CA-015257, at 11–12.

31 Id.

32 See Cole v. Gene by Gene, Ltd., No. 1:14-cv-00004, 2017 WL 2838256 (D. Alaska June 30, 2017).

33 Id. at *3; Alaska Stat. Ann. § 18.13.010(a) (West 2017).

34 Cole, 2017 WL 2838256, at *3; Alaska Stat. Ann. § 18.13.020.

35 Cole, 2017 WL 2838256, at *4.

B *Justifications for Genetic Conversion Claims*

Despite the widespread historical distaste, courts seem more open to genetic conversion claims now than they were in the past. Perhaps part of this willingness is because some plaintiffs will have no other remedy. The lion's share of legal protections related to genetics cover clinical care or research. For example, actions for breach of fiduciary duty and informed consent cover medical treatment.[36] Moore could recover because the person who engaged in the unconsented conduct with his genetic material was his treating physician. While not including a private right of action, the Common Rule, which applies to government-funded research, provides ethical standards regarding the collection and use of biospecimens.[37] Yet outside of those two contexts, individuals have little recourse when someone uses their genetic material or their genetic data without their consent. Absent actionable genetic property rights, they remain vulnerable to such intrusions. Far from dehumanizing people, genetic conversion could protect them.

For example, without conversion, the Perlmutters would have had no grounds to sue. Peerenboom owed the Perlmutters no special duty of care, nor was he planning to do research on their cells. Beyond a handful of state laws criminalizing unconsented genetic testing[38] or the testing company's terms of service,[39] nothing stopped Peerenboom from collecting the Perlmutters' DNA and testing it. Even if Peerenboom had run afoul of a genetic stalking law or a service term, those violations would not give the Perlmutters any legal relief. Notably, the genetic testing in *Peerenboom* was forensic. Yet the same reasoning would hold true for any form of direct-to-consumer genetic testing. Peerenboom could have gained information about the Perlmutters' familial relationships, geographic ancestry, or medical risk, and the Perlmutters would have been powerless to stop him.

Similarly, the company and Cole had no special relationship. He was neither a patient nor a research subject. To be sure, the company outlined its obligations to Cole in its terms of service.[40] However, it is not clear that its alleged sharing of his data actually breached any of those terms; Cole filed only statutory claims. Terms of

36 See Greenberg v. Miami Children's Hosp. Research Inst., Inc., 264 F. Supp. 2d 1064, 1069 (S.D. Fla. 2003); Moore v. Regents of Univ. of Cal., 793 P.2d 479, 483 (Cal. 1990); Dobbs et al., supra note 3, at § 308, 310; see also Pegram v. Herdrich, 530 U.S. 211, 235 (2000) (providing that a physician making a treatment decision to benefit an HMO or himself would violate a fiduciary duty).

37 See 45 C.F.R. §§ 46.101(a), 46.103 (2018); see also U.S. Dep't of Health & Human Servs., Federal Policy for the Protection of Human Subjects ("Common Rule") (Mar. 18, 2016), www.hhs.gov/ohrp/regulations-and-policy/regulations/common-rule/index.html (indicating that subpart A of 45 CFR part 46 is usually referred to as the "Common Rule").

38 Elizabeth Joh, DNA Theft : Recognizing the Crime of Nonconsensual Genetic Collection and Testing, 91 B.U. L. Rev. 665, 667–68 (2011).

39 See, e.g., Frequently Asked Questions, FamilyTree DNA, www.familytreedna.com/learn/faq/(last visited July 2, 2019) ("Even if you paid for the test of a friend or relative, they need to be the one to consent . . . we ask that you practice ethical testing and kit conservatorship").

40 Subsequently, FamilyTree DNA and GEDmatch changed their law enforcement policies. See Sara Zhang, A DNA Company Wants You to Help Catch Criminals, The Atlantic (Mar. 29, 2019),

service may, therefore, not adequately protect consumers' interests. Terms may be silent on certain key issues, their provisions may be unenforceable, and contract law provides only limited remedies. Without a right to recover for genetic conversion, consumers may be unable to meaningfully recover for the misuse of their DNA by consumer genetic companies.

And despite the criticisms, actions for genetic conversion will not chill research or impede clinical care. Recall that consent is a defense to conversion. It therefore stands to reason that genetic conversion would only be actionable when the alleged converter failed to get adequate permission. Physicians and researchers – who already face legal and ethical obligations to obtain informed consent – should then have nothing to fear. Recognizing genetic conversion claims will simply ensure that stewards of genetic material and genetic information are transparent and obtain adequately broad consent for their actions. Reinforcing these existing norms is particularly important in the context of consumer genetics, where other legal and ethical duties do not readily apply.

Importantly, genetic conversion empowers plaintiffs to seek relief for the unconsented use of their DNA. As noted, Contreras argues against genetic property interests in favor of other sources of protection for consumers.[41] However, breaches of contract may provide only limited remedies, agency enforcement may not include private rights of action, and states are extremely variable with respect to their statutory provisions. An action for genetic conversion is thereby still a necessary legal innovation.

IV APPLYING GENETIC CONVERSION

While consumers could meaningfully benefit from viable genetic conversion claims, that reality alone does not justify recognizing these causes of action. Here I turn to how actions for genetic conversion could play out.

A *Law*

DNA presents some unique challenges for establishing the elements of conversion. As noted, conversion typically involves tangible property, potentially making claims for the conversion of tissue stronger than claims for the conversion of data. However, that general practice did not dissuade the *Peerenboom* court from recognizing a data-based genetic property right. Other courts could likewise choose to acknowledge property interests in either genetic material, genetic data, or both.

The underlying property interest is not the only hurdle for genetic conversion claims. To establish conversion, the plaintiff must show that the interference with

www.theatlantic.com/science/archive/2019/03/a-dna-company-wants-your-dna-to-catch-criminals/586120/.

41 See Contreras, supra note 24.

the property right was substantial. Yet what does it mean for someone to interfere with your genetic ownership rights? Proving that genetic material or data has lost its value to the plaintiff could be surprisingly difficult. Pilar Ossorio sums up this issue nicely: "If a researcher creates an immortalized cell line from my cells and licenses that cell line to a biotechnology company for a million dollars, that will not prevent me from traveling on my vacation, writing a play, or getting a pet."[42] Hence, a plaintiff must show that the defendant controlled her genetic material or data in such a way that it meaningfully violated her rights. For instance, plaintiffs could demonstrate that the act of conversion violated their privacy or their dignity. Thus, courts hearing genetic conversion cases may need to take an inclusive view of what constitutes substantial interference.

Determining the appropriate remedy for genetic conversion also raises questions. Damages in the amount of the converted property's market value at the time of the conversion – plus damages for the loss of the converted property's use – are the normal remedy. Yet most often, genetic material and data only gain monetary value after the conversion, when the research has been successfully commercialized. Applying the longstanding historical rule that plaintiffs are only entitled to the value of the property at the time of the conversion,[43] an individual could not then attempt to co-opt the research proceeds. That said, if the conversion caused some kind of demonstrable cost or harm, a plaintiff could cast the negative impact as flowing from the conversion. Perhaps plaintiffs could then recover damages for those violations, such as the dignitary harms felt by the Perlmutters. Actions for conversion also give plaintiffs the opportunity to forgo damages and seek the return of the property itself. This remedy could be particularly valuable in certain circumstances when the actual physical sample has personal or symbolic value to the plaintiff.

B *Case Studies*

We can now revisit some of the genetic conversion claims described in Sections I and II to consider how they might unfold after withstanding a motion to dismiss. Because *Cole* raises a statutory and not a tort claim, the analysis focuses on *Moore*, *Greenberg*, and *Perlmutter*.

Imagine that *Moore* were happening right now. If the court recognized that Moore had an actionable property interest, does that mean that he would recover handsomely for genetic conversion? Probably not. Even assuming a property interest, it is not clear whether Moore experienced a substantial interference. Further, recall that abandonment is a complete defense to conversion. The California Supreme Court pointed out that Moore had no expectation that he would retain

42 Pilar N. Ossorio, Property Rights and Human Bodies, in Who Owns Life? 232 (David Magnus et al. eds., 2002).

43 Restatement (Second) of Torts §§ 222A, cmt. c (Am. Law Inst. 2018).

his spleen following its removal.[44] His intent to have his spleen removed was clear: after all, he agreed to a splenectomy. Showing up on the day of the surgery was an overt act confirming that intent. Moore then arguably abandoned his spleen in the operating room. As I will discuss shortly, *Moore* is distinguishable from *Perlmutter* on this issue. Yet whether Moore abandoned his rights in his data – had he raised a data-based claim – would be a different matter.

As part of his conversion claim, Moore sought a proprietary interest in the subsequent research. This remedy is simply unavailable in actions for conversion. Even if Moore had prevailed, he would have only been entitled to the value of his cells at the time of conversion – or their return, which he surely did not want – plus any additional damages. Even in a world of actionable genetic conversion, *Moore* would have turned out largely the same. Lack of informed consent and breach of fiduciary duty would still be his strongest legal claims. A conversion action would therefore not pose the kind of chilling effect to research that the California Supreme Court feared.

Greenberg might also end up with a very similar outcome. As in *Moore*, assume a legally recognized property right. Substantial interference and the available defenses again become the sticking points. The plaintiffs sought out a research relationship and gave their genetic material with the express purpose of facilitating genetic research. They objected not to the research itself but to its commercialization. Far from converting their genetic property, the researcher used it in precisely the way that they desired: to find a genetic link for Canavan's disease. The later commercialization is a separate issue. Consent could thereby be a valid defense. A person cannot transfer title to her car and then object if the new owner drives it for Lyft. Likewise, the *Greenberg* plaintiffs relinquished their property interests by donating their tissue. However, they did contribute significantly to the research through their actions. Thus, unjust enrichment – not conversion – is the appropriate legal remedy.

The Perlmutters, by contrast, may well have a valid claim for genetic conversion. First, the court acknowledged the presence of their genetic property rights. Second, Peerenboom and his associates seem to have exercised control over their DNA in a way that deprived the Perlmutters of their rights. By surreptitiously taking the Perlmutters' genetic material and obtaining their genetic information, the defendants violated those rights. Unlike Moore, the Perlmutters had no clear intent to abandon their DNA, and unlike the *Greenberg* plaintiffs, they did not consent to its testing. Third, with respect to remedies, they did not seek the return of their genetic information.[45] They can therefore recover damages for the market value of their

44 Moore v. Regents of Univ. of Cal., 793 P.2d 479, 488–89 (Cal. 1990) ("Moore clearly did not expect to retain possession of his cells following their removal.").

45 Order granting in part the counterdefendant's motions to dismiss the counterclaim and dismissing the counterclaim in part, Peerenboom v. Perlmutter, No. 2013-CA-015257, at 12 (Fla. Cir. Ct. Jan. 23, 2017).

data – probably nothing – plus any additional costs and compensation for any harms that resulted from the conversion. In fact, they could even be entitled to punitive damages if they can establish that the defendants engaged in serious misconduct with a reckless or malicious intent.[46]

But what does this analysis mean for consumer genetics? To be sure, a case as factually bizarre as *Peerenboom* might seem like a dubious basis for genetic conversion claims. While it does highlight the potential need for these causes of action, other kinds of scenarios also justify allowing plaintiffs to recover for genetic conversion. Consider this example. Imagine that a testing company told its customers in its terms of service that customers would maintain ownership of their information[47] and that it would not share their genetic data without a court order.[48] It later changes its terms of service and sells access to the database. Upon learning of the sale, several consumers stop using the services. Thus, the consumers neither abandoned their genetic property interests nor consented to the sale. Should they want to form a class and sue,[49] their potential causes of action would be breach of contract (assuming they did not consent to the change and the terms are enforceable) and genetic conversion. In such a case, a genetic conversion claim serves two important functions. First, it gives plaintiffs access to greater remedies than the relatively modest relief available under breach of contract. Second, an action for genetic conversion provides an additional incentive for direct-to-consumer companies to be good actors and, as a result, to be transparent and to obtain adequate consent.

V CONCLUSION

In 1990, the California Supreme Court dismissed Moore's genetic conversion claim, reasoning that it was an inappropriate extension of that tort. In so doing, the court both overstated the concerns posed by such a doctrine and failed to recognize its promise. Thirty years later, claims of genetic conversion make far more sense. Genetics is no longer a thing of the future. It is part of millions of people's lives right now. The genetic era has demonstrated a real need for these legal actions, particularly in the area of consumer genetics. Hopefully, going forward, more courts will take a cue from *Peerenboom* and *Cole* and recognize people's rightful legal claims to their genetic property.

46 Dobbs et al., supra note 3, at § 73.

47 See, e.g., Ancestry.com, Ancestry Terms and Conditions, www.ancestry.com/cs/legal/termsandconditions (last visited Jul. 25, 2019) ("You always maintain ownership of your data"); 23andMe, Terms of Service, www.23andme.com/about/tos/ (last visited July 2, 2019) [hereinafter 23andMe ToS] ("Any Genetic Information derived from your saliva remains your information.").

48 See 23andMe ToS, supra note 47 ("23andMe is free to preserve and disclose any and all Personal Information to law enforcement agencies or others if required to do so by court order.").

49 Though class certification in *Cole* ultimately failed, the issue is beyond the scope of this chapter. See Cole v. Gene by Gene, Ltd., No. 1:14-cv-00004, 2017 WL 2838256 (D. Alaska June 30, 2017).

4

Direct-to-Consumer Genomics and Personal Health Data

Jorge L. Contreras

I INTRODUCTION

Regular reports of the mishandling of personal data by firms like Facebook, Yahoo!, Target, and Quest Diagnostics have given rise to heightened public concern over data privacy and protection, particularly when genetic and health information are involved. Responding to these concerns, direct-to-consumer (DTC) genetic testing services such as Ancestry.com have publicly stated that "You always maintain ownership of your data."[1] Similarly, the popular GEDmatch genealogy DNA matching site claims that both DNA and genealogy data "remain the property of the person who uploaded it."[2]

These DTC services join a growing chorus of academics, patient advocates, and health care professionals who are calling for the recognition of personal property rights (ownership) in individual health data.[3] In response, a host of would-be data intermediaries has arisen seeking to profit from brokering data transactions on behalf of individuals.[4] Six US states have enacted legislation purporting to grant individuals ownership of their genetic information (though one, Oregon, repealed its legislation a few years later).[5] Even former President Barack Obama has echoed the intuitive

1 Ancestry.com, Ancestry Terms and Conditions, www.ancestry.com/cs/legal/termsandconditions(last visited May 28, 2019) [hereinafter Ancestry.com Terms].

2 GEDmatch, GEDmatch.Com Terms of Service and Privacy Policy - Revised December 9, 2019, www.gedmatch.com/tos_read.php(last visited Dec. 9, 2019).

3 For an overview of the debate over health data propertization, see, e.g., Jessica Roberts, In Favor of Genetic Conversion, in Consuming Genetics (I. Glenn Cohen et al., eds. 2022) [hereinafter Roberts, Genetic Conversion]; Jorge L. Contreras, The False Promise of (Health) Data Ownership, 94 N.Y. U. L. Rev. 624 (2019) [hereinafter Contreras, False Promise]; Jorge L. Contreras, Genetic Property, 105 Geo. L.J. 1, 30 (2016) [hereinafter Contreras, Genetic Property]; Jessica L. Roberts, Progressive Genetic Ownership, 93 Notre Dame L. Rev. 1105, 1158–9 (2018); Misha Angrist, Do You Belong to You?, Genome (Jan. 2, 2018), www.genomemag.com/do-you-belong-to-you/#.

4 See Contreras, False Promise, supra note 3, at 627–28 (describing data intermediaries).

5 See Anya E. R. Prince, Comprehensive Protection of Genetic Information: One Size Privacy or Property Models May Not Fit All, 79 Brook. L. Rev. 175, 195–98 (2013) (discussing laws in Alaska, Colorado, Georgia, Louisiana, and Florida). The first state to enact legislation recognizing a property

appeal of individual data ownership, stating that "if somebody does a test on me or my genes . . . that's mine."[6]

Yet these intuitive appeals are unconvincing upon closer consideration. Unlike parts of the human body, which data propertization advocates often analogize to genetic information, information *about* one's body is not *part of* one's body. Moreover, the individual who is the source of this information typically expends little or no effort to create it. In most cases, it is detected and recorded by skilled professionals (physicians, pathologists, medical examiners) who then analyze it without material assistance from the individual. As a result, arguments regarding the ownership of one's body and the fruit of one's labor (what have been termed Lockean arguments) are not particularly apt in the case of pure information.[7]

What's more, recognizing a personal property right in individual genetic data would represent a significant departure from current US law, which has held for more than a century that data – objective information and facts – cannot be owned as property.[8] As Justice Louis Brandeis famously wrote more than a century ago, facts are "free as the air to common use."[9] This longstanding principle has been applied consistently to information ranging from the news of the day,[10] stock recommendations,[11] and sports scores[12] to the sequence of naturally occurring human DNA.[13] Both state and federal courts have expressly rejected property-based conversion claims for health data, even when the users of that data have otherwise been found liable for violations of ethical and fiduciary duties.[14]

interest in genetic information was Oregon. Genetic Privacy Act, Or. Rev. Stat. Ann. § 659.715(1) (1995). However, Oregon repealed this legislation in 2001. See Or. Public Health Div., History of Oregon's Genetic Privacy Law 3 (2007); Genetic Research Advisory Comm., Assuring Genetic Privacy in Oregon (Nov. 15, 2000) (recommending repeal) [hereinafter Oregon Report].

6 Julie Hirschfeld Davis, President Weighs in on Data from Genes, N.Y. Times, Feb. 25, 2016, at A15. But see Jorge L. Contreras, Letter to the Editor: The President Says Patients Should Own their Genetic Data. He's Wrong., 34 Nature Biotech. 585 (2016) (critiquing President's statement).

7 See I. Glenn Cohen, Is There a Duty to Share Healthcare Data?, in Big Data, Health Law, and Bioethics 209 (I. Glenn Cohen et al., eds., 2018), at 212–14.

8 Feist Publ'ns, Inc. v. Rural Tel. Serv. Co., 499 U.S. 340, 344–45 (1991); Int'l News Serv. v. Assoc. Press, 248 U.S. 215, 234 (1918).

9 Int'l News Serv., 248 U.S. at 250 (Brandeis, J., dissenting).

10 See id. at 234.

11 Barclays Capital Inc. v. Theflyonthewall.com, 700 F. Supp. 2d 310, 313, 344–45 (S.D.N.Y. 2010), rev'd in part sub nom. Barclays Capital Inc. v. Theflyonthewall.com, Inc., 650 F.3d 876 (2d Cir. 2011).

12 Nat'l Basketball Ass'n v. Motorola, Inc., 105 F.3d 841 (2d Cir. 1997).

13 Ass'n for Molecular Pathology v. Myriad Genetics, Inc., 569 U.S. 576 (2013).

14 See, e.g., Wash. Univ. v. Catalona, 490 F.3d 667, 673 (8th Cir. 2007) (denying researcher's ownership claims to biobanked specimens and associated data even after research subjects purported to assign rights to him); Greenberg v. Miami Children's Hospital, 264 F. Supp. 2d 1064 (S.D. Fla. 2003) (denying plaintiffs' claims to a share of the profits that a research institution made from discoveries based on their children's genetic data); Moore v. Regents of the Univ. of Cal., 51 Cal. 3d 120, 138 (Cal. 1990) (rejecting conversion claims when physicians extracted utilized patient's cells and tissue without his consent and in violation of physician fiduciary duties). For a discussion of these cases in the context of conversion claims, see Roberts, Genetic Conversion, supra note 3.

Stare decisis aside, the propertization of genetic and other individual health data raises a number of concerns. Assigning ownership rights to personal health information would give individuals powerful rights to control, and exclude others from exploiting, information that has significant value for biomedical research and public health monitoring, thus increasing the cost and difficulty of these socially beneficial activities.[15] Moreover, property law, if strictly applied to health information, would likely result in more mischief than it cures, as a result of infinite duration, hereditability, dead hand control, and intractable administrability issues.[16] Finally, property rights in individual health data are simply unnecessary in view of existing common law privacy, fiduciary, and other tort claims as well as existing federal and state regulatory regimes that protect the privacy of health records, govern the conduct of biomedical research, and prohibit discrimination on the basis of genetic information.[17]

In this chapter, I argue that existing contractual, regulatory, and liability regimes are sufficient to protect individuals from harms that could arise from DTC genomic testing, and that the propertization of individual health data to achieve these same ends is both undesirable and unnecessary.[18] Section II addresses contractual mechanisms embodied in the DTC relationship. Section III addresses federal agency oversight of DTC practices. Section IV turns to federal and state legislation and regulation designed to protect individual genetic and other health data, and Section V addresses common law and statutory tort remedies available to individuals whose information has been mishandled or misappropriated.

15 See Contreras, False Promise, supra note 3, at 638, 646; Jorge L. Contreras & Francisca Nordfalk, Liability (and) Rules for Health Information, 29 Health Matrix 179, 192–95 (2019).

16 See generally Contreras, False Promise, supra note 3, at 639–56 (analyzing the application of common law property to health data, both in its absolute form and as modified by a range of limitations and exceptions).

17 See id. at 660.

18 Roberts argues that there are at least some cases in which none of the contractual, regulatory, or tort theories discussed in this chapter would support an individual's claim that his or her genetic information has been improperly obtained or used, thus supporting the need for a separate property conversion claim. Roberts, Genetic Conversion, supra note 3. In particular, she cites Peerenboom v. Perlmutter, No. 2013-CA-015257 (Fla. Cir. Ct. Jan. 23, 2017), a case involving the acquisition of DNA from a discarded water bottle, to support this point. While I acknowledge that the facts in cases such as *Peeren boom* might not lead to a cognizable claim under any of the theories advanced in this chapter, I do not view this as an undesirable outcome. The law need not supply a cause of action for every instance in which individuals feel that they have been aggrieved, and there seems to be no compelling policy rationale under the facts of *Peeren boom*, whether moral, instrumentalist, systemic, or otherwise, to recognize Peerenboom's claim. Indeed, it has long been held that, as a matter of property law, discarded items are considered to be abandoned, and ownership thereof may be claimed by anyone taking possession. As a result, the DNA information gleaned from Perlmutter's discarded water bottle, along with his fingerprints, hair, and skin cells left nearby, are all fair game to one seeking information about him. The court's interpretation of Florida's unusual statute to give Peerenboom a cause of action for conversion in this case strikes me as wrong. But given that the *Peeren boom* case does not relate to DTC genomics, I will not address it further in this chapter.

II CONTRACTUAL MECHANISMS FOR DATA PROTECTION

The handling and use of both data disclosed to the DTC provider by its customers (name, contact details, payment details, demographic and physical information, health history, and survey responses), as well as data generated by the provider from the customer's biological material and online activity (DNA sequence, genotype, health profile, ancestry, and browsing history), are addressed by a range of contractual mechanisms offered by DTC providers themselves (online agreements, policies, and terms of use). These mechanisms typically detail the circumstances under which the DTC provider may disclose data about a customer to others, including corporate partners and researchers, and the uses to which that data may be put. In many cases, customers must give their affirmative consent to particular uses or sharing of data.[19]

In 2018, leading DTC genomics providers including 23andMe, Ancestry, MyHeritage, and Helix expressed support for a set of "Privacy Best Practices for Consumer Genetic Testing Services" developed by the Future of Privacy Forum.[20] These best practices require that data collectors build into their data usage policies and practices features to promote transparency, consent, accountability, security, data integrity, and the like.

These privacy mechanisms are essentially contractual in nature. The DTC provider makes its privacy policy available for consumers to read and requires their agreement before offering services to them. The provider, in turn, must comply with the representations and warranties that it makes in the agreement. A failure to do so would result in a breach of contract, which is actionable by affected consumers.[21]

While these contractual mechanisms may strike some as ineffective and unlikely to elicit meaningful agreement – an objection that has been raised with respect to the entire range of "boilerplate" agreements that, for better or worse, pervade the

[19] See, e.g., 23and Me, Full Privacy Statement, https://www.23andme.com/about/privacy/#Full (last visited May 28, 2019) ("Your Genetic and Self-Reported Information may be used for 23andMe Research only if you have consented to this use by completing a Consent Document."). According to one recent report, 80 percent of 23andMe customers opt-in to the company's data sharing practices. Julian Segert, Understanding Ownership and Privacy of Genetic Data, Science in the News Blog (Nov. 28, 2018), http://sitn.hms.harvard.edu/flash/2018/understanding-ownership-privacy-genetic-data/.

[20] Carson Martinez, Privacy Best Practices for Consumer Genetic Testing Services, Future of Privacy Forum (Jul. 31, 2018), https://fpf.org/2018/07/31/privacy-best-practices-for-consumer-genetic-testing-services/ [hereinafter Privacy Best Practices] (announcing release of Future of Privacy Forum, Privacy Best Practices for Consumer Genetic Testing Services).

[21] Jessica Roberts, in advocating a property-based conversion action for unauthorized use of genetic information, argues that contractual terms of use may not adequately protect consumer interests. Roberts, Genetic Conversion, supra note 3. Roberts cites, in particular, the plaintiff's action in *Cole v. Gene by Gene, Ltd.*, No. 1:14-cv-00004, 2017 WL 2838256 (D. Alaska June 30, 2017), which was a statutory action under the Alaska Genetic Privacy Act, an Act that appears to sound in property law. However, the plaintiff in that case failed to bring a claim for breach of the defendant's terms of use. Id. It is not clear whether any such breach occurred, or what the terms of use actually provided.

modern information economy[22] –many of the same criticisms have been leveled at the "informed consent" model that has been used for decades in federally funded human subjects research.[23] Though the informed consent model has been found to give research subjects little meaningful understanding of underlying risks and benefits,[24] and has shown itself to be amenable to manipulation of various kinds,[25] it is still viewed as an indispensable mechanism for protecting individual privacy and respecting individual autonomy in the context of human subjects research.[26] Thus, the use of contractual mechanisms by DTC providers is, at worst, on par with such consent practices.[27] In some consumer contexts, contracts and other consumer-facing documents must contain special warnings and notifications to alert consumers of particularly important information. For example, consumer credit card agreements must highlight certain information such as the annual percentage rate, issuance fees, and finance charges, in a tabular format and in plain and easy-to-understand language.[28] Likewise, advertisements for prescription drug products must include information about known side effects and counterindications of the

22 See, e.g., Margaret Jane Radin, Boilerplate: The Fine Print, Vanishing Rights, and the Rule of Law (2012).

23 Informed consent, as it is understood in the bioethics community, requires a significantly higher degree of understanding and volition than the legal doctrine of contractual assent. For example, obtaining informed consent from the subject of a medical procedure includes explaining the associated risks and benefits to the individual in a manner that the individual understands, confirming that understanding, allowing the individual to ask questions, and carefully delineating the scope of the consent. See Nat'l Comm'n for the Prot. of Human Subjects of Biomedical & Behavioral Research, The Belmont Report: Ethical Principles and Guidelines for the Protection of Human Subjects of Research § C.I (1979) (Informed Consent). Contractual assent, on the other hand, simply requires that a contracting party manifest its assent to abiding by the contract terms "even in the absence of informed assent to these terms." Florencia Marotta-Wurgler, Omri Ben-Shahar, and Oren Bar-Gill, Adoption of Standard Contract Terms, ALI Advisor (Apr. 27, 2017), http://www.thealiadviser.org/consumer-contracts/adoption-standard-contract-terms/.

24 See, e.g., Barbara A. Koenig, Have We Asked Too Much of Consent?, 44 Hastings Cent. Rep. 33, 33 (2014); Patrick Taylor, When Consent Gets in the Way, 456 Nature 32, 33 (2008).

25 Howard Brody, Transparency: Informed Consent in Primary Care, 19 Hastings Center Rep. 5, 5 (1989).

26 See General Requirements for Informed Consent, 45 C.F.R. § 46.116 (2018) [hereinafter the Common Rule]. Of course, DTC providers are not technically required to obtain "informed consent" from customers under the Common Rule so long as they are not conducting medical research funded by the federal government or directed to the approval of a drug or device.

Nevertheless, some commentators versed in the traditions of bioethics tend to think – inaccurately, I believe – that all interactions with individuals, whether or not involving medical procedures, require informed consent. See Contreras, Genetic Property, supra note 3, at 6–7 (arguing that overly expansive interpretations of informed consent requirement "inappropriately grant[] individuals excessive and inappropriate control over genetic data").

27 Nevertheless, Professors James Hazel and Christopher Slobogin recently found in a study of ninety DTC genomics providers' privacy policies that the majority of such policies failed to conform to recognized fair information practice principles. James W. Hazel & Christopher Slobogin, Who Knows What, And When?: A Survey Of The Privacy Policies Proffered By U.S. Direct-To-Consumer Genetic Testing Companies, 28 Cornell J.L. & Pub. Pol. 35 (2018).

28 See Credit and Charge Card Applications and Solicitations, 12 C.F.R. § 1026.60(a)(2) (2019).

drug.[29] By the same token, Ifeoma Ajunwa proposes that DTC providers display prominent online disclaimers "alerting potential consumers that there is a high potential that their genetic information may be intercepted by third parties on the Internet and that this information may be used for a variety of nefarious purposes including both genetic discrimination and genetic identity theft."[30] While the actual language and ultimate effectiveness of such notifications may be debated, it is clearly possible to require that important contractual provisions be highlighted for consumers.

Moreover, contract law has adapted over the years to the mechanisms of online contracts of adhesion, particularly in the consumer context. In most cases, contractual terms that are unconscionable will not be enforced against a consumer, even if contained in an otherwise valid agreement.[31] Thus, DTC providers are, for all practical purposes, constrained from including in their customer agreements and policies terms that significantly overreach or otherwise take advantage of consumers.[32]

In the event of a violation of contractual data usage terms by a DTC provider, individual remedies for breach of contract are well-understood.[33] If a DTC provider violates the terms of its data usage agreement with a consumer, the consumer will, at a minimum, have an action for damages. If the violation is particularly egregious, punitive damages may also be awarded. In some cases, equitable relief may also be available, possibly including revocation of the agreement or a court-ordered prohibition on unauthorized usage of the data in question. But, most importantly, contract-based expectation damages seek to redress the wrong suffered by the injured party – to place him or her in the position that he or she would have been in absent a breach of the contract by the other party. If the injury suffered is small, then damages should be small. This approach contrasts with that offered by property-type rules, in which a property owner may seek to prevent an encroachment on his or her

29 See Prescription Drug Advertising, 21 C.F.R. § 202.1(e) (2008).

30 Ifeoma Ajunwa, Genetic Testing Meets Big Data: Tort and Contract Law Issues, 75 Ohio St. L.J. 1225, 1256–57 (2014).

31 Restatement (Second) of Contracts, § 208 (Am. Law Inst. 1981) ("If a contract or term thereof is unconscionable at the time the contract is made a court may refuse to enforce the contract, or may enforce the remainder of the contract without the unconscionable term, or may so limit the application of any unconscionable term as to avoid any unconscionable result.").

32 See Contreras, Genetic Property, supra note 3, at 46–47 (describing, in the context of biomedical research, actions that could be prohibited as beyond the scope of permissible data usage: attempting to reidentify individuals from genetic data and uses other than biomedical research, such as insurance underwriting and direct marketing).

33 Failures to comply with consumer agreement policies and terms, regrettably, are not uncommon in health-related applications. See Kit Huckvale, John Torous & Mark E. Larsen, Assessment of the Data Sharing and Privacy Practices of Smartphone Apps for Depression and Smoking Cessation, 2 JAMA Network Open (Apr. 19, 2019) (" In this cross-sectional study of 36 top-ranked apps for depression and smoking cessation available in public app stores, 29 transmitted data to services provided by Facebook or Google, but only 12 accurately disclosed this in a privacy policy.").

property even if the encroachment would cause little or no actual harm.[34] Thus, contract-type damages can offer a more proportional and logical remedy for violations of rules relating to individual health data than can property-type remedies.

One potential concern relating to contractual mechanisms, particularly in the consumer context, is that a number of rights and remedies may be waived through contract. Such waivers can cover both procedural avenues of redress – such as agreements to resolve disputes through confidential arbitration as opposed to litigation[35] – as well as substantive remedies such as the right to seek punitive and consequential damages and injunctive relief.

Finally, despite the boilerplate nature of most DTC consumer agreements, when individuals are sufficiently motivated, and when the genetic material or data that they possess is sufficiently valuable, they have been able to negotiate far more favorable terms with researchers wishing to access and use that data. Perhaps the best known example of this approach is PXE International (PXEI), an organization founded in 1995 by the parents of children suffering from *pseudoxanthoma elasticum* (PXE), a rare and potentially lethal genetic disorder.[36] In order to facilitate research on the disease, PXEI assembled tissue and blood samples from PXE patients and made them accessible to researchers only under strict contractual terms. The PXE biorepository soon became a critical resource for genetic investigation of PXE and eventually helped investigators to identify the gene responsible for the disorder. When a patent application was filed covering the gene and its mutations, per the terms of the arrangement, PXEI members were listed as coinventors, and the patent itself was assigned to PXEI.[37] Admittedly, the PXEI situation is a rare one, but perhaps such tailored contractual structures, and the extra administrative overhead they entail, are only justified in rare cases when individual genetic data is of significant value.

Thus, whether contractual mechanisms are standardized "click-through" contracts or customized and negotiated agreements, DTC customers have the opportunity to protect their rights and limit permitted uses of their data through them, or simply to opt not to provide data to any DTC provider.[38]

34 Contreras & Nordfalk, supra note 15, at 195–203 (comparing application of property versus liability-type rules to misuse of personal health data).

35 Cf. Epic Systems Corp. v. Lewis, 138 S. Ct. 1612 (2017) (upholding contractual forced arbitration clauses in employment agreements); Italian Colors Rest. v. Am. Express, 570 U.S. 228 (2013) (upholding a contractual forced arbitration clause and class action waiver in antitrust case).

36 See Sharon F. Terry et al., Advocacy Groups as Research Organizations: The PXE International Example, 8 Nature Rev. Genetics 157, 157–58 (2007); Sharon F. Terry & Charles D. Boyd, Researching the Biology of PXE: Partnering in the Process, 106 Am. J. Med. Genetics 177, 180 (2001).

37 Terry et al., supra note 36, at 162; Terry & Boyd, supra note 36, at 179–80.

38 In the DTC context, genetic information can only be obtained with the consent of the individual (distinguishing this context from others (e.g., criminal investigation) in which involuntary collection of genetic information is possible). As such, the initial entitlement to control this information lies squarely with the individual. Contreras & Nordfalk, supra note 15, at 203. In fact, some (including the author) have argued that the contractual terms of use applicable to some DTC sites may be so restrictive that beneficial biomedical research is stymied. See Jorge L. Contreras, Kyle Schultz, Craig

III AGENCY OVERSIGHT AND ENFORCEMENT

In addition to traditional contractual mechanisms, governmental oversight and regulation exist to protect individual data and privacy. Since the early days of Internet commerce, the US Federal Trade Commission (FTC), which is authorized to police unfair and deceptive business practices, has monitored the collection and use of consumer data by online vendors.[39] In recent years, the FTC has investigated and brought actions for deceptive data claims and practices against prominent companies including Uber, Vizio, BLU, and AshleyMadison.com.[40]

The FTC has also been active in policing the data security practices of health care and DTC providers. In 2014, it filed charges against two companies, Genelink, Inc. and foru International, for a range of false advertising claims pertaining to the companies' nutrigenetic products.[41] In addition, the FTC charged the companies with engaging in unfair and deceptive trade practices by failing to maintain adequate and reasonable data security for their customers' personal information.[42] These claims were settled, with the companies agreeing to "establish and maintain comprehensive data security programs and submit to security audits by independent auditors every other year for 20 years."[43] Two years later, the FTC found medical testing company LabMD liable for data security practices "lacking even basic precautions to protect the sensitive consumer information maintained on its computer system."[44]

In late 2017, Senator Chuck Schumer (D-NY) sent a letter to the FTC asking the agency to "investigate and ensure that the privacy policies of all DNA test kits are clear, transparent, and fair to consumers."[45] The Senator concluded: "The last gift any of us want to give away this holiday season is our most personal and sensitive information, so that is why we are asking the FTC to step in, take a hard look at this industry and ensure there are across-the-board protections to safeguard consumers and ensure good research continues."[46] The FTC responded quickly with an open

C. Teerlink, Tim Maness, Laurence J. Meyer, Lisa A. Cannon-Albright, *Legal Terms of Use and Public Genealogy Websites*, J.L. & Biosciences, LSAA063, 1–24 (2020).

39 See Fed. Trade Comm'n, Privacy Online: Fair Information Practices in the Electronic Marketplace (2000); Fed. Trade Comm'n, Privacy & Data Security Update: 2016, 1 (2017).

40 See Press Releases, Fed. Trade Comm'n, Privacy and Security Enforcement, www.ftc.gov/news-events/media-resources/protecting-consumer-privacy/privacy-security-enforcement (last visited May 30, 2019).

41 Press Release, Fed. Trade Comm'n, FTC Approves Final Consent Orders Settling Charges that Companies Deceptively Claimed Their Genetically Modified Nutritional Supplements Could Treat Diseases (May 12, 2014), www.ftc.gov/news-events/press-releases/2014/05/ftc-approves-final-consent-orders-settling-charges-companies.

42 Id.

43 Id.

44 Opinion of the Commission, LabMD, Inc., F.T.C. Docket No. 9357, at 1 (July 28, 2016), www.ftc.gov/system/files/documents/cases/160729labmd-opinion.pdf.

45 Press Release, Office of Senator Charles E. Schumer (Nov. 26, 2017), www.schumer.senate.gov/newsroom/press-releases/schumer-reveals-popular-at-home-dna-test-kits-are-putting-consumer-privacy-at-great-risk-as-dna-firms-could-sell-your-most-personal-info-and-genetic-data-to-all-comers-senator-pushes- feds-to-investigate_ensure-fair-privacy-standards-for-all-dna-kits.

46 Id.

letter to consumers, urging them to pay attention to DTC firms' privacy policies, choose privacy options carefully, and recognize the inherent risks of submitting DNA to a DTC provider.[47] Today, the FTC maintains on its website additional information and cautionary guidance for consumers concerning DTC-GT.[48] Though not confirmed by the agency, press reports have recently suggested that the FTC may be formally investigating DTC providers including 23andMe and Ancestry.[49]

The FTC is not the only federal agency that has been active in policing genetic testing providers. In 2019, the US Department of Health and Human Services Office of Inspector General issued a Fraud Alert regarding a genetic testing company that offered free genetic test kits in exchange for Medicare beneficiaries' Medicare numbers and other personal information.[50]

These examples illustrate that federal agency oversight and enforcement do exist as viable backstops to purely contractual mechanisms for data privacy and protection in the area of DTC genomics.

IV PROTECTIVE LEGISLATION AND REGULATION

Governmental regulation of the DTC industry is currently in a state of flux. In recent years, the FTC, FDA, and various state attorneys general have each asserted some degree of oversight over DTC providers, particularly those that offer health-related information to their customers.[51] However, these regulations pertain primarily to the laboratory procedures implemented by the DTC provider and the accuracy of its advertising. However, most DTC genomics providers are not regulated under the federal regimes governing human subjects research – the Common Rule (as they are not federally funded researchers nor are they seeking approval of a new drug or medical device)[52] or the HIPAA Privacy Rule (as they are not health care providers).[53] Nevertheless, to the extent that increased protection for individual

47 DNA Test Kits: Consider the Privacy Implications, Fed Trade Comm'n (Dec. 12, 2017), www.consumer.ftc.gov/blog/2017/12/dna-test-kits-consider-privacy-implications.

48 Direct-To-Consumer Genetic Tests, Fed. Trade Comm'n (Feb. 2018), www.consumer.ftc.gov/articles/0166-direct-consumer-genetic-tests.

49 Marcus Baram, The FTC is investigating DNA firms like 23andMe and Ancestry over privacy, FastCompany (Jun. 5, 2018), www.fastcompany.com/40580364/the-ftc-is-investigating-dna-firms-like-23andme-and-ancestry-over-privacy.

50 U.S. Dept. Health and Human Servs., Office of Inspector General, Fraud Alert: Genetic Testing Scam (Jun. 3, 2019), https://oig.hhs.gov/fraud/consumeralerts/alerts/geneticscam.asp?utm_source=website&utm_campaign=geneticscam.

51 The laboratories that analyze DTC customer biological samples must be certified under the Clinical Laboratory Improvement Amendments of 1988 (CLIA). Pub. L. No. 100-578, 102 Stat. 2903 (codified as amended at 42 U.S.C. § 263a (2006)).

52 See Common Rule, supra note 26 (governing human subjects research conducted using federal funding or with respect to the approval of drugs or medical devices).

53 See 45 C.F.R. §§ 160, 164 (2003) (hereinafter HIPAA Privacy Rule) (pertaining to the use and handling of protected health information by health care providers and related entities).

health data is desired, it would not be a stretch to amend and expand these existing regulatory frameworks to include within their scope DTC providers and various other stewards of individual health data.

But even without the expansion of these existing regulatory frameworks, important legislation protecting individuals from abuse of their genetic information currently exists, most notably the US Genetic Information Nondiscrimination Act of 2008 (GINA).[54] GINA prohibits discrimination by employers and health insurers on the basis of an individual's genetic information. The conduct prohibited by GINA is far reaching, as the statute bars even the collection of employee genetic information by an employer.[55] Employment-based actions under GINA are filed by aggrieved employees with the Equal Employment Opportunity Commission (EEOC), and then advance through an administrative process which is subject to appeal to the courts.[56] While GINA has been criticized for failing to cover certain types of employers (including the military) and insurers (including life and long-term disability carriers),[57] its basic framework is sound. Thus, an expansion of GINA's scope to market sectors that are currently omitted would go a long way toward preventing discrimination based on genetic information in a comprehensive fashion.[58]

In addition to existing legislative and regulatory regimes, new legislation and regulation can be enacted specifically to address the privacy and security of data held by DTC providers. In the context of biomedical research, I have previously proposed regulatory requirements regarding enhanced data security for individual genetic information.[59] Along these lines, regulatory and administrative penalties for the misuse of individual health data already exist for a few specific data repositories.[60]

Such prohibitions could also be enacted with respect to the data held by DTC genomics providers. For example, states such as California have recently enacted sweeping data privacy laws that apply across the board to entities holding individual

[54] Genetic Information Nondiscrimination Act of 2008, Pub. L. No. 110-223, 122 Stat. 881 (2008) (codified as amended in scattered sections of 29 and 42 U.S.C.) [hereinafter GINA]. Other statutes prohibiting discrimination on the basis of medical condition also exist. See, e.g., Sharon Hoffman, Big Data and the Americans with Disabilities Act, 68 Hastings L.J. 777 (2017) (arguing that the ADA should be interpreted to prohibit discrimination on the basis of predictive medical testing).

[55] GINA § 202(b).

[56] GINA § 207.

[57] For two critical assessments of GINA on its tenth anniversary, see Bradley A.Arehardt & Jessica L. Roberts, GINA, Big Data, and the Future of Employee Privacy, 128 Yale L.J. 710 (2019); Barbara J. Evans, The Genetic Information Nondiscrimination Act at Age 10: GINA's Controversial Assertion that Data Transparency Protects Privacy and Civil Rights, 60 Wm. & Mary L. Rev. 2017 (2019).

[58] See Contreras, Genetic Property, supra note 3, at 44–46 (proposing expansions of GINA); see also Leslie E.Wolf at al., The Web of Legal Protections for Participants in Genomic Research, 29 Health Matrix 1, 53–63 (2019) (discussing state law nondiscrimination legislation that, in many respects, goes beyond the protections offered by GINA).

[59] Contreras, Genetic Property, supra note 3, at 47.

[60] See Contreras & Nordfalk, supra note 15, at Part III (describing administrative restrictions and penalties for misuse of data housed in the Utah Population Database and Statistics Denmark).

data.[61] Four states (California, Maryland, New York, and Virginia) have enacted laws governing human subjects research that is not covered by the Common Rule,[62] and several more have laws pertaining specifically to the use and disclosure of genetic information.[63] Notably, as Leslie Wolf and coauthors have recently pointed out, a handful of states have enacted legislation that purports to protect individual genetic information from being disclosed even in response to a subpoena or court order, protections that go well beyond what is available under federal regulations such as the HIPAA Privacy Rule.[64] Likewise, the National Institutes of Health offer a Certificate of Confidentiality that permits federally funded researchers to refuse to disclose sensitive personal information about research subjects even in the face of subpoenas or other legal requests.[65]

This being said, there is a danger of states overregulating data usage and imposing restrictions that are inconsistent across jurisdictions. As Wolf and coauthors note: "[T]he quantity of state laws [relating to the protection of participants in genomic research] is striking Applicable state laws are not just numerous, they are extremely variable."[66] This degree of variability and inconsistency has been viewed by some critics as potentially harmful to research across state lines.[67] Even more significantly, DTC providers, which offer services to consumers across the country, will be most affected by the variability in this patchwork of state privacy and other regulations.

V LIABILITY RULES FOR DATA PROTECTION

In addition to contractual and administrative remedies, individuals whose personal health data has been used in an impermissible or abusive manner often have a range of private remedies including common law and statutory tort actions for violations of

61 California Consumer Privacy Act of 2018, Cal. Civ. Code §§ 1798.100-.199 (West 2018).

62 See Wolf at al., supra note 58, at 27–31.

63 See id. at 31–34, 44–49.

64 See id. at 50–52 (discussing legislation in Texas, Delaware, Illinois, Nevada, Oklahoma, Oregon and Utah). Such state legislation is also likely to be far more potent than the largely hortatory declarations by DTC providers that they will not willingly disclose customer information for law enforcement purposes. See, e.g., Ancestry.com Terms, *supra* note 1 ("[W]e ... will not share your Genetic Information with law enforcement unless compelled by valid legal process.").

65 42 U.S.C. § 241(d) (2012); 21 U.S.C. § 872(c) (2012); Protection of Identity — Research Subjects, 42 C. F.R. § 2a (2013); see also Leslie E.Wolf et al., Certificates of Confidentiality: Protecting Human Subject Research Data in Law and Practice, 43 J.L. Med. & Ethics 594 (2015) (observing that "questions persist about the strength of Certificate protections, and the evidence on which to judge their strength is scant").

66 Id. at 98.

67 See, e.g., Jeannie Baumann, Patchwork of Privacy Laws Muzzle Medical Studies Across States, Bloomberg Law (May 28, 2019), https://news.bloomberglaw.com/pharma-and-life-sciences/patchwork-of-privacy-laws-muzzle-medical-studies-across-states ("A wave of state privacy bills targeting tech giants like Facebook and Google is prompting warnings that the measures could mire biomedical research in red tape and slow innovation").

privacy, deceit, fraud, and breach of fiduciary duty.[68] Jessica Litman, in assessing a range of legal mechanisms for the protection of individual data, notes that "[p]hysicians are routinely held to owe fiduciary duties to their patients, and thus unauthorized disclosure of patient information is actionable in tort."[69] Likewise, in the well-known case *Moore v. Regents of the University of California*, even though the court denied Mr. Moore's property-based claims relating to the misuse of his biological materials and associated discoveries, he prevailed against the health care providers that violated a range of common law duties owed to him.[70]

This being said, it would be difficult to characterize a DTC provider as a health care provider owing a fiduciary duty of care toward its customers, just as fiduciary arguments failed in *Greenberg v. Miami Children's Hospital* with respect to researchers removed from actual contact with the patients in question.[71] To overcome this barrier, Jack Balkin has recently introduced the idea of an information fiduciary, "a person or business who, because of their relationship with another, has taken on special duties with respect to the information they obtain in the course of the relationship."[72] This concept, if adopted by courts, could offer a tort-based avenue to assess liability for intentional breaches of trust relating to health data. As such, remedies such as those awarded in *Moore* could be made available to DTC customers whose data is used in a manner inconsistent with the relationship of trust established.

Unintentional violations of trust may also occur with respect to health data – namely the types of data leaks and breaches that have gained international attention over the past several years.[73] In 2006, two state negligence cases established the very real possibility of tort liability for the inadvertent disclosure of personal health information by a health care provider.[74] In view of the likelihood of negligent releases of personal data, Jay Kesan and Carol Hayes have proposed the recognition

68 See Contreras, Genetic Property, supra note 3, at 40–41 (discussing claims for deception, breach of fiduciary duty, fraud, and deceit).

69 Jessica Litman, Information Privacy/Information Property, 52 Stan. L. Rev. 1283, 1308 (2000); see also Ajunwa, supra note 30, at 1249–52 (discussing breach of fiduciary duty claims in the health care context).

70 Moore v. Regents of the Univ. of Cal., 793 P.2d 479, 493 (Cal. 1990); see also Roberts, Genetic Conversion, supra note 3 (discussing Moore case and fiduciary claims).

71 264 F. Supp. 2d 1064, 1072 (S.D. Fla. 2003) ("There is no automatic fiduciary relationship that attaches when a researcher accepts medical donations.").

72 Jack M.Balkin, Information Fiduciaries and the First Amendment, 49 U.C. Davis L. Rev. 1183, 1209 (2016).

73 See Jay P. Kesan & Carol M. Hayes, Liability for Data Injuries, 2019 U. Ill. L. Rev. 295, 297–99 (2019) (examples of data breaches); Ajunwa, supra note 30, at 1225–28 (describing data breaches in health care industry).

74 Acosta v. Byrum, 638 S.E.2d 246 (N.C. Ct. App. 2006) (negligent disclosure of information caused by psychiatrist's negligent release of computer password); Herman v. Kratche, No. 86697, 2006 WL 3240680 (Ohio Ct. App. Nov. 9, 2006) (negligent invasion of privacy caused by transmission of patient's medical records to her employer instead of her health insurer); see also Ajunwa, supra note 30, at 1243–44 (collecting cases).

of a general "legal duty to secure data" upon which tort claims may be brought following data breaches and leaks.[75] This approach is reasonable and could both offer consumers greater peace of mind when entrusting their data to DTC providers and encourage DTC providers to bolster the security measures that they use to secure customer data.

Private actions grounded in tort law generally give rise to remedies that are measured in terms of monetary awards (so-called liability rule remedies).[76] These awards can include both compensatory damages for loss of value and emotional distress, as well as punitive damages. Nevertheless, unlike it does for demonstrable economic loss in the presence of a breached duty (unauthorized withdrawals from a bank account, for example), US tort law does not offer particularly generous remedies for purely dignitary harms.[77] Litman, writing nearly two decades ago, thus observed that tort remedies probably "would be more effective in deterring misuse of data than in actually compensating victims for the loss of their data privacy."[78] Kesan and Hayes also recognize difficulties recovering monetary damages in such actions and recommend an expansion of remedies for data breaches.[79] With Nordfalk, I have assessed the desirability of liability rule (rather than property rule) structures for health data, and acknowledge the comparative weakness of private tort law remedies in this area. We suggest that such liability rules are best adopted in tandem with administrative and regulatory rules that are enforceable by governmental agencies, such as those discussed in Sections III and IV above.[80]

Thus, even in the context of DTC services governed by contractual arrangements, individuals have a range of ex post liability remedies in the event of data misuse or mishandling, again making a resort to property law both unnecessary and inadvisable.

75 Kesan & Hayes, supra note 73, at 320, 356. Ifeoma Ajunwa goes further, arguing that liability for unauthorized disclosure of genetic information should be governed under a strict liability standard, much as product liability claims are. Ajunwa, supra note 30, at 1259. I am not convinced that a strict liability standard is appropriate for data breaches, particularly given uncertainties regarding the efficacy of technological protection measures in the face of as-yet unknown and undeveloped cyber-intrusion techniques. Certainly, it seems overly punitive to subject a hospital or DTC genomics provider to a strict liability standard when they have relied on otherwise reasonable security measures.

76 This nomenclature finds its roots in the seminal law review article, Guido Calabresi & A. Douglas Melamed, Property Rules, Liability Rules, and Inalienability: One View of the Cathedral, 85 Harv. L. Rev. 1089 (1972).

77 See, e.g., Russell Fraker, Reformulating Outrage: A Critical Analysis of the Problematic Tort of IIED, 61 Vand. L. Rev. 983, 1000–01 (2008); William L. Prosser, Intentional Infliction of Mental Suffering: A New Tort, 37 Mich. L. Rev. 874, 877 (1939) ("If the plaintiff is to recovery every time that her feelings are hurt, we should all be in court twice a week."); Ajunwa, supra note 30, at 1254.

78 Litman, supra note 70, at 1311 n.126.

79 Kesan & Hayes, supra note 73, at 359; cf. Marian K. Riedy & Bartlomiej Hanus, Yes, Your Personal Data Is at Risk: Get Over It!, 19 SMU Sci. & Tech. L. Rev. 3, 6 (2016) (proposing the establishment of an administered data breach compensation fund along the lines of those created after mass disasters).

80 Contreras & Nordfalk, supra note 15, at 207 (proposing a combination of liability rules and governmental oversight in lieu of "property" rules to govern individual health data).

VI CONCLUSION

Customers of DTC-GT today are protected by a combination of contractual mechanisms, government oversight, and statutory law. While none of these existing legal mechanisms is perfect, each can be amended, improved, and expanded. However, few benefits would be gained by DTC customers, or individuals in general, from propertizing genetic data. On the contrary, the propertization of this data could have severe consequences for biomedical research, public health, and the health care system well beyond the comparatively small DTC testing industry. As a result, the movement toward propertization of genetic data should be resisted, both by DTC providers and the health care industry more broadly. Instead, the focus of policy efforts should be on the improvement of DTC providers' privacy policies and practices, the strengthening of agency oversight of DTC provider handling and use of individual data, and the adoption and implementation of enhanced laws and regulations protecting individual privacy and data security with respect to genetic and health information.

5

Governance in the Era of CRISPR and DIY-Bio

Regulatory Guidance of Human Genome Editing at the National and Global Levels

Scott J. Schweikart

I INTRODUCTION

Human genome editing[1] is a powerful biomedical tool, which has great potential but which is also coupled with risks.[2] The process has received considerable national press and scrutiny following the "birth of twin girls whose genome was edited during in vitro fertilization."[3] The news of so-called "CRISPR-babies" prompted a wave of foreboding news headlines[4] and calls for a moratorium on germline editing.[5] This event highlighted the urgency in this newfound era of CRISPR[6] – where genome editing is now more efficient and affordable[7] – to consider how human genome editing should be properly and ethically regulated. Critically, regulation must consider the two major categories of implementers of this technology: Big-Bio (corporations and universities) and DIY-Bio (biohackers, individuals, and

[1] National Academy of Sciences, Engineering, and Medicine, Human Genome Editing: Science, Ethics, and Governance 1 (2017), http://nap.edu/24623(suggesting that the language "genome editing" be used instead of "gene editing," as it is a more accurate and encompassing term).

[2] Amy Gutmann & Jonathan D. Moreno, Keep CRISPR Safe: Regulating a Genetic Revolution, 97 Foreign Aff. 171, 171 (2018) (noting the tension between the promise and risk of genome editing and explaining that while advances in genome editing "could bring vast benefits to society," such technology "raises risks both for individuals and for society as a whole").

[3] R. Alto Charo , Rogues and Regulation of Germline Editing, 380 New Eng. J. Med. 976, 976 (2019) (describing how Chinese scientist He Jiankui shocked the world in November, 2018 when he announced the birth of twin girls whose genomes were modified using CRISPR technology).

[4] See, e.g., Julia Belluz, Is the CRISPR baby controversy the start of a terrifying new chapter in gene editing?, Vox (Jan. 22, 2019), www.vox.com/science-and-health/2018/11/30/18119589/crispr-gene-editing-he-jiankui.

[5] See Charo, supra note 3, at 976 (noting that while "calling for a moratorium may feel satisfying, it does little to stop rogue actors"); Eric Lander et al., Adopt a Moratorium on Heritable Genome Editing, 567 Nature 165, 165 (2019) (calling for an "international framework" where nations "voluntarily commit to not approve any use of clinical germline editing unless certain conditions are met").

[6] CRISPR is short for clustered regularly interspaced palindromic repeats. National Academy of Sciences, Engineering, and Medicine, supra note 1, at 65.

[7] See Arthur L. Caplan et al., No Time to Waste: The Ethical Challenges Created by CRISPR, 16(11) EMBO Rep. 1421, 1421 (2015).

community labs). The distinction between the two is important and often overlooked when considering regulation from both national and global levels.

A national[8] regulatory approach to human genome editing – one example of which includes the federal and state agencies that help to verify and enhance safety and efficacy – will have to be applied differently to Big-Bio and DIY-Bio. Traditional regulatory levers at the national level are better designed for the larger-scale institutions of Big-Bio. Additionally, a global regulatory approach – which may involve an international treaty or other international collaborative – should also look different when applied to Big-Bio and DIY-Bio, respectively.

II DIY-BIO VERSUS BIG-BIO

Who is implementing and producing genome editing technology is an important consideration when evaluating regulatory questions. There are nominally two types of implementers of this technology: DIY-Bio and Big-Bio. DIY-Bio, short for "do-it-yourself biology," is "non-institutional science or science performed outside of professional laboratories."[9] Sometimes DIY-Bio is referred to as "biohacking," and there are ongoing debates about the precise and proper definition of these activities.[10] However, this chapter will refer to activities that are carried out by individuals or community labs, outside of the institutional realm, as DIY-Bio. DIY-Bio can include many kinds of biologically related modifications and experiments; of relevance here is the rise of bio-hacking of molecular genetics, which has recently included "modifying algae to glow" and "self-injecting nucleotides to genetically enhance muscle growth or to treat HIV or herpes."[11] Indeed, DIY-Bio has already begun to use the gene-editing technology CRISPR, reportedly for both therapeutic and enhancement purposes.[12]

As opposed to DIY-Bio, traditional sources of biological innovation and technology are found in what is sometimes described in the literature as Big-Bio

8 By "national" I mean to refer to the regulatory authority of a sovereign and to broadly include both federal and/or state governments and their respective regulatory powers.

9 Lisa C. Ikemoto, DIY Bio: Hacking Life in Biotech's Backyard, 51 U.C. Davis L. Rev. 539, 541 (2017) ("DIY biologists set up home labs in garages, space bedrooms, and closets or use community lab spaces.").

10 See Maxwell J. Mehlman & Ronald A. Conlon, Governing Non-Traditional Biology, in Consuming Genetics (I. Glenn Cohen et al. eds. 2022). Mehlman and Conlon prefer to call DIY-Bio and biohacking by the term "Non-Traditional Gene Editing," noting that DIY is not always accurate since much work takes place in "community labs" and because bio-hacking is sometimes associated with the negative connotations of computer hackers. Id.

11 Patricia J. Zettler et al., Finding a Regulatory Balance for Genetic Biohacking, in Consuming Genetics (I. Glenn Cohen et al. eds. 2022); Sarah Zhang, A Biohacker Regrets Publicly Injecting Himself With CRISPR, The Atlantic (Feb. 20, 2018), www.theatlantic.com/science/archive/2018/02/biohacking-stunts-crispr/553511/.

12 See Mehlman & Conlon, supra note 10.

("big biology").[13] For the purposes of this chapter, Big-Bio[14] will refer to large corporations and academic institutions that produce biotechnology most typically associated with large-scale government regulation, such as that from the NIH or FDA. Big-Bio has for decades been the dominant implementer of genetic- engineering technologies. For instance, CRISPR technology itself was discovered and developed by scientists working at various Big-Bio institutions like the Broad Institute of MIT and Harvard.[15]

III REGULATION OF GENOME EDITING: NATIONAL LEVEL VERSUS GLOBAL LEVEL

A *National Level*

The scope of nationally based regulation of DIY-Bio and Big-Bio must be considered. First, looking towards Big-Bio, there are already traditional regulatory entities at work, like the FDA, NIH, and EPA. These big government agencies were designed to regulate large scale entities, like corporations and other institutions. Barbara Evans explains that " [t]wentieth-century federal regulatory frameworks conceived the regulator's role as protecting consumers in two-party transactions between a discrete number of large providers of goods and services and the mass of relatively powerless consumers."[16] This is the kind of regulatory environment that is primed for Big-Bio regulation.

With regards to DIY-Bio, the traditional national regulations are an imperfect fit, and gaps are inevitable. As Evans notes, "[t]ransactions in the 21st-century sharing economy and DIY bio community often fall below the (express or discretionary) thresholds for federal regulation under the twentieth-century regulatory paradigm."[17] DIY-Bio is often composed of individuals or small groups, not the large-scale entities that traditional government regulations were designed for.[18] However, it is not that existing paradigms cannot be applied to DIY-Bio – they can be – but that policy makers are left to decide "how to better enforce existing laws before deciding

[13] Robert Bolton & Richard Thomas, The Science, Politics, and Economics of Synthetic Biology, 9 Innovations 213, 214 (2014) (referring to "big bio" as "universities, big corporations, and government agencies").

[14] There is not a precise or formal term for this group. I use Big-Bio here as a shorthand for the larger and more historically known implementers of biotechnology: universities, academic institutions, and corporations.

[15] See Eric S. Lander, The Heroes of CRISPR, 164 Cell 18, 25 (2016).

[16] Barbara J. Evans, Programming Our Genomes: Programming Ourselves: The Moral and Regulatory Limits of Self-Harm in Do-It-Yourself Gene Editing, in Consuming Genetics (I. Glenn Cohen et al. eds. 2022).

[17] Id.

[18] See id. (explaining that "the very concept of 'regulation,' as developed and practiced under the web of old statutes the Coordinated Framework rests on, fails unless there are suitable entities to regulate").

that additional authority is needed to provide effective oversight."[19] Additionally, nontraditional models of regulation, including criminal law and trade restrictions, may also be employed in the regulation of DIY-Bio. A mix of finding new ways to enforce traditional mechanisms coupled with new regulatory paradigms for the modern era will be necessary to regulate DIY-Bio with regards to human genome editing technologies.

1 Administrative Safety and Efficacy Regulations

On a national level, one of the primary ways human genome editing may be regulated is through the work of federal agencies charged with safety and efficacy, like the Food and Drug Administration (FDA) in the United States. The FDA is responsible for regulating the safety of clinical research and clinical therapies and will have some regulatory impact over genome editing technologies, notably CRISPR.[20] Evita Grant notes that "the application of CRISPR-Cas technology to the genome modification of human somatic cells *ex vivo* or *in vivo* will be subject to FDA regulations for somatic therapy and gene therapy."[21] Grant additionally argues that the FDA will likely be able to regulate CRISPR technology used with regards to "human germline cells and embryos as a form of assisted reproductive technologies (ARTs),"[22] although currently there is a policy rider "forestalling the therapeutic modification of the human germ line by prohibiting the [FDA] from considering such applications."[23]

With regards to DIY-Bio, such regulations may be more difficult to apply. The FDA or the EPA can of course have jurisdiction to implement requirements on DIY-Bio groups, such as "requiring notification and agency review before experiments take place and conducting periodic inspections."[24] However, the difficulty is enforcement, as some groups may be underground or individuals of which the government is not aware.[25]

[19] Zettler et al., supra note 11 (noting that existing regulatory mechanisms can still be applied to DIY-Bio and explaining that "in the United States, a web of laws, regulations and norms – if used – could reach a number of genetic biohacking activities").

[20] Sarah Ashley Barnett, Regulating Human Germline Modification in Light of CRISPR, 51 U. Rich. L. Rev. 553, 577 (2017) ("The FDA is responsible for ensuring the safety and effectiveness of all gene-transfer therapy products and research protocols.").

[21] Evita V. Grant, FDA Regulation of Clinical Applications of CRISPR-CAS Gene-Editing Technology, 71 Food & Drug L.J. 608, 628 (2016) (explaining that FDA will have authority over somatic cell CRISPR treatments, as such treatments fall under FDA guidance for somatic cell and gene therapy).

[22] Id. at 628–29 ("[The] FDA defines ART as: '[a]ll treatments or procedures that include the in vitro handling of human oocytes and sperm or embryos for the purpose of establishing a pregnancy.'").

[23] Russell A. Spivak, I. Glenn Cohen, & Eli Y. Adashi, Germ-line Gene Editing and Congressional Reaction in Context: Learning From Almost 50 Years of Congressional Reactions to Biomedical Breakthroughs, 30 J. L. & Health 20, 22 (2017).

[24] Mehlman & Conlon, supra note 10.

[25] Evans, supra note 16 (noting that "FDA jurisdiction exists, even if the agency might face enormous practical difficulties discovering the activity is taking place").

2 Research Funding

The other primary national regulatory mechanism comes from research funding. For example, "[t]he [National Institutes of Health (NIH)] is America's most significant public source of funding for biomedical research in the field of the life sciences."[26] One must always consider, however, that NIH funding streams will not influence private research. Farrow notes that "most industrial research is not touched by these funding streams [i.e. NIH money], as basic research is done either by industry or through industrial-academic cooperation."[27] Currently, the NIH "will not fund any research involving human germline genome modification."[28] Notably, there is the Dickey-Wicker Amendment, created in 1996 and reauthorized every year since, "that prohibits using any appropriated funding to create a human embryo or modify a human embryo 'to include a heritable modification.'"[29] Dickey-Wicker is considered a strong regulation against genome editing and often very "sticky,"[30] as it effectively cuts off federal money for any research regarding genetically modifying an embryo. Critics are concerned that with such regulations in place, the United States could be left behind as other parts of the world lead the frontier on this new technology.[31]

3 Tort Law

Another possible form of nationally based regulation is tort law. While tort law is not the most commonly seen form of administrative regulation directed from the government at large – that is, from entities like the FDA or the NIH – it can still regulate or influence certain actions, particularly in countries like the United States that have a litigious nature and a robust court system, allowing plaintiffs a forum in which to sue. Undoubtedly, at some point injuries will occur from genome-editing technologies, and medical malpractice suits will be filed. What might a tort for damages caused by gene editing look like?[32] This and other key questions will be

[26] Zachary A. Zalewski, Shining City on a Hill at the Edge of Tomorrow: CRISPR-Cas9, Dickey-Wicker, and the Inner Space Race, 28 Health Matrix 469, 498 (2018).

[27] Barry R. Furrow, The CRISPR-Cas9 Tool of Gene Editing: Cheaper, Faster, Riskier?, 26 Annals Health L. 33, 46 (2017).

[28] Grant, supra note 21, at 609 (citing a statement the NIH put out regarding funding of researching using gene- editing technologies in human embryos).

[29] Zalewski, supra note 26, at 494 (offering suggestions for how Dicker-Wicker could be reinterpreted or evaluated, so that it is not so stifling on advancements made with targeted genome editing).

[30] Spivak, Cohen, & Adashi, supra note 23, at 37 ("While these appropriations riders require yearly renewal, in the case of Dickey-Wicker they have proven very 'sticky' and suggest the ban on funding for gene editing research may be here to stay.").

[31] See Zalewski, supra note 26, at 506 ("It is precisely because the questions surrounding the current subject of TGE [targeted gene editing] are hard, that we should choose to pursue them, to accept the challenges and confront them, head on. For if we do not, we leave the door open for others to answer them for us.").

[32] See Kendall Lovell, CRISPR/Cas-9 Technologies: A Call for a New Form of Tort, 19 San Diego Int'l L.J. 407, 408 (2018) ("The novelty of the injuries that will arise [because of CRISPER-Cas9

answered over time as actions are filed and the case law develops. One fascinating aspect of this developing area of tort law is how damages stemming from germline editing will be apportioned to future generations for multigenerational injuries. As Kendall Lovell notes, "the inherent risk in CRISPER/Cas-9 gene editing is that any negligence on the part of the physician can affect future generations."[33] How tort law develops will play a crucial role in the regulation of gene editing, as tort law will instill a level of caution for clinicians and researchers, a check on their practice. Fear of liability – both for Big-Bio and DIY-Bio actors – may act as a safeguard against risky measures, although it also has the potential to stymie useful innovations in medical treatments.

4 Criminal Law

Criminal law is not a traditional or common mechanism used to regulate genome editing technology (or other biotechnologies), largely because the traditional Big-Bio players cannot be held criminally liable in the typical sense, as they are not individuals, lack the mens rea to commit a criminal act, and cannot be sanctioned with criminal penalties like prison.[34] However, with the rise of DIY-Bio, individuals are directly involved – not bodiless corporations or other entities – and can be held criminally liable and subject to criminal penalties for potential bio-hacking activity. A recent example has surfaced in Germany with regards to DIY-Bio. Recently, the German government banned anyone from doing "genetic engineering outside of a licensed facility" on penalty of a substantial fine and prison time.[35] However, critics have noted that the German criminal ban will be "difficult to enforce" and is "likely to drive more NTGE [DIY-Bio] underground."[36] The possibility of criminal penalties has also surfaced recently in the United States, where California is now investigating celebrity bio-hacker Josiah Zayner for practicing medicine without

technology] require a system that is able to balance the interests of physicians with single and multi-generational plaintiffs, while providing a realistic framework for courts to follow.").

33 Id. at 426. ("On the one hand, it is important that any tort claim proposed to address CRISPER/Cas-9 injuries account for the damage potential for multi-generational injuries, otherwise very real injuries of future generations may be invalidated. On the other hand, it is unfair to hold physicians or their practices liable for later generations under a traditional tort approach because resulting damages would seemingly have no end.").

34 See Mihailis E. Diamantis, Corporate Criminal Minds, 91 Notre Dame L. Rev. 2049, 2050 (2016). ("Though crimes typically require an actus reus and a mens rea, courts have no real theory of how corporations, which have no bodies or minds, could instantiate either. The best they have is an antiquated gimmick – respondeat superior – for holding corporations vicariously responsible for the crimes of their employees."). Hence, while there may be a role for criminal law with regards to Big-Bio – notions of vicarious liability and respondeat superior are in play – criminal law's role is less direct and more complicated than when it is applied to DIY-Bio individual actors.

35 Kristin V. Brown, Germany is Threatening Biohackers with Prison, Gizmodo (Feb. 9, 2019), https://gizmodo.com/germany-is-threatening-biohackers-with-prison-1792143993.

36 Mehlman & Conlon, supra note 10.

a license.[37] While this investigation is recent and not yet concluded, it highlights another way criminal law (in this case state criminal law regarding unauthorized practice of medicine) could be wielded to regulate individuals in the DIY-Bio space.

5 Trade Restrictions

Another regulatory approach governments can take is to restrict the sale of certain biotechnology (like CRISPR kits) to particular groups or entities.[38] Sales restrictions could be a possible tool with regards to DIY-Bio, because access restrictions may get around difficulties in enforcing other regulations. While restrictions may help regulate DIY-Bio, the drawback of this approach is that restricting access completely could be an overly restrictive solution to the problem of enforcement and thwart potentially creative and positive DIY-Bio activities.

6 Patent Law

Patent law is another area of law that may have regulatory influence on gene-editing technologies, as patents are designed to "both fund and incentivize research."[39] Hannah Mosby offers an argument for how patent law can be developed to ethically regulate human genome editing technology.[40] Mosby notes that historically US patent law had a Moral Utility Doctrine, whereby courts interpreted the "utility" requirement for accepting a patent to have a "*moral* or *beneficial* utility," such that it was good policy and moral for society.[41] However, recent court decisions have degraded the Moral Utility Principle in patent law,[42] and morality is not currently a factor in determining whether or not to grant a patent. Mosby argues that because of the ethical questions raised by CRISPR technology, adding back an evaluation of the ethics and morality of technologies during their patent application process would be useful in helping to better regulate such technologies.[43] Alta Charo also

37 Antonio Regalado, Celebrity Biohacker Josiah Zayner is Under Investigation for Practicing Medicine Without a License, MIT Technology Review (May 15, 2019), www.technologyreview.com/s/613540/celebrity-biohacker-josiah-zayner-is-under-investigation-for-practicing-medicine-without-a/.

38 See Mehlman & Conlon, supra note 10 ("[T]he government could impose mandatory restrictions on sales and shipments, enforced by inspections, sales record review, and the use of 'secret shoppers.'").

39 Hannah Mosby, Biotechnology's Great Divide: Strengthening the Relationship Between Patent Law and Bioethics in the Age of CRISPR-Cas9, 19 Minn. J.L. Sci. & Tech. 565, 566 (2018).

40 See id. at 568 (arguing in favor of "strengthening the relationship between U.S. patent law and ethics, and propos[ing] a schema for utilizing the patent prosecution process as a regulatory mechanism for ethically controversial technologies").

41 Id. at 573.

42 See id. at 574.

43 See id. at 603 ("Current biotechnological developments have brought once-dystopian ethical concerns to the forefront of public discourse, providing a renewed opportunity to establish a relationship between ethics and patent law.").

makes the point that "patent owners may place restrictions on uses permitted under the licenses they grant," which can also act as a regulatory mechanism.[44]

There is a notable example of this dynamic, where the Broad Institute of MIT and Harvard – which "holds several key patents on the CRISPR technology" – has put a license restriction on their CRISPR patents that "restricts socially controversial applications" of the technology.[45] The use of patent law is a practical reminder that in addition to the more-traditional regulatory levers of administrative agencies (like the FDA and the NIH) there are other areas within US law that, notably from an ethical perspective, can be tweaked or strengthened to allow for regulatory oversight of human genome editing.

B *Global Level*

When considering the global regulation of genome editing, we must also consider how to regulate DIY-Bio and Big-Bio. From a global perspective, it is clear that DIY-Bio has now become a "global movement."[46] Since 2008, DIY-Bio groups have "spread around the world," notably in North American and European cities, but in Asia as well.[47] These groups have created codes of ethics, notable examples being major DIY-Bio groups in North American and Europe each drafting their own codes of ethics.[48] It is important to note that "the ways in which DIY biology is 'governed' or 'regulated' takes a distinctive form: rather than being top-down it is bottom-up," meaning that it is "collectively and openly negotiated by a large group of people," as opposed to the "top-down" regulatory approach that is more fitting of institutions.[49]

With regards to Big-Bio on the global front, regulation will likely take the form of international collaboratives or declarations, as such partnerships or agreements between nations where nations agree to exercise their national regulatory authority in a unified way. Big-Bio players (companies, universities, and other research institutions) are largely operating under and subject to the rules and regulations of their home jurisdictions, hence international collaboratives and declarations are more primed for global regulation of Big-Bio. Of course, national regulations can also have effect on DIY-Bio (although as discussed earlier, there may be challenges and differences in application of national regulations to DIY-Bio versus Big-Bio), hence international collaboratives and declarations may also globally regulate DIY-Bio along with Big-Bio. Also note that while some Big-Bio entities may be

[44] Charo, supra note 3, at 978 (noting that that such restrictions were given for a patent license for "chimera-related uses of embryonic stem cells").

[45] Furrow, supra note 27, at 44.

[46] Thomas Landrain et al., Do-It-Yourself Biology: Challenges and Promises for an Open Science and Technology Movement, 7 Sys. & Synthetic Biology 115, 116 (2013).

[47] Id. at 116–17.

[48] See Joszef Keulartz & Henk van den Belt, DIY-Bio – Economic, Epistemological and Ethical Implications and Ambivalences, 12 Life Sci. Soc'y & Pol'y 1, 16 (2016).

[49] Landrain et al., supra note 46, at 125.

transacting business globally or are international in scale, they are still subject to the patchwork of national regulations spanning the globe. Thus, a treaty with the binding force of international law would have greater effect in providing a true global regulation of Big-Bio. Additionally, self-regulation of Big-Bio entities on their own initiative is possibly another pathway for global regulation (in theory) but is unlikely to ever be truly fruitful in practice, as varying economic and other incentives drive Big-Bio's behavior.[50]

1 International Collaboratives

One possible way to regulate germline editing on a global scale is to have an international treaty, or other such collaborative, that has binding force between nation states.[51] Considering the global nature and risk that editing the germline presents, such an international collaborative presents itself as an ideal regulatory solution; there is a sound argument for the creation of such an international treaty. For example, such a treaty might be a moratorium on germline editing, whereby parties to the agreement agree that such editing will not legally occur within their borders. The essence of such a treaty is that bound nations would agree to enforce their own national regulatory mechanisms (like the FDA and NIH) to satisfy their international obligations. The problem is that in practice, such a treaty has very little chance of coming to fruition.[52] However, in a theoretical sense, this may be the best solution.

2 International Declaration

Tara Melillo argues that creating an international declaration to give nations guidance of how to approach germline gene editing is a more realistic option – suggesting that the Universal Declaration on the Human Genome and Human Rights be amended to include information about germline modifications.[53] This is a possible alternative to a treaty and one that may have a more realistic chance of being implemented, while additionally carrying the benefit that "a declaration can indicate international consensus absent the complexities and complications necessary in drafting, enacting, and ratifying a treaty."[54] However, the drawback is that it is

50 See Keulartz & van den Belt, supra note 48 (noting that Big-Bio, as opposed to DIY-Bio, is "highly profit driven" with an "emphasis on economic productivity").

51 See Tara R. Melillo, Gene Editing and the Rise of Designer Babies, 50 Vand. J. Transnat'l L. 757, 785 (2017) ("In a utopian world, key countries involved in gene editing could collaborate an enact a multilateral or plurilateral treaty, prohibiting gene editing until further research occurs and the ethical implications can be better understood. Ideally, a stand-alone treaty involving China, the United Kingdom and the United States would eliminate any fear that gene editing will bypass ethical concerns to the detriment of society.").

52 See id. at 785 ("[The] current political climate hinders the likelihood of negotiating such a treaty.").

53 See id. at 786–88.

54 Id. at 789.

nonbinding. The reality is that a binding international regulatory framework for germline genome editing, while ethically ideal, is not a practical reality. That said, such a declaration could possibly be seen as guidance or a "regulatory road map" to help guide the "ecosystem of regulatory actors" already in play around the world, such as existing national regulatory agencies like the FDA and NIH.[55] Alta Charo recommends that such guidance "include stringent criteria for use of germline editing and standards for determining whether these criteria have been met, embedded within larger political structures offering vehicles for public input."[56] Providing such a road map might be the best way forward in approaching globally minded regulation of germline editing. If the road map can become a true international consensus, that can have impact, as a consensus can influence behavior.

3 International Collaboration among DIY-Bio Groups

Discussion involving international treaties and declarations often is more applicable to governance of Big-Bio, as the declarations and consensus built between nations are then expected to be transplanted to individual national schemes of federal regulation which, as discussed earlier, are better primed to govern Big-Bio. With regards to governing DIY-Bio from a global and international perspective, what may have impact is collaboration between various DIY-Bio groups that have built "community labs."[57] These labs are maintained by various DIY-Bio groups around the world, most located in Europe and North America.[58] Discussion tends to focus on the US and the European groups, which have different values: US DIY-Bio groups are focused on "market driven entrepreneurship and personal enhancement," and European groups are focused "on open access" in conjunction with "social empowerment and community building."[59] This divergence in values is reflected in codes of ethics drafted by both the US and European groups.[60] While a divergence of views among DIY-Bio groups from different countries is unsurprising, if the various groups around the world can successfully create their own international declaration or consensus[61] on how they will perform human genome editing – that is, an ethical code of conduct dictating what types of edits are

55 Charo, supra note 3, at 977.

56 Id.

57 Günter Seyfried, Lei Pei, & Markus Schmidt, European Do-It-Yourself (DIY) Biology: Beyond the Hope, Hype and Horror, 36 BioEssays 548, 548 (2014).

58 Keulartz & van den Belt, supra note 48, at 1 ("[C]urrently 26 local groups in Europe, 35 in the United States and Canada, and 11 in Latin America, Asia and Oceania.").

59 Id. at 16.

60 See id. at 16.

61 See id. at 17. A consensus between international DIY-Bio groups has been pondered, and Keulartz and van den Belt state: "The gap between the North American and the European model raises some important questions. Will one of these models take precedence over the other? Or will the tension between the two be resolved in a productive way, creating some sort of balance between grassroots entrepreneurship and social innovation?" Id.

permissible – this could have a powerful impact by filling in the gaps of any consensus that arrives between nations. Note that the "question remains to what extent a global set of ethical principles will and can be adapted and adopted in the local contexts," but the potential to reach a global consensus among groups is promising.[62] A consensus of how to implement human genome editing, from both DIY-Bio groups and key nation-states, could have a positive global impact if both consensuses work in tandem and are mindfully approached.

IV CONCLUSION

Accounting for the ethical issues and the scope of consequences that human genome editing can and will yield, it is apparent that some regulatory guidance is necessary, both at the national and global levels. Regulations will need to account for the two primary implementers of genome editing technology: Big-Bio and DIY-Bio. DIY-Bio is a relative newcomer to the scene, and one must be mindful that existing regulatory mechanisms and strategies may or may not always fit this new category of biotechnology implementers and innovators.

From a national regulatory perspective, with regards to Big-Bio, the traditional "top- down" regulatory models (such as those implemented by the FDA, NIH, and EPA) are the best models, as they are traditionally primed to influence the institutional biotechnology centers of the twentieth century. With regards to DIY-Bio, the traditional "top-down" regulations may work in some areas, but gaps will remain. Hence, jurisdictions should look to promote "bottom-up" style regulatory approaches – incentives to build proper ethical and regulatory consensus among DIY-Bio groups themselves. Additionally, nontraditional regulatory drivers, such as criminal law or trade restrictions on the selling of certain biotechnology kits, may have a role in nationally based regulation of DIY-Bio.

From a global regulatory perspective, with regards to Big-Bio, an international framework[63] can more likely be implemented through an international declaration or consensus between nations, though a binding international treaty is the theoretical ideal. With regards to DIY-Bio, such a framework can be best implemented through an international collaboration and consensus of key DIY-Bio groups and labs around the world.

62 Landrain et al., supra note 46, at 125.

63 As referenced at the outset of this chapter, current debate about what an international collaboration or consensus should ultimately be is often centered on whether or not there should be a moratorium on genome editing, particularly with regards to that of the germline. Further ethical and policy analysis regarding the scope of consequences is needed to properly determine the ideal nature and limits of a moratorium; this debate is ongoing. See Eli Y. Adashi & I. Glenn Cohen, Heritable Genome Editing: Is a Moratorium Needed?, 322(2) JAMA 104 (2019); Lander et al., supra note 5.

PART II

Privacy in the Age of Consumer Genetics

Introduction to Part II

Nita A. Farahany

The chapters in this Part discuss the existing and evolving threats to privacy and discrimination of individuals that arise from the rapid growth in direct-to-consumer genetic testing. From shortcomings in the governance of genetic privacy, to evolving trends in reproductive genetics, these authors push us to think about gaps in governance of consumer genetics through both real-world and hypothetical examples.

In *Improving Commercial Genetic Data Sharing Policy*, Kayte Spector-Bagdady focuses our attention by explaining that "the value of the DTC-PGT business model is not actually in selling genetic test results to individuals ... [but] ... from selling consumer health data to researchers." And yet, she cautions, consumers generally unwittingly share their own health data to their peril without realizing that the data is being commercialized. Spector-Bagdady, like Hazel, suggests steps beyond the Future of Privacy Forum's (FPF) self-governance guide. In particular, she argues for much greater transparency by companies including when specific instead of broad consent will be sought from consumers before sharing their data.

With a specific example of the loss of privacy that comes with DTC genomic databases, Seema Mohapatra dives into the loss of gamete-donor anonymity in *The Myth of "Anonymous" Gamete Donation in the Age of Direct-to-Consumer Genetic Testing*. The long-standing approach in the USA and in some other countries of offering anonymity to sperm donors is now "merely a façade." Mohapatra dispels the myth of anonymity, helps us to understand why it was offered and what it supports, and how legal and governance models should guide assisted-reproduction industry in the future. By recognizing that "donor anonymity no longer exists," along with its potential ramifications, Mohapatra encourages us to think about interventions that could help society better navigate this new reality.

Vardit Ravitsky turns our attention to a little-discussed but critical ethical issue arising from another aspect of reproductive genetics – in the burgeoning field of Noninvasive Prenatal Testing (NIPT) or Screening (NIPS). In *Noninvasive Prenatal Whole Genome Sequencing: Ethical and Regulatory Implications for Post-Birth Access to Information*, Ravitsky discusses the complicated ethical issues that arise when intending parents opt for NIPT but choose against terminating their pregnancy. This includes the interest of the resulting child in the privacy of their genetic information (including their right not to know this information), as well as pragmatic concerns such as how parenting may differ based on the knowledge gained through the tests. Through insightful examples from genetic testing of minors and newborn screening, Ravitsky encourages us to consider whether parents ought to have access to "nonactionable genetic information," particularly as NIPT expands to whole genome sequencing, We may need to balance the competing autonomy interests of the parents with that of the future child by considering the "characteristics of the genetic information in question," allowing certain information to be disclosed while withholding other information for the resulting child to discover instead.

We conclude Part II with a privacy frontier issue, in Yaniv Heled and Liza Vertinsky's chapter, *Genetic Paparazzi*. Heled and Vertinsky take us into the near future where "the genetic information of others, public figures in particular, makes it into the public discourse." In this future scenario, lawsuits will emerge by public figures seeking to define the "nature and scope of genetic privacy." Although public figures have a decreased expectation of privacy under the law, it remains to be seen whether the discovery and disclosure of the genetic information of public figures will go a legal step too far. While "no court has yet had to rule on the legal status of celebrities' genetic material," these authors reveal to us that celebrities have already complained about the theft of their genetic material. Through hypothetical examples, Heled and Vertinsky push us to think about the legal claims that may be brought against the "genetic paparrazi" and how those claims are likely to fare. Their conclusion – that we ought to expand our thinking about what role genetics can and should come to play in public discourse – aptly concludes this Part of the book.

6

Noninvasive Prenatal Genome Sequencing

Ethical and Policy Post-birth Implications

Vardit Ravitsky[*]

I INTRODUCTION

The discovery in 1997 of cell-free fetal DNA (cffDNA) circulating in the blood of the pregnant woman[1] opened the door to a new generation of prenatal tests that became known as Noninvasive Prenatal Testing (NIPT) or Screening (NIPS). These tests were first introduced as an additional screening test for women identified as having a high chance of carrying a fetus with Trisomy 21 but are gradually being offered as first-tier screening to all pregnant women for a growing number of conditions.

The global spread of these tests has been rapid,[2] and while a growing body of empirical research shows that women are excited about this technology,[3] a heated debate has emerged about ethical and societal concerns associated with its introduction into health care systems worldwide.[4] Many of these concerns touch on the implications of NIPT for women's reproductive autonomy and possible pressures they will experience if they wish to decline a test that is easy, safe, and performed

[*] The author would like to thank Marie-Christine Roy for her assistance with research and referencing. I would also like to thank the other members of our NIPT research team: Aliya Affdal, Stanislav Birko, Stephanie Cloutier, Charles Dupras, Hortense Gallois, Hazar Haidar, Cynthia Henriksen, Chris Kaposy, Anne-Marie Laberge, Jessica Le Clerc-Blain, Marie-Eve Lemoine, Marsha Michie, Talya Miron-Shatz, and Tierry Morel-Laforce. Work on this chapter was supported by the PEGASUS-2 project (Personalized Genomics for prenatal Aneuploidy Screening Using Maternal Blood), funded by Genome Canada, Genome Quebec, and the Canadian Institutes for Health Research.

[1] Yuk-Ming Dennis Lo et al., Presence of Fetal DNA in Maternal Plasma and Serum, 350 Lancet 485–87 (1997).

[2] See Subhashini Chandrasekharan et al., Noninvasive Prenatal Testing Goes Global, 6 Sci. Translational Med. 231 (2014); Vardit Ravitsky, Marie-Christine Roy, Hazar Haidar, Lidewij Henneman, John Marshall, Ainsley J. Newson, Olivia M.Y. Ngan, Tamar Nov-Klaiman. The Emergence and Global Spread of Non-Invasive Prenatal Testing. Annual Review of Genomics and Human Genetics. In press, 2021, https://pubmed.ncbi.nlm.nih.gov/33848430/

[3] Celine Lewis et al., Non-Invasive Prenatal Testing for Trisomy 21: A Cross-Sectional Survey of Service Users' Views and Likely Uptake, 121 BJOG 582–94 (2014).

[4] See, e.g., Jessica Mozersky et al., Toward an Ethically Sensitive Implementation of Noninvasive Prenatal Screening in the Global Context, 47 Hastings Ctr. Rep 41–49 (2017).

early in the pregnancy.[5] Other concerns touch on the impact of such an accessible test on those living with disabilities, and on the possible expansion of its use to detect a growing number of conditions, possibly leading to exacerbated eugenic social attitudes.[6]

The introduction of NIPT as a product sold by private companies has also been associated with ethical concerns regarding a commercial drive possibly leading to premature implementation of the technology broadly to increase market share.[7] Companies developing NIPT technologies have been fighting in courts over patent rights, which also raised concerns about possible monopolies and increased cost to consumers. Another avenue through which companies have been attempting to compete is the development of tests that cover a growing range of conditions, all the way to whole genome sequencing of fetal DNA.[8]

This combination of commercial drive, improved performance of the technology, and the ease and safety of the test has fueled concerns about lowering the threshold of acceptable testing to include a broader set of conditions (for example, treatable, late onset, only increased risk, etc.) and even nonmedical conditions.[9] These concerns have been addressed in the bioethics literature mostly in terms of their impact on the termination of certain pregnancies: at the individual level, concerns about pressure to test and terminate, and on the societal level, concerns about the aggregate impact of individual decisions to terminate on how society views those living with the same conditions that become easily detectable prenatally.

Meanwhile, scant attention has been given to the ethical implications of NIPT's expanded use in cases where women test the fetus but do *not* terminate their pregnancy.[10] The widespread presence of NIPT, combined with its commercial offer, improved performance, and possible use for whole-genome sequencing[11] raise

5 Stanislav Birko et al., Moving Towards Routine Noninvasive Prenatal Testing (Nipt): Challenges Related to Women's Autonomy, 2 OBM Genetics 18 (2018).

6 See Hazar Haidar, Charles Dupras, & Vardit Ravitsky, Non-Invasive Prenatal Testing: Review of Ethical, Legal and Social Implications, 5 BioéthiqueOnline (2016).

7 See Blake Murdoch et al., Non-Invasive Prenatal Testing and the Unveiling of an Impaired Translation Process, 39 J. Obstetrics & Gynaecology Canada, 10–17 (2017).

8 See, e.g., Antonio Regalado, Prenatal DNA Sequencing, MIT Tech. Rev. (Apr. 23, 2013) www.technologyreview.com/s/513691/prenatal-dna-sequencing/; Megan Allyse and Subhashini Chandrasekharan, Too Much, Too Soon?: Commercial Provision of Noninvasive Prenatal Screening for Subchromosomal Abnormalities and Beyond, 17 Genetics in Med. 958–61 (2015).

9 See, e.g ., Betsy L. Gammon et al., "I Think We've Got Too Many Tests!": Prenatal Providers' Reflections on Ethical and Clinical Challenges in the Practice Integration of Cell-Free DNA Screening, 2 Ethics Med. Pub. Health 334–42 (2016); Rachel V. van Schendel, et al., What Do Parents of Children with Down Syndrome Think About Non-Invasive Prenatal Testing (Nipt)?, 26 J. Genetic Counseling, 522–31 (2017).

10 See Zuzana Deans, Angus J. Clarke & Ainsley J. Newson, For Your Interest? The Ethical Acceptability of Using Non-Invasive Prenatal Testing to Test "Purely for Information," 29 Bioethics 19–25 (2015).

11 See Y. M. Dennis Lo et al., Maternal Plasma DNA Sequencing Reveals the Genome-Wide Genetic and Mutational Profile of the Fetus, 2 Sci. Translational Med. 61 (2010).

concerns regarding the implications of the technology for those fetuses that are brought to term and become children who have been prenatally sequenced. These "post-birth concerns" include issues such as privacy, open future, right not to know, and even pragmatic risks. This chapter discusses these concerns and explores possible conceptual and policy approaches aimed at balancing prospective parents' reproductive autonomy during pregnancy against the post-birth well-being and rights of minors.

I NIPT AND THE RATIONALE BEHIND PRENATAL TESTING

Much has been written about the complex ethical landscape underlying prenatal testing.[12] Two possible rationales justify the offer of screening and diagnostic testing to pregnant women. The first is the ethically and socially acceptable rationale of reproductive autonomy, according to which testing is meant to provide women and their families with information that would support and promote informed and free decision making about the management of the pregnancy.

However, decades of experience have shown that consent to prenatal testing is most often not informed[13] and that women do feel pressure to comply with the offer of testing.[14] Moreover, the mere existence of various tests (whether ultrasound, serum screening, or invasive tests such as Chorionic villus sampling (CVS) and amniocentesis) changes the experience of pregnancy for all women, even those who reject all forms of testing.[15] This has called into question the integrity of the claims that prenatal testing indeed promotes autonomy.

The second rationale acknowledges the social agenda behind prenatal testing. It recognizes that testing is offered based on a public health rationale that seeks to reduce the burden of disease on individuals and on society. This rationale is concealed and tacit, since unlike other forms of screening (e.g. population-base screening for cancer), in the prenatal context no preventive or treatment options are offered. The choices available to pregnant women are to either terminate or carry to term an affected fetus.

Despite challenges to the integrity of the autonomy rationale, there is an overwhelming insistence that autonomy is indeed the basis of the widespread and growing offer of testing options. As a result, testing cannot be framed as a "search

12 Vardit Ravitsky, The Shifting Landscape of Prenatal Testing: Between Reproductive Autonomy and Public Health, 47 Hastings Ctr. Rep. 34–40 (2017).

13 See Victoria Seavilleklein, Challenging the Rhetoric of Choice in Prenatal Screening, 23 Bioethics 68–77 (2009).

14 Celine Lewis, Caroline Silcock & Lyn S. Chitty, Non-Invasive Prenatal Testing for Down's Syndrome: Pregnant Women's Views and Likely Uptake, 16 Pub. Health Genomics 223–32 (2013).

15 See Barbara Katz Rothman, The Tentative Pregnancy: How Amniocentesis Changes the Experience of Motherhood (W.W. Norton & Company 1993); Rayna Rapp, Testing Women, Testing the Fetus: The Social Impact of Amniocentesis in America (Routledge 2004).

and destroy mission."[16] Testing must instead be offered for the sake of providing information that women and their families see as relevant to their decision making, whatever their decision might be. Put simply, NIPT "purely for information,"[17] that is, without any intent to terminate, is ethically acceptable since it aligns perfectly with the notion of autonomy (i.e. free and informed decision making) as underlying testing.

Once "purely for information" is acknowledged as a perfectly good justification for testing, post-birth challenges arise. Most fetuses screened by NIPT will be carried to term without being diagnosed with a serious condition. Moreover, consistent with autonomy, even for those that are diagnosed, the choice to continue the pregnancy ought to be fully supported. The growing and expanding use of NIPT consequently raises very real concerns associated with a future in which parents possess vast amounts of genetic information about their babies. Some of this information may be actionable in childhood, some may be relevant in adult life, some may have unknown significance, and some may become significant later in the life of the child as scientific discovery advances. But it will all be available to parents upon and oftentimes before birth.

Whole-genome sequencing (WGS) through NIPT, known as NIPW,[18] brings these concerns to a new level. WGS has been raising ethical concerns even in the context of consenting adults,[19] and the prenatal context creates its own unique additional concerns. Beyond the "flood" of information[20] and complicated decision-making that follows, a future in which most fetuses are sequenced may forever change, once again, the experience of pregnancy for all women, even those who decline testing.

Consider the effect ultrasound had on our perception of the fetus, and consequently on our individual and social attitudes towards pregnancy. For most pregnant women, ultrasound is no longer seen as a medical diagnostic test meant to reveal potential birth defects or developmental issues in the fetus.[21] Rather, due to its noninvasive, risk-free, pain-free nature, the cultural focus has become the opportunity to see the fetus before birth. For some, the test is experienced as the first "meeting with the baby," followed by images shared with family and friends. In a certain sense, ultrasound made the uterus transparent and created a common expectation to "peek

16 Frank H. Boehm, Having a Perfect Child, 109 Obstet Gynecol 444, 444–45 (2007).

17 Deans et al., supra note 10.

18 See Stephanie C. Chen & David T. Wasserman, A Framework for Unrestricted Prenatal Whole-Genome Sequencing: Respecting and Enhancing the Autonomy of Prospective Parents, 17 The American Journal of Bioethics, 1, 3–18 (2017).

19 Wim Pinxten & Heidi Carmen Howard, Ethical Issues Raised by Whole Genome Sequencing, 28 Best Practice & Research Clinical Gastroenterology 269–79 (2014).

20 Henry T.Greely, Get Ready for the Flood of Fetal Gene Screening, 469 Nature 289–91 (2011).

21 See Margarete Sandelowski, Channel of Desire: Fetal Ultrasonography in Two Use-Contexts, 4 Qualitative Health Research, 262–80 (1994); Josephine M. Green, Women's Experiences of Prenatal Screening and Diagnosis, in Prenatal Diagnosis: The Human Side, 37–53 (Lenore Abramsky & Jean Chapple ed., 1994).

inside the womb" before birth. NIPW may, over time, create similar cultural expectations to make the fetus transparent at the genetic level. A widespread routine offer of NIPW may lead to a cultural shift whereby prospective parents expect to "peek inside the fetus" and have a complete picture of their future child's DNA early in the pregnancy. For some, this may entail a decision to terminate the pregnancy. But for most, it would generate a new reality at birth, one in which the genome of a child is exposed from the outset.

II THE POST-BIRTH CHALLENGES OF NONINVASIVE PRENATAL WHOLE GENOME SEQUENCING (NIPW)

What could be problematic about a reality in which babies are born already sequenced? Several concerns come to mind. First, babies will lose any chance of genetic privacy. With their entire DNA known, they will be exposed from the beginning of life to all of the societal risks that have traditionally been associated with genetic information, such as discrimination and stigmatization. Second, this information will be known about them without their consent. Testing of minors for genetic information that is not actionable during childhood has long been considered ethically unacceptable precisely because people should be allowed to consent to testing when they are autonomous adults.[22] Third, prenatal sequencing would deprive children, and the adults they will become, of the "right not to know" – a notion that has emerged in the literature on genetic testing to denote the freedom people should have to refrain from knowing certain genetic information about themselves.[23] This links with the violation of their "right to an open future," another concept that describes the need to protect children from decisions that restrict their range of options later in life.[24]

Finally, the exposure of a child's DNA could lead to harmful family dynamics. Parents could, for example, favor one child over another based on a perception that a certain child had limited genetic potential and thus did not merit the investment of family resources. This scenario has been powerfully depicted in the film *Gattaca*, portraying a society in which all children are born sequenced and two brothers are coping their entire lives with genetic discrimination that profoundly impacts their lives not only at the societal level, but also within the family.[25]

Considering these issues, it seems that a strong argument can be made against allowing prenatal sequencing. However, it can also be argued that prior to birth,

22 See Jeffrey R. Botkin, Ethical Issues in Pediatric Genetic Testing and Screening, 28 Current Opinion in Pediatrics, 700–04 (2016).

23 See, e.g., Ruth Chadwick, Mairi Levitt, & Darren Shickle, The Right to Know and the Right Not to Know: Genetic Privacy and Responsibility, Cambridge Bioethics & Law (2014).

24 See Joel Feinberg, Freedom and Fulfillment: Philosophical Essays (1994); see also Dena S. Davis, Genetic Dilemmas: Reproductive Technology, Parental Choices, and Children's Futures (2d ed. 2010).

25 Andrew Niccol, Gattaca (TriStar Home Video, 1997).

parents should have complete autonomy and decisional authority regarding their fetus. While a full discussion of the legal status of the fetus in various jurisdictions and at various stages of the pregnancy goes beyond the scope of this chapter, it should be noted that NIPT can be performed as early as ten weeks of pregnancy, during the first trimester, when in many jurisdictions the fetus is not considered to have any rights and when in some cultures it does not yet have full moral status either.[26] What emerges is thus an ethical tension between the notion of parental autonomy to make decisions about prenatal testing on one hand, and protecting the future child on the other.

III POSSIBLE PRECEDENTS: GENETIC TESTING OF MINORS, NEWBORN SCREENING, AND THE BABYSEQ PROJECT

A *Genetic Testing of Minors*

Ethical arguments raised in the context of the genetic testing of minors and newborn screening (NBS) provide insights and some limited analogies to evaluate the ethics of prenatal genetic sequencing. Both involve the collection of genetic information about minors without their consent in ways that are meant to benefit them but may also pose certain risks.

Genetic testing of minors has received ample attention in the literature. Overall, predictive and carrier testing of minors are not supported by clinical guidelines[27] based on several key arguments.[28] First, there is the notion that testing minors should be limited to childhood-onset conditions, especially those that are actionable (e.g. preventable or treatable). Testing minors to obtain genetic information that would only become relevant when they are adults, even when done with the best of parental intentions, is considered by most to be unjustifiably paternalistic, as it invades the privacy of the future adult. It is also considered to narrow the future options of the prospective adult, who can no longer choose not to know, or that her parents would not have known. Finally, it is considered potentially harmful for the individual (for example, increasing anxiety or fatalistic attitudes), for family relationships (for example, causing parents to treat their child differently), and from a societal perspective (for example, producing stigma and limited opportunities associated with carrier status). While robust data on such implications is lacking, some studies suggest that "most children and families manage this type of predictive information well without significant adverse impacts," and hence recent positions are more

26 See, e.g., Hazar Haidar et al., Noninvasive Prenatal Testing: Implications for Muslim Communities, 6 AJOB Empirical Bioethics, 94–105 (2015).

27 Laine F. Ross et al., Technical Report: Ethical and Policy Issues in Genetic Testing and Screening of Children, 15 Genetic Med. 234–45 (2013); American Academy of Pediatrics, Ethical and Policy Issues in Genetic Testing and Screening of Children, 131 Pediatrics 620–22 (2013).

28 Pascal Borry et al., Presymptomatic and Predictive Genetic Testing in Minors: A Systematic Review of Guidelines and Position Papers, 70 Clinical Genetics, 374–81 (2006).

flexible and argue in favor of allowing adolescents to request testing (as opposed to young children), based on "growing support for the ability of parents to make thoughtful and appropriate decisions for their child."[29]

While WGS may not reveal any definitive information about adult-onset conditions, it may reveal increased risk. Even a recessive carrier status that will not have an impact on future health may still have substantial implications for reproductive decision making. Moreover, with the growing understanding of the genetic basis of numerous traits and the genealogical and relational implications of genetic knowledge, non-medical aspects of the genome will become increasingly significant. Hence, even if WGS would not provide information that is clinically relevant, it may still have enough meaning to justify waiting for the adult individual to decide.

B *Newborn Screening*

NBS has also received much bioethical attention, mostly because it has been implemented as a population-based program without parental consent[30] and because it has been raising dilemmas around what results to disclose to parents.[31] First introduced for conditions that were clearly justifiable due to their actionability (such as phenylketonuria, where early prevention is extremely effective), it has been gradually expanded to include less actionable conditions, but still without parental consent. Clinical guidelines have traditionally supported the mandatory offering of NBS, while promoting general education and counseling about its benefits and supporting the option of parental refusal.[32]

Traditional NBS programs have been implemented as a public health program, targeting specific conditions. They were not designed for sequencing nor for return of all results to parents. Moreover, the rationale behind NBS is not an expressed parental desire to know but rather a public health approach to screening.[33] This means that the government, based on guidance provided by an advisory committee, determines which conditions ought to be screened for in the entire population of newborns, to identify those who can benefit from early interventions, both for their individual benefit and for the societal benefit of reducing the burden of disease. As noted, parents usually do not provide consent and do not receive results unless an actionable condition is detected in their baby. NBS programs are thus far from an

29 Botkin, supra note 22.

30 See Lainie Friedman Ross, Mandatory Versus Voluntary Consent for Newborn Screening?, 20 Kennedy Institute of Ethics Journal 299–328 (2010).

31 Fiona Alice Miller, Jason Scott Robert, & Robin Z. Hayeems, Questioning the Consensus: Managing Carrier Status Results Generated by Newborn Screening, 99 American Journal of Public Health 210–15 (2009).

32 Ross et al., supra note 27.

33 National Institute of Child Health and Human Development, What is the Purpose of Newborn Screening?, www.nichd.nih.gov/health/topics/newborn/conditioninfo/purpose(last visited Feb. 9, 2020).

ideal analogy for prenatal WGS, in which parents would be initiating testing, paying for it, and expecting a full return of results.

At the same time, NBS does provide an example of a situation whereby parents are not receiving all the genetic information available about their child, despite the fact that this information exists and a third-party is in possession of it. Whereas in the case of minors the objection is to the testing itself, in the case of newborns, testing does occur but parents are not offered information unless it is actionable. This demonstrates that parental autonomy has not been seen in the past as a necessarily overriding consideration when it comes to disclosure of genetic results. NBS may thus be a possible precedent for arguing that nonactionable genetic information ought to be withheld from parents, even in cases where the screening is initiated by them and not by a public health program.

C *The BabySeq project*

More relevant to the prenatal context is the recent BabySeq project, which explores the possibility of implementing Whole Exome Sequencing in newborns to "provide objective data regarding the risks and benefits of newborn genomic sequencing in terms of the health impacts on the child, the psychosocial implications for the family, and the ways in which clinicians use the information,"[34] including the ethical and policy implications of such an offer. Some early insights from the project are indeed useful for the prenatal context as well, such as the understanding that "determining criteria for disclosure of information will be a challenge for clinicians and policymakers and will require development of decisional supports to help parents determine the information they want to learn" and that "new and more scalable materials and procedures for communicating the potential benefits and risks of learning such information would need to be developed, validated, and deployed."[35]

The BabySeq project provides a better analogy to NIPW, as both involve the collection of genetic information without the consent of those being tested. Both intend to benefit those tested, yet raise concerns about risks and violations. The objectives of the BabySeq project, as described above, therefore align perfectly with the challenges raised by NIPW. As such, the results of the project may end up being useful in the prenatal context as well. For example, development of criteria for disclosure and decisional support for parents could cut across these two contexts and be employed both before and after birth.

34 Ingrid A. Holm et al., The Babyseq Project: Implementing Genomic Sequencing in Newborns, 18 BMC Pediatrics 225 (2018).

35 Jonathan S. Berg et al., Newborn Sequencing in Genomic Medicine and Public Health, Pediatrics, Feb. 2017, at e20162252.

IV WHAT MAKES NIPW DIFFERENT?

In their 2015 paper, Deans et al. argue that "in many ways, testing a fetus 'purely for information' ... is based on similar principles to carrying out genetic tests in children" and that therefore "most of the arguments about the acceptability of testing children ... will apply."[36] However, several substantial differences distinguish these two contexts and justify a unique analysis of prenatal sequencing.

The first difference between testing minors (whether individual children or in the context of NBS) and prenatal sequencing is – obviously – that fetuses are not children. Even without exploring in depth the legal and ethical literature on the status of the fetus, it is clear that at least some critical differences exist, particularly in the very early stage of the pregnancy in which NIPT can be performed. Babies, children, and adolescents have the full moral and legal status of a person, with all the associated rights and protections. Medical – and other – practices that are not designed to protect and promote their well-being are largely considered unethical and, in some cases, illegal as well. The state may intervene in its role of *Parens Patriae* to protect children from bad decisions that even their own parents can make, if these can endanger them or negatively affect them. It is thus much easier to limit the use of genetic testing in the case of minors, than in the case of fetuses.

Moreover, arguing that parents' decision-making authority ought to be limited during pregnancy in order to protect the interests of the future child who may result from the current fetus is conceptually dangerous. If such limitations are justified in the context of genetic testing, why would they not be justified in other contexts as well? This line of argument obviously aligns with a pro-life ideological and political agenda and can lead down a path that strips women of their reproductive autonomy in relation to the pregnancy they are carrying. This is an outcome that is already evident in debates about maternal behavior during pregnancy, as in the case of fetal alcohol syndrome, where, in the name of fetal protection, women are subject to legal action and even physical limitations. While these debates touch on vast literatures and go beyond the scope of this chapter, they are mentioned here to exemplify the risk of arguing that fetuses ought to be protected from parental decisions in the same way that children ought to be.

The second difference between testing minors and prenatal sequencing is the reason underlying testing. While in the case of minors the justification is clearly linked to the well-being of the child (albeit the understanding of this well-being may be contested, that is, parents may disagree with health care providers or with the state), in the prenatal context the reason for testing may be unclear to the parents themselves. Parents may assume that they are testing in order to decide about termination but then choose to continue the pregnancy. And vice-versa, they may assume that termination is not an option in their case and then in light of the results choose to terminate after all.

[36] Deans et al., supra note 10.

The possibility of termination casts a distinct light on the debate surrounding prenatal sequencing. On the one hand, it can play a role in helping to justify such sequencing, since unexpected findings may have health implications that may lead to a decision to terminate, as in other cases of more targeted prenatal testing. On the other hand, it is a constant reminder that such sequencing is not done "for the well-being of the fetus," because prevention or treatment options are exceedingly rare and the only real alternative is termination,[37] which can hardly be described as being in the best interest of the aborted fetus (notwithstanding the rich literature on the nonidentity problem and the philosophical conundrum of comparing existence and nonexistence).[38]

The third difference between testing minors and prenatal sequencing is the context in which these are offered. While newborn screening is performed in the context of a government-run program based on a public health rationale, and genetic testing of minors is performed in a clinical context based on a medical indication, prenatal sequencing will be – at least in the foreseeable future – offered in a commercial context. It will be offered by for-profit companies as an extended service at a higher price than more limited "packages" which target specific conditions. The commercial drive to offer such testing for profit means that the best interest of the future child, or of the prospective parents for that matter, may not be at the heart of the practice. Moreover, it means that any attempt to limit such offer through regulation may end up encouraging medical tourism by pushing parents to purchase such a service in another jurisdiction with a laxer approach, as was the case with the first clinical use of mitochondrial transfer.[39]

These differences highlight the limits of what can be learned from the context of testing minors to the context of prenatal sequencing and the unique scope of post-birth issues raised by prenatal sequencing.

V CONCEPTUAL APPROACHES TO POST-BIRTH CHALLENGES

Considering the scope of the challenges prenatal sequencing may soon present, what conceptual approaches can be used to address this practice and what are their policy implications? Possible approaches range from completely banning the practice to allowing it without restriction, with several midway alternatives.

On one extreme of this spectrum is an approach that gives priority to privacy concerns, to the right of the prospective child to an open future, and to the right not

[37] Of note, the notion of sequencing to prepare, in the case of significant findings, for the birth of a child with special needs or with certain health issues, may allow to consider sequencing as being in the best interest of the baby, but not of the fetus.

[38] See, e.g., Derek Parfit, "Part Four: Future Generations," in Reasons and Persons 351–451 (1987); James Woodward, The Non-Identity Problem, 96 Ethics 804–31 (1986).

[39] Jessica Hamzelou, Exclusive: World's First Baby Born with New '3 Parent' technique, New Scientist (Sept. 27, 2016), www.newscientist.com/article/2107219-exclusive-worlds-first-baby-born-with-new-3-parent-technique/.

to know unsolicited genetic information that he or she did not consent to receiving. The implication of this approach would be a policy that bans the use of NIPT technology for sequencing and limits it to the detection of conditions that have clinical significance and are actionable in childhood. The regulation of NIPT would thus consider not only the ramifications of prenatal testing for termination decisions, but also for post-birth scenarios.

On the other end of the spectrum is an approach that gives priority to parental autonomy, leading to a policy that would allow unrestricted use of NIPT during pregnancy and unrestricted parental access to the information generated by sequencing before and after birth. This approach could be conceptually based on the notion that in the prenatal context there is no justification for considering the rights or well-being of the prospective child and hence no grounds for limiting parental access to information, regardless of legitimate post-birth concerns.

Alternatively, this approach could be conceptually based on the rejection of concerns about open future and the right not to know. Indeed, certain authors have called into question such concerns, arguing that "knowledge does not impede capabilities" and therefore testing children does not jeopardize their open future. They argued that a recognition of autonomy, in the Kantian sense of the obligation to make thoughtful and informed decisions, creates a *prima facie* duty to receive "readily accessible relevant information," including genetic information that may impact our decisions.[40]

Between these two extremes are several more nuanced approaches that are based on the characteristics of the genetic information in question. These would allow WGS but disclose only certain categories of results, such as actionable results that would be considered justifiable in the context of testing a minor, or information about conditions that are considered serious, or – at the very least – information that has some relevant medical implication. While this approach raises great challenges and would require substantial conceptual work to define and justify selected categories, it may be the best approach in terms of striking a balance between parental autonomy and respect for the well-being of prospective children. Indeed, in the context of the BabySeq project, it has already been acknowledged that "systems may need to be established that enable parents to request certain results from their child's genomic information over time, allowing them to decide iteratively as their values and perceptions of risk change or as their child attains an age to assent or consent."[41]

VI CONCLUSION

The emerging possibility of prenatal whole-genome sequencing, especially through safe and simple noninvasive cell-free fetal DNA testing and in a commercial context,

40 Rosamond Rhodes, Resisting Paternalism in Prenatal Whole-Genome Sequencing, 17 The American Journal of Bioethics 35–37 (2017).

41 Berg et al., supra note 35, at 8.

raises significant ethical and policy challenges. It would require the development of nuanced conceptual approaches that strive to strike an intricate balance between parental autonomy and the prospective child's well-being. If an approach is adopted that attempts to treat different categories of genetic information differently, sophisticated informational and educational tools would have to be developed, validated, and implemented, as has been suggested in the context of newborn sequencing. Moreover, if we move into a future where many babies are born already sequenced, and where vast amounts of genetic information is available on individuals who never consented to testing, legal protections against any type of genetic discrimination would have to be strengthened and educational efforts will have to be enhanced to promote genetic literacy.

7

The Myth of "Anonymous" Gamete Donation in the Age of Direct-to-Consumer Genetic Testing

*Seema Mohapatra**

I INTRODUCTION

In the United States, sperm donation has always been shrouded in secrecy.[1] The first reported successful donor insemination in the United States occurred in 1884, when William Pancoast, a Philadelphia physician, treated a wealthy man's infertility by sedating his wife with chloroform, without her knowledge or consent, and injected her with the sperm from his best-looking medical student.[2] Shockingly, her husband was informed of this only after the baby's birth, but agreed to keep the doctor's secret from his wife.[3] From this unseemly beginning, sperm donation has continued largely in a clandestine manner, albeit now with an organized and profitable industry behind it.[4]

The United States has long had a history of allowing anonymous gamete donation. Even as other countries have embraced a trend towards donor-conceived children receiving open access to information about their genetic origins, donor anonymity is the norm in the United States. The vast majority of sperm donors in the United States sell their sperm with the understanding that their identity will not be

* This chapter benefited from the research assistance of Levi Baysinger, Paige Ferise, and Madison Hartman and the comments and suggestions by Nita Farahany, Rachel Rebouche, Sonia Suter, and the participants of the Petrie Flom Consuming Genetics: Ethical and Legal Considerations of New Technologies Conference and Drexel Law Faculty Colloquium.

1 The main thesis of this chapter regarding the death of anonymity applies to all gametes (both sperm and eggs). However, this chapter mainly focuses upon sperm donation as an example. Prior to assisted reproduction, the person who bore a child was presumed to be the biological parent of the child. However, with the increased use of in vitro fertilization and the use of donor eggs, the pregnant person may be carrying a fetus conceived from a donor egg. Thus, similar issues of secrecy and anonymity apply to egg donation as well.

2 Sarah Zhang, The Fertility Doctor's Secret, Atlantic (Mar. 18, 2019), www.theatlantic.com/magazine/archive/2019/04/fertility-doctor-donald-cline-secret-children/583249/?fbclid=IwAR1E04lym3BwnetfodGUiUFQzLocmz2_Vx9pQyFdQIKnzUbUJ-NQoeIpk30; see also Peter G. McGovern & William D. Schlaff, Sperm Donor Anonymity: A Concept Rendered Obsolete by Modern Technology, 109 Fertility & Sterility 230, 230–31 (2018).

3 Zhang, supra note 2.

4 McGovern & Schlaff, supra note 2.

revealed. In one study, almost one third of current donors indicated that they would no longer sell their sperm if anonymity was not preserved.[5]

However, this so-called anonymity is merely a facade given the increasingly widespread use of direct-to-consumer (DTC) genetic testing. This chapter describes why gamete donor anonymity is a myth and how claiming such anonymity is harmful to both donors and those who use donor gametes. This chapter proceeds as follows: Section II of this chapter discusses how consumer genetic testing has overturned the promise of gamete donor anonymity. Section III describes the history and state of sperm donation in the United States, as well as the reasons often given for preserving donor anonymity by donors, those who use donor sperm, and sperm banks. This section also discusses the business of so-called donation. Section IV provides the legal and governance landscape for sperm banks and sperm donations in the United States. Section V suggests that at a minimum, sperm banks and the assisted reproduction industry should address the anonymity issue with vigorous self-policing.

II CONSUMER GENETIC TECHNOLOGIES AND WHY ANONYMITY IS A MYTH

As of the beginning of 2019, over twenty-six million people had undergone DTC autosomal genetic tests, and most of this testing had occurred between 2016 and 2019.[6] Studies show that a genetic database covering only 2 percent of the population could match nearly anyone in that population, especially if they are of European descent.[7] In the United States, assisted reproduction is accessed overwhelmingly by those of European descent. Thus, a legal regime that allows "anonymous" donation is misleading those parties involved with donor gametes. Although gamete donors may argue that they have a right to privacy in this context, such a right is not likely to be respected due to the state of genetic technology. Regardless of a clinic's policies, it is very likely that donor conceived children will be able to identify the person who supplied the egg or sperm that led to their existence.

The story of Danielle Teuscher is illustrative.[8] Teuscher purchased direct-to-consumer (DTC) genetic tests from 23andMe as Christmas presents for her father,

5 I. Glenn Cohen et al., Sperm Donor Anonymity and Compensation: An Experiment with American Sperm Donors, 3 J. L. & Bioscience 468 (2016).

6 Antonio Regalado, More Than 26 Million People Have Taken an At-Home Ancestry Test, MIT Tech. Rev. (Feb. 11, 2019), www.technologyreview.com/s/612880/more-than-26-million-people-have-taken-an-at-home-ancestry-test; Yaniv Erlich et. al., Identity Inference Of Genomic Data Using Long-Range Familial Searches, 362 Science 690, 690–94 (2018).

7 Carolyn Y. Johnson, Even If You've Never Taken A DNA Test, A Distant Relative's Could Reveal Your Identity, Wash. Post (Oct. 11, 2018, 2:00 PM), www.washingtonpost.com/science/2018/10/11/even-if-youve-never-taken-dna-test-distant-relatives-could-reveal-your-identity/?utm_term=.246543026ff8.

8 Jacqueline Mroz, A Mother Learns the Identity of Her Child's Grandmother. A Sperm Bank Threatens to Sue, The N.Y. Times (Feb. 16, 2019), www.nytimes.com/2019/02/16/health/sperm-donation-dna-testing.html.

friends, and her donor-conceived five-year-old daughter.[9] The 23andMe test result allowed Teuscher to unintentionally discover the identity of the sperm donor she had used to conceive her daughter.[10] The test results revealed a biological grandmother for her daughter (which was the sperm donor's mother). Teuscher reached out to the revealed paternal grandmother, as that individual had set her profile preferences to say that she was open to contact from relatives.[11] NW Cryobank, a sperm bank in Spokane, Washington, from which Teuscher had bought the donated sperm, contacted Teuscher and let her know that she could face a penalty of $20,000 for "flagrantly" violating the sperm recipient agreement she had signed by seeking the identity of the donor and contacting his family.[12] NW Cryobank also told Teuscher that they would deny her access to the four vials of sperm from the same donor that Teuscher had already purchased and was storing with NW Cryobank. [13] Teuscher had hoped to use this sperm in the future so that her daughter would have a full biological sibling and expressed devastation over the potential lost opportunity to form the family she had planned.[14]

Analyzing this real-life situation from the hypothetical viewpoints of the parties involved helps to demonstrate the relational and linked nature of DTC testing and anonymous sperm donation. It is possible, or even likely, that the sperm donor's mother had no idea that her son had ever donated sperm. Presumably, men who donate sperm for money usually do not let their mothers know about it. So, when the woman said she was open to contact from relatives, she likely did not anticipate a biological grandchild from her son's donated sperm.

We can speculate that the donor contacted NW Cryobank to complain about this breach of privacy after getting questions from his mother about the contact from Teuscher. The donor may have been shocked to hear the inquiry from his mother, when he was supposedly guaranteed anonymity by the sperm bank. Donors cannot control their relatives' use of DTC testing. In this case, the use of DTC testing by the paternal grandmother uncovered the sperm donor's past and his donor-conceived offspring. The donor's mother is not a party to any agreement with NW Cryobank, yet NW Cryobank's reputation for preserving anonymity is threatened by this testing. NW Cryobank's reaction, while likely ill-advised and too heavy-handed, was likely an attempt to preserve its reputation for preserving anonymity.

There is no need to speculate about Teuscher's motivations, as she has given several newspaper and television interviews expressing her point of view.[15] Teuscher signed the agreement that she would not seek the identity of the donor, but her

[9] Id.

[10] Id.

[11] Id.

[12] Id.

[13] Id.

[14] Id.

[15] Martha Henriques, Sperm Bank Warns Against Tracing Anonymous Donor Via DNA Test, Bio News, (Feb. 4, 2019), www.bionews.org.uk/page_141189.

daughter was not a party to that agreement. She argues that when she emailed the donor's mother, she did so to explore the independent grandparent relationship, not to identify the donor himself. Thus, according to her, this was not against the contract with the sperm bank she had signed. In this example, due to DTC testing and inadvertently violating the terms of her agreement, Teuscher may miss out on the opportunity to have full biological siblings for her daughter.

This situation is a recent example of how sperm donor anonymity is now just a myth, given the state of DTC testing in the United States. DTC testing reveals relationships such that parties uninvolved in the donor agreement or recipient agreement may nonetheless enable the sperm donor's identity to be known.

Although sperm banks may not release records identifying an "anonymous" donor, due to widespread genetic testing, these sperm banks cannot guarantee anonymity any longer. There is a duty to warn gamete donors of this fact.[16] In fact, promising gamete anonymity "may border on fraudulent."[17]

It is deceptive to gamete donors and gamete recipients to advertise "anonymous" donation for many reasons. First, the state or federal law could change (and retroactively, like it has in some countries), which would mean that the sperm bank may be forced to reveal the identity of the donor.[18] Even if the contract language protects such situations, most donors and recipients would not contemplate this happening. This possibility should be clearly disclosed to both parties: donor and recipient, and not buried in fine print.

Second, even if the sperm bank or egg agency does not reveal the identity of the gamete donor, consumer genetic testing is becoming so common that anonymity, especially in the case of a white donor, is impossible. There are many instances of people who are surprised about their genetic origins – learning that they were donor-conceived – due to consumer genetic testing.[19] Numerous examples abound. There is the woman who found out through DTC testing that her biological father was an employee at a fertility clinic, who secretly used his own sperm to inseminate her mother.[20] One donor-conceived individual was able to identify their sperm donor

16 Pascal Bony et al., Genetic Testing: Anonymity of Sperm Donors Under Threat, 496 Nature 196, 196 (2013).

17 See Naomi Cahn, The New "Art" of Family: Connecting Assisted Reproductive Technologies & Identity Rights, U. Ill. L. Rev. 1443, 1443 (2018).

18 Id.

19 See Marilyn Crawshaw, Direct-to-Consumer DNA Testing: The Fallout for Individuals and Their Families Unexpectedly Learning of Their Donor Conception Origins, 21 Hum. Fertility 225, 225–28 (2017). Some have argued that the interest in anonymity is so great that there should be limits to DTC genetic testing rather than abolishing gamete anonymity. See Abigail Hoglund-Shen, Direct-to-Consumer Genetic Testing, Gamete Donation, and the Law, 55 Fam. Ct. Rev. 472, 472 (2017). This does not appear to be a feasible solution, given the private and relational nature of consumer genetic testing. Even if a donor contract limits DTC genetic testing for the party to the contract, any relative would not be bound by that and one's genetics can be revealed through their relatives.

20 Lauren F. Friedman, At-Home Genetic Testing Reveals A Sperm-Swapping Nightmare, Business Insider (Jan. 8, 2014), http://www.businessinsider.com/23andme-test-reveals-artificial-insemination-nightmare-2014-1.

via a third cousin found on Ancestry.com and some investigation on Facebook.[21] "In the comfort of one's home, a cheek swab and a little time on social media can easily penetrate the 'anonymity' of the sperm donation process."[22] These stories are likely just the tip of the iceberg, as one's origins are often closely held, private information, not shared with reporters.

Millions of people have tested their DNA through kits that cost under $100 each using companies like 23andMe, Ancestry.com, and Family Tree DNA.[23] Most of those people are in the United States.[24] Most of these tests use autosomal DNA testing, which examines genetic material inherited from both parents and can identify other people in the database who have a DNA match.[25] The pervasive use of genetic and genomic services for genealogical or ancestry purposes can undermine the privacy and confidentiality of those who donate sperm and their relatives.[26] Autosomal markers estimate genetic similarity to another person and make an estimation of the degree of relatedness by comparing the number of markers individuals have in common.[27] These services may reveal genetically close or more distant relatives that the concerned parties were not aware of.[28] It is not realistic to request companies to stop disclosing this type of relatedness information, especially when many people only purchase these tests to find relatives and information about their background. The risk of inadvertently discovering that someone was conceived using gamete donation has increased, as has the risk of identifying family members of a gamete donor or the gamete donor himself.[29] It should be disclosed to new donors and potential recipients in writing and orally that the sperm bank can no longer guarantee anonymity due to the widespread availability of DNA ancestry and genealogical tests. Parties who are considering donating or receiving sperm should do so with the knowledge that the identity of the sperm donor can be revealed via those who are seeking information through genetic testing for recreational purposes.

III SPERM DONATION IN THE UNITED STATES

This section introduces the sperm donation industry and outlines the issue of donor anonymity from the perspective of different stakeholders involved in gamete

21 McGovern, supra note 2.

22 Id.

23 Libby Copeland, Who Was She? A DNA Test Only Opened New Mysteries, Wash. Post (July 27, 2017), www.washingtonpost.com/graphics/2017/lifestyle/she-thought-she-was-irish-until-a-dna-test-opened-a-100-year-old-mystery/.

24 Id.

25 Id.

26 See P. Borry et al., Anonymity 2.0: Direct-to-Consumer Genetic Testing and Donor Conception, 101 Fertility & Sterility 630, 630–32.

27 Id.

28 Id.

29 Id.

donation to provide a background for why anonymity (or lack thereof) may be important in decision making.[30]

A *The Sperm Market*

Sperm has often been called "America's greatest export."[31] The US sperm market is thriving is due to its large pool of sperm donors compared to much of the world. This large pool of willing donors can be attributed to the payment.

The United States also dominates the sperm market due to its favorable rules regarding sperm donor anonymity, compared with many countries.[32] For example, Britain, Sweden, Norway, Germany, Italy, New Zealand, and Australia do not allow anonymous sperm donations.[33] In the United States, however, sperm donors typically are promised anonymity.[34]

Throughout this chapter, although the term "sperm donor" is used, the vast majority of these men are not actually donating any sperm (that is, giving away their sperm for free.) In fact, sperm donors are paid between $30 and $130 per sperm sample.[35] "Sperm donor" is a term of art and the most common term for men who sell their sperm to a variety of sperm banks in the United States. The term itself obscures the fact that the sperm market is a multibillion-dollar industry, where those who purchase the sperm for use in assisted reproduction pay more for the sperm than the "donors" are paid.[36] The main financial beneficiaries of the sperm market are the sperm banks that solicit donors and sell sperm to consumers and fertility clinics.[37]

30 Although this chapter primarily focuses on sperm donations, similar issues of anonymity being compromised due to DTC testing are present in the egg donation context as well.

31 See Soo Yoen, America's Hottest Export? Sperm, Guardian (Aug. 15, 2018),www.theguardian.com/science/2018/aug/15/americas-hottest-export-sperm-fertility; see also Brooke Jarvis, Come And Get It: How Sperm Became One Of America's Hottest Exports, Verge (Apr. 2, 2013), www.theverge.com/2013/4/2/4145560/come-and-get-it-how-sperm-became-one-of-americas-hottest-exports; Sarah Kramer, America Is The Largest Exporter Of Sperm In The World – Here's Why, Business Insider (Mar. 10, 2016), www.businessinsider.com/sperm-donations-anonymity-U.S.-canada-2016-3.

32 See Yoen, supra note 31; Kramer, supra note 31.

33 See Alessandra Rafferty, Donor-Conceived Children Demand Right, Newsweek (Feb. 25, 2011), www.newsweek.com/donor-conceived-children-demand-rights-68721; Courtney Mckinney, My Father Was An Anonymous Sperm Donor. I Feel The Consequences Of That Every Day, Los Angeles Times (Mar. 18, 2018), www.latimes.com/opinion/op-ed/la-oe-mckinney-anonymous-sperm-donor-offspring-20180318-story.html.

34 Cohen et al., supra note 5.

35 Yoen, supra note 31. The reported amounts vary. Renee Almeling reported $75 per sample in her book in 2011. See Rene Almeling, Sex Cells: The Medical Market for Eggs and Sperm 69 (2011). Almeling reported $50–$100 per sample in 2007. See Rene Almeling, Selling Genes, Selling Gender: Egg Agencies, Sperm Banks, and the Medical Market in Genetic Material, 72 Am. Soc. Rev. 319, 319 (2007).

36 California Cryobank, Pricing, www.cryobank.com/services/pricing/(last visited Oct. 21, 2020) (cost of $400–900 per vial for anonymous donor vials).

37 Kimberly D. Krawiec, Sunny Samaritans and Egomaniacs: Price Fixing in the Gamete Market, 72 Law & Contemp. Probs. 59, 59 (2009). Fertility clinics themselves also make a profit from sperm, purchasing it for a lower price than they charge consumers for it. Kimberly Krawiec uses the sale of

B *Sperm Donors*

In the United States, due to the payment associated with "donating," there are many more people who are interested in selling their sperm than are actually accepted as donors.[38] Sperm banks screen men by looks (height), disease history, sperm count, and other factors.[39] Only about one in ten men who wish to be a sperm donor is actually chosen as a donor.[40] Although there may be some altruistic interest in helping to create a child, monetary compensation seems to be a greater motivator for sperm donation in the United States. One recent systematic review of studies involving donor motivations concluded that American sperm donors donate due primarily due to the financial incentive.[41]

In countries where payment is prohibited, the supply of sperm donors is much lower.[42] For example, in Canada, where payment for sperm is not allowed, 90 percent of donor sperm used in the country is imported from the United States.[43] As of 2011, Canada only had one sperm bank and thirty-five active donors in the whole country.[44]

C *Sperm Donors and Anonymity*

The promise of anonymity seems to reassure donors that there will be no long-term entanglements by donating sperm.[45] Because the main motivation to donate sperm in the United States is compensation, there is often no desire to meet or know about donor-conceived children. In studies of sperm donors, donors have indicated that anonymity helps quell concerns about future repercussions, unwanted financial liability, legal issues of responsibility, and wanting detachment from their donor-conceived children.[46] There is a fear that without anonymity, donor-conceived

gametes as an example of a "taboo trade," due to its perception by the public as unseemly due to its commodifying of bodily material.

38 See Tamar Levin, 10 Things to Know About Being a Sperm Donor, N.Y. Times (Nov. 3, 2016), www.nytimes.com/2016/11/08/health/sperm-donor-facts.html.

39 Id.

40 Id.

41 Uschi Van den Broeck et al., A Systematic Review of Sperm Donor Demographics Characteristics, Attitudes, Motives and Experiences of the Process of Sperm Donation, 19 Human Reproduction, 37, 37–51 (2013).

42 See Jarvis, supra note 31.

43 Id.

44 Id.

45 State family law changes have ensured that sperm donors are not considered a legal parent and are not required to pay any type of financial support for a donor-conceived child. Because sperm is frozen and can be used decades later, a person who donated sperm as a college student could find out decades later, when he is possibly more financially secure and has his own family, that he is a biological father of a donor-conceived child.

46 See L. R. Schover et al., The Personality and Motivation of Semen Donors: A Comparison with Oocyte Donors, 7 Hum. Reproduction 575, 575–79 (1992) (describing a survey of U.S. sperm donors in which a majority of the participants indicated they would not participate in sperm donation if it

children may be emotionally or financially burdensome to donors, who had no intention of creating such a relationship.

D *Sperm Recipients and Anonymity*

In the 1970s and 1980s, only married couples were recipients of donor sperm (often chosen by the physician, not the couple).[47] Today, however, there is a significant demographic shift. The vast majority of those using donor sperm are single mothers and lesbian couples.[48] In many of these cases, the donor-conceived individual knows the details of their origins at some point, because it is more obvious that a sperm donor was used. Some of these women may prefer anonymity because they do not want a donor complicating their independent lives. However, in many cases, these recipients of donor sperm are more open and interested in their child knowing the identity of their sperm donor. Historically, heterosexual couples favored anonymous sperm donations and matched physical characteristics of the sperm donor so that they could hide the child's donor-conceived origins. [49]

E *Donor-Conceived Individuals and Anonymity*

Donor-conceived individuals, however, are often curious about their gamete provider. A 2011 study in Human Reproduction found that 82 percent of donor-conceived offspring hoped to one day contact their donor (most frequently because they were curious about their donor's physical appearance.)[50] A 2010 study found that 92 percent of donor-conceived offspring surveyed were actively searching for their

were no longer anonymous); Lucy Frith et al., UK Gamete Donors' Reflections on the Removal of Anonymity: Implications for Recruitment, 22 Hum. Reproduction, 1675, 1675–80 (2007).

47 Ashley Fetters, Finding the Lost Generation of Sperm Donors, Atlantic (May 18, 2018), www.theatlantic.com/family/archive/2018/05/sperm-donation-anonymous/560588.

48 Id. Scott Brown, the person quoted from the article, indicated via email follow-up that this comment was based on internal survey data that he could not share. It is difficult to get specific data due to the lack of required reporting. Almeling, supra note 35 (both references) (noting that a larger proportion of single women and lesbian couples make up the customer base, based on internal surveys by two large sperm banks, Western and CryoCorp). There is no regulatory body or agency that tracks donor insemination demographics in the United States. The CDC tracks success rates and some demographic data, however, the demographic data only lists "unmarried" persons and does not consider lesbian couples within that category; The Human Fertilisation and Embryology Authority, an independent body in the United Kingdom (UK), found that a majority of persons using donor insemination in the UK are single women and lesbian couples. Human Fertilisation & Embryology Auth., Fertility Treatment 2017: Trends and Figures, 13 (2019), www.hfea.gov.uk/media/2894/fertility-treatment-2017-trends-and-figures-may-2019.pdf.

49 Susan C. Klock et al., A Comparison of Single and Married Recipients of Donor Insemination, 11 Human Reproduction, 2554 (1996); Joanna E. Scheib et al., Choosing Between Anonymous and Identity-Release Sperm Donors: Recipients and Donor Characteristics, 10 Reproductive Tech. 50 (2001); Susan C. Klock et al., Psychological Factors Related to Donor Insemination, 56 Fertility & Sterility 489 (1991).

50 Fetters, supra note 47.

donor, their donor sibling, or both.[51] A donor-conceived child's right to know the donor's identity was not even possible when sperm donation was becoming more common in the 1970s.[52] Most physicians did not even keep records of who the donor was, and many children did not ever find out that they were donor conceived.[53] For physicians who were performing inseminations using donor sperm, preserving the anonymity of the donor, for the benefit of the intended parents and the donor, was very important.[54]

More recently, though, there has been a push by donor-conceived individuals to find their donors. In the absence of records, the Donor Sibling Registry, a private nonprofit organization, attempts to connect donor conceived individuals with their siblings.[55] Some have theorized that knowing one's genetic origin is deeply important to one's sense of self. Psychologists Wellisch and Sants state that not knowing one's biological identity may cause "genealogical bewilderment," which could prevent one from developing a sense of identity and feelings of belonging.[56]

F *Sperm Banks and Anonymity*

Sperm banks purport to offer anonymity to attract donors but can no longer legitimately maintain such anonymity. Although sperm banks seem to be starting to shift their policies and advertisement, they need to do so on a more widespread basis. Sperm banks may be slow to change their statements regarding anonymity due to the decreased availability of donors if they cannot promise anonymity. Additionally, due to the broad waivers against liability sperm donors require both donors and recipients to sign, sperm banks seem to lack motivation to change their marketing, if it will affect their bottom line.

Sperm banks' websites emphasize the protection of anonymity for donors and recipients on their websites. The self-proclaimed largest sperm bank in the United States, California Cryobank (CCB), has 600 donors in its pool and has contributed to 75,000 live births worldwide.[57] CCB has several categories of donors, including ID donors who are willing to be identified and get paid more per sample of sperm, and anonymous donors.[58] CCB has a prominent Anonymous Donor Policy on its website. CCB notes that it will never destroy patient or donor files, and that once eighteen, a donor-conceived child may request information about the donor.[59]

51 Id.
52 Id.
53 Id.
54 Id.
55 Donor Sibling Registry, www.donorsiblingregistry.com/(last visited Oct. 21, 2020).
56 Fetters, supra note 47.
57 See Yoen, supra note 31.
58 Betsy Streisand, Who's Your Daddy?, US News & World Report, (Feb. 5, 2006), www.donorsiblingregistry.com/sites/default/files/images/docs/US_NewsWorld_Report_206.pdf.
59 California Cryobank, Anonymous Donor Contact Policy, www.cryobank.com/services/post-conception-services/anonymous-donor-contact-policy/ (last visited Oct. 21, 2020).

However, the contact will be facilitated by CCB only if the donor is willing, meaning that the donor could refuse contact and maintain "anonymity."[60] The Policy states that: "A parent may not, either for themselves or on behalf of their underage child, receive any additional information on their donor beyond the available profile. Any medical concerns or genetic questions should be directed to the CCB Genetic Counselors."[61]

CCB's website indicates that the only way an anonymous donor will be identified is via "mutual consent."[62] According to an article published in *The Guardian* in 2018, CCB planned to take non-anonymous donations going forward because of its concern that DTC services would render anonymity unrealistic.[63] However, as of May 2019, CCB was accepting "anonymous" donors, despite articulating that concern.[64] Another article noted that CCB instituted a policy in which all new donors must agree to a policy that gives offspring access to the donor's name, donation location, last known address, and email address when they turn eighteen.[65] Again, such policy is not evident from its website but would be a step in the right direction. More common are sperm banks, like Xytex, which guarantee anonymity to sperm donors and recipients on its website, without any warning about DTC testing reidentification.[66]

IV LEGAL LANDSCAPE OF SPERM DONATION ANONYMITY

Gamete donation, like other aspects of assisted reproduction in the United States, has been referred to as the Wild West. In the United States, there are no laws against either anonymous donation or the number of times a particular donor's sperm could be used.[67] The Donor Sibling Registry has found individuals who have hundreds of half-siblings due to the same sperm donor being used over and over again.[68]

A *Federal Laws*

Although some sperm banks and clinics allow "open donation," there is currently no federal legal requirement in the United States that requires the identity of sperm donors be known. In fact, the only federal law regarding sperm banks requires that sperm undergo extensive testing for contagious and communicable diseases.[69]

60 Id.
61 Id.
62 Id.
63 See Yoen, supra note 31.
64 California Cryobank, supra note 59.
65 Fetters, supra note 47.
66 Xytex, Frequently Asked Questions, www.xytex.com/about-xytex/frequently-asked-questions/ (last visited Oct. 21, 2020).
67 See Jacqueline Mroz, One Sperm Donor, 150 Offspring, N.Y. Times (Sept. 5, 2011), www.nytimes.com/2011/09/06/health/06donor.html (describing one donor who fathered 150 children).
68 Donor Sibling Registry, supra note 55.
69 Courtney Megan Cahill, Reproduction Reconceived, 101 Minn. L. Rev. 617, 635 (2016) (citing 21 C.F. R. § 1271)

B State Laws

Most state laws are silent on the issue of gamete donor anonymity. In 2011, Washington was the first state to require that nonidentifying medical information related to the gamete donor be made available to donor-conceived children when they turn eighteen.[70] The same statute requires that donor-conceived children be able to receive the identity of their gamete donor at the age of eighteen.[71] However, the statute has a huge loophole that allows a donor to sign an affidavit of nondisclosure at the time of donation. Most donor are signing such affidavits, skirting the underlying purpose of the law to allow identification by donor-conceived individuals.[72]

In 2015, Utah enacted a statute that required disclosure of relevant medical information to donor-conceived individuals after they turned eighteen.[73] However, this did not require or permit any identification of the donor.

C Other Laws

Although not the focus of this chapter, I have written elsewhere about how private law, such as contract law, tort law, and consumer protection law can be used creatively to hold sperm banks liable for claiming anonymity when such anonymity no longer exists.[74]

D Private Governance

Assisted reproduction in the United States has often proceeded via voluntary models of private governance. The American Society of Reproductive Medicine (ASRM) has attempted to address the concern over anonymity by recommending that clinics fully inform donors and recipients of donor gametes of their clinic's policies about information sharing and contact, but they should caution that policies cannot be guaranteed if laws or individual circumstances change and that the possibility exists of contact from offspring in the future.[75] This does not go far enough, given the prevalence of DTC testing and large ancestry and DNA databases.

70 Cahn, supra note 17 (citing Wash. Rev. Code § 26.26.750(2)(b) (2019)).
71 Wash Rev. Code § 26.26.750 (2019).
72 Cahn, supra note 17.
73 Id. (citing Utah H.B. 249).
74 Seema Mohapatra, Anonymous No More: Holding Sperm Banks Liable for the False Promise of Privacy (working paper) (on file with authors).
75 Ethics Committee of the American Society For Reproductive Medicine, Interests, Obligations, And Rights In Gamete Donation: A Committee Opinion, 102 Fertility & Sterility, 664, 664 (2014), www.Asrm.Org/Globalassets/Asrm/Asrm-Content/News-And-Publications/Ethics.

V THE WAY FORWARD: CURRENT REGULATORY REGIMES AND DEBATES

A *The Moot Bioethical Debate*

There is an active bioethical debate ongoing about whether anonymous sperm donation should be allowed. Some defend anonymity in donor-assisted conception because it protects donors and their family members from financial, emotional, or moral obligations toward children conceived with the help of their biologic material. While gamete donors may have monetary or altruistic motivations to donate, often they do not have any intention to engaged in a relationship with donor offspring. Some argue that abandonment of anonymity might lead to fewer sperm donors. They point to the examples of countries that have prohibited anonymous sperm donation and faced a shortage of donor gametes.

Some, like Naomi Cahn, have argued that there is a right to know one's genetic history. Others have argued that it is pivotal to one's identity and dignity to know their own genetic background. Still others assert that it is a violation of one's human rights to be deprived of the knowledge of one's genetic background.[76] There is also worry that removing anonymity would treat donor-conceived families differently than families created in other ways.[77]

As sympathetic as the arguments for not removing anonymity are, they are now moot. The reality is that in the United States, anonymity in gamete donation is impossible. Although some may wish that this were not the case, sperm banks need to face this reality and articulate this reality clearly to their donor and recipient clients.

B *Potential Legal Solutions*

1 Federal Action Unlikely

In other countries, like the United Kingdom and Australia, gamete anonymity has been addressed at the national level via regulation. The assisted reproductive technology (ART) industry has long resisted regulation and has instead self-policed via norms and policies set forth by the ASRM and Society of American Reproductive Technology (SART). One reason for the resistance to federal and state legal regulation in this realm is the fear that the federal or state governments will attempt to limit who is able to become a parent via ART. The adoption arena is highly regulated, and adoption regulations often did not allow single or older women or LGBTQ individuals to become parents via adoption. Sperm donation allows infertile couples to

[76] Brigitte Clark, A Balancing Act? The Rights of Donor-Conceived Children to Know Their Biological Origins, 40 Ga. J. Int'l & Comp. L. 619, 626 (2012); Martin Hevia & Carlos Herrera Vacaflor, From Recognition to Regulation: Access to In Vitro Fertilization and the American Convention on Human Rights, 25 Fla. J. Int'l L. 453, 473–78 (2013).

[77] Cahill, supra note 69.

become parents but increasingly is used by single women and lesbian couples. Given this demographic, there is a real fear that regulation will be used to limit access to gametes.

Thus, although sperm samples are subject to rigorous testing requirements by the Food and Drug Administration, it is unlikely that the federal government will (or should) step in to address gamete anonymity.

2 State Efforts: Licensing Tied to Disclosure

Washington's statute related to donor contact after age eighteen allows a donor to opt out of such contact. Given the state of DTC testing, a donor can usually be identified without such contact. Thus, the opt-out provision is likely not needed.

Perhaps licenses for fertility clinics and sperm banks to operate could be tied to a requirement that the clinic or bank disclose that sperm donor anonymity is not possible. This could be achieved with required counseling prior to donating or receiving donor gametes. A nuanced conversation is needed about this issue. Tying licensure to this requirement may help ensure that no advertising occurs regarding anonymous donation and that parties to the gamete agreement know about the risks of identity disclosure. It is not clear that this would be an efficient solution as state laws often are unwieldy, and achieving consensus is difficult.

3 Private Governance and Accreditation

The Ethics Committee of the ASRM has warned that donors and recipients of donor gametes should be counseled that "anonymity or future contact cannot be assured."[78] However, this does not go far enough. Thus, the ASRM needs to revise its policy to reflect the reality that no donors will be able to preserve their anonymity in order to give proper informed consent to both gamete donors and gamete recipients. The language of "anonymous" donation misleads all of the parties involved with donor conception. The ARSM and SART should strongly suggest that in order to remain members, clinics and bank stop using the language of anonymity. Gamete banks should remove the category of anonymous donors. Potential donors may still donate without the promise of anonymity if they are paid more. Additionally, they should be counseled that under all state law, donors will not have any financial or parental responsibility towards donor-conceived children. Similarly, potential recipients of donor sperm should be counseled that the identity of the sperm donor being known does not confer parental or decisional rights upon the donor, but rather allows their potential donor-conceived child to know their donor's identity and medical background. The end of anonymity need not mean the end of a supply of gamete donors.

[78] Ethics Committee, supra note 75.

C Possible Ramifications

From other countries' experiences, we see that once rules and laws related to anonymity are established, supply dips significantly.[79] Although there are passionate debates about the need to preserve anonymity to ensure that there are enough sperm and egg donors available for those who seek assisted reproduction, those arguments are no longer tenable due to DTC testing and the genetic databases in existence. Thus, the ASRM needs to revise its policy to reflect the reality that no donors will be able to preserve their anonymity in order to give proper informed consent to both gamete donors and gamete recipients. The language of "anonymous" donation misleads all of the parties involved with donor conception. Due to the state of DTC testing, this gives donors a false sense of privacy. Acknowledging that we now have a system of open donation is in the best interests of all of the parties involved: the donor, recipient of donor gametes, and a donor-conceived child.

The reality is that donor anonymity no longer exists. The practical ramifications of this reality – the potential lack of donors – is outweighed by the need for the donor and recipient of donor gametes to have a realistic view that even in cases where the donor wishes to remain anonymous, that is no longer possible due to the advent of consumer genetic technologies.

79 See Yoen, supra note 31.

8

Improving Commercial Genetic Data-Sharing Policy

*Kayte Spector-Bagdady**

I INTRODUCTION

In the summer of 2018, the pharmaceutical company GlaxoSmithKline (GSK) and the direct-to-consumer personal genetic testing (DTC-PGT) company 23andMe announced a four-year, $300 million equity investment deal to jointly use 23andMe's massive genetic and health information database for drug research and development.[1] Some 23andMe consumers reacted angrily to their data being shared like this[2] – despite this potential being discussed in the 23andMe Terms of Service[3] and the collaboration being one of hundreds of data-sharing agreements between 23andMe and industry, nonprofits, and academia over the past decade.[4] In fact, with the genetic data of over ten million consumers,[5] and one billion related phenotypic data points,[6] 23andMe is likely the largest genetic and health information database in the world.[7]

* The author would like to thank Dr. John Z. Ayanian, Dr. Nita Farahany, Prof. Holly Fernandez Lynch, and Prof. W. Nicholson Price II for their thoughtful feedback on a prior version of this article. This work was funded by the National Center for Advancing Translational Sciences (UL1 TR 002240) and the National Human Genome Research Institute (K01HG010496).

1 GSK and 23andMe Sign Agreement to Leverage Genetic Insights for the Development of Novel Medicines, GlaxoSmithKline (July 25, 2018), www.gsk.com/en-gb/media/press-releases/gsk-and-23andme-sign-agreement-to-leverage-genetic-insights-for-the-development-of-novel-medicines ("GSK and 23andMe today unveiled an exclusive four-year collaboration that will focus on research and development of innovative new medicines and potential cures, using human genetics as the basis for discovery. [. . .] Additionally, GSK has made a $300 M equity investment in 23andMe.").

2 See, e.g., Megan Molteni, 23andMe's Pharma Deals Have Been the Plan All Along, Wired (Aug. 3, 2018), www.wired.com/story/23andme-glaxosmithkline-pharma-deal ("But some customers were still surprised and angry, unaware of what they had already signed (and spat) away.").

3 Terms of Service, 23andMe, www.23andme.com/about/tos/ (last visited Oct. 21, 2020).

4 Kayte Spector-Bagdady et al., Genetic Data Partnerships: Academic Publications with Privately Owned or Generated Genetic Data, 21 Genetics in Medicine 2827–29 (2019).

5 23andMe for Healthcare Professionals, 23andMe, https://medical.23andme.com/ (last visited Oct. 21, 2020) ("23andMe has more than 5 million customers worldwide.").

6 Kayte Spector-Bagdady, "The Google of Healthcare": Enabling the Privatization of Genetic Bio/Databanking, 26 Annals of Epidemiology 515–19 (2016).

7 John T. Wilbanks & Eric J. Topol, Stop the Privatization of Health Data, 535 Nature 345–48 (2016).

In the same week that 23andMe announced the GSK deal, major DTC-PGT companies, including 23andMe and the Future of Privacy Forum, released a proposed industry self-governance document entitled *Privacy Best Practices for Consumer Genetic Testing Services* ("Privacy Best Practices").[8] But these professional standards for DTC-PGT are not yet up to par to protect consumer privacy. Given recent research establishing the privacy risks to genetic and health data[9] and a lack of clarity regarding informed consent standards for secondary research with privately derived data,[10] this chapter will make several recommendations regarding how industry can strengthen these privacy practices moving forward to improve both transparency and trust. Given the foundational strength of health data for medical advances in both the private and public sphere, contributors have the right – and researchers have the obligation – to understand how DTC-PGT data are being commercialized and how consumers are providing consent.

II THE DIRECT-TO-CONSUMER PERSONAL GENETIC TESTING MODEL

The DTC-PGT industry was launched in 2007, for the first time giving consumers access to their genetic information without a clinician intermediary.[11] Potential benefits to such direct access include empowering individuals to better understand their own health, facilitating access to genetic data and information without paying for or going to a clinician, or even helping people to make better health choices.[12] Criticisms of the industry include a potential lack of understanding of complex health data as well as some genetic tests not relevant or actionable for a given consumer.[13] But, as the price of genetic testing has gone down and the speed of data generation and analysis has gone up, the DTC-PGT industry has grown exponentially.[14] And yet – despite the US Food and Drug Administration's (FDA) almost exclusive focus on the accuracy and reliability of the information that

8 Future of Privacy Forum, Privacy Best Practices for Consumer Genetic Testing Services (July 31, 2018), https://fpf.org/wp-content/uploads/2018/07/Privacy-Best-Practices-for-Consumer-Genetic-Testing-Services-FINAL.pdf ("The Best Practices provide a policy framework for the collection, retention, sharing, and use of Genetic Data generated by consumer genetic and personal genomic testing services.").

9 See Luc Rocher, Julien M. Hendrickx, & Yves-Alexandre de Montjoye , Estimating the Success of Re-Identifications in Incomplete Datasets Using Generative Models, 10 Nature Commc'n 3069 (2019).

10 See Spector-Bagdady et al., Genetic Data Partnerships, supra note 4.

11 Patricia J. Zettler, Jacob S. Sherkow & Henry T. Greely, 23and Me, the Food and Drug Administration, and the Future of Genetic Testing, 174 JAMA Internal Medicine 493–94 (2014).

12 See Robert C. Green & Nita A. Farahany, Regulation: The FDA is Overcautious on Consumer Genomics, 505 Nature 286–87 (2014).

13 See Valerie Gutmann Koch , PGTandMe: Social Networking-Based Genetic Testing and the Evolving Research Model, 22 Health Matrix 33 (2012).

14 Research and Markets, Global Consumer DNA (Genetic) Testing Market: Forecasts from 2018–2023 (2018), www.researchandmarkets.com/research/w4fsmm/global_928?w=5(last visited Nov.1, 2020).

companies provide *consumers*[15] – the value of the DTC-PGT business model is not actually in selling genetic test results to individuals. Its primary revenue comes from selling consumer health data to researchers.[16]

We know from the empirical health policy literature that people are concerned about the commercialization of their health data.[17] People specifically lack trust in the pharmaceutical industry.[18] Despite this lack of trust, the majority of people do not think of uploading their own health data into private platforms, such as "wellness apps" or industry websites, as "commercializing" their own information.[19] Participants also generally do not read detailed terms and conditions – even when sharing sensitive health data.[20] For example, a recent study (which queried cancer patients that had enrolled in a precision medicine trial), found that *none* recalled consenting to future commercialization of their data even though the terms of service had clearly specified that possibility.[21] Genetic data has added risks above general health data including unforeseen risks for blood relatives (such as the recent reidentification case leading to the Golden State killer via publicly accessible genealogy sites).[22] A recent *Science* article projected that almost 60 percent of European-descent individuals have a blood relative in a genetic database.[23] In fact, almost all Americans can be reidentified with fifteen demographic attributes,

15 Green & Farahany, supra note 12; Kayte Spector-Bagdady & Elizabeth Pike, Consuming Genomics: Regulating Direct-to-Consumer Genetic and Genomic Information, 62 Neb. L. Rev. 701–02 (2014).

16 Matthew Herper, Surprise! With $60 Million Genentech Deal, 23andMe Has a Business Plan, Forbes (Jan. 6, 2015), www.forbes.com/sites/matthewherper/2015/01/06/surprise-with-60-million-genentech-deal-23andme-has-a-business-plan/#5fbe51dd2be9.

17 Kayte Spector-Bagdady et al., Encouraging Participation And Transparency In Biobank Research, 37 Health Affairs 1313 (2018).

18 Christine R. Critchley & Dianne Nicol, Understanding the Impact of Commercialization on Public Support for Scientific Research: Is it About the Funding Source or the Organization Conducting the Research, 20 Public Understanding Sci. 347 (2011) ("[T]he results reveal that support drops significantly when scientific research is funded by private rather than public interests, and even more so when it is conducted in a private company rather than a public university.")

19 Kirsten Ostherr et al., Trust and Privacy in the Context of User-Generated Health Data, 5 Big Data & Soc'y 2 (2017) ("Members of the general public expressed little concern about sharing health data with the companies that sold the devices or apps they used. . .").

20 Id. at 6 ("While users were generally aware that consenting to a company's terms of use constitutes a legal contract, very few reported actually reading those agreements before consenting to them. One participant commented: 'Do I ever read 'terms of use'? Did I actually read the consent form I just signed? No. I just agree to everything like I do for all of my Apple updates. Agree. Agree. Done.'").

21 Kayte Spertor-Bagdady et al. "My Research is Their Business, but I'm Not Their Business": Patient and Clinician Perspectives on the Commercialization of Precision Oncology Data, 25 Oncologist 622 (2020).

22 Thomas Fuller, How a Genealogy Site Led to the Front Door of the Golden State Killer Suspect, NY Times (Apr. 26, 2018) www.nytimes.com/2018/04/26/us/golden-state-killer.html.

23 Yaniv Erlich et al., Identity Inference of Genomic Data Using Long-Range Familial Searches, 362 Science 690 (2018) ("We project that about 60% of the searches for individuals of European descent will result in a third-cousin or closer match, which theoretically allows their identification using demographic identifiers.").

genetic data notwithstanding.[24] This raises the real potential for genetic discrimination, some of which is not protected under federal or state law.[25]

Despite these concerns, when researchers use genetic data that is privately derived for their academic publications, they often disclose little regarding the pedigree of the data or type of consent. In fact, while the number of academic publications using private genetic data has increased rapidly since 2011, the type of contributor consent is unclear in such publications almost half of the time.[26]

There is much good that can come from being able to analyze and share genetic data resources at this scale, and many recent scientific advances have been founded in both private and private-public collaborations.[27] But there is a tension between allowing consumers the autonomy to access genetic and health information directly and contractually accept related terms and conditions,[28] and protecting them from a lack of clarity and transparency in the commercial genetic-data-research industry.

III IMPROVING CLARITY AND TRANSPARENCY IN COMMERCIAL HEALTH DATA RESEARCH

The *Privacy Best Practices* recommendations highlight ensuring continued "consumer trust" as a foundational goal,[29] but improving commercial health data policy need not and should not be done in a health policy data vacuum. What builds contributor trust in data sharing is an empirical question to which there are already many answers. From both the perspective of building a sustainable business model to which consumers will contribute and continuing to meet best practices for disclosure and consent in secondary research, there are two specific shortcomings in these recommendations that need to be improved upon: (1) when and if deidentified individual-level consumer health data will be shared with third parties, and (2) whether express consent should be required to share identifiable individual-level data (Table 8.1).

Regulatory protections for health data, including the Health Insurance Portability and Accountability Act (HIPAA) and Subpart A of the Federal Policy for the Protection of Human Subjects (the Common Rule), are founded in whether health

24 Rocher et al., supra note 9.

25 Kayte Spector-Bagdady et al., Analysis of State Laws on Informed Consent for Clinical Genetic Testing in the Era of Genomic Sequencing, 178 Am. J. Med. Genetics 81–8 (2018).

26 Spector-Bagdady et al., Genetic Data Partnerships, supra note 4.

27 See, e.g., Craig L. Hyde et al., Identification of 15 Genetic Loci Associated with Risk of Major Depression in Individuals of European Descent, 48 Nat. Genetic 1031–36 (2016).

28 Neil Richards & Woodrow Hartzog, The Pathologies of Digital Consent, 96 Wash. U. L. Rev. 1461–504 (2019).

29 Future of Privacy Forum, supra note 8 ("By developing these responsible guidelines, we hope to ensure continued innovation and consumer trust within the consumer genetic and personal genomic testing industry.").

TABLE 8.1 *Future areas for commercial health data management improvement*

Area	Proposed Best Practice	Room for improvement
	Deidentified health data	
Whether individual level consumer health data may be shared as long as deidentified	Companies may not share deidentified genetic data or health data analyzed in conjunction with genetic data without consent	Companies should disclose if individual level de-identified health data may be shared with third parties
	Specific versus broad research consent	
Whether consumers should give consent to research generally or a research plan specifically	Separate "express consent" must be required for sharing identified, individual-level data	Companies should clarify and researches disclose when specific consent in necessary

data are readily and individually identifiable.[30] If data are identifiable, they are generally protected; if data are deidentified, they are generally not. Genomic data, and in particular large-scale sequencing data, confound this paradigm because even if genomic data are not identifiable in and of themselves, they are still uniquely identifiable to only one person.[31] With rapidly advancing genetic technologies, and the online proliferation of identifiable information, it has become generally accepted that it is possible for genomic data to be reidentified.[32] The new *Privacy Best Practices* accepts this position and commits to not sharing individual-level genetic data or health data analyzed in conjunction with individual-level genetic data without consent.

But many DTC-PGT companies are also collecting health data that are not genetic.[33] And contributors to these databanks have concerns about sharing their deidentified health data with third parties,[34] in addition to recent research showing the inherent re-identifiability of demographic data as well.[35] The *Privacy Best*

[30] 45 C.F.R. § 160.103 (2019) ("*Protected health information* means individually identifiable health information."); 45 C.F.R. § 46.102(e) (2019) ("*Human subject* means a living individual about whom an investigator [whether professional or student] conducting research … [o]btains, uses, studies, analyzes, or generates identifiable private information or identifiable biospecimens." (emphases in original)).

[31] Presidential Commission for the Study of Bioethical Issues, Privacy and Progress in Whole Genome Sequencing 64 (Oct. 2012), https://bioethicsarchive.georgetown.edu/pcsbi/sites/default/files/PrivacyProgress508_1.pdf.

[32] MelissaGymrek et al., Identifying Personal Genomes by Surname Inference, 339 Science 321–24 (2013) ("This study shows that data release, even of a few markers, from one person can spread through deep genealogical ties and lead to the identification of another person who might have no acquaintance with the person who released his [or her] genetic data. The propagation of information through shared male lines amplifies the range of identification, allowing ~135,000 records to potentially target several million U.S. males.").

[33] See, e.g., Spector-Bagdady, The Google of Healthcare, supra note 6.

[34] See Reshma Jagsi et al., Perspectives of Patients with Cancer on the Ethics of Rapid-Learning Health Systems 35 J. Clinical Oncology 2315–23 (2017).

[35] Rocher et al., supra note 9.

Practices appear to specifically *not* protect nongenetic health data (for example, from self-reported surveys, questionnaires, or online user interfaces). But when companies post separate research-consent documents, it would be reasonable for consumers to believe that *no* health data will be shared unless they agree. Companies should disclose to consumers if deidentified individual-level nongenetic health data may be shared with third parties – even if they do not specifically consent.

A second issue surrounds specific versus broad research consent. "Broad consent" generally refers to consent for unspecified future research within a set of basic terms and conditions.[36] "Specific consent" generally discloses the risk and plans for a distinct study.[37] However, it is unclear when DTC-PGT companies are requiring third-party researchers to obtain specific consent to research rather than relying on standard broad consent forms. But, again, we know that even when people sign broad consent agreements, there are certain kinds of research protocols (e.g., those that are sensitive or controversial) that often later make them change their minds when told specifically.[38]

The *Privacy Best Practices* discuss "separate express consent" being required for sharing identified health data with third parties, but do not clarify what that means or in which circumstances specific consent will be solicited. Companies should be transparent regarding what kinds of protocols will require specific consent and researchers should be clear whether they obtained broad versus specific consent in subsequent publications.[39]

IV CONCLUSIONS

The DTC-PGT market is rapidly reaching more consumers, but more critical is its dominance in the commercial genetic data market – a position that gives it influence over many important future advances in health. Privacy best practice standards will be a major area for improvement in the coming years both from a regulatory and professional standards perspective. Given existing empirical data regarding contributor preferences and re-identifiability of data, additional clarity and transparency in sharing deidentified health data and specific consent versus broad consent are necessary for the achievement of true "best practices" for the DTC-PGT industry.

36 Christine Grady et al., Broad Consent for Research with Biological Samples: Workshop Conclusions, 15 Am. J. Bioethics 34–42 (2015).

37 Id.

38 Raymond G. De Vries, et al., Understanding the Public's Reservations About Broad Consent and Study-by-Study Consent for Donations to a Biobank: Results of a National Survey 11 PLoS One 1, 8 (2016) ("For practical reasons, blanket consent must remain, but people need – at a minimum – to be put on notice that their specimens may be used in research they consider to be objectionable. Our data confirm that this information is material to the decision to donate, and thus consent given without this information cannot be considered truly informed.").

39 See Spector-Bagdady et al., Genetic Data Partnerships, supra note 4.

9

Genetic Paparazzi

Yaniv Heled and Liza Vertinsky

I INTRODUCTION

As genetic sequencing technologies become faster, cheaper, and more informative, they are making their way into many different facets of our lives. We are becoming accustomed to using and sharing our own genetic information, whether it be to investigate ancestry, to further medical research, to detect diseases, establish paternity, or to inform our reproductive choices. It is not hard to imagine a future in which the genetic information of others, public figures in particular, makes it into the public discourse. The media industry will be ready to capitalize on this interest, and it may only be a matter of time before genetic disclosures are published alongside candid photographs of celebrities on tabloid pages. Genetic paparazzi with swabs and sterile tubes in hand will seek out and analyze discarded genetic materials from the celebrities they pursue, publishing the results, and lawsuits will follow.

This chapter provides an overview of the legal landscape in which genetic paparazzi lawsuits will unfold and explores the legal questions that genetic paparazzi will raise about the nature and scope of genetic privacy. We begin with the anticipated emergence of genetic paparazzi and two hypotheticals based on real events to illustrate the legal questions that will arise when genetic paparazzi scenarios reach the courtroom. The chapter concludes with some thoughts on how the choices that courts make in genetic paparazzi cases might impact how we think about genetic privacy, for better or for worse.[1]

II GENETICS AND THE MEDIA

Madonna has long been worried about her genetic privacy, even going so far as to appoint teams to sterilize her dressing room after concert tours to ensure that no

[1] For a broader discussion about how channeling legal questions about genetics and public figures into narrowing pathways may impact how we think about genetics and the law, and for a more detailed analysis of the hypotheticals discussed in this Chapter, see Yaniv Heled and Liza Vertinsky, *Genetic Paparazzi: Beyond Genetic Privacy*, 82 Ohio State Law Journal 403 (2021).

trace of her genetic material is left behind. [2] While many have considered this level of concern over the natural shedding of skin, hair, and body fluids to be paranoia, Madonna's desire to guard against risks to her genetic privacy may well be prophetic.[3]

The cost and speed of genetic sequencing has fallen dramatically over the past decade and access to genetic sequencing technology has expanded.[4] While it took $2.7 billion and more than a decade for the Human Genome Project to complete the first sequencing of the human genome,[5] by 2008 the human genome could be sequenced for less than $1.5 million and in only four months.[6] By 2009, some labs were offering a price of $5,000 for sequencing a human genome, and companies such as Illumina promise the option of decoding our genome for a mere $100 at some point in the future, yielding results within hours rather than days or months.[7] With the availability of fast, low cost, accessible, and informative genetic testing has come a similarly dramatic increase in the number of Americans who have undergone genetic testing. It is estimated that some twenty-six million Americans have taken a direct-to-consumer genetic test, while many others have undergone genetic testing for health care purposes or in connection with law enforcement activities.[8] The growing number and volume of uses of genetic technologies is likely to impact not only our familiarity with and interest in genetic information, but also how we think about genetic privacy – particularly in areas already subject to diminished privacy interests, such as in criminal law contexts or – as is the subject of this chapter – in the case of public figures.[9]

[2] See Clemmie Moodie, Madonna Appoints a DNA Team to Sterilize Her Dressing Room After She Has Used It, Mirror (June 23, 2012), www.mirror.co.uk/3am/weird-celeb-news/madonna-appoints-dna-team-sterilise-907641.

[3] See Ben Locwin, Madonna May Suffer from "DNA Paranoia," Genetic Literacy Project (Feb. 19, 2016), https://geneticliteracyproject.org/2016/02/19/madonna-may-suffer-dna-paranoia.

[4] See, e.g., Kris Wetterstrand, The Cost of Sequencing the Human Genome, National Human Genome Institute, www.genome.gov/about-genomics/fact-sheets/Sequencing-Human-Genome-cost (last updated Oct. 30, 2019).

[5] Tom Ulrich, Can DNA Sequencing Get Any Faster and Cheaper?, Broad Institute Blog (Sept. 13, 2016), www.broadinstitute.org/blog/opinionome-can-dna-sequencing-get-any-faster-and-cheaper.

[6] Meredith Wadman, James Watson's Genome Sequenced at High Speed, 452 Nature 788–89 (2008).

[7] See Mathew Herper, The New Fast Gene Machine, Forbes (Sept. 17, 2009) www.forbes.com/forbes/2009/1005/revolutionaries-science-genomics-gene-machine.html?sh=1f3b542622f3; Mathew Herper, Illumina Promises to Sequence Human Genome for $100 — But Not Quite Yet, Forbes (Jan. 9, 2017) www.forbes.com/sites/matthewherper/2017/01/09/illumina-promises-to-sequence-human-genome-for-100-but-not-quite-yet/?sh=cdbb0d7386d2.

[8] Megan Molteni, The US Urgently Needs New Genetic Privacy Laws, Wired (May 1, 2019), www.wired.com/story/the-us-urgently-needs-new-genetic-privacy-laws/; Antonio Regalado, More than 26 Million People have Taken an at-Home Ancestry Test, MIT Tech. Rev. (Feb. 11, 2019), www.technologyreview.com/s/612880/more-than-26-million-people-have-taken-an-at-home-ancestry-test.

[9] For other ways in which genetic technologies are impacting both our concepts of privacy and the realities of what can be private, see Chapter 13, Generational Failures of Law & Ethics: Rape, Mormon Orthodoxy, and the Revelatory Power of AncestryDNA (Augustie-Adams) and Chapter 6, Noninvasive Prenatal Testing (Ravitsky).

"Public figures," people of public importance or fame, or even those who have been thrust into fame by newsworthy events, have a diminished expectation of privacy under the law. [10] Utilizing this legal shield to the fullest, a lucrative industry has emerged around the lives and actions of celebrities and other figures of public interest, one that has been driven and shaped by entrepreneurial paparazzi and the visual glimpses they have provided into the private lives of the famous people they follow.[11] The paparazzi have continued to push at the boundaries of what is public and what is private, utilizing new technologies that continuously test the limits of privacy in their efforts to capture ever more unique (and often more intrusive) images of public figures.[12] The reward that the paparazzi can claim from the sale of their photographs increases dramatically when they are able to capture something of unique public interest. Since the growth of social media has allowed public figures to present the image and information *they* want directly to the public, paparazzi have had to find new opportunities either in partnership with public figures or by finding aspects of public lives that have previously remained hidden. Genetic sequencing technologies promise to provide paparazzi with glimpses into previously hidden dimensions of the public figures they pursue.

Public interest in the genetics of celebrities predates the availability of and familiarity with genetic sequencing, but until recently the information available was extremely limited.[13] Genetic sequencing and testing technologies and the information they provide offer promising insights into public figures (albeit with widely varying accuracy and validity) including ancestral links, genetic predispositions for certain kinds of disease, propensities for certain kinds of behaviors, and guesses about the purported genetic source of certain physical and character traits. Enterprising and entrepreneurial paparazzi now have the technology to go further, and deeper, into the public figures they pursue, an option that may become more attractive to paparazzi as their traditional sources of income diminish.[14]

As public comfort with and interest in genetics increases, and the speed, ease, and affordability of the technology make it ever more accessible, opportunities for

10 See, e.g., Shlomit Yanisky-Ravid & Ben Zion Lahav, Public Interest Versus Private Lives – Affording Public Figures Privacy in the Digital Era: The Three Principle Filtering Model, 19 J. Const. L. 975 (2017).

11 See, e.g., Kim McNamara, The Paparazzi Industry and New Media: The Evolving Production and Consumption of Celebrity News and Gossip Websites, 14 Int'l J. Cultural Stud. 515 (2011); Elizabeth Day, Paparazzi! How an Unloved Profession Has Shaped Us, Guardian (Mar. 1, 2014), www.theguardian.com/media/2014/mar/02/paparazzi-unloved-profession-major-french-exhibition.

12 See generally Robin Barnes, Outrageous Invasions: Celebrities' Private Lives, Media, and the Law (2010).

13 See, e.g., Nicola C. Ho et al., Famous People and Genetic Disorders: From Monarchs to Geniuses – A Portrait of Their Genetic Illnesses, 118 Am. J. Med. Gen. 187–96 (2003).

14 See Claudia Roesenbaum, How the Fast Times of the Paparazzi Came to a Screeching Halt, BuzzFeed News, Oct. 15, 2015, www.buzzfeednews.com/article/claudiarosenbaum/downfall-of-the-paparazzi.

genetic paparazzi to capitalize on the genetics of public figures will grow. Indeed, discussions about the genetic information of presidential candidates have already entered the news in a limited way, as a result of recent pressure on Elizabeth Warren to back up her claims to Native American ancestry.[15] While demands for the genetic information of presidential candidates has not gone further in this election cycle (at least not yet), there may well be more public demand for the genetic information of presidential candidates in the future.[16] Public interest in and commercial opportunities to exploit the genetic information of celebrities are also likely to grow.

III WHAT GENETIC PAPARAZZI CASES MIGHT LOOK LIKE

Given the advances in technology and the public interest in delving ever deeper into the lives of public figures, the emergence of "genetic paparazzi" seems not only probable but imminent.[17] While no court has yet had to rule on the legal status of celebrities' genetic material and information put to media use, complaints from celebrities about the alleged theft of their genetic material have already made their way into courts. Madonna recently brought a lawsuit against an online auction house and the auctioneer, a long-time friend, to stop the auctioning of personal items such as a hairbrush with Madonna's hair still entwined. [18] In her complaint, Madonna expressed concern over the possible auctioning of her genetic material.[19] Although the court never reached this issue, finding instead that her claims were barred by the statute of limitations, it will not be long before similar celebrity complaints make their way onto the docket. Once they do, courts will be pushed to determine the legal status of genetic materials and information taken by "genetic paparazzi"[20] from celebrities or other public

[15] See Astead Herdnon, Elizabeth Warren Stands by DNA Test. But Around Her Worries Abound, N.Y. Times (Dec. 6, 2018).

[16] See, e.g., Robert Lee Hotz, Gene Screen: Will We Vote Against a Candidate's DNA, WSJ (Oct. 31, 2008), www.wsj.com/articles/SB122539728499285289.

[17] See Nicolle Strand, Shedding Privacy Along with Our Genetic Material: What Constitutes Adequate Legal Protection Against Surreptitious Genetic Testing, 18 AMA Journal of Ethics 264–71 (2016); Teneille R. Brown, Double Helix, Double Standards: Private Matters and Public People, 11 J. Health Care L. & Pol'y 295–376 (2008).

[18] See Ciccone v. Gotta Have It! Collectibles Inc. et al., No. 156454/2017 (Sup. Ct. N.Y., Apr. 23, 2018).

[19] Michelle Kaminsky, Madonna Loses Fight to Reclaim Tupac's Letter, Other "Highly Personal Items," Forbes (Apr. 23, 2018), www.forbes.com/sites/michellefabio/2018/04/23/madonna-loses-fight-to-reclaim-tupacs-letter-other-highly-personal-items/?sh=723b97b38b0c (discussing Madonna's complaint, including concerns about genetic privacy, as she stated "I understand that my DNA could be extracted from a piece of my hair ... it is outrageous and grossly offensive that my DNA could be auctioned for sale to the general public.").

[20] For the purpose of this analysis, we define "genetic paparazzi" as individuals who pursue information, including genetic information, about public figures that might be of public interest with the intent to sell such information to potential publishers. We are by no means the first to coin the term "genetic paparazzi" or to imagine the commercial implications of non-consensual genetic testing of celebrity DNA. See, e.g., supra note 17. See also e.g. Mara Thompson, Genetic Paparazzi: Could Celebrity DNA Become Public Domain?, Ga. St. U. News (Apr. 28, 2020), https://news.gsu.edu/2020/04/28/genetic-

figures[21] and used for media purposes. Since no court has yet had to confront a genetic paparazzi case as such, we employ two hypotheticals to explore what genetic paparazzi cases might look like and how courts will likely handle the issues such cases are expected to raise.

Hypothetical 1: It is a close presidential race and the public is particularly eager to learn more about the intelligence, fiscal responsibility, and integrity of each candidate. A genetic paparazzo who closely follows Presidential Candidate's campaign is able to obtain a used napkin and half eaten sandwich left behind by Presidential Candidate during a campaign lunch at a local museum. The genetic paparazzo sends the napkin and sandwich to a laboratory, which is able to extract Presidential Candidate's genetic material from the napkin and have it sequenced. From the results, the paparazzo learns that Presidential Candidate – now in his late forties – has a mutation on the gene that is known to cause Huntington's Disease[22] as well as several genetic markers that have been associated with early onset Alzheimer's disease [23] and the "gambling gene." [24] The genetic paparazzo then writes up the findings and sells the story, along with excerpts from the report of the genetic results to a major newspaper, which publishes it promptly.

Hypothetical 2: Famous Celebrity has long been known for her beautiful voice[25] and her unique style, but also for her sometimes erratic behavior, tumultuous personal life, and prolonged absences from the limelight while in rehab and psychiatric institutions. Famous Celebrity's hairbrush, with her hair entwined, is being offered for sale by an auction house. The auction house acquired the hairbrush legally from Famous Celebrity's college roommate, who kept the hairbrush after Famous Celebrity abandoned it when she dropped out of college to pursue a career in entertainment. A genetic paparazzo purchases the hairbrush and immediately proceeds to have the genetic material in the hair sequenced and analyzed in an out-of-state laboratory. The results show that Famous Celebrity's genetics include

paparazzi-could-celebrity-dna-become-public-domain/ [https://perma.cc/MWW6-9XNT]; A. Pollack, DNA Evidence Can Be Fabricated, Scientists Show, New York Times August 17, 2009.

21 We think of "pubic figures" in the same way that the Supreme Court does, encompassing people of public importance or celebrity or even those who have been thrust into fame by newsworthy events. See, e.g., Yanisky-Ravid & Lahav, supra note 10. See also Gertz v. Robert Welch, Inc., 418 U.S. 323 (1974) (outlining distinction between public and private figures in the context of defamation case); Curtis Publishing Co. v. Butts, 388 U.S. 130 (1967) (same).

22 See Mayo Clinic, Huntington's Disease, Symptoms & Causes, www.mayoclinic.org/diseases- conditions/huntingtons-disease/symptoms-causes/syc-20356117 (last visited Mar. 12, 2020).

23 For an interesting discussion of the challenges associated with genetic tests for diseases such as Alzheimer's disease, see Chapter 15, Losing Our Minds? Direct-to-Consumer Genetic Testing and Alzheimer's Disease (Largent).

24 See Daniela Sabbatini da Silva Lobo et al., Addiction-Related Genes in Gambling Disorders: New Insights from Parallel Human and Pre-Clinical Models, 20 Molecular Psychiatry 1002–10 (2015); Angela Ibáñez et al., Pathological Gambling and DNA Polymorphic Markers at MAO-A and MAO-B Genes, 5 Molecular Psychiatry 105–09 (2000). See also Lee Hotz, supra note 16.

25 See, e.g., Robert T.Sataloff, Genetics of the Voice, 9 J. Voice 16–19 (1995).

several genetic markers that have previously been associated with increased likelihood of developing bipolar disorder, as well as the "infidelity gene."[26] The genetic paparazzo then sells the results to a prominent tabloid, which publishes them in its next issue.

Presidential Candidate and Famous Celebrity can, and no doubt will, bring a variety of legal claims against the genetic paparazzi as well as the labs that sequence the DNA and the media outlets that publish the genetic information. Foremost among these will be claims of privacy and rights of publicity. But, public figures have diminished rights of privacy and limitations on their rights of publicity, and additional legal protections are afforded to the press.[27] Courts hearing such cases will be in the uncomfortable position of deciding just how far inside of public figures the press is allowed to peer and in doing so will shape the way we think about both genetics and privacy.

IV GENETIC PAPARAZZI VERSUS GENETIC PRIVACY

The genetic paparazzi hypotheticals described above foreshadow some of the tensions that will arise when courts are asked to determine the nature and scope of rights that public figures have over the genetic materials that they leave behind, particularly when the resulting materials and information are obtained and used by the press. In a world where public figures have almost no right to privacy but possess strong rights of publicity, and where genetics is increasingly a part of public conversation and discourse, can public figures expect to protect their genetics from public view?

To answer this question, courts will begin by looking to the existing web of laws governing privacy and publicity rights of public figures – limited as they are by protections to freedom of speech and freedom of the press – and state genetic privacy laws.[28] Claims for conversion might also emerge as a possible legal pathway for disputes over the ownership and use of genetic materials and information,[29] and a property-based approach to genetics is reflected in at least a few state genetic privacy statutes.[30]

[26] See generally Richard Friedman, Infidelity Lurks in Your Genes, N.Y. Times (May 22, 2015), www.nytimes.com/2015/05/24/opinion/sunday/infidelity-lurks-in-your-genes.html (discussing research suggested as providing biological basis for infidelity). But see John Horgan, "Infidelity Gene" Hyped in the News, Scientific American (May 25, 2015), https://blogs.scientificamerican.com/cross-check/infidelity-gene-hyped-in-the-news/.

[27] See Jamie Nordhaus, Celebrities' Rights to Privacy: How Far Should the Paparazzi Be Allowed to Go, 18 Rev. Litg. 285–316 (1999).

[28] For an overview of privacy laws as they apply to genetics, see also E. Wright et al., The Law of Genetic Privacy: Applications, Implications, and Limitation, J. L. & Biosci. (May 14, 2019).

[29] Some scholars have suggested a property rights approach to securing genetic privacy. See, e.g., Jessica Roberts, Progressive Genetic Ownership, 93 Notre Dame L. Rev. 1105–72 (2018); Jessica Roberts, In Favor of Genetic Conversion: An Argument for Genetic Property Rights, Petrie-Flom Ct'r (2019) (working paper); Natalie Ram, DNA by the Entirety, 115 Colum. L. Rev. 873–940 (2015).

[30] See AS § 18.13.010, C.R.S.A. § 10-3-1104.7, F.S.A. § 760.40, O.C.G.A. § 33-54-1, and LSA-R.S. 22:1023. These states employ a property-based approach to genetic privacy. See also National Conference of State Legislatures, State Genetic Privacy Laws, http://pierce.wesleyancollege.edu/faculty/hboettger-

Privacy While not the only starting point, Presidential Candidate and Famous Celebrity are likely to rely heavily on privacy claims in response to the actions of the genetic paparazzi. Modern US privacy law consists of a complex web of state and federal laws and regulations that govern the ways that information can be acquired, accessed, stored, and used.[31] The concept of privacy underlying the law is itself amorphous and elusive, varying with the contexts in which privacy issues are raised and with the technologies that determine what is accessible as a practical matter and what is not.[32] Regardless of the source of support, however, the right to privacy is limited by First Amendment protections to freedom of speech and freedom of the press and Fourth Amendment prohibitions on unreasonable searches and seizures.[33]

Most of the existing cases dealing with surreptitious collection of genetic information have occurred in the criminal law context, providing constitutional arguments for privacy of genetic material and information grounded in the Fourth Amendment.[34] At the state level, tort based privacy rights provide individuals with some control over the gathering, sharing, and use of information about themselves,[35] but such rights are limited by determinations about what are reasonable expectations of privacy, subjects of legitimate public interest, and acceptable and unacceptable intrusions.[36] Recently state and federal legislatures have shown interest in increasing the regulation of consumer biometric data, however, with potential implications for genetics.[37]

The right to privacy is also balanced against the right of the public to access and share newsworthy information. [38] While there is no fixed formula for balancing

tong/docs/hbt%20public%20folder/FYS/State%20Genetic%20Summary%20Table%20on%20Privacy%20Laws.htm.

31 See, e.g., Neil Richards et al., Understanding American Privacy, in Research Handbook on Privacy and Data Protection Law: Values, Norms and Global Politics (Gloria González Fuster, Rosamunde van Brakel & Paul De Hert eds. 2018).

32 See, e.g., Richard A. Posner, The Right of Privacy, 12 Ga. L. Rev. 393–422 (1978). See also Ken Gormley, One Hundred Years of Privacy, 1992 Wis. L. Rev. 1335–442 (1992).

33 See Richards et al., supra note 31 (discussing how US privacy law is bifurcated between public and private regimes).

34 See, e.g., Holly Fernandez, Genetic Privacy, Abandonment and DNA Dragnets: Is Fourth Amendment Jurisprudence Adequate?, 35 Hast. Ct'r Rep. 21–23 (2005).

35 See Restatement (Second) of Torts § 652A (1977).

36 See Solveig Singleton, Privacy Versus the First Amendment: A Skeptical Approach, 11 Ford Intell. Prop. Media & Ent. L.J. 97–154 (2001).

37 A few states, such as California with its recent amendments to the California Consumer Privacy Act, have expanded privacy protections over commercial use of biometric data, and federal legislators are following suite, debating the need for tougher regulations on the collection of consumer health and biometric information. See, e.g., Jill Cowan & Natasha Singer, How California's New Privacy Law Affects You, N.Y. Times (Jan. 3, 2020). See also Heather Landi, Lawmakers Taking Steps to Create Federal Data Privacy Law with Tougher Regulation of Biometric, Health Data, FierceHealthcare (Dec. 5, 2019).

38 See, e.g., Shulmann v. Group W. Productions, 18 Cal. 4th 200 (1998). See also Reporters Committee for Freedom of the Press, Courts Wrestle with Defining Newsworthiness in Privacy Cases, www.rcfp.org/journals/news-media-and-law-fall-2015/courts-wrestle-defining-newsw (last visited Nov. 1, 2020).

individual privacy interests against the interest in allowing the media to publish without fear of liability, and while standards for newsworthiness vary, courts share a tendency to give deference to the press in their determinations of what is newsworthy.[39]

Against this backdrop, both Presidential Candidate and Famous Celebrity will find their right of privacy limited by the public's "right to know" and to discuss information of public concern. They will find that the newsworthiness of much of their lives often supersedes the "right to be let alone."[40] The strength of their claims to violations of privacy for obtaining their genetic material, analyzing it, and disclosing their genetic information will also be limited by existing social norms governing what should, and should not, be regarded as legitimate subjects of public discourse and what should be protected as private facts.[41]

Rights of Publicity Famous Celebrity in particular will be quick to assert a violation of her rights of publicity based on misappropriation of her commercially valuable genetic identity. This approach will require courts to think about genetic material and information as a manifestation of identity, one protected by a property interest. They will have to weigh this property interest against the right of the public and the press to access and share information about Famous Celebrity.

Conversion Genetic paparazzi will argue that the genetic materials they collect have been abandoned, and that there is not (and perhaps should not) be an ownership interest in them. Such claims will raise difficult questions about the nature of possession, abandonment, and intentionality with respect to a person's shed genetic material and the information it contains. [42]

State Genetic Privacy Laws From a genetic paparazzi's vantage point, about half of the states appear to have laws that would make it illegal to carry out one or more of the acts involved in a genetic paparazzi scenario, and in seven states some of these acts would even be considered a crime.[43] But while the state genetic privacy statutes create legal risks for genetic paparazzi as well as labs involved in analyzing the genetic materials and publishers involved in publication of the information, the landscape of genetic privacy statutes includes important gaps and potential areas of weakness. Not all states have genetic privacy statutes and those that do vary in the

39 See Danielle Keats Citron, Mainstreaming Privacy Torts, 98 Cal. L. Rev. 1805–52 (2010).

40 See, e.g., Nordhaus, supra note 27; Yanisky-Ravid & Lahav supra note 10; Jennifer Rothman, The Right of Publicity: Privacy Reimagined for a Public World (2018).

41 See Daniel Solove, The Virtues of Knowing Less: Justifying Privacy Protections Against Disclosure, 53 Duke L.J. 967–1066 (2003) (examining the legal basis for distinguishing between information of public and private concern).

42 See, e.g., Chapter 3, In Favor of an Action for Genetic Conversion (Roberts).

43 These states are Alaska, Delaware, Florida, Nevada, New Jersey, New York, and Oregon. State genetic privacy laws vary in nature and scope, but they typically seek to restrict specified groups (e.g. employers, insurers, any third party) from carrying out specified activities (e.g. collecting DNA samples, analyzing such samples, etc.) without consent.

scope and nature of coverage. In addition, at least some of the statutes might face a First Amendment challenge similar to the ones seen in the context of privacy and defamation lawsuits. Finally, as a practical matter, given the lucrative nature of the information obtained, some genetic paparazzi will no doubt be ready to take the legal risks involved.

V COURT DECISIONS AND GENETIC PAPARAZZI

The issue of nonconsensual analysis and use of genetic materials has already come before the courts in the criminal law context, and commentators have made predictions about what the decision might look like in situations outside of criminal law.[44] Most have concluded that the current legal framework is inadequate to protect against nonconsensual collection, testing, sequencing, analysis, publication, and use of genetic material and information.[45] We reach the same conclusion in the context of genetic paparazzi cases.

But we suggest that this inadequacy of genetic privacy, while interesting in itself, reveals a much bigger challenge with fitting genetics into existing legal frames. When courts confront genetic paparazzi cases, they will seek to fit the legal status of genetic materials and information into existing legal categories and to adapt questions about genetics into existing bodies of law – mostly those designed to address the privacy and publicity rights of public figures in media contexts. But in so doing, they will, inevitably, fail to capture some important aspects of genetic materials and information while overemphasizing other aspects.[46]

Focusing on privacy as the lens through which to evaluate use of genetic materials and information will lead courts to ask questions about reasonable expectations of privacy and legitimate public interests in access. But focusing on these issues ignores the fact that our genetic information is shared with other people, including ancestors, living relatives, and current and future children. It also makes the analysis of how to regulate genetics dependent on changing social contexts and social expectations, rather than anchoring our analysis in more fundamental rights and concerns about human dignity and human identity, both integral aspects of human genetics.

Thinking about genetic information and materials through a publicity lens is also problematic, leading to a focus on the property-like aspects of genetics and an

[44] See, e.g., Mark Rothstein, Genetic Stalking and Voyeurism: A New Challenge to Privacy, 57 U. Kan. L. Rev. 539– 78 (2009); Elizabeth E. Joh, Reclaiming "Abandoned" DNA: The Fourth Amendment and Genetic Privacy, 100 Nw. U. L. Rev. 857–84 (2006); June Mary Z. Makdisi, Genetic Privacy: New Intrusion a New Tort? 34 Creighton L. Rev. 965–1026 (2001); Elizabeth E. Joh, DNA Theft : Recognizing the Crime of Nonconsensual Genetic Collection and Testing, 91 B.U. L. Rev. 665–700 (2011); Teneille R. Brown, Double Helix, Double Standards: Private Matters and Public People, 11J. Health Care L. & Pol'y 295–376 (2008).

[45] See, e.g., Rothstein, supra note 44; Makdisi supra note 44; Joh 2011, supra note 44.

[46] See A Theory of Genetic Interests (working paper) (on file with authors).

analysis of the commercial value of genetic property interests. This could fuel a commodification of genetics within the law, which raises a plethora of other issues and potential ramifications that exceed the scope of this chapter.[47]

If the rights of the press to share genetic information were to predominate in a genetic paparazzi case, as they might in some cases – particularly in contexts such as presidential races – we might be left with court decisions that emphasize the public interest in accessing the genetic information and materials of public figures. Such decisions may even be read as encouraging a view of the procurement and analysis of genetics as speech for First Amendment purposes. The idea of genetics as speech has already come up in the context of question about the patenting of genetic sequences and the constitutionality of rules limiting the sharing of genetic information obtained from research.

Genetic paparazzi cases will force courts to address areas of potential conflict between the diminished expectations of privacy that public figures have under federal and state law, the protections afforded to the press, and the strict construal of genetic privacy provided by a number of state genetic privacy statutes. The ways in which courts resolve these competing legal conceptions of genetic privacy in the context of genetic privacy cases will, thus, impact other areas in which questions about the role of genetics within the law is taking shape.

In sum, when genetic paparazzi cases such as the two hypotheticals discussed above hit the courtroom, courts will face challenging questions about how to balance competing interests in and access to a variety of very new and different kinds of materials and information. Relying on the existing web of privacy and publicity laws, and even less utilized pathways such as conversion, could yield legal conceptions of genetic privacy that are both inadequate and, ultimately, unsatisfying. We conclude that instead of fitting genetic paparazzi cases into the existing legal framework, we should think more carefully about the role that genetics does, could, and should, play in public discourse and in the media and how this could be reflected in the law.

VI CONCLUSION

Genetic technologies are opening up new possibilities for a media industry intent on publicizing every aspect of the lives of public figures. Expanding public familiarity with and uses of genetic technologies will ensure a reader-base ready and interested in consuming stories about celebrity genetics whenever they hit the press. If and when genetic information appears alongside candid photographs in tabloid pages, lawsuits will follow, and courts will be pressed to determine just how far inside public figures the press and the public it serves are allowed to peer. Considering hypothetical genetic paparazzi cases raises new questions about the scope and limits

47 See, e.g., Chapter 4, Direct to Consumer Genetics and Personal Health Data (Contreras).

of genetic privacy that courts and policymakers will have to consider. This chapter has suggested some of the ways in which genetic paparazzi cases will challenge how we think about genetic privacy, and perhaps how we think about genetics more generally. Perhaps it also reveals the inadequacy of genetic privacy laws to handle the complex and multidimensional nature of genetics.

PART III

Tinkering with Ourselves: The Law and Ethics of DIY Genomics

Introduction to Part III

Henry T. Greely

The three chapters in this Part of the book take an interesting turn from the rest of the book, one akin to a jumping off a flat page and into a new dimension, a new universe. These three chapters are not, primarily, about *consuming* genomics, but about how people, often consumers, who are not "the usual suspects," are *producing* genomics, sometimes their own genomics. And, as in science fiction (and perhaps in science fact), the laws of nature are not necessarily the same in parallel universes, so the human laws dealing with this space – whether called DIY gene editing, nontraditional gene editing, or genetic biohacking – are not quite the same as those in the consuming space. And each of our chapters sees this new universe, and its laws, from a different angle, with a different lens.

In the first Chapter, *Programming Our Genomes, Programming Ourselves: The Moral and Regulatory Challenge of Regulating DIY Gene Editing*, Barbara Evans takes on the challenging task of examining the regulation of Do-It-Yourself (DIY) genetic editing under existing US law, the tangled set of provisions from different statutes and regulations from different agencies known, without apparent irony, as "The *Coordinated* Framework." Evans notes the problems commonly identified in the Coordinated Framework: inapt definitions, underpowered agencies, and an overwhelming surge of new activity. She cuts through that to a deeper problem: "The very concept of 'regulation,' as developed and practiced under the web of old statutes the Coordinated Framework rests on, fails unless there are suitable entities to regulate." New kinds of transactions are happening – from business to business, business to consumer, consumer to consumer, and consumer to self – that challenge the practical, as well as merely legal, limits of our regulatory schemes. And she argues that before trying to reinvent regulation, we need to ask ourselves whether regulation is justified, applying Joel Feinberg's analysis of paternalism to focus particularly on DIY gene editing of humans by those same humans.

The second Chapter, *Governing Nontraditional Gene Editing*, by Max Mehlman and Ronald Conlon, describes much the same territory but from a very different vantage point. Mehlman and Conlon dive deep into what they call the "Nontraditional Gene Editing (NTGE) Community," describing some of its many manifestations. They look at iGEM, the international genetically engineered machine competition; at various community labs; and at the surprising role of the Federal Bureau of Investigation. They then lay out a wide range of governance approaches, a full dozen by my count, ranging from prohibition to laissez-faire. The most fascinating part of the chapter, to me, is their discussion of regulatory treatment of somewhat similar earlier "nontraditional" uses of four regulated technologies: ham radio, sport rocketry, home brewing, and computer hacking. They draw lessons from those precedents to guide a governance approach to NTGE.

In the final Chapter in this Part, *Finding a Regulatory Balance for Genetic Biohacking*, the authors, Patti Zettler, Christi Guerini, and Jake Sherkow, apply yet a different lens, and name, to some of the same activities discussed by the earlier authors. They focus more closely on a particular set of actors, the unknown number of thousands of "enthusiasts, followers, biohackers, and citizen scientists" in the USA. This chapter reviews government regulation but also looks hard at the roles of "private regulation," notably through patents, contracts, and torts, as well as voluntarily adopted guidelines. It argues for carefully adapted and applied regulatory approaches, urging that "policymakers should consider whether existing oversight mechanisms can be used in more effective ways – whether that means better engagement, more or more finely tailored enforcement, or some other approach – to mitigate genetic biohacking's risks while amplifying its potential."

These three chapters each look at genomic research done outside the confines of industry, academia, or government laboratories. Each sees part of the same beast, but different parts. And each brings a different approach to play: ethical analysis of paternalism, the histories of hobbyist "science," and the world of private law and informal "regulation." The result is a Part filled with diverse and interesting insights; a Part that, I think you will agree, is more than the sum of its component chapters.

10

Programming Our Genomes, Programming Ourselves

The Moral and Regulatory Challenge of Regulating Do-It-Yourself Gene Editing

Barbara J. Evans[*]

I INTRODUCTION

In 2015, the Obama Administration launched an effort to update the United States' biotechnology regulatory framework. One component of that effort was a landscape study of novel biotechnology products expected to enter the market within five to ten years and whether there was an adequate federal regulatory framework in place to address the consumer safety, environmental, workplace safety, biosecurity, and other hazards they might present.

In 2017, the US National Academies of Science, Engineering, and Medicine (NASEM) published that landscape study, *Preparing for Future Products of Biotechnology*.[1] The study argued that a focus on products arriving in five to ten years meant the United States would have to rely mainly on the Coordinated Framework for Regulation of Biotechnology (Coordinated Framework), which is the existing scheme of federal oversight dating back to 1986.[2] The landscape study assumed that major legal reforms take longer than ten years to complete by the time Congress enacts new legislation, courts hear legal challenges, and federal agencies promulgate regulations implementing the new statutes.[3] That assumption seems even more prophetic now, after a change of presidential administration in 2017 redefined priorities for regulatory reform.

This chapter explores some of the practical and ethical challenges of regulating do-it- yourself (DIY) genomic technologies under the Coordinated Framework. A 2013 survey found that DIY genomics mostly involves simple activities such as extracting DNA; purifying proteins; genetically engineering bacteria, yeast, cells, or

[*] Professor Evans served on the committee that prepared the 2017 *Preparing for Future Products of Biotechnology report* that is cited in this chapter. She has no financial conflicts of interest to disclose.

[1] National Academies of Science, Engineering, and Medicine [NASEM], Preparing for Future Products of Biotechnology (2017), www.nap.edu/catalog/24605/preparing-for-future-products-of-biotechnology (last visited Apr. 7, 2020).

[2] See Coordinated Framework for Regulation of Biotechnology, 51 Fed. Reg. 23302 (June 26, 1986).

[3] NASEM, supra note 1 at 68.

plants; or testing oneself for the presence of a particular gene.[4] Editing one's own genome has not yet been a major focus of DIY activity.[5] Even so, this chapter devotes some attention to the challenge of overseeing DIY tools that could eventually enable people to alter their own genomes and engage in human genome self-editing. While not yet a major focus of DIY activities, self-editing of one's own genome is foreseeable in the not-too-distant future.

II THE COORDINATED FRAMEWORK

Successes in recombinant DNA technology in the late 1970s and early 1980s sparked concern that a flood of new biotechnology products might require new types of regulation. Congress considered but did not enact special biotechnology legislation for the United States.[6] Instead, in 1984, a Working Group on Biotechnology under the auspices of the White House Cabinet Council on Natural Resources and the Environment called for existing federal agencies – such as the Food and Drug Administration (FDA), the Environmental Protection Agency (EPA), the US Department of Agriculture (USDA), and the Occupational Safety and Health Administration (OSHA) – to regulate biotechnology products using their existing statutory authorities.[7] This led, in 1986, to the adoption of a Coordinated Framework to clarify the division of responsibilities among the various agencies.[8]

Under the Coordinated Framework, each agency has only the powers conferred by its regular enabling statutes. For example, the FDA exercises its authority under the Federal Food, Drug, and Cosmetic Act (FFDCA) and the Public Health Service Act; the EPA regulates under the Toxic Substances Control Act and various other statutes; and the USDA implements the Plant Protection Act, the Federal Meat Inspection Act, and several other acts.[9] The Coordinated Framework confers no new, biotechnology-specific regulatory powers. The Coordinated Framework has been updated twice: in 1992 and in the closing hours of the Obama Administration in January 2017.[10] The 2017 update expressly avoided addressing human genome editing and other

4 Daniel Grushkin, Todd Kuiken & Piers Millet, Seven Myths and Realities About Do-it-Yourself Biology, Woodrow Wilson Int'l Center for Scholars Synthetic Biology Project (2013), https://perma.cc/CX7W-73D5 (last visited Apr. 7, 2020).

5 Id.

6 NASEM, supra note 1, at 70.

7 Id.

8 Coordinated Framework for Regulation of Biotechnology, supra note 2.

9 Modernizing the Regulatory System for Biotechnology Products: An Update to the Coordinated Framework for Biotechnology Products (2017), https://obamawhitehouse.archives.gov/sites/default/files/microsites/ostp/2017_coordinated_framework_update.pdf (last visited Apr. 7, 2020).

10 Id.; Exercise of Federal Oversight Within Scope of Statutory Authority: Planned Introductions of Biotechnology Products Into the Environment, 57 Fed. Reg. §§ 6753–62 (Feb. 27, 1992).

biotechnologies subject to FDA regulation as human medical products, leaving policy to be clarified by the FDA.[11]

This approach invites criticism that the US biotechnology regulatory framework is a jumbled collection of old federal statutes designed for products predating the advent of modern genomics.[12] Thus, the FDA struggles to regulate CRISPR-Cas9 therapies today, using drug regulations rooted in the 1938 FFDCA[13] and biologics authorities dating back over a century to a time when diphtheria antitoxin and smallpox vaccine were the cutting edge of biomedicine.[14] Emerging products can fall through gaps in the regulatory jurisdiction these statutes confer, and even when agencies do find jurisdiction, their regulatory powers are not always well tailored to the risks of the products now emerging.[15] The modest 2017 update to the Coordinated Framework continued to rely on the same underlying statutes and did not alter this reality.

The problem is not simply that emerging biotechnology products are novel and sometimes do not fit within traditional jurisdictional definitions – such as "drug," "biological product," "device," "food," "pesticide," "plant pest," and "chemical" – that Congress allows federal agencies to regulate.[16] And the problem is not just that agencies' powers – such as the power to conduct a premarket review of safety and effectiveness, the power to inspect manufacturing facilities, or the power to require adverse event reporting or postmarketing evidence collection – are a poor fit for the risks the regulators now must manage (although, in many instances, the fit is indeed quite poor). Moreover, while the scope, scale, pace, and complexity of biotechnology innovation threatens to overwhelm existing regulatory agencies,[17] it is not true that simply expanding those agencies (for example, by tripling or quadrupling their staffing and budgets) would solve the problem.

Doing more of the same regulatory activities may not suffice, because the problem is more fundamental. The very concept of "regulation," as developed and practiced under the web of old statutes the Coordinated Framework rests on, fails unless there are suitable entities to regulate. This problem is salient in the age of direct-to-consumer (DTC) and DIY biotechnology. The next section explores trends underlying this problem.

III THE COORDINATED FRAMEWORK'S REGULATORY LANDSCAPE, DISRUPTED

The Coordinated Framework and the twentieth-century regulations it comprises cast regulators as benevolent entities standing between – and mediating the

[11] Update to the Coordinated Framework (2017), supra note 9.
[12] Id. (listing key statutes).
[13] Pub. L. No. 75-717, 52 Stat. 1040 (1938).
[14] Peter Barton Hutt, Richard A. Merrill & Lewis Grossman, Food and Drug Law: Cases and Materials, 1123 (4th ed. 2014).
[15] See NASEM, supra note 1 at 11.
[16] See id. at 209–12 (listing key definitions).
[17] Id. at 10.

relations of – "product developers," on the one hand, and "the public and society," on the other hand.[18] The product developers, under this traditional paradigm, mainly are "US and international corporations, research organizations, small- and medium-sized enterprises" engaged in commercial development, manufacturing, or distribution of biotechnology products.[19] The public and society are cast in a passive role, simply buying and using products that corporate product developers think they ought to have, although members of the public do sometimes engage in "[u]nregulated domestic production and use" – for example, if they cook a pie at home instead of purchasing a pie manufactured by a "product developer."[20] This is the orderly twentieth-century regulatory landscape for which the Coordinated Framework was designed.

There is no question that traditional product developers will continue playing major roles in the biotechnology industry, but with new players alongside them. "A key, new element associated with the development of biotechnology products in the United States is the multiplicity of different players that intersect and collaborate in flexible but robust entrepreneurial ecosystems."[21] The National Academies' landscape study surveyed trends reshaping the biotechnology industry.[22] These trends include DIY biotechnology, including gene editing technologies practiced in people's homes or at community laboratories; nontraditional funding sources such as crowdsourced funding for biotech research and development; and smaller-scale and decentralized manufacturing that could leave regulators bereft of the well-staffed, well-financed, compliance-oriented regulated entities that US regulations depend on to generate most of the data on which regulators base their decisions.[23] Important research activities now happen outside the reach of the ethical and safety norms traditionally tied to public research funding and voluntarily embraced by responsible, compliance-oriented corporate actors.[24] The National Academies' landscape study highlighted four emerging business models.

The first involves new business-to-business transactions. For example, contractors provide bioinformatics services and laboratories synthesize DNA fragments and other molecules for traditional product developers.[25] Twentieth-century regulations attach to some but not all of these new players. As an example, the FDA's definition of a regulable "drug" includes "a component" of a finished drug product,[26] so a contract lab synthesizing chemicals for a drug developer seemingly falls under FDA oversight. But what of the contract bioinformatics service provider whose

18 See id. at 20, Fig. 1-1 (portraying this relationship).
19 Id.
20 Id.
21 Id. at 36.
22 Id. at 27–66.
23 Id. at 33–38.
24 Id. at 85.
25 Id. at 36.
26 21 U.S.C. § 321 g(1)(4).

software helps design or screen the safety of the finished drug? Information services are not a "drug component," even when they might critically affect the safety and efficacy of the finished drug.

A second emerging model includes new business-to-consumer activities.[27] Some of these lie in the jurisdiction of existing federal statutes. Thus, the FDA can regulate DTC-GT services, such as 23andMe, if their test reports imply they are "intended for use in the diagnosis of disease . . . or in the cure, mitigation, treatment, or prevention of disease."[28] Yet FDA officials have signaled that the agency does not view "data-only" DTC testing services – those that merely report a person's genetic variant data without making any interpretive statements about their potential health impacts – as medical devices.[29] Nor is it clear that the FDA can regulate the stand-alone genetic interpretation services to which consumers can then turn to help them decipher the clinical significance of their "data-only" results.[30]

Part of the problem here is that modern biotechnology platforms (products used to make other biotechnology products) blur the distinction between products traditionally characterized as "wet-lab" (such as DNA/RNA, enzymes, vectors, cells, sequencing prep kits) and "dry-lab" (such as computer-aided design software and informatics tools).[31] This blurring facilitates a disaggregation, unbundling, and remixing of the activities traditionally involved in creating and delivering a new medical product. The FDA has authority to regulate entities that (1) manufacture or distribute *products* (as opposed to services) and which (2) do so with intent for the products to be used in diagnosing, treating, or preventing a disease or health condition.[32] Modern technology platforms sometimes split the act of manufacturing or distributing the product (e.g., synthesizing a strand of DNA) from the act of forming intent for how it should be used (that is, for clinical versus nonclinical purposes). This splitting may leave no single player engaged in the full array of activities that, when done together, unleash the FDA's regulatory power. For example, if an individual contracts with a laboratory to synthesize a chemical and distributes that chemical to others with an intent for medical use, the individual unquestionably would trigger FDA jurisdiction. However, if the individual injects the chemical in herself, she is a consumer rather than a distributor and seemingly escapes FDA oversight. The FDA regulates manufacturers and distributors, not consumers.

27 See NASEM, supra note 1, at 36.

28 21 U.S.C. § 321(h)(2).

29 Dan Vorhaus, DTC Testing and the FDA: Is There an End in Sight to the Regulatory Uncertainty?, Privacy L. Rep. (June 16, 2011), https://theprivacyreport.com/2011/06/16/dtc-genetic-testing-and-the-fda-is-there-an-end-in-sight-to-the-regulatory-uncertainty (last visited Apr. 7, 2020).

30 See Gail H. Javitt & Katherine Strong Carner, Regulation of Next Generation Sequencing, 42 J.L. Med. & Ethics 9–21 (2014).

31 See NASEM, supra note 1, at 5.

32 See, e.g., 21 U.S.C. § 321(g)(1) (drugs); id. § 321(h) (devices, including diagnostic devices).

A third emerging trend involves new consumer-to-consumer transactions.[33] If a person genetically edits yogurt cultures or synthesizes a new molecule at home and then distributes these products to others (whether as a gift or for a price), that person is manufacturing a product that may fall under FDA regulation as a dietary supplement, food additive, medical food, cosmetic, or drug, depending on the products' intended use.[34] FDA jurisdiction exists, even if the agency might face enormous practical difficulties discovering the activity is taking place.

However, if the person designates her home laboratory as a community lab and charges others a fee to visit her lab and follow her published instructions to synthesize their own genetically edited yogurt cultures and molecules, this laboratory operator is providing a service, rather than selling a medical product, and seemingly falls outside the FDA's jurisdiction. Furthermore, the publication of instructions may qualify as scientific speech that enjoys First Amendment protections. Persons using the community laboratory to manufacture products could fall under the FDA's jurisdiction if they sell or distribute their products to others, but they – rather than the laboratory operator – would be responsible for showing that their products are safe, effective, and compliant with the FDA's other requirements.

The fourth emerging model is DIY biotechnology in which the individual is both producer and consumer.[35] Professor Lisa Ikemoto points out that DIY practitioners are not necessarily scientific amateurs; many are trained professional scientists who perhaps work in an academic or corporate laboratory by day but pursue hobbies or extracurricular projects in their free time.[36] The projects vary widely. Many are non-health-related and threaten few, if any, environmental or social impacts: for example, developing a genetic test to detect whether one's sushi is the type of fish it purports to be or to infer which of the neighbors' dogs is soiling one's front yard.[37] Other projects, however, do sound in biomedicine: for example, synthesizing low-cost insulin[38] or injecting oneself with CRISPR gene-editing chemicals.[39] Other DIY projects threaten impacts on the environment or on agriculture, for example, developing genetically modified plants or animals[40] for open release into the environment.

These four new business models, in some instances, place the manufacturing of biotechnology products outside the reach of current product safety and environmental regulatory frameworks, such as those administered by the FDA, EPA, and USDA.

33 See NASEM, supra note 1, at 36.
34 See 21 U.S.C. §§ 321(ff), 321(s), 360ee(b)(3), 321(i), 321(g)(1).
35 NASEM, supra note 1, at 36.
36 See Lisa C. Ikemoto, DIY Bio: Hacking Life in Biotech's Backyard, 51 U.C. Davis L. Rev. 539–68 (2017).
37 See, e.g., id. at 543.
38 Id.
39 See Molly Campbell, Meet Josiah Zayner, The Biohacker Next Door, Technology Networks (June 21, 2019).
40 See NASEM, supra note 1, at 46–47.

Regulators and law enforcement agencies attempting to engage with these new players – out of concern, for example, for potential bioterrorism risks – at times have embraced a light-handed regulatory approach out of fear that strongly enforced, compulsory standards might only drive activities deeper underground.[41]

IV CHALLENGES OF REGULATING DIY PRODUCERS

The trends just described empower individuals to experiment with and manufacture DIY biotechnology products that once might have required a large organization to assemble. Software tools are available to help people design strands of DNA that perform specific functions, such as causing a cell to detect and react to specific environmental stimuli.[42] Such tools empower users, even laypeople with "no special knowledge of genetic engineering," to design a strand of DNA or a guide RNA for CRISPR editing system that can imbue cells with desired characteristics.[43] Standard biological parts are available, as are laboratories that can synthesize DNA and RNA to order.[44]

In the scenario just described, the parties from which the individual buys input goods and services may or may not fall under FDA regulatory oversight. The software vendor seemingly lacks any specific intent with respect to the molecules its software is capable of designing, nor is the software vendor engaged in manufacturing the molecules its software designs. A contract laboratory manufactures the molecules but may be agnostic about their intended use. For many genetic sequences and other molecules individuals now can order, there is no basis to infer any particular intent from the mere fact that an order was placed: Was it ordered for a therapeutic use as opposed to a preclinical research use or for use in a hobby, and was it ordered for insertion in a plant, an animal, a human, or simply for an inanimate chemistry experiment?

The federal government does have a program in place to track laboratory shipments of a very small set (about sixty-five) of biological agents (e.g., the Ebola virus) that have such narrow uses – and such high potential for harm – that anyone who orders such items can be presumed to have improper intent.[45] Other, less sinister agents, however, lend themselves to a wide range of possible research, hobby, or health-related uses, whether in humans, animals, plants, or microbes and cells. The DIY practitioner who forms the intent for how the molecule will be used might not engage in manufacturing or distributing it, and thus might not trigger FDA oversight. Even when DIY practitioners theoretically can be regulated, a host of

41 Id. at 73.

42 Anne Trafton, A Programming Language for Living Cells: New Language Lets Researchers Design Novel Biological Circuits, MIT News (Mar. 31, 2016).

43 Id.; see also NASEM, supra note 1, at 28–33.

44 NASEM, supra note 1, at 28–33.

45 Id. at 73 (describing the Federal Select Agent Program administered by the US Department of Agriculture and the Centers for Disease Control).

logistical, practical, and other challenges can make it hard for traditional twentieth-century regulatory agencies to regulate them effectively.

Similar problems arise in the sharing economy exemplified by ride-hailing services like Uber and Lyft and home-sharing services like Airbnb.[46] As with DIY biotechnology, "scale is a defining feature and fundamental challenge of the sharing economy."[47] Twentieth-century federal regulatory frameworks conceived the regulator's role as protecting consumers in two-party transactions between a discrete number of large providers of goods and services and the mass of relatively powerless consumers. The sharing economy encompasses an immense number of three-party transactions among small providers, small consumers, and platforms that bring them together and facilitate their transactions. In aggregate, the scale of this economy is massive, with almost half of Americans engaged in some aspect of the sharing economy.[48]

Notably absent from the sharing economy are the discrete, large providers of goods and services that were the targets of twentieth-century-style regulatory scrutiny. Under the twentieth-century regulatory paradigm, a regulator can order hotels to implement security standards and accommodate consumers with disabilities, knowing who the hotels are and where they are located, confident that their scale of operations can bear the compliance costs, and with a credible threat of conducting inspections to verify that the standards are met. But "when everything is small, the regulatory challenge is immense."[49] How is a regulator to enforce standards against everybody renting a spare room through home-sharing services like Airbnb?

Some twentieth-century regulations expressly exclude small actors from regulation. Examples include labor laws and workplace safety regulations that stratify requirements depending on how many people a business employs.[50] The FDA's regulations generally do not stratify requirements based on the size of the *manufacturer*, although there is some stratification based on the market size of the *product*: for example, the FDA has a statutory exemption easing regulatory burdens on custom devices, such as orthodontic appliances, that are tailored to individual patients and sold in quantities of five or less per year,[51] but the companies that make custom devices often are significantly scaled businesses. A drug or biological product is eligible for orphan drug designation under the FDA's regulations if it serves small-scale markets, but the scale in question is still quite a large market: the drug must be aimed at a rare disease or condition affecting fewer than 200,000

46 See Kellen Zale, When Everything is Small: The Regulatory Challenge of Scale in the Sharing Economy, 53 San Diego L. Rev. 949–1016 (2016).

47 Id. at 950.

48 Id. at 952, 955 n.6.

49 Id. at 950.

50 See, e.g., id.; Equal Employment Opportunity Commission, Small Business Requirements, www.eeoc.gov/employers/smallbusiness/requirements.cfm (last visited Apr. 7, 2020. 2019).

51 FFDCA, § 520(b).

patients per year.[52] Moreover, the companies that manufacture orphan drugs to serve these "small" markets may be large pharmaceutical companies themselves.

Even when regulators like the FDA and EPA could, in theory, regulate small-scale, at-home operators, they often exercise discretion and focus regulatory efforts on the larger players. The FDA has never been in the business of prosecuting moms who manufacture chicken soup with the intent that it be used for "the diagnosis, cure, mitigation, treatment, or prevention of" the common cold within their families – although, in theory, the FDA might have jurisdiction based on mom's curative claims.[53] Mom is involved in a personal, noncommercial distribution within the home or to sick friends. Only if Mom goes into business selling her soup in arm's-length transactions with strangers is the FDA likely to take note. Similarly, the EPA tends to focus on large-scale commercial and industrial polluters rather than at-home infractions, such as the hobbyist who pours paint-thinner down the kitchen sink.[54] Individuals' decisions to commute to work in their own cars have a large aggregate environmental impact, but the EPA does not send enforcement letters telling people not to do it.[55] Law relies on other mechanisms to shape these decisions – for example, high gasoline taxes or fuel-efficient speed limits – instead of bringing EPA's coercive regulatory powers to bear.[56]

Transactions in the twenty-first-century sharing economy and DIY bio community often fall below the (express or discretionary) thresholds for federal regulation under the twentieth-century regulatory paradigm. Twentieth-century regulations worked well precisely because regulators drew distinctions, such as between commercial or large-scale activities that should be regulated, on the one hand, and personal or small-scale activities that merit leniency, on the other hand.[57]

There are various justifications for excluding small-scale endeavors from regulation. Some of these have long existed, whereas others are emerging in the twenty-first-century sharing economy. They include: (1) the de minimis nature of personal, small-scale activities and the tenuous link between such activities and interstate commerce; (2) concerns about privacy impacts and regulatory invasions on constitutionally protected precincts such as the home;[58] (3) the fact that information regulators need in order to regulate individual providers may reside not with those individuals, but rather with platforms (such as Uber or Airbnb) that broker the transactions but are not themselves engaged in the regulated activity. This raises questions about regulators' jurisdiction to force information disclosure, and there are concerns about consumer

52 21 C.F.R. pt. 316.
53 See 21 U.S.C. § 321(g)(1).
54 See Michael P. Vandenbergh, From Smokestack to SUV: The Individual as Regulated Entity in the New Environmental Law, 57 Vand. L. Rev. 515–628 (2004).
55 Id.
56 Id.
57 See Zale, supra note 46, at 950.
58 See Griswold v. Connecticut, 381 U.S. 479 (1965); Katrina Fischer Kuh, When Government Intrudes: Regulating Individual Behaviors that Harm the Environment, 61 Duke L. J. 1111–82 (2012).

privacy when the entity reporting data is not the regulated entity; (4) doubts about the wisdom of visiting the fixed costs of being regulated on small actors;[59] (5) doubts about the cost-effectiveness and feasibility of enforcing regulatory norms on diffuse, tiny enterprises;[60] and (6) the possibility that social norms or other community-based mechanisms may be better suited than regulation is to shape behavior in these contexts.[61] For all of these reasons, the agencies covered by the Coordinated Framework traditionally have focused on large commercial and industrial operators, as opposed to individuals.

The distinctions – commercial versus personal, large-scale versus small-scale – are now breaking down. "Small-scale activities that once fit criteria for light or no regulation" are now occurring in volumes that threaten to marginalize consumer-safety regulators if they continue to restrict their focus to commercial, large-scale actors.[62] There is a sense that safety regulators need to step up their oversight of small-scale DIY genomics, yet the regulatory model they inherited from the twentieth century leaves them ill-equipped for this task. Regulatory jurisdiction over individual, noncommercial actors is sometimes unclear. Federal agencies like the FDA are good at interpreting their jurisdiction broadly and in ways that let them regulate things that need to be regulated, and courts tend to let them do so. A classic example is the 1969 case, *U.S. v. Bacto-Unidisk*,[63] which let the FDA to stretch its drug jurisdiction to regulate a product that, by modern standards, was unquestionably a device, because doing so was "consistent with the [FFDCA's] overriding purpose of protecting the public health."[64]

Even when the FDA's jurisdiction is clear (or can be stretched to cover DIY genomics), the available regulatory tools – such as FDA inspections – can raise constitutional concerns when the inspected facility is a person's home. Commercial entities that seek FDA clearance or approval to market their products in effect are consenting to FDA inspections of their facilities: turning an FDA inspector away is a prohibited act under the FFDCA and might cause one's product to be deemed adulterated or misbranded.[65] In contrast, an FDA inspector who shows up at a person's home might first need to obtain a warrant to enter the premises.[66] The staffing and budgets required to enforce regulations against thousands of tiny at-home operations could make regulation, as we knew it in the twentieth century, unworkable, especially if DIY genomics grows more widespread than it is today.

59 See Zale, supra note 46, at 965–67.
60 Id. at 964; Albert Lin, Herding Cats: Governing Distributed Innovation, 96 N.C. L. Rev. 945–1012 (2018).
61 See Zale, supra note 46, at 967–68.
62 Id. at 956–57.
63 374 U.S. 784 (1969).
64 Id. at 798.
65 FFDCA, §§ 301(f), 21 U.S.C. § 331(f).
66 See Zale, supra note 46, at 961–64; U.S. Const. amend IV.

Updating the Coordinated Framework, as last done in 2017, fails to address a deeper problem: the old statutes and regulations that the Coordinated Framework "coordinates" exhibit a lack of fit for the new context of DIY genomics. Coordinating old, twentieth-century regulations is not necessarily the best way to ensure effective regulation for the twenty-first century.

V BEFORE REINVENTING THE REGULATIONS, THE QUESTION IS, "SHOULD WE?

The regulatory challenges just described might be addressed through some sort of clever reinvention of existing regulatory frameworks. Before embarking on that project, however, a basic question must be resolved: How paternalistic do we want our regulations to be? If an at-home practitioner of DIY genomics, being an adult of sound mind, wishes to edit her genome and turn her skin glow-in-the-dark green, is it really the federal government's role to stop her? Would doing so feed a new social scourge, *wildism* – the view that people with pure, natural, wild-type human genomes are physically or morally superior to those who take advantage of future opportunities to edit their genomes? In this context, there is room to debate what constitutes self-harm.

Joel Feinberg's *Harm to Self* explores how far governments can go in banning self-harming conduct without infringing on citizens' autonomy.[67] He explains nuances that clarify the meaning of paternalism and distinguish it from other principles that justify governmental intervention to protect individual and public safety. He identifies ten coercion-legitimizing (liberty-limiting) principles that justify governmental interference with people's actions by means of laws and regulations.[68] By his analysis, the United States' Food and Drug laws and consumer protection laws are not paternalistic.[69] Rather, they are grounded in a completely different principle, a "Harm Principle" against allowing one party to visit harm on others.[70] The FDA's drug-safety regulations apply coercion not to the protected class of individuals (drug consumers), but to medical product manufacturers and distributors.[71] The legitimizing principle is that government can bring coercive force to bear on product manufacturers and distributors to keep them from harming consumers.[72]

Feinberg's conclusion – that the FDA's regulatory framework is not paternalistic – may strike readers as philosophical hairsplitting that is a little hard to swallow. After all, the FDA is the agency that fought to keep Laetrile out of the hands of dying cancer patients who wanted to try it.[73] The Supreme Court did not ground that

67 Joel Feinberg, Moral Limits of the Criminal Law, Volume 3: Harm to Self (1989).
68 Id. at xvi–xvii.
69 Id. at 21.
70 Id. at xvi–xvii.
71 Id. at 21.
72 Id.
73 U.S. v. Rutherford, 442 U.S. 544 (1979).

decision on paternalistic principles, but observers smelled a definite whiff of paternalism in the air: "The Supreme Court accepted FDA's arguments that it was important to protect individuals suffering from a potentially fatal disease from rejecting conventional therapy in favor of a drug with no demonstrable curative properties."[74] The FDA also brought us *Abigail Alliance v. Von Eschenbach*[75] – again protecting a dying person from the risky behavior of taking an unapproved drug – and the lesser-known case *Kessler v. Benten*.[76] The *Benten* case stands out because the FDA's coercive force was applied not to a product manufacturer, but to a woman who purchased a drug (mifepristone, which blocks action of the female hormone progestin) overseas for her own personal use, only to have it confiscated at a US port of entry. These examples call to mind the distinction between de jure discrimination (policies directly designed to discriminate) and de facto discrimination (facially neutral policies that have a discriminatory impact). If Feinburg is right that the FDA's regulations are not grounded in de jure paternalism, there seems to be de facto paternalism at times.

Setting aside this contradiction for a moment, Feinberg's analysis is useful to the discussion of DIY editing of one's own genome. Feinberg defines the Harm Principle, which refers to the notion that it is appropriate to regulate an actor in order to prevent or reduce harms to persons other than the actor.[77] The Offense Principle involves regulating an actor in order to keep the actor from inflicting serious offense on other people.[78] The Offense Principle might encompass, for example, regulating DIY gene editing to keep people from modifying their own bodies in ways that other people find scary, grotesque, or offensive to civilized norms of bodily integrity. Feinberg recognizes these two principles as the only two possible justifications for coercion that are consistent with liberal principles.[79]

He goes on to define Legal Paternalism as the notion that governments can apply coercion to an actor to prevent the actor from self-harm (physical, psychological, or economic).[80] John Stuart Mill strongly rejected Legal Paternalism as a legitimate basis for state coercion, regarding the prevention of self-harm as grounds to remonstrate with, entreat, persuade, or reason with a person, but not as grounds for "compelling him or visiting him with harm if he do otherwise."[81]

Feinberg acknowledges, though, that "the view that the state has a right to protect people from their own folly seems to provide the rationale for many [laws] that nobody would wish to repeal."[82] He distinguishes "presumptively non-blameable"

74 Hutt et al., supra note 14 at 952.
75 495 F.3d (D.C. Cir. 2007), cert. denied 128 S. Ct. 1069 (2008).
76 799 F.Supp 281, cert. denied 515 U.S. 1084 (1992).
77 See Feinberg, supra note 67, at xvi–xvii.
78 Id.
79 Id. at 3.
80 Id. at xvii.
81 Id. at 3 (quoting Mill).
82 Id. at 4.

paternalism (for example, laws that protect children and others who are genuinely vulnerable) from "presumptively blameable" paternalism.[83] This latter category includes two things: (1) well-intentioned "benevolent paternalism" that ostensibly protects people for their own good but, in fact, overrides the will of well-informed, competent adults who were not vulnerable and did not need or want protection, and (2) "nonbenevolent paternalism" that purports to protect people but, in fact, is directed at other goals such as increasing worker productivity or reducing the costs of doing business.[84] An example of nonbenevolent paternalism would be to argue that granting people access to unapproved cancer drugs might be unsafe for them, when the real concern is that patients might stop enrolling in clinical trials if they could try the drugs without doing so.

Feinberg recognizes a position of "soft paternalism" (or "soft antipaternalism") in which law allows people to consent to self-harm but makes sure their consent is truly voluntary and well informed – that is, that their expressed will really is their will and not the product of misinformation, coercion, etc.[85] Under this view, law has a valid role to play in ensuring the validity of consents. This view is reflected in major US research regulations such as the Common Rule,[86] which allows people to consent to risky research but polices their consents to make sure they are informed and reflect people's true will.

Once it is established that people are competent and well-informed adults who freely consent to self-harm, the antipaternalistic view is that law should let them do so.[87] The reality is that law has never done this, at least not since Wright's case in the 1600s.[88] In that English case a man consented to have another person cut off his hand, for the seemingly rational reason that doing so would increase the man's earnings as a beggar. The perpetrator, when charged with mayhem, advanced the man's consent as a defense, but to no avail. The man's consent was not valid, because to consent to such a thing deprived the King of the able work capacity of one of his subjects.[89]

Wright's case points to nuances that Feinberg's analysis partly addresses. First, there is a difference between "single-party" self-harm (doing harm to oneself) and "two-party" cases in which a person enlists the aid of others to inflict the harm.[90] Feinberg dwelled on the question of whether a person's consent to self-harm should, or should not, exculpate the second party who aids in a self-harming scheme.[91] That

[83] Id. at 5.
[84] Id.
[85] Id. at 13–14.
[86] 45 C.F.R. 46, subpt. A.
[87] See Feinberg, supra note 67, at 2.
[88] See Arthur Ripstein, Force and Freedom: Kant's Legal and Political Philosophy 133 (2010); Vera Bergelson, The Right to be Hurt: Testing the Limits of Consent, 75 Geo. Wash. L. Rev. 165–236 (2007).
[89] See Bergelson, supra note 88 at 173.
[90] See Feinberg, supra note 67, at 9.
[91] Id. at 10.

is an interesting question, but it is not the main question we need to answer in connection with DIY genomics. That question is: Does one's right to self-harm encompass a right to inflict potential harms on others by involving them as accomplices? Such harms could include moral harms, feelings of guilt, or legal risks for enabling people's desire to edit their own genomes. If so, the reason to restrict DIY genomics is not Legal Paternalism (preventing harm to the individual) but rather the Harm Principle (keeping the individual from inflicting harms on accomplices).

Feinberg recognizes that most of the laws we label as paternalistic are, in reality, "mixed paternalistic laws" that draw on more than one of the above principles for their rationales. A given law may be simultaneously motivated by "the need to protect the directly restricted party himself; but also to protect third parties from indirect harm, and even the general public from a kind of diffuse harm."[92] This mixed rationale is seen, for example, in rules that restrict individuals' access to return of results and data generated during genomic research. There is "benevolent paternalistic" concern for the individual, who may misunderstand research-quality data and incur medical and psycho-social harms as a result.[93] But there also is "non-benevolent paternalism" in the concern that individuals may waste scarce health care resources in their quest to make sense of the data, or that the research institutions that generated the data may lose control over valuable data resources, or that returning results may take time and money that reduces research productivity.[94] Such rules actually draw, in part, on the Harm Principle – that is, the desire to prevent harm to others, including a concern that returning low-quality genetic test results may trigger a cascade of costly testing for the person's family members to rule out the possibility that they, too, may be at risk.[95]

Rules have conscious and unconscious rationales as well as stated and unstated ones.[96] The notion of "mixed paternalism" helps make sense of some of the FDA cases cited earlier in this section. The access to experimental drugs plaintiffs sought in *Abigail Alliance* not only, in the FDA's view, might expose them to risk but also might deter enrollment in clinical trials, which are an essential part of the FDA's program to protect the public. In the *Benten* case, the woman whose mifepristone was confiscated stated she intended to use it to induce an abortion. Confiscating the drug may have seemed justified under the Harm Principle, to protect the fetus. It is possible the case might have gone differently, had she stated she was importing the

92 Id. at 16.

93 National Academies of Science, Engineering, and Medicine, Committee on the Return of Individual-Specific Research Results Generated in Research Laboratories, Returning Individual Research Results to Participants: Guidance for a New Research Paradigm (Jeffrey R. Botkin et al., eds., 2018), http://nationalacademies.org/hmd/reports/2018/returning-individual-research-results-to-participants.aspx?_ga=2.125510026.1285413390.1534711400-1676621809.1532099289 (last visited Apr. 7, 2020).

94 Id.

95 Thomas M. Morgan, Genomic Screening: The Mutation and the Mustard Seed, 46J. L., Med., Ethics 541–46 (2018).

96 Feinberg, supra note 67, at 16.

drug to treat a fibroid tumor, another use that has some evidentiary support. The FDA often takes a non-paternalistic stance by letting people import limited quantities of unapproved drugs for their own use, for example, letting people import unapproved pork and beef insulin for their own use even while warning them that these products carry a risk of prion diseases such as mad cow disease.[97] The *Benten* case may be an outlier, influenced by the fact the drug was an abortifacient.

Before embarking on a program to build an effective regulatory framework for DIY genomics, we need, to the extent possible, to be clear what our motives are. Some uses of DIY genomics raise concerns under Harm Principle – for example, desperate parents editing the genomes of children with rare genetic disorders. Who will protect that child? The FDA, in theory, could require parents to obtain investigational new drug (IND) applications before injecting their kids with gene-editing substances. Such experiments are sponsor-investigator studies (with the parent doubling as study sponsor and investigator), which removes a level of research oversight. Some officials at the FDA have suggested that the agency can regulate sponsor-investigator studies even if the studies are noncommercial in nature with no intent to submit data from the study to the FDA.[98] But how would the FDA know the experiment is occurring? If not the FDA, are state children's protective services agencies equipped to oversee parental editing of children? A first step might be for legislatures to amend reporting statutes to add signs of gene editing to the list of things physicians, teachers, and others who work with children already must report.

Feinberg identifies various other justifications that are sometimes put forward for coercive laws and regulations.[99] One of these is "Legal Moralism," which prohibits actions that may cause no harm or offense to anybody – neither to the actor nor to other people – but which seen inherently immoral or capable of visiting free-floating harms on society or on morality in general.[100] Legal Moralism resembles "the wisdom of repugnance" or "yuk factor," sometimes cited as grounds to reject human cloning.[101]

If Legal Moralism is why we wish to regulate certain DIY genomic activities – for example, genetic enhancement – then we need to be explicit about that fact. And we will need to face the fact that the FDA is not the appropriate regulator. Congress authorizes the FDA to review the safety and effectiveness of medical products, but not to pass judgment on their morality. This is seen in a stream of FDA-cleared and approved products (e.g., breast implants for the indicated use of cosmetic enhancement) that present unresolved moral issues (for example, does it benefit society to

97 FDA, Questions and Answers on Importing Beef or Pork Insulin for Personal Use (Oct. 28, 2015); FDA, Is it Legal for Me to Personally Import Drugs? (Mar. 28, 2018). FDA, Personal Importation (Aug. 3, 2018).

98 Lynn Henley, FDA Clinical Investigator Training Course: How to Put Together an IDE Application, Food & Drug Admin. sl.12 (Nov. 14, 2013).

99 See Feinberg, supra note 67, at xvi–xvii.

100 Id. at xvii.

101 Leon R. Kass, The Wisdom of Repugnance, The New Republic 17–26 (June 2, 1997).

sell products that prey upon women's body-image anxieties, which remake women to fulfill the adolescent fantasies of men, and which divert scarce surgical resources that might better be deployed on other things?). The FDA is not the right agency to regulate DIY genomics, if the risks society wishes to address are rooted in the wisdom of repugnance. If I, an adult of sound mind, choose to edit my genome to grow rabbit ears on top of my head, is it legitimately the FDA's role to stop me? The agency's role is to protect me from harms inflicted by others – not to protect me from myself.

VI CONCLUSION

Much of the current discussion about regulating DIY genomics centers on whether federal agencies already have legal authority to do so, and if not, how to craft governmental or nongovernmental oversight mechanisms to fill the gaps. Before resolving those questions, however, there needs to be a dialogue about what the aims of regulation are and what principles future regulations should be designed to serve. This dialogue has begun, but it still feels unfinished. Before rushing to regulate DIY genomics, we need to say why.

11

Governing Nontraditional Gene Editing

Maxwell J. Mehlman and Ronald A. Conlon

I INTRODUCTION

Advances in gene editing technology make it increasingly possible for individuals to experiment with editing genes in humans and other organisms outside of traditional, regulated settings. These experiments could yield significant societal benefits, including important scientific advances. But these experiments also pose risks – to the subjects, the environment, the public, and the experimenters themselves. The question is whether the current relatively laissez-faire regulatory approach to these experiments achieves an appropriate balance between the potential risks and benefits and, if not, what alternate regulatory approaches could be implemented.

II BACKGROUND

Gene editing is being conducted not only in traditional university and corporate settings but in nontraditional settings such as basements, garages, and collective community labs. Some call these experiments "do-it-yourself biology,"[1] but that is a misnomer, since many are carried out in community labs or with the help of virtual community groups and friends. Others refer to the experiments as "bio-hacking,"[2] but the negative connotations of "hacking" are at odds with the potential benefits from these efforts, which include broader science education, a larger pool of scientific talent, and above all, scientific innovation; after all, Steve Jobs and Bill Gates did early work in their garages, and the first Apple was unveiled at a local electronics hobby club. Still others call this type of experimentation "citizen science,"[3] but this lumps active, hands-on experimenters with more passive public participation in projects such

[1] Thomas Landrain et al., Do-it-yourself Biology: Challenges and Promises for an Open Science and Technology Movement, 7 Systs. & Synthetic Biology 115 (2013).

[2] Heidi Ledford, Garage Biotech: Life Hackers, 467 Nature Biotechnology 650 (2010) [hereinafter "Garage Biotech"]; Günter Seyfried, Lei Pei, & Markus Schmidt, European do-it-yourself (DIY) biology: Beyond the Hope, Hype and Horror, 36 Bioessays 1 (2014).

[3] Julian Guthrie, Do-it-yourself biology grows with technology, SF Gate (Dec. 20, 2009), http://www.sfgate.com/science/article/Do-it-yourself-biology-grows-with-technology-3277834.php.

as NIH's "All of Us" program. In lieu of "do-it-yourself biology," "biohacking," or "citizen science," therefore, the authors use the term "nontraditional gene editing" (NTGE).

The NTGE community is highly diverse.[4] Some of its members are employed in traditional biological institutions but pursue NTGE in their free time on projects of personal interest;[5] others are amateurs who pursue NTGE individually and in teams in private homes and community laboratories. Some rebel against the hierarchy and specialization of academic and corporate biology.[6] Some reject intellectual property rights and insist on an open-source approach,[7] while others actively seek to commercialize their discoveries.[8] Some are public about their work, while others are secretive.[9]

While amateur biology has a long and storied history, interest in NTGE markedly increased around the start of the new millennium. In 2003, an international synthetic biology competition for high school and college students called the "International Genetically Engineered Machine" (iGEM) was founded at MIT "to show that it does not take a doctoral degree to design a biotechnology product."[10] The 2008 announcement of the creation of a synthetic genome[11] increased interest in genetic engineering, including in NTGE settings. In 2009, Mac Cowell and Jason Bobe launched a group of nontraditional biologists which they called "DIYBio."[12] Local, community, and regional workspaces called "labs" were established, including BioCurious in Silicon Valley and GenSpace in New York.[13] Relatively inexpensive equipment began to become available, including equipment produced by the experimenters themselves through reverse engineering.[14]

4 Alessandro Delfanti, Biohackers: The Politics of Open Science 153 (2013).

5 Victoria Stodden, Open Science: Policy Implications for the Evolving Phenomenon of User-led Scientific Innovation, 9 J. Sci. Comm. 1 (2010).

6 Landrain et al., supra note 1; Seyfried et al., supra note 2; Hanno Charisius, Richard Friebe, & Sascha Karberg, Becoming biohackers: Learning the game, BBC (Jan. 21, 2013), http://www.bbc.com/future/story/20130122-how-we-became-biohackers-part-1.

7 Ledford, Garage Biotech, supra note 2; Seyfried et al., supra note 2; Delfanti, supra note 4.

8 Biohackers of The World, Unite, Economist: Technology Quarterly 12 (2014); Andrew Fazekas, DIY biology: How amateur scientists are playing with genetic code, Yahoo News (Sept. 16, 2015), https://ca.news.yahoo.com/blogs/geekquinox/diy-biology–how-amateur-scientists-are-playing-with-genetic-code-191755522.html#.

9 Ledford, Garage Biotech, supra note 2.

10 Erik Parens, Josephine Johnston, & Jacob Moses, Ethical Issues in Synthetic Biology: An Overview of the Debates 15 (2009).

11 Daniel G. Gibson et al., Complete Chemical Synthesis, Assembly, and Cloning of a Mycoplasma genitalium Genome, 319 Science 1215 (2008).

12 Delfanti, supra note 4; Landrain et al., supra note 1; Ledford, Garage Biotech, supra note 2; Seyfried et al., supra note 2; Presidential Commission for the Study of Bioethical Issues, New Directions: The Ethics of Synthetic Biology and Emerging Technologies (2010).

13 Delfanti, supra note 4; Landrain et al., supra note 1; Charisius et al., supra note 6.

14 Landrain et al., supra note 1; James Bloom, The geneticist in the garage, Guardian (Mar. 18, 2009), http://www.theguardian.com/technology/2009/mar/19/biohacking-genetics-research.

Traditional biological experimentation is highly regulated by the government, the biotech industry, and the scientists themselves in settings that are relatively visible and accountable.

NTGE is not generally so controlled, though it is not completely without oversight or guidance. Some community NTGE laboratories exert some degree of control over their members; GenSpace in New York, for example, only permits the conduct of Biosafety Level 1 experiments.[15] One of the purposes for creating DIYBio in 2009 was "for amateur biotechnologists . . . to think through . . . safety and regulations for individuals working outside of traditional settings."[16] In 2011, a North American DIYbio Congress adopted a code of ethics, and in 2013, DIYBio launched an "Ask a Biosafety Expert" (ABE) Service staffed by volunteers who respond to questions from experimenters.[17] But advisory consultations were optional and the code is vague and hortatory (for example, "Adopt safe practices").[18]

The only external monitoring of nontraditional biologists who operate independently is by the FBI. When concerns were raised about biosafety and biosecurity after 9/11,[19] the FBI began actively monitoring NTGE, and raided the basement lab of an art professor in 2004 on suspicion that his wife had died from exposure to a dangerous biological organism that he was using in his art.[20] By and large, however, the FBI has pursued engagement and cooperation rather than confrontation, sending agents to NTGE meetings, conferences, and labs, and even funding iGEM.[21]

15 About the Lab, GenSpace, www.genspace.org/the-lab

16 Stodden, supra note 5, at 9.

17 Information About Self-Administration of Gene Therapy, FDA (Nov. 21, 2017), www.fda.gov/vaccines-blood-biologics/cellular-gene-therapy-products/information-about-self-administration-gene-therapy; Sara Tocchetti & Sara Angeli Aguiton, Is an FBI Agent a DIY Biologist Like Any Other? A Cultural Analysis of a Biosecurity Risk, 40 Sci. Tech. & Human Values 825 (2015); Heidi Ledford, Biohackers Gear Up for Genome Editing, 524 Nature 398 (2015) [hereinafter "Biohackers"].

18 Codes, DIY Bio, https://diybio.org/codes/ (last visited Oct. 22, 2020).

19 Bloom, supra note 14; Gaymon Bennett et al., From Synthetic Biology to Biohacking: Are We Prepared?, 27 Nature Biotechnology 1109 (2009); Arthur Caplan et al., No Time to Waste—The Ethical Challenges Created by CRISPR, 1 6 EMBO Reports 1421 (2015); Michele Garfinkel et al., Synthetic Genomics: Options for Governance 66 (2007); Kenneth A. Oye, Maureen O'Leary, & Margaret F. Riley, Revisit NIH Biosafety Guidelines, 357 Science 627 (2017).

20 Sarah Kellogg, The Rise of DIY Scientists: Is It Time for Regulation?, Washington Lawyer, May 2012. As Kellogg describes, "In May 2004, Kurtz [Steven J. Kurtz, an art professor at the State University of New York at Buffalo] and his wife, Hope, had been preparing commissioned works when Hope Kurtz died at their home. Her husband called 911. Her death was later determined to be of natural causes. In attending to Hope Kurtz, emergency personnel observed Petri dishes containing bacteria cultures and food-testing equipment that was considered suspicious. They contacted the Federal Bureau of Investigation (FBI). Authorities later told Kurtz he was being investigated for bioterrorism, and, eventually, Kurtz and Robert E. Ferrell, former chair of the University of Pittsburgh's Department of Human Genetics, were indicted on mail and wire fraud for their alleged efforts to obtain biological organisms from a lab that was not allowed to sell to individuals. In April 2008, a federal judge dismissed the mail and wire fraud charges against Kurtz, noting that there was insufficient proof to go forward. Ferrell was fined $500 after pleading guilty to a count of mailing an injurious article, a misdemeanor." Id.

21 Tocchetti & Aguiton, supra note 17; Ledford, Biohackers, supra note 17.

Some commentators have argued that NTGE did not require additional oversight because much of it was conducted in community labs that followed accepted safety guidelines, because there was no reason to expect NTGE experimenters to be more likely to desire to cause mischief or harm than researchers in traditional settings,[22] and above all, because NTGE experiments were relatively unsophisticated due to experimenters' lack of knowledge, skill, funding, equipment, and access to materials.[23]

The introduction of CRISPR/Cas9, however, has significantly expanded gene editing capabilities by increasing the efficiency of gene editing and making it near universal. Gene editing previously was practical only in a very limited number of cells and organisms, but CRISPR/Cas9 can be used to edit any cell or organism with a sequenced genome and with a way to introduce nucleic acids and/or protein. Reagent introduction can be difficult for some target cells and organisms, but easier for others (for example, direct injection into muscle, inhalation of aerosolized particles, microinjection of fish or amphibian eggs).[24] Indeed, one indication of the potential of CRISPR/Cas9 is its February 2016 addition to the US list of weapons of mass destruction, the only biotechnology so listed.[25]

NTGE has already begun to deploy CRISPR/Cas9.[26] As the principal investigator of the Synthetic Biology Project at the Woodrow Wilson Center states, "the equipment and reagents that are needed to use CRISPR-Cas9 are already readily available."[27] Some say that CRISPR/Cas9 is still so technically-demanding that only simple NTGE experiments on organisms such as E. coli and brewer's yeast can be expected.[28] Others predict more advanced experiments.[29] Experimenters can

22 Todd Kuiken, Learn from DIY Biologists, 531 Nature 167 (2016); Howard Wolinsky, The FBI and Biohackers: an Unusual Relationship, 17 EMBO Reports 793 (2016).

23 Landrain et al., supra note 1; Ledford, Biohackers, supra note 17; Presidential Commission, supra note 12; Katrine Bosley et al., CRISPR Germline Engineering—The Community Speaks, 33 Nature Biotechnology 478 (2015).

24 See Hao Yin, Kevin J. Kauffman, & Daniel G. Anderson, Delivery Technologies For Genome Editing, 16 Nature Revs. Drug Discovery 387 (2017).

25 Antonio Regalado, Top U.S. Intelligence Official Calls Gene Editing a WMD Threat, MIT Tech. Rev. (Feb. 9, 2016), www.technologyreview.com/s/600774/top-us-intelligence-official-calls-gene-editing-a-wmd-threat/.

26 Kristen V. Brown, Inside the garage labs of DIY gene hackers, whose hobby may terrify you, Project Earth (Mar. 29, 2016), https://projectearth.us/inside-the-garage-labs-of-diy-gene-hackers-whose-hobby-1796423884; Ellen Jorgensen, How DIY bio-hackers are changing the conversation around genetic engineering, Wash. Post (May 24, 2016), https://geneticliteracyproject.org/2016/05/24/crispr-fueling-rise-genetic-engineering-biohacker-labs/; Emily Baumgaertner, As D.I.Y. Gene Editing Gains Popularity, "Someone Is Going to Get Hurt," N.Y. Times (May 14, 2018), www.nytimes.com/2018/05/14/science/biohackers-gene-editing-virus.html.

27 Kuiken, supra note 22.

28 Kuiken, supra note 22; Jorgensen, supra note 26.

29 Wolinsky, supra note 22; Sarah R. Carter et al., Synthetic Biology and the U.S. Biotechnology Regulatory System: Challenges and Options (May 28, 2014), www.wiley.law/media/publication/279_full-report.pdf; Catherin Jefferson, Filippa Lentzos, & Claire Marris, Synthetic Biology and Biosecurity: Challenging the "Myths," 2 Frontiers Public Health 1 (2014).

select target organisms from the increasing number of organisms with sequenced genomes and obtain reagents and viral vectors from commercial suppliers, in some cases, by circumventing sales restrictions.[30] NTGE gene editing already may be taking place to combat human disease[31] and to enhance performance.[32] Two recent FDA approvals of gene therapies are likely to spark a resurgence of interest in improving gene delivery methods for therapeutic purposes, which could be used by NTGE for human somatic gene editing.[33] In addition, while recent research into the first generation of gene drive systems has shown that their spread may be limited by host genome mutation[34] schemes to make gene drive more persistent have already been developed and more can be expected.[35]

More advanced NTGE gene editing experiments could raise significant safety and ethical concerns.[36] Would undesirable transgenes be placed in food or crops? Would engineered microbes cause adverse environmental or health effects? Would they be released intentionally or accidentally into the environment with gene drives, and thus have the potential to alter entire populations? Would researchers edit genes in animals without proper regard for animal welfare? NTGE experimenters already are injecting themselves with edited genes.[37] Are they taking adequate precautions?

30 BioMaster, Does NEB Send to Private Individuals?, in DIYBio. 2016, Google Groups; Emily Mullin, A biotech CEO explains why he injected himself with a DIY herpes treatment on Facebook Live, MIT Tech. Rev. (Feb. 5, 2018), www.technologyreview.com/s/610179/a-biotech-ceo-explains-why-he-injected-himself-with-a-diy-herpes-treatment-live-on-stage/.

31 Brown, supra note 26; Rowan Jacobsen, Hacking Your Genes Has Never Been Easier, Outside (Sept. 6, 2017), www.outsideonline.com/2238276/ultimate-life-hack.

32 Adele Peters, Modifying Your Genes Is Just An Injection Away—If You're Feeling Lucky, Fast Company (Oct. 10, 2017), www.fastcompany.com/40477808/genetic-modification-is-just-an-injection-away-if-youre-feeling-lucky; Brian Wang, CRISPR muscle boosting gene therapy at few thousand dollars per year will go mainstream, Next Big Future (Nov. 18, 2017), www.nextbigfuture.com/2017/11/diy-biohacking-with-crispr-gene-therapy-for-muscle-boosting-myostatin-inhibitor.html.

33 FDA approval brings first gene therapy to the United States, Food and Drug Administration (Aug. 30, 2017), www.fda.gov/news-events/press-announcements/fda-approval-brings-first-gene-therapy-united-states; FDA approves CAR-T cell therapy to treat adults with certain types of large B-cell lymphoma, Food and Drug Administration (Oct. 18, 2017), www.fda.gov/news-events/press-announcements/fda-approves-car-t-cell-therapy-treat-adults-certain-types-large-b-cell-lymphoma.

34 Jackson Champer et al., Novel CRISPR/Cas9 gene drive constructs reveal insights into mechanisms of resistance allele formation and drive efficiency in genetically diverse populations, 13 PLoS Genetics e1006796 (2017).

35 Jackson Champer et al., Reducing resistance allele formation in CRISPR gene drive, 115 Proc. Nat'l Acad. Sci. 5522 (2018).

36 ASGCT Statement on DIY Gene Therapy, Am. Soc. Gene & Cell Therapy (Dec. 7, 2017), www.asgct.org/research/news/december-2017/asgct-statement-unregulated-diy-gene-therapy.

37 Mullin, supra note 30; David Grossman People Are Treating Themselves With DIY Gene Therapies and the Government Is Getting Worried, Popular Mechanics (Feb. 8, 2018), www.popularmechanics.com/science/health/a16691487/fda-gene-therapy-concern-crispr/; Tom Ireland, 'I want to help humans genetically modify themselves', Guardian (Dec. 24, 2017), www.theguardian.com/science/2017/dec/24/josiah-zayner-diy-gene-editing-therapy-crispr-interview; Jessica Lussenhop, Why I injected myself with an untested gene therapy, BBC News (Nov. 21, 2017), www.bbc.com/news/world-us-canada-41990981.

If experimenting in others, are they obtaining voluntary informed consent? It must be stressed that serious safety and ethical concerns would arise not only if NTGE gene editing experiments were successful, but also if the apparent ease and relatively low cost of these techniques led to overly ambitious experiments that failed, causing harm to the environment and to human and nonhuman subjects.

Aside from FBI monitoring, there appears to be little external oversight of NTGE gene editing. California passed a law in July 2019 stating that,

> except as permitted by federal law, a person shall not sell a gene therapy kit in this state unless the seller includes a notice on the seller's internet website in a conspicuous location that is displayed to the consumer prior to the point of sale, and on a label on the package containing the gene therapy kit, in plain view and readily legible, stating that the kit is not for self-administration.[38]

The Environmental Protection Agency regulates microbial pesticides under the Federal Insecticide Fungicide and Rodenticide Act, as well as other recombinant DNA microbes and algae "intended for general commercial and environmental applications" under the Toxic Substances Control Act,[39] but "the reach of the law is limited to commercial or commercial research and development activities [and] it is unclear that … noncommercial research efforts by DIY users are covered."[40]

The Department of Agriculture's Animal and Plant Health Inspection Service (APHIS) regulates field trials and commercial introduction only of plants genetically engineered through the use of known "plant pests," and has acknowledged that it lacks the authority to regulate crops modified with the latest gene editing techniques.[41]

The Food and Drug Administration regulates research on genetically modified food, food additives, and human and animal drugs and biologics, and has asserted authority over human gene therapy, but its oversight over NTGE is unclear if no commercial product results.

The government is in the process of revising its Coordinated Framework for the Regulation of Biotechnology Products to cope with new gene editing techniques, but it is not clear if the framework will extend to noncommercial research, and in any event, it will not cover experiments in humans.[42] NIH oversight is limited to research that is federally funded or conducted at academic institutions that receive federal funding. Intentional or reckless releases of engineered bioterror agents would

38 S.B. 180, 2019–2020 Reg. Sess. § 2 (Cal. 2019).

39 Executive Office of the President Office of Science and Technology Policy, Coordinated Framework for Regulation of Biotechnology, 51 Fed Reg. 23302 (1986).

40 Presidential Commission, supra note 12.

41 Emily Waltz, CRISP R-edited crops free to enter market, skip regulation, 34 Nature Biotechnology 582 (2016).

42 Clarifying Current Roles and Responsibilities Described in the Coordinated Framework for the Regulation of Biotechnology and Developing a Long-Term Strategy for the Regulation of the Products of Biotechnology, 80 Fed. Reg. 62538 (2015).

be crimes,[43] and humans whose health or property were harmed by such a release or by other types of unethical experimentation might seek to recover damages in civil suits[44]; but it may not be possible to hold the experimenters accountable because their identities may not be known, they may not be subject to US legal jurisdiction (for example, they may not be extraditable from a foreign country), or they may not have the assets to pay court-awarded damages.

To date, NTGE has not caused any known serious harm, and as noted earlier, the prevailing view has been that it was unlikely to because of its technological limitations. In light of growing NTGE gene-editing capabilities, the question is whether the current governance NTGE is appropriate.

III GOVERNANCE GOALS

Different stakeholders arguably have different views about what the goals of NTGE governance should be. NTGE experimenters presumably want NTGE governance to maximize their freedom to experiment, enjoyment, sense of accomplishment, the advancement of science, the counterculture nature of their activities, and at least for some, financial gain. Traditional biologists in university and corporate settings who do not moonlight in NTGE, along with their university and corporate employers, might be expected to prefer a governance approach that protects the public and promotes scientific advancement but that limits NTGE interference with their careers, status, and personal and institutional financial well-being. For example, NTGE could significantly disrupt traditional biology patenting strategies by creating "prior art" that defeats claims of novelty or nonobviousness by traditional innovators,[45] or by leading courts to determine that a person having ordinary skill in the art would find the invention obvious in the light of the prior art.[46] Patent disruption of this sort would be particularly disruptive to biotech startups, for whom patents serve as durable assets to attract venture capital.[47]

NTGE stakeholders also include the potential subjects of NTGE experimentation. Lower organisms arguably do not have any cognizable interests at stake, although changes that affect them could also have expanding environmental consequences that affect more sentient creatures. NTGE governance should avoid causing suffering to animals and should accord human subjects, at least when they are

43 18 U.S.C. § 175 (2018) (biological weapons); 18 U.S.C. § 2332a (2018) (weapons of mass destruction).

44 E. Haavi Morreim, Litigation in Clinical Research: Malpractice Doctrines versus Research Realities, 32 J.L. Med. & Ethics 474 (2004).

45 35 U.S.C. § 102(a)(1) (2018).

46 35 U.S.C. § 103(a) (2018).

47 See Stuart J.H. Graham, Ted Sichelman, Robert P. Merges & Pamela Samuelson, High Technology Entrepreneurs and the Patent System: Results of the 2008 Berkeley Patent Survey, 24 Berkeley Tech. L.J. 1255 (2010).

not the experimenters themselves, recognized legal and ethical rights associated with autonomy, beneficence, and justice.[48]

Overriding other interests are the interests of the public. Paramount among these are health, safety, and well-being. While this might seem to call for a highly restrictive governance approach, the public also has an important interest in the advancement of science, which NTGE experimentation may foster, and which also promotes national interests such as defense and international competitiveness. The ideal governance approach therefore should seek to maximize the potential benefits from NTGE while minimizing the potential harms by permitting the greatest amount of experimentation consistent with acceptable levels of safety and the well-being of subjects. Less clear is the extent to which the NTGE governance approach should protect the interests of traditional biologists at the expense of the freedom to experiment and potential resulting advances in science.

IV GOVERNANCE OPTIONS

Governance options for NTGE range from a completely laissez-faire approach to criminalization. Neither of these extremes is appropriate; the former would preclude even the limited oversight currently exercised by the FBI to protect against bioterrorism, while the latter, although adopted in Germany,[49] seems too draconian in light of the potential benefits from NTGE, extremely difficult to enforce, and likely to drive more NTGE underground, which would make it more difficult to detect objectionable experimentation.

A range of governance options lie between these two extremes:

(1) The FDA could regulate NTGE as it does human cellular and gene therapy experiments through its Center for Biologics Evaluation and Research (CBER), requiring notification and agency review before experiments take place and conducting periodic inspections.

(2) Federal and/or state government could restrict access to material and equipment.[50] Some commercial suppliers of viral vectors and other materials do this now voluntarily, selling only to experimenters with addresses at traditional university or corporate settings, but NTGE experimenters have found ways around this, for example, by having shipments sent to what seem like corporate addresses.[51] The government could impose mandatory

48 The Belmont Report, Office of the Secretary of Health and Human Services (Apr. 18, 1979), http://www.hhs.gov/ohrp/regulations-and-policy/belmont-report/read-the-belmont-report/index.html.

49 Tim Collins, Germany cracks down on BIOHACKERS: DIY geneticists may face jail time following fears they could create bioweapons, Daily Mail (Feb. 10, 2017), www.dailymail.co.uk/sciencetech/article-4211206/Biohackers-Germany-face-jail-time.html.

50 Parens et al., supra note 10; Garfinkel et al., supra note 19; Oye et al., supra note 19.

51 BioMaster, supra note 30; Mullin, supra note 30.

restrictions on sales and shipments, enforced by inspections, sales record reviews, and the use of "secret shoppers."

(3) The government could place restrictions on entry (for example, licensure, registration, certification, training requirements).

(4) The government could levy Pigouvian taxes and/or grant subsidies (for example, permit fees, discounts or waivers for compliance with government requirements).

(5) Federal and state laws could create statutory private rights of action for harm from experiments.

(6) NTGE experimenters could regulate themselves. They could establish clearer and more comprehensive codes and standards than the DIYBio code mentioned earlier. More community labs could be established with experimental requirements and limitations, and labs could encourage experimentation in their facilities by providing access to sophisticated equipment and materials, perhaps subsidized by the government or the private sector. Members of the NTGE community also could monitor NTGE activities[52] and take various actions against experimenters who appeared to be acting irresponsibly.

(7) The government and/or the NTGE community could disseminate information and best practices.

(8) The NTGE community could adopt voluntary moratoria on certain types of research.

(9) The NTGE community could create more advisory bodies similar to the DIYBio Ask a Beiosafety Expert program.

(10) The government or the NTGE community could facilitate or require that NTGE use IRBs and other biosafety committees.

It is important to understand that these governance options are not mutually-exclusive.

They, or certain aspects of them, can be combined, and multi-level approaches could be employed that varied depending on the type of experiment. For example, research in community labs could be largely self-governed, while the government might exert greater regulatory control over experiments outside of those labs.

V HISTORICAL ANALOGIES

Useful insights about possible governance approaches can be gleaned by examining historical analogues such as ham radio, amateur rocketry, home brewing, drones and model airplanes, and computer hacking.

Ham radio emerged in the early twentieth century. Potential public benefits such as facilitating emergency communication during natural disasters were identified, but also concerns about interference between amateurs and government or

[52] Ledford, Garage Biotech, supra note 2; Economist, supra note 8; Ledford, Biohackers, supra note 17.

commercial channels. In response, Congress passed the Radio Act of 1912, which required amateur operators to be licensed and restricted them to a single wavelength of 200 meters. This caused a drop-off in ham radio use, leading operators in 1914 to organize the American Radio Relay League (ARRL) to represent and lobby for their interests. The value of ham radio was recognized during the First World War, but the practice was conducted under military supervision. The Navy wanted to continue to control the practice after the war, but the ARRL opposed this and independent amateur radio returned. In 1927, the federal Radio Act gave authority over amateurs to the Federal Communications Commission. In the 1950s, the FCC created different classes of amateur licenses, but there were few differences between what the classes could do, so in the 1960s, the FCC adopted "incentive licensing," which gave higher classes greater access to wavelengths. Localities imposed restrictions and zoning rules to control the location of ham radio towers, which led to litigation. The FCC has issued a preemptive ruling stating that local governments must reasonably accommodate amateur operations, but they may still zone for height, safety, and aesthetics concerns.[53] In addition to being licensed by the FCC, operators must notify the commission if they propose to erect tall antennas near airports and must apply for call signs. Violations of FCC requirements come with criminal penalties.[54]

Amateur or "sport rocketry" enthusiasts have created two interest groups, the National Association of Rocketry and the Tripoli Rocketry Association, which have adopted safety codes,[55] represent members' interests by lobby legislatures and bringing lawsuits against government regulators, and offer liability insurance to their members.[56] Both organizations belong to the National Fire Protection Association, a nongovernmental public safety organization that promulgates model fire safety codes to govern aspects of sport rocketry such as where and how rockets can be launched, and which are adopted as is or in modified form by state and local jurisdictions and enforced by fire marshals. The Federal Aviation Administration regulates aspects such as the maximum height that sport rockets may reach. The Bureau of Alcohol, Tobacco and Firearms requires permits for "toy" rockets that move in interstate commerce, only grants permits to US citizens over the age of eighteen who pass a background check, and limits propellants to 62.5 grams. The US Department of Transportation also regulates propellants as explosives under rules harmonized with BATF. Legal violations carry both civil and criminal penalties.[57]

53 Federal preemption of state and local regulations pertaining to amateur radio facilities, 101 F.C.C. 2d 952 (1985); Pentel v. City of Mendota Heights, 13 F.3d 1261 (8th Cir. 1994).

54 For the history of ham radio regulation, see Jim Maxwell, Amateur Radio: 100 Years of Discovery, QST (Jan. 2000), www.arrl.org/files/file/About%20ARRL/Ham_Radio_100_Years.pdf.

55 See Safety Codes, National Association of Rocketry (2020), www.nar.org/safety-codes-2/; Safety Code, Tripoli Rocketry Association (2017), www.tripoli.org/SafetyCode.

56 For details on laws and regulations, see Laws and Regulations, National Association of Rocketry (2020), www.nar.org/find-a-local-club/section-guidebook/laws-regulations/.

57 For a history of the role of amateur rocket clubs in rocketry, see Oliver Morton, The Moon (2019).

Home brewers, in an interesting twist, are represented by the American Home Brewers Association, which is a division of the commercial Brewers Association. No license is required; New Jersey at one point attempted to impose a licensing requirement, but backed off after lobbying opposition.[58] Federal law, enforced by the BATF, prohibits sale, and limits home production to 100 gallons per year per adult, with a maximum of 200 gallons per household. Some state laws restrict alcoholic content and shipment. Violations carry criminal penalties.[59]

Congress passed a law in 2015 that governs both commercial and recreational drones.[60] The two uses must be kept separate. With the passage of the National Defense Authorization Act of 2017, the FAA began requiring registration (for a $5 fee) if the weight of the recreational drone exceeded .55 pounds, prohibits weights over 55 pounds unless specially certified, and restricts operation near airports. Recreational drone operators are represented by a number of organizations, including the Academy of Model Aeronautics and the Drone Advocacy Network.

Computer hacking initially was viewed relatively positively as a way of proofing software applications, but attitudes began to shift in the 1980s as more people began using personal computers, and in 1986 Congress enacted the Federal Computer Fraud and Abuse Act, which criminalizes hacking. Until the 1990s, hackers often worked together in actual or virtual groups, but this fell off after the Secret Service began sting operations; thereafter, hackers could gain immunity from prosecution for informing on others. After 2010, "hacktivist" groups began to emerge, such as Anonymous; they typically function on the "Dark Web," releasing government documents and unfavorable information about targeted individuals.

VI LESSONS LEARNED FROM HISTORICAL ANALOGIES AND PRELIMINARY RECOMMENDATIONS

What lessons can be learned from these historical analogies? First, all but one of the activities, computer hacking, enjoys a substantial degree of self-regulation. Substantial self-regulation seems appropriate at this time for NTGE. It is likely to afford the greatest degree of experimental freedom to its practitioners; is in keeping with their antiestablishment values; reflects the lack of known, serious, adverse experimental events; capitalizes on NTGE experimenters' knowledge of what others are doing; and reduces the degree to which experimenters would be driven underground, which could increase risks to subjects and the public by decreasing community awareness and potential oversight.

58 For a history of home brewing regulation, see Statutes, American Home Brewers Association (2020), https://www.homebrewersassociation.org/homebrewing-rights/statutes/.

59 Id.

60 See Drone Laws in the United States of America, UAV Coach (2020), https://uavcoach.com/drone-laws-in-united-states-of-america/.

Self-regulation of analogous activities, however, has been facilitated by organizations that represent amateurs' interests (although in the case of home brewing, under the aegis of a commercial trade association) and NTGE does not have any comparable entities; DIYBio is relatively inactive currently, and community labs do not have any umbrella organization.

Forming organizations to represent NTGE experimenters generally and community lab and their experimenters in particular would be a substantial boon to self-regulation. They could issue concrete guidelines, establish NTGE IRBs, and cooperate with the government to forestall greater government regulation. Some more independent-minded and antiestablishment NTGE experimenters might view these organizations with skepticism, but taking a page from the insurance offered by amateur rocketry groups, buy-in could be fostered by offering benefits to members beyond representing their interests, such as access to equipment and/or materials and advanced expert advice.

Another element of self-regulation could be a degree of self-monitoring. NTGE experimenters could be on the lookout on the Web and social media for inappropriate experiments. Miscreants could be publicly identified; excluded from community labs, incubators, and events, including conferences and iGEM;[61] and, in extreme cases, reported to potential suppliers and/or to government authorities such as the FBI.

Moreover, external regulation of the historical analogues tends to be introduced in waves reflecting growth and risk-increasing changes in the activities in question. It therefore seems sensible to phase in any increased external oversight of NTGE only as NTGE capabilities expand, as risks to subjects and the public are perceived to increase, or as unfortunate incidents occur, rather than to immediately impose a significant degree of external regulatory oversight.

To facilitate NTGE self-regulation, the government should follow the lead of the FBI and work cooperatively with the NTGE community, providing guidance and encouragement, but making it clear that inadequate self-regulation is likely to lead to more direct government intervention. Ideally, the community will act resolutely; from its perspective, the worst case is failure to act, followed by publicity about a high-risk or harmful experiment that triggers government overreaction.

VII CONCLUSION

Nontraditional scientific research is an important contributor to scientific and medical advances. In determining how to regulate gene editing in nontraditional settings, society must balance the potential benefits and risks, allowing for experimental freedom within an adequate margin of safety. The nontraditional gene editing community will play a key role in any oversight scheme.

61 Economist, supra note 8.

12

Finding a Regulatory Balance for Genetic Biohacking

Christi Guerrini, Jacob S. Sherkow, and Patricia J. Zettler[*]

I INTRODUCTION

"Biohacking" has emerged as a cultural and scientific phenomenon. Although there is no consensus on the precise definition of "biohacking," the term generally describes biological investigations and interventions that are conducted outside of institutional scientific settings by individuals who may not have traditional scientific training.[1] Easier access to biological information and resources has enabled biohacking to flourish. Its participants often describe their activities as motivated by a belief in a right to "do science," a high value placed on bodily autonomy, and a view that traditional scientific institutions and regulations have systematically failed to benefit society.[2] It is difficult to quantify the number of individuals worldwide who participate in biohacking, given disagreement about what counts as biohacking, the constant flux of individuals entering and leaving biohacking communities, and the communities' decentralized natures. As one estimate, the DIYbio Google Groups counted over 5,000 members in early 2020.[3] As another estimate, a 2017 Brookings Institute report estimated that there were 30,000 "enthusiasts, followers, biohackers and citizen scientists" in the United States alone.[4]

* We thank Barbara Evans, Hank Greely, Max Mehlman, and the participants in the 2019 Petrie Flom Center Annual Conference for thoughtful comments and discussion. We also thank the participants in the 2018 interview study discussed in this chapter for sharing their biohacking and citizen science insights and experiences.

1 See Amelia Fiske et al., Conceptual and Ethical Considerations for Citizen Science in Biomedicine, in Personal Health Science 195, 198–99, 204 (Nils B. Heyen et al., eds. 2019); see also Barbara J. Evans, Programming Our Genomes, Programming Ourselves: The Moral and Regulatory Limits of Self-Harm in Do-It-Yourself Gene Editing, in Consuming Genetics (I. Glenn Cohen, et al., eds. 2020); Maxwell J. Mehlman and Ronald A. Conlon, Governing Non-Traditional Biology, in Consuming Genetics (I. Glenn Cohen, et al., eds. 2020).

2 See Lisa C. Ikemoto, DIY Bio: Hacking Life in Biotech's Backyard, 51 U.C.D. L. Rev. 548, 548–54 (2017); Daniel Grushkin et al., Woodrow Wilson Ctr., Seven Myths and Realities About Do-it-Yourself Biology 4 (2013), https://www.wilsoncenter.org/sites/default/files/7_myths_final.pdf.

3 DIY Google Groups, https://groups.google.com/forum/#!members/diybio.

4 Bart Kolodziejczyk, Do-It-Yourself Biology Shows Safety Risks of an Open Innovation Movement, Brookings Inst. (Oct. 9, 2017), https://www.brookings.edu/blog/techtank/2017/10/09/do-it-yourself-biology-shows-safety-risks-of-an-open-innovation-movement/.

Molecular genetics – the modification of genetic coding and expression – has become a popular focus of biohacking. Alongside the rise of direct-to-consumer testing services that provide access to raw genetic data, cheap and easy gene-editing techniques, such as CRISPR, are now available. "Genetic biohacking" activities are diverse and include, among other things, modifying algae to glow, altering nonhuman animals to increase their size, and self-injecting nucleotides to genetically enhance muscle growth or to treat HIV or herpes.[5]

At the same time, the November 2018 announcement that a scientist in China used CRISPR to genetically modify viable human embryos – allegedly resulting in the birth of the first "CRISPR babies" – has reinvigorated concerns about the distribution of genetic technologies.[6] For genetic biohacking, these concerns may be heightened by a belief that mechanisms to regulate the activity are absent or inadequate to address its risks. But, as this chapter details, genetic biohacking is likely subject to numerous oversight mechanisms, both public and private.[7] Before calling for additional regulations, regulators and policymakers should evaluate these extant mechanisms.

Some of our assessment is informed by semistructured interviews led by one author (Christi J. Guerrini), from August to December 2018, with thirty-eight individuals who lead, participate in, or study genomic biohacking and other citizen science initiatives.[8] Data were collected and coded according to methods detailed elsewhere;[9] we share select data relevant to regulatory, liability, and safety issues. Although biohacking occurs throughout the world, we focus on the US regulatory environment because the United States is the home of the first community laboratories and where many highly publicized examples of genetic biohacking have occurred.

II GOVERNMENT REGULATION

In the United States, various public laws and regulations govern some aspects of genetic biohacking. These include an appropriations rider in federal law effectively

5 See Patricia J. Zettler, Christi J. Guerrini & Jacob S. Sherkow, Regulating Genetic Biohacking, 365 Science 34 (2019); see also Alex Pearlman, Biohackers are Using CRISPR on Their DNA and We Can't Stop It, New Scientist (Nov. 15, 2017), https://www.newscientist.com/article/mg23631520-100-biohackers-are-using-crispr-on-their-dna-and-we-cant-stop-it/.

6 See Eli Y. Adashi & I. Glenn Cohen, The Ethics of Heritable Genome Editing: New Considerations in a Controversial Area, 320 JAMA 2531 (2018); Henry T. Greely, CRISPR'd Babies: Human Germline Genome Editing in the 'He Jiankui Affair', 6 J.L. Biosci. 111 (2019). The scientist was an academic, using professional resources, and is not generally described as having engaged in biohacking. See generally id.

7 See Christi J. Guerrini, G. Evan Spencer & Patricia J. Zettler, DIY CRISPR, 97 N.C. L. Rev. 1399 (2019).

8 These interviews were conducted as part of a broader study to understand values, preferences, and processes related to managing the outputs of genomic biohacking and other citizen science initiatives. The study was approved by the Baylor College of Medicine Institutional Review Board (H40925). Data is attributed to interviewees by their assigned interview numbers.

9 Christi J. Guerrini et al., Core Values of Genomic Citizen Science: Results from an Interview Study BioSocieties (2020), https://doi.org/10.1057/s41292-020-00208-2.

prohibiting research with human embryos that are modified or created to include a heritable genetic modification.[10] There are also laws that regulate environmental impacts,[11] as well as regulations[12] and policies[13] applicable to federally funded research.[14]

Of all federal agencies, the US Food and Drug Administration (FDA) has the most extensive power to regulate the public-health impacts of genetic biohacking. In November 2017, following reports of biohacking by means of genetic self-experimentation, FDA explained its authority over biohacking, stating that it considered "any use of CRISPR/Cas9 gene editing in humans to be gene therapy," subject to the same premarket approval and other requirements that apply to gene therapy products.[15] The agency's jurisdiction is so broad, in part because many things biohackers use – such as raw biological materials, traditional drug products, and biohacking "kits" – are arguably "drugs" under US law.[16] The Federal Food, Drug, and Cosmetic Act (FFDCA) defines drugs as "articles" "intended for use in the diagnosis, cure, mitigation, treatment, or prevention of disease" or "intended to affect the structure or any function of the body of man or other animals."[17]

So defined, a product's "intended use" is crucial to placing it within FDA's jurisdiction.[18] The agency may rely on "any relevant source" of evidence to prove a product's intended use, including, for example, statements on a website that a kit can be used to modify a gene, treat an illness, or enhance the body's function. The agency may also determine intended use from nonpublic statements, statements made in the past, and product design.[19] Moreover, distributing products at no charge – which some biohackers do – is not, alone, sufficient to evade FDA's jurisdiction, which requires only that an item, or one of its components, is

10 Consolidated Appropriations Act, 2018, Pub. L. No. 115-141, § 734, 132 Stat. 389, 389 (2018).

11 R. Alta Charo & Henry T. Greely, CRISPR Critters and CRISPR Cracks, 15 Am. J. Bioethics 11, 11–17 (2015).

12 Protection of Human Subjects, 45 C.F.R. § 46 (2018).

13 U.S. Dep't Health & Human Serv., NIH Guidelines for Research Involving Recombinant or Synthetic Nucleic Acid Molecules (Apr. 2019), https://osp.od.nih.gov/wp-content/uploads/NIH_Guidelines.html.

14 Notably, some US institutions interpret federal human research subject protections to cover researchers' participation in their own interventions. See, e.g., Emily Mullin, Who Says You Need Permission to Study Yourself?, Medium (Sept. 27, 2018), https://medium.com/neodotlife/who-says-you-need-permission-to-study-yourself-1c347a25c10c; Johns Hopkins Med. Office of Human Subjects Res., Investigators as Study Participants (Self-Experimentation), Johns Hopkins Med. (July 2005), https://www.hopkinsmedicine.org/institutional_review_board/guidelines_policies/guidelines/self_experimentation.html.

15 FDA, Information About Self-Administration of Gene Therapy (Nov. 21, 2017), https://www.fda.gov/BiologicsBloodVaccines/CellularGeneTherapyProducts/ucm586343.htm.

16 For a more detailed discussion of FDA's jurisdiction, see Guerrini, Spencer & Zettler, supra note 7.

17 21 U.S.C. § 321(g)(1) (2018). Certain kinds of articles – such as human-gene-therapy products – also meet the definition of a biological product in the US Public Health Service Act. 42 U.S.C. § 262(i) (2018).

18 21 C.F.R. § 201.128 (2018).

19 See, e.g., 82 Fed. Reg. 2193, 2199 (Jan. 9, 2017).

distributed across state or national boundaries.[20] As its November 2017 statement indicated, FDA likely has jurisdiction over many materials used in US genetic biohacking activities, especially those promoted on the internet and shipped directly to consumers.

At the same time, FDA lacks jurisdiction over genetic experimentation, including self-experimentation, undertaken with materials distributed without an intent that they be used in humans or animals.[21] DIY CRISPR kits intended only for the modification of bacteria, for example, do not fall within FDA's purview. Likewise, FDA's powers do not extend to simple information about biohacking when it is not provided by or on behalf of distributors of biohacking materials. Although the agency regulates certain information provided by entities marketing products – such as labeling and, in some circumstances, advertising – it does not oversee information about products unconnected to the entities marketing them.[22] Many self-help guides, standards, and FAQs developed by and distributed among biohackers – such as one group's instruction manual for creating an epinephrine autoinjector at home, the "EpiPencil"[23] – thus likely fall outside FDA's authority. Excepting circulation of this kind of information, FDA's authority still applies to many interactions where genetic biohacking materials are exchanged or distributed.[24]

There are benefits to FDA's broad authority. FDA, through its longstanding role in assessing drugs and biological products, has developed expertise to assess the safety and effectiveness of genetic biohacking. This expertise can be used to protect individuals from the distribution of unsafe or ineffective interventions, which may

20 21 U.S.C. § 331 (2018).

21 To be clear, biohacked foods for humans and animals – such as yogurt modified to contain custom bacteria – generally fall within FDA's purview. For more details on FDA's authority over foods, including "biotechnology foods," see National Academies of Sciences, Engineering and Medicine, Preparing for Future Products of Biotechnology 80, 80–86 (2017) and Peter Hutt, Richard Merrill, & Lewis Grossman, Food and Drug Law: Cases and Materials 317, 317–639 (4th ed. 2013).

22 The extent to which FDA can regulate even information provided by entities marketing products has been the subject of First Amendment challenges in various contexts. For just a small selection of literature discussing this issue, see, e.g., Micah L. Berman, Manipulative Marketing and the First Amendment, 103 Geo. L.J. 497 (2015); Nathan Cortez, Do Graphic Tobacco Warnings Violate the First Amendment?, 64 Hastings L.J. 1467 (2013); Aaron S. Kesselheim & Michelle M. Mello, Prospects for Regulation of Off-Label Drug Promotion in an Era of Expanding Commercial Speech Protection, 92 N.C. L. Rev. 1539 (2014); Lars Noah, Truth or Consequences?: Commercial Free Speech vs. Public Health Promotion (at the FDA), 21 Health Matrix 31 (2011); Christopher T. Robertson, The Tip of the Iceberg: A First Amendment Right to Promote Drugs Off-Label, 78 Ohio St. L.J. 1019 (2017); Joshua M. Sharfstein & Alta Charo, The Promotion of Medical Products in the 21st Century: Off-Label Marketing and First Amendment Concerns, 314 JAMA 1795 (2015).

23 Introducing the EpiPencil, Four Thieves Vinegar (Sept. 19, 2016), https://fourthievesvinegar.org/blog/2016/09/introducing-the-epipencil.

24 Another question that may arise is whether certain genetic interventions are procedures within the practice of medicine and outside FDA oversight. See, e.g., Jordan Paradise, U.S. Regulatory Challenges for Gene Editing, 13 SciTech Lawyer 10, 13 (2016); see also Barbara J. Evans, Distinguishing Product and Practice Regulation in Personalized Medicine, 81 Clinical Pharmacology & Therapeutics 288 (2007). We discuss the blurry line between medical practice and medical products regulation later in this chapter.

be particularly important where patients undertake do-it-yourself (DIY) techniques for conditions that otherwise have available, effective treatments. The lure – and relatively low price – of genetic biohacking materials might result in patients foregoing effective therapeutic options, akin to cancer patients seeking cheaper, albeit ineffective, "alternative therapies." Equally important, FDA plays a critical role in inducing the production of scientifically credible information about interventions by requiring safety and efficacy information prior to distribution.[25] In the absence of oversight, commercial purveyors of reagents and materials for genetic biohacking have every incentive to market their products widely and little incentive to ensure such marketing is supported by robust evidence – similar to makers of tonics, tinctures, and patent medicines in the nineteenth century.[26]

Yet, there are also burdens associated with FDA regulation. For one, as explained by biohackers in interviews, it is difficult to comply with regulations that are incomprehensible to lay persons (or anyone who is not an FDA specialist): "If the laws are just clear for everyone going in, and there's just a place that in plain English they can interpret these things, without paying a lawyer to interpret it, I think we could get along really well and understand where the perimeter is." (Int. 15). Outdated regulatory frameworks also seem to frustrate biohackers' good-faith efforts at compliance. Another interviewee stated: "I think that they don't have a framework to deal with some of these new technologies, so they're trying to fit that into some old ideas on how we regulate things. And I think that that is difficult because it obviously doesn't work" (Int. 37). Other costs of FDA regulation include delayed access to or underinvestment in the development of medical interventions, which has led some patients and their family members to contact biohackers for help. One biohacker described these conversations as follows: "'Hey, I have X genetic disease. Can you fix me?' Or, 'Can you tell me how to fix myself?' You have to tell these people no, and it's heartbreaking." (Int. 5). Although there is no unrestricted legal or ethical right to experimental drugs,[27] there is a vein of US culture that has long emphasized free choice of medical interventions without government interference.[28] Consistent with this "health libertarianism," for example, recently passed state and federal "Right To Try" laws allow patients

[25] See Rebecca S. Eisenberg, The Role of FDA in Innovation Policy, 13 Mich. Telecomm. & Tech. L. Rev. 345, 347 (2007); see also Amy Kapczynski, Dangerous Times: The FDA's Role in Information Production, Past and Future, 102 Minn. L. Rev. 2357 (2018); Catherine M. Sharkey, Direct-to-Consumer Genetic Testing: The FDA's Dual Role As Safety and Health Information Regulator, 68 DePaul L. Rev. 368 (2019).

[26] See generally Joseph Gabriel, Medical Monopoly: Intellectual Property Rights and the Origins of the Modern Pharmaceutical Industry (2014).

[27] See Abigail Alliance for Better Access to Dev. Drugs v. von Eschenbach, 495 F.3d 695, 703 (D.C. Cir. 2007); Alex John London, Social Value, Clinical Equipoise, and Research in a Public Health Emergency, 33 Bioethics 326, 326 (2018).

[28] See Lewis A. Grossman, The Origins of American Health Libertarianism, 13 Yale J. Health Pol'y L. & Ethics 76, 80 (2013).

to access experimental interventions without FDA authorization in some contexts.[29]

This reality does not mean that regulators like FDA are unaware of these burdens. Consistent with norms around free choice and the agency's own resource limitations, FDA often chooses not to enforce certain requirements when serious public-safety, health, or welfare risks are not implicated. FDA might therefore exercise such enforcement discretion over genetic biohacking activities that do not pose serious public-health concerns. More practically, it may be difficult for FDA to identify violations by genetic biohackers who work exclusively in private settings and do not publicly discuss their activities.[30] Although a 2013 survey conducted by the Woodrow Wilson Center suggests the number of these individuals may be small,[31] concerns about the safety of their activities may persist if they are – as some have worried[32] – perhaps a little too comfortable working in the legal and ethical margins.

To fill this gap, some states may take steps to regulate genetic biohacking, as California did in August 2019 when it enacted the first "CRISPR law."[33] Consistent with FDA's 2017 statement, the law requires sellers of "gene therapy kit[s]" to inform consumers, on websites and in labeling, that the kits are "not for self-administration."[34] Earlier in 2019, California's Department of Consumer Affairs began to investigate Josiah Zayner, PhD, a well-known biohacker and founder of an online retailer of DIY CRISPR kits, for the "unlicensed practice of medicine."[35] While the line between FDA's jurisdiction and that of state medical boards is, at best, fuzzy, and definitions of

29 See, e.g., Lewis A. Grossman, AIDS Activists, FDA Regulation, and the Amendment of America's Drug Constitution, 42 Am. J.L. & Med. 741 (2016); Holly Fernandez Lynch, Patricia J. Zettler & Ameet.Sarpatwari , Promoting Patient Interests in Implementing the Federal Right to Try Act, 320 JAMA 869 (2018); Patricia J. Zettler & Henry T. Greely, The Strange Allure of State Right-to-Try Laws, 174 JAMA Internal Med. 1885 (2014).

30 See, e.g., Henry T. Greely, Take Care!, STAT (Mar. 14, 2016), https://www.statnews.com/2016/03/14/crispr-do-it-yourself/#Greely.

31 Cf. Grushkin et al., supra note 2, at 6–7, 9, 15 (reporting that 6 percent of respondents of a survey of biohackers favored complete privacy in response to the question, "What are your feelings about transparency and sharing your work?," and 8 percent reported conducting experiments exclusively at home).

32 See Ctr. for Global Security Research, Independent Biotechnology: The Innovation-Regulation Dilemma 7 (2016), https://cgsr.llnl.gov/content/assets/docs/Independent_Biotechnology_Workshop_SummaryNOV2016.pdf [hereinafter CGSR].

33 See Press Release, Sen. Ling Ling Chang, Governor Signs Senator Chang's Bill to Address Human Biohacking (July 31, 2019), https://chang.cssrc.us/content/governor-signs-senator-chang-s-bill-address-human-biohacking.

34 Cal. Bus. & Prof. Code Ann. § 22949.50 (2020).

35 Josiah Zayner (@jzayner), Instagram (May 14, 2019), https://www.instagram.com/p/BxdcemZF5uf/?utm_source=ig_twitter_share&igshid=1pkcfktaku9jt; Emily Mullin, Celebrity Biohacker Josiah Zayner is under Investigation for Practicing Medicine Without a License, MIT Tech. Rev. (May 15, 2019), https://www.technologyreview.com/s/613540/celebrity-biohacker-josiah-zayner-is-under-investigation-for-practicing-medicine-without-a/. California's investigation of Dr. Zayner was closed in late 2019. Kristen V. Brown, Biohacker Investigation is Dropped by California Medical Board, Bloomberg (Oct. 19, 2019), https://www.bloomberg.com/news/articles/2019-10-15/biohacker-investigation-is-dropped-by-california-medical-board.

the practice of medicine vary between states, genetic biohacking seems unlikely to qualify as medical practice when it involves only self-experimentation.[36]

In this way, biohacking has now joined other more traditional scientific activities in raising questions about the appropriate intersection of state and FDA regulation.[37] California's efforts raise the specter of state enforcement against genetic biohackers – particularly those who attempt to, or represent that they can, diagnose or treat others' conditions. If medical practice laws do not allow states to reach biohacking, they may seek to regulate biohacking through other means, such as new biohacking-specific legislation. Such developments may be unwise given states' relative lack of expertise in evaluating the safety or effectiveness of the tools of genetic experimentation. In addition, state efforts to regulate biohacking may give unwarranted rhetorical credence to the notion that genetic biohacking is necessarily medical in nature, whereas many biohackers report that their work is not medical but conducted for philosophical, political, recreational, or experimental reasons.[38]

III PRIVATE REGULATION

In addition to being regulated by public agencies, genetic biohacking is also potentially subject to US laws that private actors enforce.[39] Patent owners can impose ethical and public-health restrictions on licensees, such as the Broad Institute's licenses for its CRISPR patents to Monsanto on conditions that Monsanto avoid certain research activities involving human germline cells – eggs and sperm – and tobacco.[40] Patent owners can enforce these restrictions through litigation or the threat of litigation, and even without licenses, they can file lawsuits to prohibit or end conduct posing security, environmental, or public-health risks. Such an approach assumes, of course, that patent owners are aware of such activities and are willing and able to fund such lawsuits. But patent owners of genetic technologies, often active developers themselves, are typically well-positioned to understand their technologies' social and ethical risks. They may also have selfish interests in ensuring that such technologies are developed away from regulatory oversight – interests that would be served by helping to minimize harms to third parties.

In addition, the United States has a robust system of private governance through tort law and tort avoidance. The fear of injuries – and large verdicts from tort suits –

36 See Patricia J. Zettler, Toward Coherent Federal Oversight of Medicine, 52 San Diego L. Rev. 427, 435 (2015).

37 See Patricia J. Zettler, Pharmaceutical Federalism, 92 Ind. L.J. 845, 846 (2017).

38 See Guerrini et al., supra note 9.

39 See Stephen M. Maurer, Self-Governance in Science 63 (2017).

40 See Christi J. Guerrini et al., The Rise of the Ethical License, 35 Nature Biotech. 22, 24 (2017); cf. Jorge L. Contreras, Patent Pledges, 47 Ariz. St. L.J. 543, 590–92 (2015) (describing "philanthropic" patent pledges that are made with the outward goal of promoting public welfare).

often drives the development of safety mechanisms for consumer products, from lawnmowers to airplanes.

Distributors of genetic biohacking materials may similarly self-regulate to avoid claims by people injured by genetic biohacking materials, even when distributors may have defenses against such claims – for example, that the injured persons assumed the risks of biohacking. Some biohackers are quite aware of these responsibilities. As one interviewee explained:

> So if you're going to be providing the materials for a gene therapy, you have to be explicitly aware that the second you put it out there, somebody will inevitably use it, and if something goes wrong, it's your fault. I mean, assuming they followed the directions properly and you can only account for user error so much. But assuming everything was done properly, if something goes wrong, it's still your fault. (Int. 26).

Apart from legal mechanisms, participants in biohacking activities can use voluntary mechanisms to promote safety.[41] Many biohacking activities are undertaken in community laboratories that have adopted safety policies[42] consistent with the Biosafety in Microbiological and Biomedical Laboratories guidance document developed by the Centers for Disease Control and the National Institutes of Health.[43] These policies describe rules for handling and disposing of materials, as well as prohibitions of certain activities. Members of community laboratories usually must sign agreements acknowledging safety rules and penalties for noncompliance (including expulsion) and also separately demonstrate their safety knowledge by passing a test or completing a class.[44] Moreover, community laboratories generally endorse the codes of ethics developed by DIYbio.org,[45] which was founded in 2008 "with the mission of establishing a vibrant, productive, and safe community of DIY biologists."[46] Even outside community laboratories, many who engage in biohacking activities prioritize safety. As explained by one interviewee who maintains a home laboratory: "A lot of biohackers, even though it may seem like we're

41 See Todd Kuiken, Governance: Learn from DIY Biologists, 531 Nature 167, 167 (2016).

42 See Grushkin et al., supra note 2, at 5.

43 See U.S. Dep't Health & Human Serv., HHS Publication No. (CDC) 21-1112, Biosafety in Microbiological and Biomedical Laboratories (Deborah E. Wilson & L. Casey Chosewood eds., 5th ed. 2009).

44 See, e.g., Baltimore under Ground Science Space (BUGSS) Membership Application and Agreement, Baltimore under Ground Science Space, https://bugssonline.org/wp-content/uploads/2018/05/BUGSSmembership-agreement.pdf (last visited Apr. 26, 2021); BioCurious Membership Agreement, BioCurious (June 7, 2017), https://docs.google.com/document/d/e/2PACX-1vQHZZvoERCqR1HJuGTq2-xga-Pip_kl4x5kzMtx08wQAvg6tNE8yxtYjTBTesaE3akEmh7dJJfTkKjj/pub; What Happens After Joining?, BioCurious, https://biocuriosity.wordpress.com/join/what-happens-after-joining/ (last visited Oct. 22, 2020).

45 Draft DIYbio Code of Ethics from North American Congress, DIYbio (July 2011), https://diybio.org/codes/code-of-ethics-north-america-congress-2011/.

46 An Institution for the Do-it-Yourself Biologist, DIYbio, https://diybio.org/ (last visited Oct. 22, 2020). As of this writing, the active status of DIYbio is unclear even as its ethics code remains influential.

crazy people, are very conscious of potentials for harm" (Int. 5). Another concurred: "[D]on't hurt other people. I guess that's kind of the rule that a lot of biohackers follow is don't hurt other people." (Int. 1).

Biohackers also rely on each other for materials and information, which in turn discourages secrecy and enables individuals to monitor one another's conduct.[47] Some biohackers might even be described as aggressively public about their activities. One interviewee explained intentionally taking this approach in part to promote safety: "It's kind of this hushed tones, 'don't be too loud or you'll draw attention' kind of thing. I'm not a fan of that because that doesn't make it safe for kids. Kids shouldn't be like: 'Okay, now we're going to close the windows and do some science.' Right. That should never be a thing." (Int.15).

Like government-enforced rules, these private mechanisms present benefits and burdens. On one hand, privately enforced regulatory mechanisms – whether based on law or voluntary codes – are often quicker to respond to concerns than are government processes. Additionally, private entities bear the costs of such enforcement, and, although an expert government regulator may not be involved, this approach draws on the extensive knowledge of patent owners and members of biohacking communities more generally. On the other hand, private actors may not be inclined to regulate conduct that poses risks to the public but not the private actors themselves, leading to socially undesirable outcomes. Private actors also may not be able to afford to undertake consistent enforcement, and penalties – particularly where the underlying "rules" are purely voluntary – may simply be ineffective deterrents. Moreover, in practice, biohackers working outside of community laboratories are subject to few, if any, even voluntary rules.[48]

IV MOVING FORWARD

In the United States, a web of laws, regulations, and norms – if used – could reach a number of genetic biohacking activities. Although there are gaps in both public and private regulatory mechanisms (and questions about how rigorously both are and can be enforced), such problems are not unique to genetic biohacking. Other emergent technologies share genetic biohacking's potential for decentralized manufacturing and DIY applications,[49] including

47 Cf. CGSR, supra note 32, at 7 (noting that isolation can be an impediment to DIY biology).

48 However, they may be subject to community safety and ethics norms that are enforced through online platforms where biohackers engage with one another. See, e.g., Biohack.me, https://forum.biohack.me/ (last visited Oct. 22, 2020]); DIYbio Google Groups, https://groups.google.com/forum/#!forum/diybio (last visited Oct. 22, 2020).
Facebook is also a popular online location for biohacker discussion and engagement. See Elliot Roth, A Guide to DIYbio (Updated 2019), Medium (Feb. 16, 2019), https://medium.com/@ThatMrE/a-guide-to-diybio-updated-2019-abd0956cdf74 (noting active biohacker Facebook groups).

49 See, e.g., Albert C. Lin, Herding Cats: Governing Distributed Innovation, 96 N.C. L. Rev. 945, 946 (2018); see also Maxwell J. Mehlman & Ronald A. Conlon, Governing Non-Traditional Biology, in Consuming Genetics (I. Glenn Cohen, et al., eds. 2020).

neurohacking,[50] fecal microbiota transplantation,[51] and DIY manufacturing of traditional pharmaceuticals (and other products that pose public health risks, such as guns).[52]

Whatever regulatory mechanisms apply to genetic biohacking, they will not achieve perfect compliance. Violations are inevitable. As the announcement of the so-called CRISPR babies underscored, even with significant international agreement about ethical norms if not national prohibitions, "rogue" scientists may nonetheless move forward.[53] Concern that regulators would prohibit genetic biohacking based on a rogue biohacker's actions was a common theme during interviews. As one biohacker explained: "If you do something, you should be held accountable for it. You particularly, not the whole [biohacking] movement. That's the bigger underlying worry, is that the whole movement will be blamed if one person messes up." (Int. 15).

Policymakers, regulators, and private actors should therefore carefully examine how to better enforce existing laws before deciding that additional authority is needed to provide effective oversight of genetic biohacking. As stakeholders work to provide solutions, one important consideration is that FDA, despite its power and expertise, is not the only option for overseeing genetic biohacking's public health impacts. Nor are enforcement actions the only option available to the agency for the authority it does have. Educational and engagement strategies, such as the Woodrow Wilson Center's 2018 workshop that brought together regulators and biohacking supporters to discuss safety and ethical concerns,[54] can supplement FDA oversight where either the agency lacks authority or enforcement actions are unwarranted. Such strategies can help private actors to understand the risks their materials and genetic biohacking activities pose, as well as bolster FDA's role in protecting consumers and fostering innovation. Likewise, public regulators, such as FDA, would benefit from engaging with stakeholders to better understand genetic biohacking activities, their participants' perspectives, and the drawbacks and advantages of self-governance by various genetic biohacking communities.

The agency should understand, however, that regardless of its efforts, some biohackers will resist government regulation. One biohacker summarized this

50 See Anna Wexler, The Social Context of 'Do-It-Yourself' Brain Stimulation: Neurohackers, Biohackers, and Lifehackers, 11 Frontiers Human Neurosci. 224 (2017).

51 See Diane Hoffman et al., Improving Regulation of Microbiota Transplants, 358 Science 1390 (2017); Erika Lietzan, Access Before Evidence and the Price of the FDA's New Drug Authorities, 53 U. Rich. L. Rev. 1243 (2019); Rachel E. Sachs & Carolyn A. Edelstein, Ensuring the Safe and Effective FDA Regulation of Fecal Microbiota Transplantation, 2 J.L. & Biosci. 396 (2015).

52 See Jenna E. Gallegos et al., The Open Insulin Project: A Case Study for "Biohacked" Medicines, 36 Trends Biotechnol. 1211, 1211 (2018).

53 R. Alta Charo, Rogues and Regulation of Germline Editing, 380 New Eng. J. Med. 976, 976 (2019).

54 Todd Kuiken, Eleonore Pauwels & Sarah W. Denton, The Rise of the New Bio-Citizen: Ethics, Legitimacy, and Responsible Governance in Citizen-Driven Biomedical Research and Innovation, Woodrow Wilson Center (July 8, 2018), www.wilsoncenter.org/article/the-rise-the-new-bio-citizen-workshop.

perspective: "The government does not belong in my 'blank'. They don't belong in my bed, they don't belong in my house, they don't belong et cetera. They don't belong in my lab." (Int. 11). Another interviewee lamented:

> Legislation consistently hampers growing industries and biotech is a growing industry, and just like every other technology, it was developed in garages, it was developed in people's kitchens, you know? . . . . That's where innovation has come from. People who are passionate and able to make those things happen. And legislating them and making them hide and not allowing them access to tools and information, all it does is hurt us as a people. (Int. 4)

Indeed, policymakers, regulators, and others should recognize that some current biohacking projects seek to develop innovative solutions to important public-health problems, and other projects may have the potential to lead to unexpected results that may well serve the public health.[55] These consideration are arguably the reasons for the Department of Health and Human Services' open innovation initiatives[56] and FDA's Naloxone App Competition.[57] Biohacking activities may also uncover defects or deficiencies in traditional research protocols, analogous to "white hat" hacking in the computer context.[58] Enjoining such biohacking activities before they can bear fruit seems unwise for innovation policy.

In sum, different kinds of genetic biohacking activities pose different risks and merit different oversight approaches. Permitting the distribution of a DIY copy of a validated (but perhaps expensive) gene-editing technology shown to be safe and effective for a disease, for example, might raise concerns about the quality of the intervention and preserving incentives for innovation for the original creator. Permitting the distribution of a DIY version of an unvalidated gene-editing technology intended to treat a serious disease, on the other hand, would also raise questions about whether patients were receiving a safe and effective treatment or modern-day snake oil. Likewise, genetic biohacking intended to alter an individual's appearance or enhance performance raises different concerns than do interventions intended to

55 Cf. Nikolaus Franke, Julia Bauer & Philipp Tuertscher, The Seven IP Commandments of a Crowdsourcing Community: How Self-Organized Norms-Based IP Systems Overcome Imitation Problems (working paper), https://www.researchgate.net/profile/Philipp_Tuertscher/publication/281116194_The_seven_IP_commandments_of_a_crowdsourcing_community_How_self-organized_norms-based_IP_systems_overcome_imitation_problems/links/55f29e6f08aedecb6902176c/The-seven-IP-commandments-of-a-crowdsourcing-community-How-self-organized-norms-based-IP-systems-overcome-imitation-problems.pdf (describing a crowdsourcing approach as likely leading to "surprising solutions").

56 U.S. Dep't of Health & Human Servs., About Open Innovation, https://www.hhs.gov/cto/initiatives/open-innovation/about/index.html (last visited Oct. 22, 2020).

57 FDA, 2015 Naloxone App Competition (Dec. 16, 2016), https://www.fda.gov/news-events/public-health-focus/2016-naloxone-app-competition.

58 See Jonathan Sackner-Bernstein, Design of Hack-Resistant Diabetes Devices and Disclosure of Their Cyber Safety, 11 J. Diabetes Sci. Tech. 198, 199 (2017) (describing "white hat" hacking for discovering flaws in an infusion pump).

treat or prevent disease.[59] Policymakers and regulators must assess the validity of concerns about genetic biohacking based on the nature of the risks and benefits that particular activities pose and the likelihood that each will come to pass. Before concluding more regulatory authorities are needed, regulators and policymakers should consider whether existing oversight mechanisms can be used in more effective ways – whether that means better engagement, more or more finely tailored enforcement, or some other approach – to mitigate genetic biohacking's risks while amplifying its potential.

[59] See, e.g., Henry T. Greely, Remarks on Human Biological Enhancement, 56 U. Kan. L. Rev. 1139, 1139 (2008); Matt Lamkin, Regulating Identity: Medical Regulation as Social Control, 2016 B.Y. U. L. Rev. 501, 501 (2016); Gary Marchant et al., Regulatory Frontiers: Integrating Social and Ethical Concerns Into Regulatory Decision-Making for Emerging Technologies, 11 Minn. J.L. Sci. & Tech. 345, 345 (2010); Maxwell J. Mehlman, How Will We Regulate Genetic Enhancement?, 34 Wake Forest L. Rev. 671, 702 (1999).

PART IV

Consumer Genetics and Identity

Introduction to Part IV

Carmel Shachar

Part IV, *Consumer Genetics and Identity*, focuses on the personal impact that consumer genetic technologies can have. The reader is asked to consider how genetic information forces individuals to reevaluate their family histories and patients to consider their medical futures. At the same time, Part IV also reminds the reader that identity goes beyond an individual, that we are defined by other characteristics such as race. Each chapter also considers the role that genetic testing can play in supporting or undermining self-determination.

A theme throughout the Part is the interplay between an individual and family. Both Kif Augustine-Adams in her chapter, *Generational Failures of Law and Ethics: Rape, Mormon Orthodoxy, and the Power of AncestryDNA*, and Natalie Ram in her chapter, *Investigative Genetic Genealogy and the Problem of Familial Forensic Identification*, wrestle with whether genetic information is the property of an individual or shared among family members.

Augustine-Adams approaches this duality from a very personal perspective. She shares the story of her mother, a sexual assault survivor who gave a daughter up for adoption and kept that adoption a secret for decades. Augustine-Adams then shares her own story, that of discovering a previously unknown sibling through her family's use of AncestryDNA. The two stories intersect in a powerful narrative as her mother accepts her loss of privacy due to a relative's choice to use consumer genetic testing. Natalie Ram is deeply concerned with this loss of privacy through familial actions, considering the role that genetic testing played in several high-profile arrests.

She notes that individuals can be ensnared through the choices of distant family members because of the shared nature of genetic information. Both Augustine-Adams's mother and these criminal suspects stand to experience great distress due to their involuntary connection to DNA databases. These chapters suggest that we should reconsider the balance between individual privacy and use of consumer genetic technologies.

Another theme throughout the Part is how genetic information does and does not define us. Jonathan Kahn in his chapter, *Precision Medicine and the Resurgence of Race in Genomic Medicine*, traces the use of diversity and race in genomic medicine. He argues that there is a tendency to simplify genetics into preexisting racial concepts and that this simplification both undermines the utility of genetic technologies while also reinforcing problematic groupings. Genetic technologies can give us the ability to under the complexities of human diversity. We will miss out on this potential, he argues, if we allow people's identities to be squashed into racial categories. Emily Largent, in her chapter, *Losing our Minds? Direct-to- Consumer Testing and Alzheimer's Disease*, considers the effect that testing for a marker of Alzheimer's Disease can have on patients. This test can radically reshape patients' expectations for the future, defining them in one stroke as someone who may end their life with a debilitating disease. Does this mean that we should not allow this test to be offered direct-to-consumer (DTC)? Largent argues that self-determination is a powerful goal, and that consumers should be empowered to plan for their futures by having DTC access to this testing.

How does consumer genetic technologies change the way we view ourselves, our bodies, our families, and our communities? The contributors to Part IV document all the different ways we are defined by the results of genetic testing and how testing can undermine or support our attempts at self-determination. Tread carefully, they warn, to avoid forcing individuals into categories that do not accurate reflect them or undermining an individual's choice to keep certain information private. But allow access to these technologies when they can facilitate important life choices they also caution.

13

Generational Failures of Law and Ethics

Rape, Mormon Orthodoxy, and the Revelatory Power of Ancestry DNA

Kif Augustine-Adams[*]

I INTRODUCTION

I opened the glass shower door and stumbled, fully clothed, inside. "She is my sister," I whispered, collapsing against my husband's wet body. "Her original birth certificate has my mother's name." An hour later, I knocked on my parents' front door. Drawing my eighty-one-year-old mother into the backyard to gather some rhubarb, away from my father's dementia and flashes of anger, I turned to her and said, as gently as I could, "I learned today through AncestryDNA about the baby." Her face froze, then fell. Shaking and deeply ashamed, she told me about Thanksgiving weekend 1959, the empty apartment in Ogden, Utah, the Air Force boyfriend, her cries of protest and physical struggle when she realized what was happening. I held my mother close as I reeled in shock at both a new sister and how she came to be. "Mom, that is rape. That is date rape." "We didn't call it that back then," she said simply. Until Ancestry.com's DNA testing service, AncestryDNA, prompted me to ask, she had never told anyone – not a single soul – about the rape.

[*] I relate this story with the permission of my mother and my sister. While the particulars of this story are specific to my family, its general outlines – and shock – represent the experiences of a multitude of others. See, e.g., Amy Dockser Marcus, Two Sisters Bought DNA Kits. The Results Blew Apart Their Family, Wall St. J. (Feb. 1, 2019, 11:18 AM), https://www.wsj.com/articles/two-sisters-bought-dna-kits-the-results-blew-apart-their-family-11549037904; DNA Detectives Group, Facebook, https://www.facebook.com/groups/DNADetectives/ (last visited Feb. 16, 2020). For related, but distinct scenarios, see also Jacqueline Mroz, A Mother Learns the Identity of Her Child's Grandmother. A Sperm Bank Threatens to Sue, N.Y. Times (Feb. 16, 2019), https://www.nytimes.com/2019/02/16/health/sperm-donation-dna-testing.html (limited anonymity for the relatives of sperm donors in an age of consumer DNA testing); Malin Fezehai, The Disappeared Children of Israel, N.Y. Times (Feb. 20, 2019), https://www.nytimes.com/2019/02/20/world/middleeast/israel-yemenite-children-affair.html (consumer DNA tests identify children kidnapped and adopted as infants in Israel in 1950s); Erin Blakemore, Argentinian Grandmothers Are Using DNA to Track Down Stolen Children, Smithsonian Mag. (Sept. 3, 2015), https://www.smithsonianmag.com/smart-news/argentinian-grandmothers-are-using-dna-track-down-stolen-children (DNA testing of grandmothers helps identify grandchildren stolen during Argentina's "Dirty War," 1976–83). DNA tests also facilitate genetic surveillance of populations in ways that raise considerable human rights concerns. See Sui-Lee Wee, China Uses DNA to Track Its People, With the Help of American Expertise, N.Y. Times (Feb. 21, 2019), https://www.nytimes.com/2019/02/21/business/china-xinjiang-uighur-dna-thermo-fisher.html.

Only three people even knew about the pregnancy: her older half-sister whom she told in case she died in childbirth, my father who married her anyway, and a religious leader to whom she confessed her purported sin.

The ethical implications of DNA testing are particularly fraught for people like my mother, deeply orthodox Latter-day Saints. Within the Mormon faith, the obligation to discover and build the relational structure of family across generations forms a core religious duty. Long before the idea of DNA even existed, Mormons fulfilled that religious duty through serious genealogical research, creating elaborate family group sheets and detailed pedigree charts going back generation after generation after generation. The genealogical data created by members of the Church of Jesus Christ of Latter-day Saints provided the foundation upon which companies like Ancestry.com began and continue to build. That family history work likewise facilitates religious rituals within Latter-day Saint temples where husbands, wives, and children are "sealed" to each other to create eternal cross-generational webs of family. By identifying shared DNA, consumer genetic tests confirm and reinforce those webs of religious duty, except when they do not.

At the same time that it celebrates cross-generational webs of family, the Latter-day Saint faith maintains a highly conservative sexual orthodoxy that prohibits pre- and extra-marital sex, historically charging women to maintain the boundaries of chastity against men's sexual aggressiveness. The fulfillment of religious duty through the biotechnology of DNA testing revealed my mother's pain, a secret she considered sin. DNA testing discounted her repentance, identifying her purported sin to others, despite her own silence and claim to anonymity.

Across time, law failed my mother in many ways. Neither law nor society nor her religious community recognized as rape the violence she experienced that Thanksgiving weekend in 1959. Washington State, where my sister was born in 1960, promised my mother anonymity in a closed adoption, but changed its laws decades later without informing her.

Although she chose anonymity and silence for fifty-seven years, the relational nature of shared DNA and DNA testing made that anonymity and privacy ultimately impossible. Even if someone chooses anonymity for herself, unless all of her biological relatives do the same, she is always at risk of identification and publicity through shared DNA and genealogical databases like Ancestry.com. If law and ethics recognize an individual's right to privacy, her claim to both autonomy and anonymity, how should it account for the relational nature of shared DNA that makes complete privacy, complete anonymity impossible?

II THE LAW AND CULTURE OF RAPE: UTAH, 1959

In 1959, for adult women like my mother, the gendered delineation of rape in Utah law, as in so many other states, depended on her resistance and his violence. From the 1950s through the early 1970s, Utah Code § 76–53-15 defined rape as "an act of sexual intercourse accomplished with a female, not the wife of the perpetrator.... Where she resists, but her resistance is overcome by force or violence."[1] His actions alone, however forceful, however vile, did not establish rape.

What constituted sufficient resistance on her part to transform his actions into rape? In 1937, the Utah Supreme Court held in *State v. Roberts* that requiring a woman to resist "to her uttermost capacity to prevent penetration" was "too strict."[2] The court softened the historic rule of resistance identified in its 1898 case *State v. McCune* to follow "the trend of the more modern decisions."[3] Utah would be modern – a woman's utmost resistance would not be required – but without a clear of articulation of what resistance made violent intercourse rape. Eight years later, in 1945, the Utah Supreme Court took an apparent step back toward utmost resistance. In *State v. Whittinghill*, the court again cited the 1898 *McCune* case, but this time with approval: "[I]n order to convict, the jury must be satisfied, beyond a reasonable doubt, not only that the defendant had the ability and intended to gratify his passions on the person of the woman assaulted, but that he intended to do so at *all* events, and notwithstanding *any* resistance on her part."[4] The facts in *Whittinghill* demonstrated the point. If a woman's "mild resistance, uncleanliness or ordinary evidence of the menstrual period" sufficed to deter a man, then he couldn't have had an intent to rape, even if he put his hands up her skirt and touched her private parts, even if he admitted that "it was his intention to have sexual intercourse" with her, because maybe, just maybe, he had touched her "for the purpose of arousing [her] passion ... expecting her to submit to intercourse."[5] If she submitted, however reluctantly, she had not resisted, at least not sufficiently. The offense of rape was not in sexual intercourse itself, but in the violence that accomplished it over a woman's resistance.

The jury instructions at issue in the 1949 case, *State v. Beeny*, cited *Roberts* for the proposition that utmost resistance was not required, then set forth a standard of reasonableness: "The law requires that the woman do what her age, strength, the surrounding facts and all attending circumstances make it reasonable for her to do in order to manifest opposition to the act of sexual intercourse."[6] However, neither *Beeny* nor its reasonable resistance standard were reported in the annotations to Utah Code § 76–53-15 and no Utah appellate court ever relied on its decision.

1 Utah Code Ann. § 76–53-15 (1953).

2 State v. Roberts, 63 P.2d 584, 587 (1937).

3 Id.

4 State v. Whittinghill, 163 P.2d 342, 344 (1945) (italics added).

5 Id.

6 State v. Beeny, 203 P.2d 397, 399 (1949). Between 1953 and Thanksgiving 1959, no other rape cases on appeal to the Utah Supreme Court focused on the standard for evaluating a victim's resistance. In 1961, in State v. Horne, 364 P.2d 109 (1961), the Utah Supreme Court again referenced the 1937 *Roberts* case for the proposition that the utmost resistance rule was obsolete and, without citing the case, reiterated the reasonable resistance rule found in *Beeny*: "The law does not require that a woman shall do more than her age, strength, the surrounding facts, and all attending circumstances make it reasonable for her to do in order to manifest her opposition." 364 P.2d at 399.

Rather, a clipped annotation to the 1953 version of Utah Code Annotated § 76–53-15 focused instead on *Whittinghill*'s retrograde reliance on *McCune*: "General rule, for purposes of crime of rape, requires not only that there should have been force, violence, or fraud, but also that utmost reluctance and resistance on part of woman should appear. *State v. McCune* . . . followed and approved in *State v. Whittinghill*."[7] The annotations likewise overread dicta in *McCune* itself for the proposition that resistance must be continual: "Where, from all of circumstances, it should appear that, although when prosecutrix was first laid hold of by force and violence it was against her will, she did not afterwards resist because, in some degree, she voluntarily consented to what was then done to her, defendant should not be convicted of rape."[8] If she did not continue to resist after the first violence, she "in some degree" voluntarily consented. His violence was not her rape.

I doubt my mother ever looked up the definition of rape in the Utah Code or agonized over the explicating case law, either before or after Thanksgiving weekend 1959. Yet, here I sit more than a half-century later, doing just that. I am a Harvard-trained lawyer and a law professor of nearly twenty-five years, well-schooled in hypotheticals, cases, statutes. When I read the Utah statute and its case law, I see potential arguments to vindicate my mother. I can see that the annotations to the code consistently overread the resistance requirement set forth by the Utah Supreme Court.

As a probation officer for the juvenile court in Ogden, my mother most likely was aware of the law's general parameters, but her sense of its true meaning came from life, not analyzing books. And, yet, the annotations confirm my mother's intuitive sense. She let him into her apartment. She kissed him. Resistance, when she realized what was happening, was too little, too late, legally, practically, socially, religiously. "We didn't call it that back then."

My mother grew up in Brigham City, Utah, the descendant of hardscrabble pioneers, European converts, and top Mormon aristocracy. Her own parents' more relaxed approach to religion spurred her toward deep orthodoxy and orthopraxis. To attend church, she would walk from the family farm, where the Bear River Migratory Bird Refuge now stands, along Forest Street, past the red-brick and concrete-block Union Pacific depot where her grandfather had worked, past the water spigots at Pioneer Park where her family filled barrels on Saturdays to cart culinary water back to the farm, three miles alone into town. To keep the Word of Wisdom, the Latter-day Saint dietary code, she gave up the coffee so beloved by her Danish forbearers, which they continued to drink in gallons even after they converted. She earned awards for exceptional church activity and service, attended weekday religious classes, everything. As a first-generation college student, she chose, of course, the religious Brigham Young University (BYU), still in Utah but much further from

7 Utah Code Ann. § 76-53-15 (1953).
8 Id.

home than several public institutions. She fulfilled her religious duties in family history and genealogy, creating a fan-like pedigree chart that traced her lineage back generation after generation to allow temple ordinances for her ancestors who had not known the blessings of the Mormon faith. Her lineage links back to the requisite English nobility in the 1500s, back far enough in Denmark and its Scandinavian neighbors to include Thor and Odin, and, in a different line, Adam, although curiously, not Eve.

Within this Mormon milieu, David O. McKay, president of the Church, made clear that chastity was "the crown of beautiful womanhood."[9] Over and over, in the Church's general conferences, in regular Sunday meetings, and within the Church educational system, religious leaders counseled young people regarding sexuality. J. Reuben Clark, Jr., recalled from government service as US Ambassador to Mexico in the 1930s to serve as an apostle and one of two counselors in the Church's First Presidency, emphatically stated: "Please believe me when I say that chastity is worth more than life itself. . . . It is better to die chaste than to live unchaste. The salvation of your very souls is concerned in this."[10] Antoine R. Ivins, a member of the First Council of Seventy which supervised the Church's worldwide missionary work, highlighted the intransigent stain of sexual sin: "The physical dangers from the non-observance of the law of chastity can well be overcome, but I have never yet found anybody who could say that the moral effects of its infringement could be entirely overcome and forgotten."[11] As a member of the Quorum of the Twelve Apostles governing the Church in tandem with the First Presidency, Delbert L. Stapley equated sexual sin with violent crime as "the most serious sin short of committing murder is that of immorality."[12] Resist to the utmost, even death. Repent, but you can never be fully forgiven. Sex consorts with murder.

In February 1953, a few months shy of my mother's high school graduation, Mark E. Petersen, also a member of the Quorum of the Twelve Apostles, gave a devotional address at BYU entitled simply "Chastity." The address became a pamphlet that circulated for years among members of the Latter-day Saint Church.[13] In stentorian voice, Petersen echoed the same dire warnings of a multitude of previous church leaders. He chided young women against bare shoulders, sheer blouses, and visible bellies to protect their virtue and to avoid leading young men into sin.[14] Many

9 David O. McKay, One Hundred Twenty-Second Annual Conference, Conference Reports of the Church of Jesus Christ of Latter-day Saints 87 (April 5, 1952).

10 J. Reuben Clark, Jr., One Hundred Ninth Annual Conference, Conference Reports of the Church of Jesus Christ of Latter-day Saints 138 (October 9, 1938).

11 Antoine R. Ivins, One Hundred Twenty-Fourth Annual Conference, Conference Reports of the Church of Jesus Christ of Latter-day Saints 51 (April 4, 1954).

12 Delbert L. Stapley, One Hundred Twenty-Seventh Semi-Annual Conference, Conference Reports of the Church of Jesus Christ of Latter-day Saints 122 (October 7, 1956).

13 See Mark E. Petersen, Chastity (Feb. 3, 1953), https://speeches.byu.edu/talks/mark-e-petersen_chastity/; Mark E. Petersen, Chastity: An Apostle Speaks to Youth about the Sacredness of Sex in Its Holy Mission (1953).

14 See Chastity: An Apostle Speaks to Youth about the Sacredness of Sex in Its Holy Mission, supra note 13, at 8.

a young man's "moral downfall began with a girl's immodest dress" on the dance floor.[15] He warned against "petting parties" where "so many of our lovely girls allow boys to handle their bodies, and . . . [o]ccasionally the girls handle the bodies of the boys."[16] He concluded with force. "Virtue is more important to you than your life. Protect it above your life. If the time ever comes when you must choose between the two, then sacrifice your life but under no circumstance sacrifice your virtue."[17]

In 1961, post-childbirth and engaged, my mother approached Elder Petersen for absolution sufficient to marry my father in an Latter-day Saint temple. She wanted to be sealed to him. She wanted their future children to be born under the covenant in that eternal cross-generational web of family her genealogical pedigree chart inscribed. Confessing her sin demonstrated repentance, contingent worthiness. How could it be anything but sin? She was still alive.

III THE LAW AND CULTURE OF ADOPTION: WASHINGTON STATE, 1960 TO 2013

Before she began to show, my mother resigned her position with the juvenile courts, hefted a suitcase with her monogram SRN onto a bus, and headed to distant Seattle. Except for an older half-sister whom my mother swore to secrecy in case she died in childbirth, my mother chose absolute privacy. A pseudonym matching the SRN on her suitcase guaranteed it, until a social worker barked at her for lying and insisted she use her real name. When the time came, another social worker whisked the newborn to waiting parents, a double-blind transfer characteristic of the times. Although anonymity closed the adoption and its records, my mother wanted the child's family to be Latter-day Saint too so the child could be sealed through temple ordinances to her parents. She would have her own eternal web of family, just not my mother's. Throughout the process, indeed her entire life, my mother relied on Washington adoption law and representations made to her regarding it: "[A]ll records of any proceeding hereunder shall be sealed and shall not be thereafter open to inspection by any person except upon order of the court for good cause shown, and thereafter shall again be sealed as before."[18] No one would know.

In 1990, Washington State amended its law to allow limited breach of sealed adoption records to a court-appointed confidential intermediary upon petition by an adoptee or birth parent.[19] The intermediary's job was to "search for and discreetly contact the birth parent or adopted person" and then to make "a discreet and confidential inquiry . . . as to whether or not that person will consent to having his

[15] Id.
[16] Id.
[17] Id. at 11; see also Chastity, supra note 14.
[18] Wash. Rev. Code § 26.32.150 (1955).
[19] See Wash. Rev. Code § 26.33.343 (1992) (codifying 1990 Wash. Sess. Law 145).

or her present identity disclosed."[20] If that person refused disclosure, the confidential intermediary reported to the court and made no further contact.[21]

In October 1993, for adoptions finalized after that date, Washington modified the adoption information rule again. The new rule changed the underlying presumption to disclosure rather than sealed records, unless a birth parent affirmatively filed a nondisclosure affidavit.[22] The new rule did not affect my mother directly, given the 1960 date of my sister's adoption.

Twenty years later, on July 28, 2013, a seismic shift occurred as the default assumption of the 1993 law became the standard for all adoptions in Washington State, no matter when they had occurred.[23] A birth parent had one year, until July 1, 2014, to file a nondisclosure form to prevent release of an original birth certificate to an adoptee, no matter how long ago the adoption. The new rule stood in diametric opposition to the sealed records provision of Revised Code of Washington § 26.32.150 (1955) upon which my mother continued to rely for absolute privacy. Moreover, Washington made little to no effort to inform birth parents – not even those whose no-contact responses to confidential intermediaries rested in court files – that the default assumption had changed, that they needed to fill out a nondisclosure form to maintain the privacy and confidentiality that they and the law had presumed for decades.

In the summer of 2013, shortly before the law changed again, Judith, a court appointed confidential intermediary, found my mother. My sister was searching for her birth family under the 1990 law. Judith made the required "discreet and confidential inquiry" in a letter addressed to my mother by her married name at her home address in Provo, Utah, the same home with the rhubarb in the back where I would later learn of the rape. Judith's letter held three enclosures: a letter from my sister, identified only by her first name; her photograph; and a letter from her mother. My mother replied on July 1. In response to specific questions, she provided basic medical information. In response to unasked questions, she said that she had repented as best she could, but her immorality haunted her still. She wanted no contact. Then, my mother destroyed everything Judith's envelope contained. She drafted her reply on the computer, but did not save it, so no one – not her children, not my father – would stumble across it. She chose absolute privacy.

IV THE REVELATORY POWER OF ANCESTRYDNA

On March 19, 2017, I used AncestryDNA's messaging center to contact a DNA match to my daughter's test that I did not recognize. I myself had not tested. "Dear J," I wrote, "I see that AncestryDNA predicts that you are close family or a first cousin

20 Id.
21 See id.
22 See Wash. Rev. Code § 26.33.345 (1994) (codifying 1993 Wash. Sess. Law 81).
23 See Wash. Rev. Code § 26.33.345 (2014) (codifying 2013 Wash. Sess. Law 321).

match. From the other shared matches, I'm guessing that you are somehow related to my Utah lines." J wrote back almost immediately. "Have you asked R? I think that may be where you want to start." Oblivious to the import of her suggestion that I first talk with my mother, I instead conjured plausible scenarios in my head, a late-life indiscretion on my grandfather's part, an aunt's youthful fling. I forged ahead, "I'd love to hear what you know." J's response shifted the tectonic plates of my life. "I was born in Seattle in August 1960 and I was adopted at birth. According to my original birth certificate and then also the DNA test, R is my birth mother." After I emerged from the shower in soaked pants and sweater, I called her and we talked, two complete strangers whom AncestryDNA revealed to be sisters.

Three weeks after my sister and I first spoke, I wished her Happy National Siblings' Day in a private email. My mother continued, as was her prerogative, to choose no contact and as much privacy as she could retain under the circumstances. I knew and my husband knew, but my siblings, their spouses, and her thirty-one grandchildren did not. She asked me not to tell them.

Despite nine additional pregnancies, eight live births, and every other measure of worthiness and conceivable repentance, she was still deeply ashamed of her perceived sin. She worried that we would all somehow think less of her, consider her a hypocrite for flaunting the values of Mormon orthodoxy with which she raised us. She feared losing our love. Every single day for months, I tried to assure my mother that all her children would love her the same – even more, as I did – if they knew. Every time I saw or talked with one of them, I guarded a miserable silence, mutely honoring what remained of the privacy and autonomy that I, with my query to J and AncestryDNA had cleft. I felt deep ambivalence that my silence acceded to my mother's perceptions of fault and shame and would speak more loudly to her than my words of blamelessness. Nonetheless, hers was not my story to tell, even to my siblings, despite the DNA we all share.

Anytime she had the option, my mother chose privacy. The law in Washington State in 1959 respected that choice, as did Judith and the 1990 confidential intermediary law. The 2013 law did not, but my sister's restraint mitigated its potentially devastating effects. Soon after the law changed, my sister exercised her right to obtain her original birth certificate that contained my mother's name, but she refrained from contacting her, informed by my mother's no-contact decision in July 2013. Even when I saw the shared match between her and my daughter on AncestryDNA and first inquired, my sister referred me back to my mother. She honored my mother's choice of privacy, at considerable personal expense.

In August 2017, two weeks before my sister's fifty-seventh birthday, my mother sent an email to my siblings. She began with Lewis Carroll: "'The time has come', the Walrus said 'to speak of many things – of shoes – and ships – and sealing wax – of cabbages – and kings'." She told them about our sister, softening the rape, because, despite everything I could say, she still was not entirely convinced it was not her fault. She asked them for privacy, no visitors or phone calls for a week. I sat with her on her back-porch swing holding her hand while she cried and cried and cried. She felt her choices had run out.

In the months surrounding my mother's backyard revelation of rape, Brigham Young University, the same institution that she had attended as an undergraduate Sociology major and where I now taught law, exploded with its own sexual assault scandal. The scandal wrote my mother's experience at an institutional level, half a century later. Victims alleged that reporting a sexual assault to the Title IX Office could result in an investigation and punishment of the victims by the University's Honor Code Office, the office charged with enforcing behavioral rules that include a prohibition on nonmarital sexual activity.[24] In my view, the various disciplinary offices of the University had a hard time distinguishing between sex and rape, as did my mother, because of a laser focus on chastity rather than on consent. A more robust understanding of consent and the neurobiology of sexual assault would also have helped to counter aspects of a religious culture that could still, in the 2010s, blame and shame victims, usually women, for the violence of perpetrators, usually men. While the University ended up largely accepting and implementing the excellent recommendations made by its internally convened Advisory Council on Campus Response to Sexual Assault, significant work remains to be done within Latter-day Saint culture.[25] The historic chastity lessons of Church elders die hard.

V THE SYNERGISTIC POWER OF DNA TESTING AND MASSIVE ONLINE DATABASES

DNA is both a unique physical identifier – like retinal patterns, iris variations, and fingerprints – and a distinctly relational one, in ways no other biological attribute is or can be. Confirmation of specific identity may require an individual DNA test, but the relational nature of shared DNA means that an exceptionally confident prediction of identity can occur even if an individual herself has not tested, as long as biological relatives have. The DNA test of her granddaughter, my daughter, not her own, breached my mother's absolute privacy – that and my inability to leave well enough alone. An October 2018 study published in *Science* predicts that only 2 percent of a target population need participate in a genetic database to provide a third cousin match to 99 percent of that population and a second cousin match to

24 See Erin Alberty et al., BYU students say victims of sexual assault are targeted by Honor Code, Salt Lake Trib. (Apr. 12, 2016), https://www.sltrib.com/news/2017/07/27/byu-students-say-victims-of-sexual-assault-are-targeted-by-honor-code/; Erin Alberty, BYU students who reported sex assaults say they faced presumption of guilt, Salt Lake Trib. (May 19, 2016), https://www.sltrib.com/news/crime/2016/06/08/byu-students-who-reported-sex-assaults-say-they-faced-presumption-of-guilt/; Erin Alberty, Students: BYU Honor Code leaves LGBT victims of sexual assault vulnerable and alone, Salt Lake Trib. (Aug. 16, 2016), https://www.sltrib.com/news/crime/2016/09/01/students-byu-honor-code-leaves-lgbt-victims-of-sexual-assault-vulnerable-and-alone/.

25 See Advisory Council on Campus Response to Sexual Assault, Brigham Young Univ., Report of the Advisory Council on Campus Response to Sexual Assault (Oct. 7, 2016), https://news.byu.edu/sites/default/files/AdvisoryCouncilReport.pdf.

65 percent.[26] In other words, only a shockingly low percentage of individuals need test before everyone is identifiable. Moreover, the number of individuals testing has grown exponentially. A 2018 Genome Biology article predicts "upwards of 100 million genotyped individuals" by 2021 with the result that "the power of genealogical algorithms to infer matches will increase, until the likelihood of matching a relative, *if* you have close relatives (at least in the United States) will converge up on total certainty."[27]

Of course, the larger the group of biological relatives who test and the closer their familial relationship to the individual in question, the more readily that individual can be identified. In the Latter-day Saint tradition, that group of biological relatives is large. Moreover, enough people with Mormon heritage have tested with AncestryDNA that its DNA Story feature can link individuals with a meta-family called Mountain West Mormon Pioneers, beyond their personal matches. Even without her granddaughter's DNA test, it was only a matter of time before one of my mother's thousands of other relatives tested and asked my sister who she was.

That individual identification through relatives' DNA is possible does not mean it is easy, yet. Identification requires puzzling through the meaning of shared centimorgans and percentages of DNA, significant sleuthing through genealogical records, and building extensive family trees to discover the right connections. The Latter-day Saint religious commitment to genealogy and family history makes that sleuthing and tree building infinitely more possible than it would otherwise be. The benefit is not just religious or recreational. The pedigree charts and family group sheets that faithful Mormons like my mother created over generations form the backbone for significant medical research through the Utah Population Database (UPDB). The UPDB began in the 1980s when the University of Utah identified "more than 185,000 Utah families on 'Family Group Sheets' from the archives of the Latter-day Saint Church's Family History Library."[28] Over time, the UPDB has contributed to a number of important gene discoveries, including for cardiac arrhythmia (KCNH2).[29] The UPDB's success with cardiac arrhythmia and KCNH2 is my mother's as well. Beyond paper group sheets, her individual family members have contributed blood, DNA samples, and EKGs, to study the sudden death caused by Long QT Syndrome in a Utah cluster within the extended Christensen clan. The Christensens, including my mother's great-grandfather Jens

26 See Yaniv Erlich et al., Identity Inference of Genomic Data Using Long-range Familial Searches, 362 Science 690 (Oct. 11, 2018).

27 Razib Khan & David Mittelman, Consumer genomics will change your life, whether you get tested or not, Genome Biology (Aug. 20 2018), https://genomebiology.biomedcentral.com/articles/10.1186/s13059-018-1506-1 (citing Vladimir Shchur & Rasmus Nielsen, On the Number of Siblings and p-th Cousins in a Large Population Sample, 77 J. Mathematical Biology 1279 (2018)).

28 Family Health Records, Utah Population Database, https://uofuhealth.utah.edu/huntsman/utah-population-database/data/family-records.php (last visited Feb. 16, 2020).

29 See Utah Population Database, https://uofuhealth.utah.edu/huntsman/utah-population-database/ (last visited Feb. 16, 2020).

Niels Christensen, converted to Mormonism in their native Denmark then emigrated to Brigham City in the 1870s.

Ancestry.com benefits in a different way from the foundational genealogical records created by the religious compliance of orthodox Mormons. It monetizes and profits from them. Founded as a genealogy and family history publisher three decades ago by two Brigham Young University graduates in the Mormon mecca of Utah County, it continues its long-standing, mutually beneficial relationship with the Church of Jesus Christ of Latter-day Saints and its members. Ancestry.com's incredible databases of twenty billion records developed in part through reliance on the Church's efforts to preserve world records through microfilming, which began in 1938 as the destructive forces of war engulfed Europe, and later through digitization.[30] Tens of thousands of Latter-day Saint church members then volunteered millions of hours indexing those records. Concentrated recent efforts include indexing the 1930 Mexican census and the 1940 US census. While that volunteer indexing is primarily done for the Latter-day Saint Church-owned and free database FamilySearch, FamilySearch has shared the fruits of much of its volunteer labor with Ancestry.com. In turn, Ancestry.com provides free access to its databases to Latter-day Saint church members.

These massive, searchable, online databases of billions of records magnify exponentially the revelatory power of DNA testing. Beyond the parent-child relationship which it identifies specifically, AncestryDNA groups individual DNA matches more generally as close-family, first cousin, second cousin, third cousin, or fourth cousin with an associated degree of likelihood ranging from extremely high for relationships from parent-child through fourth cousin, to very high, high, good, and moderate for relationships fifth to eighth cousins distant. In the real world, the "close family" group encompasses genetic relationships from grandparent/grandchild to siblings to half-siblings to aunts, uncles, nieces, nephews. The various cousin categories likewise catch highly varied real-life biological relationships. Within AncestryDNA's rough categories, the researcher herself must sleuth out the actual relationships and put names and contact information to the DNA data, a challenging task made even remotely possible through the microfilming, digitizing, indexing, and reviewing of world records to transform them into searchable form.

VI CONCLUSION

What then is the solution to the power of consumer DNA testing and the synergistic force of massive online databases of genealogical records to reveal identity even when an individual has chosen anonymity for herself, particularly where rape may be involved? By the mid-1990s, all states in the USA had passed rape shield laws that

30 See R. Scott Lloyd, Preserving the World's Records, Church of Jesus Christ of Latter-day Saints: Church News (Jan. 22, 2013), https://www.lds.org/church/news/preserving-the-worlds-records?lang=eng&_r=1.

protected the privacy of sexual assault victims by limiting inquiry into their past sexual conduct in court cases.[31] However, state level efforts to protect a victim's identity from public disclosure more broadly failed federal constitutional muster. For example, in the 1975 case *Cox Broadcasting Corporation v. Cohn*, the US Supreme Court held unconstitutional a civil damages award entered against a television station for broadcasting the name of a rape-murder victim.[32] Freedom of the press under the First Amendment would not allow the state of Georgia to impose civil damages for the publication of truthful information legally obtained.[33] Similarly, in *Florida Star v. BJF* in 1989, the Supreme Court found a First Amendment violation where a civil damages award was based on a Florida statute that made it a criminal misdemeanor to "print, publish, or broadcast . . . in any instrument of mass communication" the name of a sexual assault victim.[34] Despite state law's inability to protect public disclosure of an assault victim's identity under the US Constitution, many media companies maintain internal policies that prohibit disclosure of that identity, absent explicit consent.[35] The challenge with consumer DNA testing, however, is its incommensurability. It identifies shared DNA, oblivious to the circumstances through which that sharing occurred, whether sex within a marriage or sex outside of it or rape or in vitro fertilization or donor gametes or any other of myriad scenarios.

Companies like Ancestry.com have attempted various means to limit the revelatory power of their consumer DNA tests or at least to create the perception of choice regarding the degree of privacy and anonymity an individual wants for herself. When an individual tests, AncestryDNA's privacy settings allow her to limit whether and how others can see her information. She can limit the report to an ethnicity profile and forego viewing DNA matches or being listed as a DNA match to others. She can choose a "participant display name" that masks her real name. She can choose whether to link to a family tree and, if she does, whether to make that tree public or private or even invisible to other searchers. If she makes her tree public or permits others to access her private tree under most roles, the current biographical information of living people is blinded, except for their gender. She can even completely delete her DNA results.[36]

For any individual, however, all of the perceived autonomy, privacy, and anonymity offered by AncestryDNA's privacy settings is an illusion. Setting those privacy markers to their most strict on an account may delay that individual's identification,

31 See, e.g., Michelle J. Anderson, From Chastity Requirement to Sexuality License: Sexual Consent and a New Rape Shield Law, 70 Geo. Wash. L. Rev. 51 (2002); Nat'l Dist. Attorney's Ass'n, Rape Shield Statutes (Mar. 2011), https://ndaa.org/wp-content/uploads/NCPCA-Rape-Shield-2011.pdf.

32 Cox Broadcasting Corporation v. Cohn, 420 U.S. 469 (1975).

33 See id.

34 Florida Star v. BJF, 491 U.S. 524 (1989).

35 See id.

36 See Privacy for Your AncestryDNA Test, Ancestry, https://www.ancestry.com/cs/legal/PrivacyForAncestryDNATesting (last visited March 5, 2020).

but as long as other biological family members test and share and query, identification *will* happen, irrespective of individual choice. The genealogical information available to massive online databases like Ancestry.com and FamilySearch may lag under privacy laws like the European Union's 1995 Data Protection Directive and Mexico's 2010 Federal Law on Protection of Personal Data, but unless all relatives make the same choices regarding the use of their data, the risk of identification remains. The relational nature of DNA makes absolute privacy, complete anonymity, individual autonomy impossible. The burden of that impossibility weighs most heavily upon the blameless and unnecessarily repentant people like my mother whom law, society, and religious culture have already failed.

14

Precision Medicine and the Resurgence of Race in Genomic Medicine

Jonathan Kahn

I INTRODUCTION

In his 2015 State of the Union address, President Obama announced the launch of a new Precision Medicine Initiative (PMI) that aimed "to bring us closer to curing diseases like cancer and diabetes, and to give all of us access to the personalized information we need to keep ourselves and our families healthier,"[1] committing 215 million dollars to the PMI in the 2016 budget.[2] At the heart of the PMI is a drive to create a massive database of volunteers who would supply their genetic and health information. This initiative has since been rechristened the *All of Us* program and describes itself as "creating a research community of one million people who will share their unique health data."[3] While much of the public-facing materials for the *All of Us* program emphasizes the "individualized" aspect of precision medicine, they also stress the need "to engage a community of participants that reflects the diversity of America."[4] But what does "diversity" mean in this context?

According to the *All of Us* materials, it means people "from all ages, ethnicities, and walks of life," and "from all regions of the country."[5] So, from the outset, the program is categorizing individual participants into particular groups. On one level, this makes good sense for many reasons, not least of which is that capturing such

[1] Barack Obama, President, Remarks by the President in State of the Union Address (Jan. 20, 2015), https://obamawhitehouse.archives.gov/the-press-office/2015/01/20/remarks-president-state-union-address-January-20–2015.

[2] See Fact Sheet, Office of the Press Sec'y, White House, President Obama's Precision Medicine Initiative (Jan. 30, 2015), https://www.whitehouse.gov/the-press-office/2015/01/30/fact-sheet-president-obama-s-precision-medicine-initiative.

[3] Program Overview, *All of Us* Research Program, https://www.joinallofus.org/en/program-overview (last visited Feb. 17, 2020).

[4] Id. ("[W]e're asking one million people to lead the way to provide the types of information that can help us create individualized prevention, treatment, and care for all of us The *All of Us* Research Program is part of the Precision Medicine Initiative. Precision medicine is health care that is based on you as an individual.").

[5] What Makes *All of Us* Different, *All of Us* Research Program, Nat'l Inst. of Health, https://allofus.nih.gov/about/program-overview/what-makes-all-us-different (last visited Apr. 10, 2020).

significant social and cultural variables as race,[6] class, and environmental exposure can help us better understand persistent health disparities in this country. It is one thing, however, to declare an interest in looking at interactions among genes, race, and environment; it is quite another to follow through in practice. Even as over the past decade biomedical researchers have declared an increasing interest in exploring the complexities of gene-environment (GxE) interactions in relation to racial groups, the environment often falls out of the picture in practice such that the findings raise the dangerous specter of reifying race as a genetic category.[7]

From the outset, *All of Us* recruitment materials foreground racial diversity over environment, class, or region. Thus, for example, the program has produced ethnic-specific brochures targeted at "Asian American," "African American," and "Hispanic American" communities.[8] The only thing differing across these brochures is the pictures of people serving as exemplars of potential volunteers. There are no class- or region-specific brochures. Even more notable is the absence of any brochures targeted specifically at "White" or "European" Americans, while there is one for the "General Community" – yet another example of the category "White" being used as an unmarked norm in biomedical research and practice.

The foregrounding of race at this point in the story of the development of genomic research and practice is both unsurprising and bewildering. Unsurprising because, no matter how often certain geneticists and social scientists declare the incoherence and invalidity of using race as a genetic category, others repeatedly insist on introducing it into the center of the genomic enterprise. Bewildering because many of the researchers and clinicians involved in the run up to the *All of Us* program are keenly aware of some of the dangers of foregrounding racial categories in genetic research, yet persist in their belief that the benefits of using race in this way outweigh any potential risks.

This was not how it was supposed to be. For those studying the use of racial categories in biomedical research and practice, invoking President Clinton's declaration in 2000 upon the completion of the first draft of the human genome that "the

6 In this article, I will be using the terms race and ethnicity interchangeably – for my purposes they both mean race. I find that many researchers use the term ethnicity, which is more commonly understood to apply to smaller cultural or linguistic groups, when they are really talking about race, which is often popularly (and mistakenly) understood to have a biological basis.

7 Race, of course, is a complex and contested concept. For my part, I generally agree with sociologists Michael Omi and Howard Winant who approach race as "an unstable and decentered complex of social meanings constantly being transformed by political struggle." Michael Omi & Howard Winant, Racial Formation in the United States: From the 1960s to the 1990s 55 (2d ed. 1994). Nonetheless, while I assert that race is not a genetic category, it can have biological consequences resulting, for example, in health disparities. As epidemiologist Nancy Krieger puts it, race- based health differences can be understood as "biological expressions of race-relations." Nancy Krieger, if "race" is the answer, what is the question? – on "race," racism, and health: a social epidemiologist's perspective, Is Race "Real"? (June 7, 2006), http://raceandgenomics.ssrc.org/Krieger/#31.

8 See Community Resources, *All of Us* Research Program, https://www.joinallofus.org/en/community/community-resources (last visited Feb. 17, 2020).

only race we are talking about is the human race"[9] has become almost cliché. For many, the sequencing of the human genome, which showed the overwhelming similarity among all human beings, was embraced as opening a new era where race would no longer be understood as a coherent or viable biological category inhering in some essential attribute of racialized bodies.

Subsequent events, however, demonstrated the persistent power of race as a useful and convenient category for organizing many aspects of ongoing biomedical projects. Far from a turning point, the completion of the Human Genome Project (HGP) marked merely a new chapter in an ongoing struggle over constructing the relationship between race and genetics that goes back over a century.[10]

The basic organization of the *All of Us* program is fundamentally framed in racial terms with its repeated emphasis on the need to construct a database around the concept of "diversity." Diversity thus has emerged as a central organizing theme of this massive government-sponsored enterprise, perhaps as a way to avoid explicitly invoking race. Given the fraught history of previous initiatives that utilized racial categories in biomedical research and practice, it behooves us therefore to take a close look at just what is meant here by "diversity," consider how it is being used, and what purposes it is meant to serve.

II "DIVERSITY" IN GENOMIC RESEARCH AND PRACTICE

The basic concept of diversity has played a prominent role in modern large-scale genomic enterprises at least since the inauguration of the Human Genome Diversity Project (HGDP) in the early 1990s.[11] In this early iteration, leading geneticists, such a Luca Cavalli- Sforza, conceived of "diversity" largely in terms of "isolated indigenous populations" around the world that some felt were in danger of losing their genetic distinctiveness due to modern developments that facilitated the mixing of populations.[12] Cavalli-Sforza suggested the project abandon the category "race" altogether, instead using terms such as "group" or "population."[13] The HGDP eventually faltered in the face of mounting criticism that, despite the caveats, the Project was nonetheless essentializing certain

9 William Clinton, President, Remarks by the President, Prime Minister Tony Blair of England (via satellite), Dr. Francis Collins, Director of the National Human Genome Research Institute, and Dr. Craig Venter, President and Chief Scientific Officer, Celera Genomics Corporation, on the Completion of the First Survey of the Entire Human Genome Project (June 26, 2000), https://www.genome.gov/10001356/june-2000-white-house-event/.

10 See Jonathan Marks, Human Biodiversity: Genes, Race, and History 99, 99–116 (2017).

11 See Answers to Frequently Asked Questions About the Human Genome Diversity Project, Human Genome Diversity Project, https://www.verslo.is/home/Raungreinar/lif/Itarefni/Liftaekni/Human%20genome%20diversity%20project(e).htm (last visited Feb. 17, 2020).

12 Jenny Reardon, Race to the Finish: Identity and Governance in an Age of Genomics 1 (2009).

13 Id. at 4–5.

indigenous groups as somehow genetically "pure."[14] Additionally, indigenous activists mounted various objections to it as a form of "biocolonialism" that exploited vulnerable populations.[15]

Emerging more or less concurrently with the HGDP during the 1990s, the HGP was less concerned with diversity per se, focusing instead on the basic task of providing the first draft of a full sequence of an individual human genome. It was more explicitly premised on the idea that since humans were 99.9 percent genetically the same, a model genome would serve for all populations.[16] Additionally, the HGP foregrounded the idea that sequencing the human genome would lead to great improvements in human health.

The focus on health connected this enterprise to other major federal health initiatives of the 1990s, notably the National Institutes of Health (NIH) Revitalization Act of 1993, which mandated that efforts be undertaken to include representation of women and minorities in federally funded clinical research,[17] and the Food and Drug Modernization Act of 1997, which encouraged the same.[18] The mandates were largely motivated by the laudable desire to address longstanding race-based health disparities caused by years of unjust social policies. But, unlike other civil rights laws, such as the Voting Rights Act or Fair Housing Act, health-based civil rights initiatives risked conflating social with biological differences to a far greater degree because they addressed the ways in which social, economic, and political inequality literally became manifest in the bodies of people of color.[19]

Thus, even as President Clinton stood at the White House in 2000 declaring the unity of the human race, powerful federal mandates were actively structuring the production and categorization of health-related data along racial lines. By that time, we had moved from the HGDP's conceptualization of diversity in terms of genetically isolated indigenous populations toward the broad race-based social categories of the census. And so, the stage was well-set for the emergence of race-based therapeutics, as exemplified by the case of BiDil, the first drug ever approved by the Food and Drug Administration (FDA) with a race-specific indication: to treat heart failure in black patients. [20]

[14] Jonathan Marks, The Human Genome Diversity Project: Good FOR If Not Good AS Anthropology, Anthropology Newsletter, Apr. 1995, at 72, 72.

[15] Indigenous Peoples Opposition to the HGDP, Indigenous Peoples Council on Biocolonialism, http://www.ipcb.org/resolutions/htmls/summary_indig_opp.html (last visited Feb. 17, 2020).

[16] See e.g., Genome Map, 291 Science 1218, 1218 (Feb. 16, 2001).

[17] National Institutes of Health Revitalization Act of 1993, Pub. L. No. 103–43, § 131, 107 Stat. 122 (1993).

[18] Food and Drug Administration Modernization Act of 1997, Pub. L. No. 105–115, 111 Stat. 2296 (1997).

[19] See Jonathan Kahn, Race in a Bottle: The Story of BiDil and Racialized Medicine in a Post-Genomic Age 67 (2012).

[20] See id., at 48.

III RACE AS STEPPING STONE

Shortly after President Clinton's declaration, the FDA granted approval to a company called NitroMed to conduct a race-specific drug trial exclusively in self-identified African American subjects. Four years later, it granted approval for BiDil.[21] It did not matter to the FDA that the race-specific drug trial said nothing about whether BiDil worked *differently* in black people than anyone else for the simple reason that there were no comparison populations in the trial. All that mattered was that the trial showed efficacy in self-identified blacks. [22]

The BiDil experience demonstrates that, far from being rendered irrelevant by the sequencing of the human genome, race continued to gain new salience as federal mandates and commercial incentives drove the biologization of this categorization. In the case of BiDil, the turn to race was propelled largely by NitroMed's desire to capitalize on an underlying race-specific patent that extended its effective monopoly over the drug for thirteen years.

Nevertheless, even those who were wary of such genetic constructions of race touted BiDil as a sort of interim measure to get us to an era of truly individualized pharmacogenomic medicine where the need to use racial categories would fade away.[23] Thus, for example, Lawrence Lesko of the FDA's Center for Drug Evaluation Research, asserted that race-based medicine could be a stepping stone to the higher goal of "targeted treatment" (i.e. treatment where race need no longer be taken into consideration).[24]

BiDil prompted discussions of the need to use racial categories more broadly in order to drive forward the then (and continuing) unrealized promise of pharmacogenomics – that aspect of precision medicine which aimed to deliver, as NIH Director Frances Collins put it, "the right drug, at the right dose, for the right person." [25] The BiDil model of using racial groups as a proxy for individualized genetic differences soon devolved from an interim measure to a basic structuring premise of next generation genomic research.

IV FROM STEPPING STONE TO FOUNDATION: THE SHIFT TO "PRECISION" MEDICINE

A critical turning point in race's transition from bug to feature of federally sponsored genomic enterprises came in 2011 with the publication of a report by the National Research Council called, *Toward Precision Medicine: Building a Knowledge*

21 See id.

22 See id., at 92–99.

23 See id., at 157–93.

24 Ben Harder, The Race to Prescribe, Sci. News (Apr. 12, 2005), https://www.sciencenews.org/article/race-prescribe.

25 Francis S. Collins, The Language of Life 231 (2011).

Network for Biomedical Research and a New Taxonomy of Disease.[26] The critical rhetorical shift in this report was from "personalized" to "precision" medicine. As Charles Sawyer, cochair of the committee issuing the report, later noted:

> We consciously spent a considerable amount of time on whether we were talking about personalized medicine or precision medicine With the term "precision medicine," we are trying to convey a more precise classification of disease into subgroups that in the past have been lumped together because there wasn't a clear way to discriminate between them.[27]

The report itself noted that while, technically, "personalized medicine" did not "literally mean the creation of drugs or medical devices that are unique to a patient," nonetheless, "this term is now widely used, including in advertisements for commercial products, and it is sometimes misinterpreted as implying that unique treatments can be designed for each individual."[28] It posited that the term precision medicine is preferable because it avoids this confusion and would allow a clearer focus on "the ability to classify individuals into subpopulations that differ in their susceptibility to a particular disease, in the biology and/or prognosis of those diseases they may develop, or in their response to a specific treatment." [29]

Precision medicine then, is *not* about the individual – at least not primarily. It is about classifying people into "subgroups" or "subpopulations." Just what sort of groups or populations are we talking about here? Of course, ultimately the goal is classification based on relevant genotype. But, as with those who originally called the use of race in BiDil a "stepping stone," the foregrounding of group classification in precision medicine is transforming this stepping stone into an institutionalized foundation for one of the largest biomedical research enterprises ever undertaken by the federal government: the Precision Medicine Initiative.

We see the trend toward the reification of race as genetic at work in an extensive analysis of the rhetorical shift from "personal" to "precision" medicine published by Jeungst et al. in 2016. The authors cite an interview with one senior editor of a genomics journal who says that "the way I look at personalized medicine is whereby we can stratify patient groups respective of ancestry, ethnicity, into individuals who are more likely to respond using novel technologies."[30] More broadly, among the 143 interviews conducted with an array of parties involved in genomic medicine, Jeungst et al. found that the "overwhelming sense among respondents was that genomic medicine would remain at the group level, stratified by empiric

[26] Comm. On a Framework for Developing a New Taxonomy of Disease, Nat'l Research Council, Toward Precision Medicine: Building a Knowledge Network for Biomedical Research and a New Taxonomy of Disease (2011), https://www.ncbi.nlm.nih.gov/books/n/nap13284/pdf/.

[27] Id., at 249.

[28] Id., at 124.

[29] Id., at 125.

[30] Eric T. Jeungst et al., From 'Personalized' to 'Precision' Medicine: The Ethical and Social Implications of Rhetorical Reform in Genomic Medicine, 46 Hastings Ctr. Rep. 21, 23 (2016).

genomic disease risk associations and, to lesser degrees, generalizations from racial and ethnic ancestry."[31]

The broader embrace of the rhetorical shift from a focus on individuals to groups is evident at the federal level in a 2016 statement from Muin Khoury, the founding director of the Centers for Disease Control and Prevention's Office of Public Health Genomics, where he states that:

> A strong rationale for the shift towards precision medicine was laid out in a 2011 report from the National Research Council (NRC) The report expressed concern that the use of the term "personalized medicine" could imply that treatments and preventions are being developed uniquely for each individual. After all, isn't medicine supposed to be personalized to begin with? On the other hand, the focus of 'precision medicine' is to explore how treatment or prevention approaches can be developed based on the combination of genetic, environmental, and social factors which could be targeted to individuals or populations.[32]

Khoury's embrace of precision medicine and its focus on groups is certainly understandable given his public health orientation. But the "populations" he is referring to here are being actively constructed by the Precision Medicine Initiative's *All of Us* program around race. The move from the individual to the group is not simply a matter of creating neutral genetically characterized "populations;" it was and continues to be, almost inexorably, a matter of race.

V "DIVERSITY" AND THE ENTANGLEMENT OF RACE AND GENETICS

This brings us back to the concept of "diversity" and its deployment in the construction of "precision medicine" generally and the *All of Us* program in particular. What exactly are advocates of "precision" medicine talking about when they invoke "diversity" and what are their rationales for structuring genomic enterprises around this concept? Broadly speaking there are four basic types rationales for diversity: technical, medical, political, and commercial.

We see three of the rationales expressed concisely in the single assertion from leading NIH researchers that "[i]ncreased attention to diversity will increase the accuracy, utility and acceptability of using genomic information for clinical care."[33] The focus on accuracy goes to the idea of improving the technical aspects of genomic discovery; utility goes to serving the medical ends of improving health outcomes; and acceptability addresses political concerns that under-represented groups have a seat at the table of genomic advancement, particularly as it relates to addressing persistent race-based

[31] Id.

[32] Muin J. Khoury, The Shift from Personalized Medicine to Precision Medicine and Precision Public Health: Words Matter!, Centers for Disease Control & Preventing: Genomics & Precision Pub. Health (Apr. 21, 2016), https://blogs.cdc.gov/genomics/2016/04/21/shift/.

[33] Lucia Hindorff et al., Prioritizing Diversity in Human Genomics Research, 19 Nature Reviews Genetics 175, 175 (2018).

health disparities.[34] The commercial rationale for diversity is evident in the idea that one core goal of the PMI is "is to reinvigorate stagnating therapeutic R&D," in part by using subgroup analysis to rescue otherwise failed drugs. [35]

One group of leading researchers from the NIH defines "genomic diversity" simply as "variation in alleles and allele frequency" that is "inherent within and across human populations."[36] But clearly, when the *All of Us* materials reference "diversity" they are speaking of something very different from simple genetic diversity; they do not have brochures directed to people defined by their genetic makeup. As so clearly identified by Jeungst et al., state-sponsored public health initiatives are invariably, as a practical matter, going to be organized around socially identifiable "visible groups" such as race.[37]

Researchers may be interested in genomic diversity but as a practical matter we are back to using racial diversity as a means to get at such genomic variation. But, as used by these researchers, diversity means something more. The same group of NIH researchers who provided the above referenced definition of "genomic diversity" go on to explain that, in the context of critiques of the "representativeness" of genomic databases and related research initiative, the term "diverse" can "refer to the characteristics related to peoples' ancestry and to the physical and social environments in which they live and receive health care."[38] Here we have the additions of physical and social environment, as well as geography, to the concept of diversity.[39]

With specific reference to building the cohort of volunteers to populate what would soon become known at the *All of Us* program, in 2015 the NIH's Precision Medicine Working Group argued that "[t]he PMI cohort should broadly reflect the diversity of the U.S." and went on to define this diversity as follows:

> The U.S. is a diverse society. Americans comprise diverse social, racial/ethnic, and ancestral populations living in a variety of geographies, social environments, and economic circumstances. The U.S. population includes people with extreme wealth and people living in abject poverty and with varying access to social, educational, and other resources Racial and ethnic diversity do not just reflect genetic ancestry; they are social constructs rooted in cultural identity and shaped by historic and current events, which influence an individual's behavior, place of residence, and life opportunities.[40]

34 See, e.g., Courtney R. Lyles et al., The New Era of Precision Population Health: Insights for the *All of Us* Research Program and Beyond., 16 J. Translational Med. 211, 212 (2018); Jose Flores et al., Addressing Diversity and Inclusion in Human Genetics Research, 175 Cell 303 (2018).

35 Lori Knowles et al., Paving the Road to Personalized Medicine: Recommendations on Regulatory, Intellectual Property and Reimbursement Challenges, 4 J. L. & Biosciences 453, 455 (2017).

36 Hindorff et al., supra note 33.

37 Juengst, et al., supra note 30, at 28.

38 Hindorff et al., supra note 33.

39 See Russ B. Altman et al., A Research Roadmap for Next-Generation Sequencing Informatics, 8 Sci. Translational Med. 1, 3 (2016).

40 Precision Med. Initiative Working Grp., The Precision Medicine Initiative Cohort Program – Building a Research Foundation for 21st Century Medicine 23 (Sept. 17, 2015), https://www.nih.gov/sites/default/files/research-training/initiatives/pmi/pmi-working-group-report-20150917-2.pdf.

So, here we have an explicit caveat cautioning that racial and ethnic diversity are "social constructs," yet they are deemed nonetheless to "reflect genetic ancestry."

If we now connect discussions of the meaning of diversity back to the rationales for diversity, we see some potentially problematic ambiguity in terminology that presents a heightened danger of revitalizing misbegotten understandings of race as an essentially genetic construct. One of the critical rationales for this drive to diversify the cohort is not only to promote medical progress in general, but to address social justice concerns of race-based health disparities.[41] In this regard, the intermixing of social and genetic constructs might seem warranted insofar as health disparities are the products of complex social and biological factors. On the one hand, this all seems a fairly straightforward and necessary to understanding the wide array of variables that need to be taken into account to comprehend and address the complex dynamic of GxE interactions. On the other hand, when dealing with the interplay of social and genetic factors in relation to race, it is imperative to rigorously maintain clear boundaries to avoid the dangers of geneticizing race in general, and health disparities, in particular.

Note that "genomic diversity" was earlier defined by leading NIH researchers as "variation in alleles and allele frequency."[42] This is not quite the same thing as variation of "genetic ancestry." Variation due to genetic ancestry is only one subset of the wider variety of genetic variation that can occur through such mechanisms as random mutation, genetic drift, and clinal variation. The underlying logic of the idea of combined technical, medical, political, and commercial rationales runs something like this: In order to find efficient and cost-effective medical interventions to address the genomic basis of disease, particularly those diseases disproportionately affecting under-represented minority populations, we need to find those genetic variants that play a causal role in such diseases.

The goal is to find relevant causal genetic variants. To do this, researchers need to construct databases that contain a sufficient range of genomic variation, that is, "diversity," to identify causal variants. Genomic diversity then becomes constructed in terms of "genetic ancestry," which in turn becomes "continental ancestry," which becomes African, Asian, European, Indigenous American, which in turn becomes race. Even those researchers sensitive to using race in such contexts nonetheless seem to find no other way to accomplish their goals. For example, Ramos, Callier, and Rotimi argue that, "[a]lthough race and ethnicity are inadequate proxies for individual genetic variation, the success of personalized medicine will depend on how well we understand genetic variation among ethnically diverse populations."[43] Race, it seems, is the proxy we cannot do without.

[41] See, e.g., Lyles et al., supra note 34; Flores et al., supra note 34.

[42] Hindorff et al., supra note 33.

[43] Edward Ramos et al., Why Personalized Medicine Will Fail if We Stay the Course, 9 Personalized Med. 839, 842 (2012).

But what exactly is it a proxy for? Is it a proxy for continental ancestry? Perhaps, but continental ancestry itself is really a proxy for genetic ancestry; and genetic ancestry itself does not get at what we really want but is only a means to the end of identifying patterns of differing allele frequencies; and yet still it is not simply differing allele frequencies that we want; we want those differences that correlate with particular health conditions; and then we do not want simple correlation, we want causal genetic variants; next, even if we identify causal variants, we need to understand about their penetrance and expressivity; and finally once we have figured all that out, we need to then begin the entirely distinct process of trying to come up with some sort of interventions that will actually be of clinical utility – which, of course, is the ultimate promise behind the billions of dollars being committed to the PMI.

Further complicating matters is that fact that advocates of diversity in biomedical research are using the social category of race not only as a proxy for genetic factors, but also for other nonbiological factors such as environment, economic status, or social experiences of racism, all of which can influence disease etiology. This piling of proxy upon proxy facilitates the reification of race not only by blurring critical distinctions between social, geographical, and biological constructs, but also by facilitating the elision of the very social and geographical factors that "diversity" is supposed to capture in the search for understanding the complexities of GxE interactions in shaping human health.

Advocates of diversity in precision medicine research (PMR) have acknowledged this danger. For example, Sabetello et al. recently noted that "[a]lthough PMR is expected to extend beyond race and genomics to include environmental and lifestyle factors on health interventions and outcomes, the latter have historically been neglected."[44] But, in a 2016 review of research purporting to explore gene-environment interactions (GEI), Darling et al. tellingly showed how "GEI researchers expansive conceptualizations of the environment ultimately yield to the imperative to molecularize and personalize the environment."[45] This molecularization of the environment occurs as researchers "seek to 'go into the body' and re-work the boundaries between bodies and environments," which, in turn, leads from a shift in "efforts to understand social and environmental exposures outside the body, to quantifying their effects inside the body." [46]

In programs such as *All of Us*, race serves not only as a proxy for genetic ancestry (or continental ancestry, etc.), but also for social circumstances, such as environment and class. Indeed, using race as a social proxy is central to the entire enterprise

44 Maya Sabatello et al., Trust, Precision Medicine Research, and Equitable Participation of Underserved Populations, 18 Am. J. Bioethics 34, 35 (2018).

45 Katherine Weatherford Darling et al., Enacting the Molecular Imperative: How Gene-Environment Interaction Research Links Bodies and Environments in the Post-Genomic Age, 155 Soc. Sci. & Med. 51, 51 (2016).

46 Id.

of addressing health disparities. Consider, for example, Khoury et al.'s discussion of how diversity in research cohorts promotes health justice:

> To learn what interventions work for whom, data on each individual need to be compared with data from large, diverse numbers of people to identify population subgroups likely to respond differently to interventions In addition, new biomarkers promise to improve the understanding of disease natural history. For example, epigenetics is providing insights into the impact of the environment on gene expression throughout life with the possibility of targeted interventions. There is also strong suspicion that cumulative epigenetic changes due to environmental stressors may explain population health disparities in the burden of various diseases among disadvantaged populations.[47]

Here, diversity is connected to different environments, but then reduced to its epigenetic impact within the bodies of diverse populations – the sort of molecularization discussed by Darling et al. The environment fades out of the picture and molecularized race rises to the fore.

The unfortunate dynamic we are left with then can be summarized roughly as follows:

(1) In the 1990s, even as the HGP was leaning toward President Clinton's confident declaration that "the only race we are talking about is the human race,"[48] the federal government was developing standards and guidelines that encouraged, and in some cases mandated, the use of racial categories in biomedical research, largely in a laudable effort to address persistent health disparities.

(2) After 2000, as the HGP largely failed to deliver on the grand promises of truly personalized medicine, race emerged as a stepping stone and interim proxy for refining genomic research, again in service of the promise of ultimately achieving truly personalized genomic medicine.

(3) After 2011, in part fueled by the rationale of addressing the same health disparities that were the target of various nongenomic federal initiatives of the 1990s, the stepping stone of race becomes a foundation of all future research as the concept of diversity became a central feature of constructing massive new federal databases seeking to uncover differing allele frequencies among certain human "subpopulations." The focus here is less on uncovering the genetic basis for common diseases and more on "health equity" as a new promise of genomics.

(4) In practice, the sorts of GEI studies that provide a central rationale for racially diverse research cohorts molecularize the environment by directing their gaze inward to the racialized bodies of affected individuals.

47 Muin J. Khoury et al., Precision Public Health for the Era of Precision Medicine, 50 Am. J. Preventive Med. 398, 399 (2016).

48 Clinton, supra note 9.

What we are left with is a sort of double-pronged re-reification of race as genetic: first, through the conflation of socially defined racial groups with distinctive and discrete genetic clusters; and, second, through the molecularization of social phenomena that disparately impact racial groups. The former threatens to reinvigorate dangerous, reductive, and racist constructions of race as genetic; the latter threatens to geneticize health disparities themselves, both blaming the victims and directing attention away from the sociopolitical initiatives that need to be undertaken in order to address such problems.

These are not new problems. Since the completion of the HGP, many have drawn attention to these dangers.[49] In this latest version, reification is being driven by the concept of diversity. It is a concept ready-made for conflating racial and genetic categories because diversity itself has roots in both worlds; a dual pedigree of biodiversity – or, as E. O. Wilson's popular 1992 book characterized it, "The Diversity of Life"[50] – and social diversity driving racial justice, ensconced into jurisprudence, law, and policy, for example, through Justice Powell's opinion in *Bakke v. Regents of the University of California*.[51] Diversity is a useful concept but, like race itself, it can be hard to define and even harder to use in a productive way that avoids the dangers of genetic essentialism and racial reification, hence the need to identify and address these challenges in each new manifestation.

49 See, e.g., Lundy Braun, Race, Ethnicity, and Health: Can Genetics Explain Disparities?, 45 Persp. Biology & Med. 159 (2002); William W. Dressler, Race and Ethnicity in Public Health Research: Models to Explain Health Disparities, 34 Ann. Rev. Anthropology 231 (2005); Chandra L. Ford & Nina T. Harawa, A New Conceptualization of Ethnicity for Social Epidemiologic and Health Equity Research, 71 Soc. Sci. & Med. 251 (2010); Timonthy Caulfield et al., Race and Ancestry in Biomedical Research: Exploring the Challenges, 1 Genome Med. 8 (2009); Kahn, supra note 19, at 200–19.

50 See Edward O. Wilson, The Diversity of Life (1992); see also Jonathan Marks, Human Biodiversity: Genes, Race, and History (1995).

51 438 U.S. 265, 313–14 (1978).

15

Losing Our Minds?

Direct-to-Consumer Genetic Testing and Alzheimer's Disease

Emily Largent

I INTRODUCTION

In 2017, personal genetics company 23andMe received US Food and Drug Administration (FDA) approval to provide consumers with information about ten genes linked to health risks. At the time, the FDA noted that this was the first direct-to-consumer (DTC) test authorized to "provide information on an individual's genetic predisposition to certain medical diseases or conditions."[1] One of these ten genes, apolipoprotein E (APOE), is associated with late-onset Alzheimer's disease (AD), which affects individuals sixty-five years of age and older.[2]

Presently, most experts recommend against genetic testing for AD because the results can be difficult to interpret and are of limited clinical utility. By offering DTC APOE testing, 23andMe is diverging from current clinical best practices, but also responding to the desire of some individuals to know their genetic risk. Thus, the debate over potential harms and benefits of allowing consumers to have direct access to this information – as well as the tension between paternalism and the individual's right to know – is particularly salient in connection with APOE.[3] This makes APOE an excellent case study for thinking through the implications of DTC-GT, as well as what exactly companies like 23andMe are and should be selling to consumers.

[1] News Release, Fed. Drug Admin., FDA allows marketing of first direct-to-consumer tests that provide genetic risk information for certain conditions (Apr. 6, 2017), https://www.fda.gov/newsevents/newsroom/pressannouncements/ucm551185.htm.

[2] See Alzheimer's Disease Genetics Fact Sheet, Nat'l Inst. on Aging, https://www.nia.nih.gov/health/alzheimers-disease-genetics-fact-sheet (last visited Feb. 20, 2020). Early-onset AD is an uncommon form of the disease the affects people younger than sixty-five. Early-onset AD is linked to genes other than the APOE gene. Id.

[3] See George Annas & Sherman Elias, 23andMe and the FDA, 370 N. Eng. J. Med. 985, 986 (2014).

II AD, APOE, AND ME

Appreciating the current controversies around DTC-GT for APOE requires an understanding of dementia, AD, APOE, and current clinical practice around APOE testing.

Worldwide, an estimated forty million people have dementia.[4] Dementia is not a specific disease but a general label for progressive cognitive and functional impairments significant enough to interfere with an individual's daily life. Unsurprisingly, dementia is one of the most feared conditions of old age, often decried as a fate worse than death.[5] The causes of dementia vary. AD is the most common, accounting for sixty to eighty percent of dementia cases. At present, one in ten adults over the age of sixty-five – or 5.8 million Americans – have dementia caused by AD.[6] AD is an irreversible, progressive brain disorder characterized by the development of amyloid plaques, tangles of tau protein, and neurodegeneration.[7] It slowly destroys memory and thinking skills, erodes physical capabilities, and eventually results in death. The rate of disease progression varies widely; though many variables influence life expectancy, people live an average of three to ten years after diagnosis.[8]

APOE is a susceptibility gene that has been linked to AD. Individuals inherit one copy of APOE from each parent. There are at least three alleles, or variants, of the APOE gene: ε2, ε3, and ε4. Of these, ε2 is the least common variant and appears to reduce the risk of AD. The most common variant, ε3, does not seem to affect AD risk. In contrast, the ε4 allele increases AD risk, although the reason for this is not entirely clear.[9] For the ten to fifteen percent of the general population who are ε4-heterozygotes, lifetime risk for AD is 25 to 40 percent.[10] For the 1 to 2 percent of individuals who are ε4-homozygotes,[11] lifetime risk for AD exceeds 50 percent.[12] It bears emphasizing that possession of an ε4 allele is neither necessary nor sufficient to cause AD:

4 See Philip Scheltens et al., Alzheimer's Disease, 388 Lancet 505, 506 (2016).

5 See, e.g., Emily B. Rubin et al., States Worse than Death among Hospitalized Patients with Serious Illnesses, 176 JAMA Internal Med. 1557 (2016).

6 See Alzheimer's Association, 2019 Alzheimer's Disease Facts and Figures 17 (2019), https://www.alz.org/media/documents/alzheimers-facts-and-figures-2019-r.pdf.

7 Our understanding of AD as a clinicopathologic state, defined by observable signs and symptoms, is evolving toward a biological rather than a syndromal definition. See generally Clifford R. Jack et al., NIA-AA Research Framework: Toward a Biological Definition of Alzheimer's Disease, 14 Alzheimer's & Dementia 535, 536 (2018); Clifford R. Jack et al., A/T/N: An Unbiased Descriptive Classification Scheme for Alzheimer Disease Biomarkers, 87 Neurology 539 (2016).

8 See generally O. Zanetti et al., Life Expectancy in Alzheimer's Disease, 49 Archives of Gerontology & Geriatrics 237 (2009).

9 See, e.g., Jungsu Kim et al., The Role of Apolipoprotein E in Alzheimer's Disease, 63 Neuron 287, 288 (2009).

10 See Doris T. Zallen, "Well, Good Luck with That": Reactions to Learning of Increased Genetic Risk for Alzheimer Disease, 20 Genetics Med. 1462, 1462 (2018).

11 See Jing Qian et al., APOE-related Risk of Milk Cognitive Impairment and Dementia for Prevention Trials: An Analysis of Four Cohorts, PLOS Med., Mar. 21, 2017.

12 See Scheltens et al., supra note 4, at 507.

not all people with AD have an ε4 allele,[13] and not all people who have an ε4 allele will develop AD.

Genetic testing in the clinical setting is typically driven by the hope that it will illuminate presymptomatic risk, improve diagnosis, clarify prognosis, or inform treatment. There is at present little benefit from APOE testing along these dimensions. With respect to risk, APOE is a susceptibility gene, not a deterministic one. Thus, APOE speaks to only part of an individual's risk for AD. Research suggests that ε4 carriers "may be more vulnerable to environmental factors, and thus, lifestyle interventions may greatly modify dementia risk" among these particularly susceptible individuals.[14] Yet, risk-reduction strategies for ε4 carriers are the same as for the general population – lifestyle modifications and medical management of comorbidities.[15] APOE status is not sufficient to make a diagnosis of AD after the onset of symptoms. Given the low frequency of the ε4 allele in the population, the presence or absence of ε4 alleles is generally not helpful to distinguish AD from other causes of dementia.[16] As there is currently no disease-modifying therapy for AD, treatment recommendations do not depend on APOE status.[17]

As a result, most clinicians recommend against clinical APOE testing. Further, the American College of Medical Genetics and the National Society of Genetic Counselors issued joint practice guidelines recommending against APOE testing in 2011[18] and reaffirmed the guidelines as recently as June 2018.[19] The National Institute on Aging, the primary federal agency supporting and conducting AD research, also recommends against genetic testing for AD except in limited circumstances.[20]

13 See Richard Mayeux et al., Utility of the Apolipoprotein E Genotype in the Diagnosis of Alzheimer's Disease, 338 N. Eng. J. Med. 506, 508 (1998) (explaining that roughly half of those who develop late-onset AD have no ε4 alleles at all).

14 Miia Kivipelto et al., Aplipoprotein E ε4 Magnifies Lifestyle Risks for Dementia: A Population-Based Study, 12 J. Cellular & Molecular Med 2762, 2762 (2008).

15 See generally Cara L. Berkowitz et al., Clinical Application of APOE in Alzheimer's Prevention: A Precision Medicine Approach, 5 J. Prevention of Alzheimer's Disease 245 (2018).

16 See Peter J. Newmann et al., Public Attitudes about Genetic Testing for Alzheimer's Disease, 20 Health Aff. 252 (2001).

17 If a disease-modifying therapy is found, APOE testing may become more informative; at present, APOE genotype is sometimes used in clinical trials for dosing, risk stratification, or sample enrichment (e.g., ensuring enrollment of participants more likely to progress to dementia due to their genotype).

18 See Jill S. Goldman et al., Genetic Counseling and Testing for Alzheimer Disease: Joint Practice Guidelines of the American College of Medical Genetics and the National Society of Genetic Counselors, 13 Genetics Med. 597 (2011).

19 See Jill S. Goldman et al., Genetic Counseling and Testing for Alzheimer Disease: Joint Practice Guidelines of the American College of Medical Genetics and the National Society of Genetic Counselors, 21 Genetics Med. 2404 (2019), https://www.nature.com/articles/s41436-019-0559-1.

20 See Alzheimer's Disease Genetics Fact Sheet, supra note 2 ("Genetic testing is used by researchers conducting clinical trials and by physicians to help diagnose early-onset Alzheimer's disease. However, genetic testing is not otherwise recommended.").

III APOE AND 23ANDME

23andMe is a personal genomics company named for the twenty-three pairs of chromosomes in a typical human cell. 23andMe began offering DTC-GT in 2007 and first added APOE results in April 2011.

The company entered into negotiations with the FDA about its personal genome service (PGS) in July 2009.[21] Based on 23andMe's description of the PGS "as consisting of a software program that analyzes genetic test results that are generated by an external laboratory in order to generate a patient specific test report," the FDA concluded that the PGS was "a diagnostic device and subject to all applicable requirements of the [Federal Food, Drug, and Cosmetic] Act."[22] The FDA expressed concern that 23andMe was not taking appropriate steps toward premarket approval.[23] Nevertheless, the FDA continued working with the company to ensure compliance with the relevant regulations. Finally, in July 2012, 23andMe began the process of getting clearance to sell the genetic testing kit it had already been selling for years. But in what one writer called "the single dumbest regulatory strategy I have seen,"[24] 23andMe cut off contact with the FDA and initiated new marketing campaigns that led the FDA to conclude that the company planned to expand the provision of its PGS without obtaining marketing authorization.[25]

In November 2013, the FDA sent a scathing warning letter to 23andMe ordering it to "immediately discontinue marketing the PGS until such time as it receives FDA marketing authorization for the device."[26] At the time, the FDA was particularly concerned that 23andMe was marketing the PGS as providing health reports on 254 diseases and conditions and enabling consumers to work toward risk mitigation.[27] The FDA sought assurance that the company had analytically or clinically validated the PGS for its intended uses.[28] In response, 23andMe returned to the negotiating table with the FDA.

21 23andMe has stated that the dialogue with the FDA began in 2008. See, e.g., Amanda Holpuch, 23andMe Suspends Marketing after Failing to Meet FDA Requirements, Guardian (Dec. 3, 2013, 12:35 PM), https://www.theguardian.com/science/2013/dec/03/23andme-suspends-marketing-fda-order.

22 Letter from Alberto Gutierrez, Food & Drug Admin. to Ann Wojcicki, President, 23andMe (June 10, 2010), https://www.fda.gov/media/79205/download.

23 Id. at 2.

24 Matthew Herper, 23andStupid: Is 23andMe Self-Destructing?, Forbes (Nov. 25, 2013, 3:51 PM), https://www.forbes.com/sites/matthewherper/2013/11/25/23andstupid-is-23andme-self-destructing/#3d9fa78c11c0.

25 Kelly Servick, Frustrated U.S. FDA Issues Warning to 23AndMe, Science (Nov. 25, 2013, 5:30 PM), https://www.sciencemag.org/news/2013/11/frustrated-us-fda-issues-warning-23andme#.

26 Eric Topol, The Patient Will See You Now: The Future of Medicine is in Your Hands 64 (2014).

27 *Supra* note 25.

28 Andrew Pollack, F.D.A. Orders Genetic Testing Firm to Stop Selling DNA Analysis Service, N.Y. Times (Nov. 25, 2013), https://www.nytimes.com/2013/11/26/business/fda-demands-a-halt-to-a-dna-test-kits-marketing.html.

Then, in April 2017, the FDA announced that it had reviewed data for the 23andMe genetic testing kit through the de novo premarket review pathway, [29] a regulatory pathway for novel low-to-moderate risk devices for which there is no existing substantial equivalent. As a result of this review, the FDA allowed marketing of genetic health risk tests for ten diseases or health conditions, including AD. Authorization was "supported by data from peer-reviewed, scientific literature that demonstrated a link between specific genetic variants and each of the 10 health conditions."[30]

Publicly, 23andMe CEO Ann Wojcicki celebrated this as a "major accomplishment"[31] and stated that it was "a significant step forward for 23andMe and for the adoption of personal genetics."[32] That month, the company released a set of genetic health risk reports for a variety of diseases and conditions, one of which was AD.[33]

As of summer 2019, a consumer can order a genetic testing kit and from 23andMe for 199 dollars. The individual mails in a saliva sample; then, 23andMe isolates DNA from this sample, tests it for genetic variants, and provides an online report within three to five weeks.[34] Customers log into the 23andMe website to view their results. Before clicking through to the "locked" APOE result, consumers are required to read a warning. This warning states that the results they are about to access "are about serious diseases that may not currently have an effective cure or treatment" and that people who "have been diagnosed with anxiety or depression" may experience "emotional difficulty" as a result.[35] Once accessed, the report discloses whether the individual has any ε4 alleles and notes that "[y]our risk for Alzheimer's disease also depends on other factors, including lifestyle, environment, and genetic variants not covered by this test."[36] The report clarifies that "[t]his test does not diagnose Alzheimer's disease or any other health conditions."[37]

29 News Release, supra note 1.

30 In November 2017, the FDA announced plans to make it easier for DTC-GT companies to bring genetic health risk tests to market. Companies that offer genetic health risk tests will undergo a one-time review to establish accuracy, reliability, and relevance; and subsequent tests could be released without consulting the agency. Essentially, this opens the same review process that 23andMe benefited from in April 2017 to other genetic testing companies. See Statement, Food & Drug Admin., Statement from FDA Commissioner Scott Gottlieb, M.D., on implementation of agency's streamlined development and review pathway for consumer tests that evaluate genetic health risks (Nov. 6, 2017), https://www.fda.gov/NewsEvents/Newsroom/PressAnnouncements/ucm583885.htm.

31 Adam Bluestein, After a Comeback, 23andMe Faces Its Next Test, Fast Company (Aug. 9, 2017), https://www.fastcompany.com/40438376/after-a-comeback-23andme-faces-its-next-test.

32 Good News About Health Reports, 23andMe: Blog (Apr. 6, 2017), https://blog.23andme.com/news/good-news-health-reports/.

33 Id.

34 See How 23andMe Works, 23AndMe, https://customercare.23andme.com/hc/en-us/articles/227968028-How-23andMe-works (last visited Feb. 20, 2020).

35 Sharon Begley, Before you send your spit to 23andMe, what you need to know, PBS Newshour (Apr. 9, 2017, 12:20 PM), https://www.pbs.org/newshour/health/23andme-need-know.

36 23andMe, Sample Report, https://medical.23andme.org/wp-content/uploads/2017/09/Alzheimer_two_e4_female.pdf.

37 Id.

23andMe's genetic reports are not equally relevant or informative for all ethnic groups. The company's database has notable gaps – "especially among Africans, Middle Easterners, Central Asians, Southeast Asians, and indigenous Americans"[38] – with implications for the identification of disease-causing variants and generalizability of results. For example, "[t]he prevalence of the ε4 allele is consistently found to be higher in African Americans than non-Hispanic whites, but it is inconsistently related to Alzheimer's disease or cognition in this population."[39] 23andMe's disclosure around this is somewhat limited, as testing reports state that "[t]he ε4 variant included in this test is found and has been studied in many ethnicities. Detailed risk estimates have been studied the most in people of *European* descent."[40] The report also provides citations to scientific literature about risk in people of non-European descent if consumers wish to know more.

IV THE SIGNIFICANCE OF DTC APOE RESULTS

APOE can largely be distinguished from the other health-related genetic variants for which 23andMe now tests, such as alpha-1 antitrypsin deficiency, hereditary thrombophilia, and Celiac disease. AD is a serious and stigmatized neurodegenerative disease characterized by a subtle onset that uniquely inhibits self-determination and well-being and for which there is no disease-modifying therapy. Thus, questions about the appropriate balance between disclosure and protection come to the fore in unique ways.

This tension between some individuals' desire for disclosure and others' impulse for protection can be captured in a pair of anecdotes. On the one hand, some individuals who learn they have one or more ε4 alleles find that the information enables them and their families to better understand, plan for, and address the prospect of cognitive and functional impairments.[41] A man who learned he was an ε4-homozygote described this process as "proactive anticipation" of AD.[42] On the other hand, a woman who inadvertently learned from 23andMe that she was at higher risk for developing AD called the information "devastating" and noted the possible implications for herself, for her husband (who might one day be her caregiver), and for her children (whom she assumed had each inherited an ε4 allele).[43] She also spoke to the stigma associated with AD, which she apparently

[38] Sarah Zhang, 23andMe Wants Its DNA Data to Be Less White, Atlantic (Apr. 23, 2018), https://www.theatlantic.com/science/archive/2018/04/23andme-diversity-dna/558575/.

[39] Lisa L.Barnes & David A. Bennett, Alzheimer's Disease in African Americans: Risk Factors and Challenges for the Future, 33 Health Aff. 580 (2014).

[40] 23andMe, supra note 36 (emphasis in original).

[41] Cf. Emily A. Largent & Jason Karlawish, Preclinical Alzheimer's Disease and the Dawn of the Pre-Caregiver, 76 JAMA Neurology 631 (2019).

[42] Cf. Daniel M. Gibbs, Early Awareness of Alzheimer Disease: A Neurologist's Personal Perspective, 76 JAMA Neurology 249 (2019).

[43] Stacey Burling, That Genetic Test under Your Christmas Treat Might Be Pandora's Box, Inquirer (Dec. 19, 2017), https://www.philly.com/philly/health/23andme-genetic-test-alzheimers-parkinsons-20171220.html.

felt despite only being at increased risk of AD.[44] Reflecting on her experience, she felt that she would not look at her APOE result if given the chance again and explained, "I wish I had known the can of worms I was opening."[45]

To move beyond anecdote and intuition, however, and to get a better sense of the dynamic to be resolved, it is important to examine the empirical evidence about disclosure of APOE results.

A *Desire for Testing*

Unsurprisingly, desire in the general population for APOE testing is variable.[46] A 2001 survey found that nearly 80 percent of respondents stated they would take a completely predictive genetic test for AD.[47] Similarly, in a 2016 survey, 75 percent of participants stated that they would take a free test that definitively predicted AD.[48] Yet, when the test was described instead as only partially predictive – that is, there is "a one in ten chance that they would not get the disease, despite a positive test, and that there was a one in ten chance that they would get it when the test said they would not" – less than half of respondents expressed interest in it.[49] Note that, as described, the partially predictive test more closely aligns with reality than the definitive test. There is no completely predictive genetic test for AD; possession of an ε4 allele is neither necessary nor sufficient to cause AD. A majority of 23andMe's consumers might choose *not* to be tested at all – or, perhaps more likely, not to "unlock" their APOE report – if they understand that APOE is merely a susceptibility gene. This underscores the importance of educating consumers about what an APOE test can actually tell them about their future chances for developing AD so that they can make an informed choice regarding testing and accessing results.

B *Emotional Impact of Testing and Understanding of Results*

A common argument against DTC-GT – and genetic testing more broadly – is that learning about genetic risk can be harmful to the

44 See id.

45 Id.

46 Anecdotally, James Watson authorized the publication of his entire genome with the exception of his APOE status because he did not wish to know his risk for AD. See Annas & Elias, supra note 3, at 987. Craig Venter, by contrast, chose to learn his APOE status and discovered he was an ε4 carrier. See Jason. Karlawish, Addressing the Ethical, Policy, and Social Challenges of Preclinical Alzheimer's Disease, 77 *Neurology* 1487, 1489 (2011).

47 See Peter J. Neumann et al., Public Attitudes about Genetic Testing for Alzheimer's Disease, 20 Health Aff. 252 (2001) (desire for testing fairly constant across race, sex, education, and health status).

48 See Meera Sheffrin et al., Desire for Predictive Testing for Alzheimer's Disease and Impact on Advance Care Planning: A Cross-Sectional Study, 8 Alzheimer's Res. & Therapy 55 (2016).

49 Neumann et al., supra note 47.

individual.[50] Yet, APOE disclosure has been found to be generally psychologically safe, "despite the frightening nature of the disease and the fact that disclosure has no clear medical benefit."[51] Although some individuals experience transient negative emotions after learning they have an increased risk of AD, researchers have not found the feelings to be associated with clinically significant levels of distress.[52] As mentioned above, 23andMe does warn consumers about potential "emotional difficulty" prior to unlocking their result.

In my own work, many ε4 carriers report that they expected their results, often because they have a family history of AD. Thus, from their perspective, genetic testing simply confirms something they have long suspected about themselves.[53] This work also shows that most ε4 carriers understand that they are at increased risk for AD, which addresses another argument often made against genetic testing: that the results will be too hard to understand.

C *Stereotype Threat*

Receiving genetic risk information has the potential to create a stereotype threat.[54] Stereotype threat is a disruptive concern that occurs when people know that poor performance on their part will confirm a negative self-relevant stereotype.[55] When experiencing stereotype threat, people often underperform compared to their potential, thereby confirming the stereotype. It has been noted that receiving genetic risk information has the potential to powerfully alter the recipient's mindset, and individuals who learn they are at high genetic risk sometimes exhibit deterministic behavioral responses and perceptions.[56]

Researchers have found that adults who know they carry an ε4 allele judge their memory more harshly and perform worse on objective verbal memory tests than ε4 carriers who did not know.[57] In contrast, older adults who know they are not an ε4 carrier judge their memory more positively than non-carriers who did not know, while doing no differently on objective memory tests.[58] Thus, DTC APOE testing may have

50 See, e.g., Wylie Burke & Bruce M. Psaty, Personalized Medicine in the Era of Genomics, 298 J. Am. Med. Assoc. 1682, 1683 (2007) ("These harms might include anxiety, discrimination, and exposure to unproven therapies or to therapies that may have serious adverse effects.").

51 Robert C. Green et al., Disclosure of APOE Genotype for Risk of Alzheimer's Disease, 361 N. Eng. J. Med. 245, 251 (2009).

52 See id.

53 See Emily A. Largent et al., Preliminary Results from the Study of Knowledge and Reactions to APOE Testing, 15 Alzheimer's & Dementia 550, 550 (2019).

54 See Tara T. Lineweaver et al. Knowledge of APOE Genotype Affects Subjective and Objective Memory Performance in Healthy Older Adults, 171 Am. J. Psychiatry 201 (2013).

55 See Claude M. Steele et al., Contending with Group Image: The Psychology of Stereotype and Social Identity Threat, 34 Advances Experimental Soc. Psychol. 379 (2002).

56 See Bradley P. Turnwald et al., Learning One's Genetic Risk Changes Physiology Independent of Actual Genetic Risk, 3 Nature Hum. Behav. 48, 48 (2019).

57 See Lineweaver et al., supra note 54.

58 See id.

adverse consequences for subjective memory and also objective memory test performance. This "could have a serious clinical impact by increasing the likelihood of false positive diagnosis of dementia or mild cognitive impairment."[59] 23andMe does not mention this phenomena, and further research is needed to better understand and address it.

D *Behavior Change*

Several studies have been undertaken to better understand the impact of APOE disclosure, especially on individuals' behavior post-disclosure. The REVEAL (Risk Evaluation and Education for Alzheimer's Disease) Study was a randomized controlled trial of APOE disclosure. The REVEAL team found that individuals who learned they had an ε4 allele were more likely than those who learned they did not to adopt AD-specific health behavior changes even "after explicitly being informed that none [of the behavior changes] were proven to prevent AD."[60] The investigators concluded that, unfortunately, individuals who seek genetic susceptibility testing appear to view AD as more "modifiable" than current scientific evidence suggests.[61] Participants in the Study of Knowledge and Reactions to APOE Testing (SOKRATES 2) also reported health behavior changes – particularly around diet, exercise, and cognitive fitness activities – undertaken to reduce their risk for developing AD.[62]

The 23andMe report notes that "lifestyle and other factors can also influence the chances of developing" AD and encourages people to consult with a health care professional. These changes, which carry little to no risk and may have benefits beyond AD prevention, are generally not cause for concern and may, in fact, be a positive outcome of DTC APOE testing. However, the ability to prevent AD through lifestyle modification should not be overstated, to avoid giving individuals false hope.[63]

E *Changes to Future Plans*

APOE testing may motivate individuals to change their future plans to account for the heightened possibility that they will develop AD in the future. For example, SOKRATES 2 found that many ε4 carriers feel "empowered" by receiving the

59 Id. at 207.

60 Serena Chao et al., Health Behavior Changes after Genetic Risk Assessment for Alzheimer Disease: The REVEAL Study, 22 Alzheimer Disease & Associated Disorders 94, 96 (2008).

61 J. Scott Roberts et al., Using Alzheimer's Disease As a Model for Genetic Risk Disclosure: Implications for Personal Genomics, 80 Clinical Genetics 407, 408 (2011).

62 See SOKRATES 2, supra note 53.

63 See World Health Org., Global action plan on the public health response to dementia: 2017–2025, 18 (2017), https://apps.who.int/iris/bitstream/handle/10665/259615/9789241513487-eng.pdf;jsessionid=E0A23152D4FA28E86109 87AA6F10A056?sequence=1.

information and use it to inform decision-making.[64] Individuals who learned they were ε4 carriers described making tradeoffs between spending money on checking items off their "bucket list" and saving money in anticipation of future expenses, and similarly between working and retiring.[65] Additionally, many ε4 carriers described changing their living situation – for example, moving to be closer to an adult child – to prepare for a future in which they may need caregiving due to cognitive decline.[66] They also discussed health planning with family members and updated their advance directives, with many indicating preferences for less intense end-of-life care.[67] The REVEAL Study found that participants with at least one ε4 allele were more likely to have purchased long-term care insurance.[68]

Such changes to future plans are generally positive and are perhaps most relevant to *why* people want to learn their APOE status even in the absence of clinical actionability. Nevertheless, future planning is not addressed by 23andMe. If 23andMe offers advice about lifestyle and other factors, generally centered around leading a healthier life, perhaps the company should also give more useful, substantive advice around estate and care planning. At a minimum, they should direct consumers to external resources, much as they provide links to academic articles on other topics. This information would likely have more practical impact for individuals with at least one ε4 allele than information on healthier life habits.

Further, the Genetic Information Nondiscrimination Act (GINA) – which protects Americans from discrimination in health insurance and employment decisions on the basis of genetic information – does not apply to the types of insurance that ε4 carriers may most desire: life, long-term care, and disability. 23andMe addresses GINA on its website and explicitly states that "GINA does not cover life, long-term care, or disability insurance providers."[69] It is unclear how many people will see this warning before they are tested or fully appreciate its implications. This important information is not, but should be, included in the 23andMe APOE report.

F *Sharing of Results*

Individuals who learn an APOE result must make decisions about disclosing that result to family members who may be affected – because they are genetically related, because they might be burdened by caregiving responsibilities in the future (i.e., if

64 SOKRATES 2, supra note 53.

65 See id.

66 See id.

67 See id.

68 See id.; see also Cathleen D. Zick. et al., Genetic Testing for Aslzheimer's Disease and Its Impact on Insurance Purchasing Behavior, 24 Health Aff. 485 (2005).

69 What is GINA?, 23andMe, https://customercare.23andme.com/hc/en-us/articles/202907820-What-is-GINA (last visited Feb. 20, 2020). Unfortunately, not all companies that offer DTC genetic testing discuss risks related to disclosure of testing results to third parties, such as insurers. See Linnea I. Laestadius et al., All Your Data (Effectively) Belong to Us: Data Practices among Direct-to-Consumer Genetic Testing Firms, 19 Genetics in Med. 513 (2017).

the individual develops dementia), or both – and also to friends and others.[70] Disclosure can have a measurable effect on the well-being of the party with whom information is shared as well as on the sharer.[71] Many individuals express reluctance to share an APOE result because they fear discrimination. Prior research on the public stigma of AD – the attitudes and beliefs of the general public toward persons with AD – and also self-stigma – which occurs when people internalize negative public attitudes – lend important context to these findings.[72] Stigma was reflected in SOKRATES 2 participants' circumspect approaches to sharing and also their concerns about how the APOE result would change how they are perceived and treated by others.

23andMe allows consumers to create sharing connections with others, in which users can share both ancestry and health information. Notably, reports that require "unlocking," including APOE reports, cannot be shared between accounts.[73] This is an important preliminary protection for consumers. However, consumers would benefit from a more robust discussion of the potential benefits and risks of sharing APOE results with others. In discussing sharing connections, the company notes, "[s]ome people are comfortable sharing this kind of information, some are not – it's a personal choice."[74] Elsewhere on its website, 23andMe cautions: "[I]t's always important to think about who the intended audience is, and to consider the impact on yourself and relatives especially when sharing sensitive insights."[75] More directive information about relevant considerations and possible consequences of sharing with family, friends, clinicians, insurers, employers, and others would be useful.

V WHY BUY DTC APOE?

Why pursue DTC APOE testing? APOE testing may appeal to consumers despite the lack of clinical utility because the result empowers them to make relevant changes to their lifestyle and, more pragmatically, future plans. In the prior sections, I have argued that APOE testing – particularly, learning that you are an ε4 carrier – imparts important information about one's risk for developing late-onset AD. Most individuals appear to comprehend and to be emotionally resilient to ε4 disclosure.

Moreover, empirical evidence suggests that knowledge of susceptibility to AD informs a cascade of subsequent decisions about management of co-morbidities, lifestyle, work-leisure tradeoffs, insurance purchases, and other medicolegal

70 See SOKRATES 2, supra note 53.

71 Cf. Largent & Karlawish, supra note 41.

72 See generally, Perla Werner et al., Family Stigma and Caregiver Burden in Alzheimer's Disease, 52 Gerontologist 89 (2011).

73 See How Sharing Works, 23andMe, https://customercare.23andme.com/hc/en-us/articles/211831798-How-Sharing-Works (last visited Feb. 20, 2020).

74 Id.

75 Sharing and Protecting Your Genetic Information, 23andMe: Blog (Nov. 30, 2016), https://blog.23andme.com/23andme-and-you/sharing-and-protecting-your-genetic-information/.

planning. The empirical evidence should lead us to conclude that many of the arguments made against APOE testing – that it is difficult to understand, that it may be harmful, and that it is not actionable – fall short. This speaks against protection and favors disclosure. In brief, genetic risk information for AD can and should be made available to those who want it.

Given the rarity of APOE testing in clinical practice, however, there are no "best practices" for 23andMe to adopt from the clinical sphere into the DTC sphere. Instead, 23andMe is at the forefront of APOE disclosure and must make thoughtful decisions about what and how to disclose. In many ways, 23andMe is capably handling this. Access to these results is entirely optional, and they are "locked" behind a message warning of possible psychological discomfort and indicating the limits of current clinical care. If one proceeds to access those results, he or she will read that APOE speaks to only part of an individual's risk for AD and that other factors also influence the chances of developing it. Yet, I would suggest that 23andMe is presently providing inadequate guidance about things that can and should be done in the aftermath of learning that you carry an ε4 allele (or two). One way to reconcile the obvious tension between paternalism and individuals' right to know their genetic risk is to provide genetic risk information in concert with robust materials addressing what to do with it, particularly around future planning and sharing.

It would, of course, be inappropriate and impractical for 23andMe to be prescriptive, given the range of values and interests consumers may have. Yet, given the state of empirical evidence on APOE disclosure, it would be possible for 23andMe to outline what things people typically consider and what they generally do with their APOE information. Moreover, 23andMe could point them to resources where they can learn more. Just as they provide citations for articles on genetic risk, they can point to relevant literature on the impact of disclosure both before and after testing. This provision of information would be better for consumers and would increase the value of what 23andMe sells.

AD is an outlier among the conditions for which 23andMe offers health predisposition reports. With perhaps the exception of Parkinson's disease, the other health-related variants for which 23andMe presently tests are linked to serious conditions that are not as stigmatized, that do not implicate identity to the same extent, and for which there are meaningful clinical interventions. For instance, a woman who learns she has a BRCA1/2 gene mutation can seek breast cancer screening at an earlier age, more frequently, or have a prophylactic mastectomy. This outlier status makes APOE and AD an excellent case study for testing our intuitions, identifying best practices, and assuaging our concerns about DTC-GT more broadly. If we can handle this hard case and adequately balance disclosure and protection, surely we can also handle the easier ones.

VI CONCLUSION

Going forward, we can reasonably expect an increase in both the genetic health risks for which DTC testing is available and also in the number of companies providing testing. To paraphrase a familiar expression, we cannot put the spit back in the bottle. There are a number of ethical and legal considerations that will gain urgency as uptake of DTC-GT increases.

My proposal here, though, focuses narrowly on what consumers are buying. We aren't losing our minds to allow DTC-GT for AD. If, however, people fear losing their minds to AD (and they do), DTC-GT companies would do well to sell them more than simply a count of their ε4 alleles. They should also sell ways to make use of that information.

16

Investigative Genetic Genealogy and the Problem of Familial Forensic Identification

Natalie Ram[*]

I INTRODUCTION

Since the April 2018 arrest of the alleged Golden State Killer,[1] law enforcement investigators have made arrests in a remarkable string of cold cases.[2] In dozens of cases, investigators compared preserved crime DNA to other DNA profiles in an online genealogy database.[3] These searches, in turn, uncovered partial genetic matches to known but distant genetic relatives of a putative suspect. Through sleuthing in the resulting family tree or trees, investigators have been able to identify

* This work is supported by a Greenwall Faculty Scholars grant. Many thanks to I. Glenn Cohen, David Jaros, Margot Kaminski, Jennifer Lynch, Nicholson Price, Sonja Ralston, Neil Richards, Jessica Roberts, Carmel Shachar, Jake Sherkow, and Matthew Tokson. This chapter benefitted from workshops at the Privacy Law Scholars Conference at the University of California Berkeley Law School and the Health Law Professors conference at Loyola Chicago School of Law. All errors are my own.

1 See Benjamin Oreskes et al., False Starts in Search for Golden State Killer Reveal the Pitfalls of DNA Testing, L.A. Times (May 4, 2018, 5:00 AM), http://www.latimes.com/local/lanow/la-me-ln-golden-state-killer-dna-20180504-story.html.

2 See Peter Aldhous, The Golden State Killer Case Has Spawned A New Forensic Science Industry, BuzzFeed (Feb. 15, 2019, 12:43 PM), https://www.buzzfeednews.com/article/peteraldhous/genetic-genealogy-dna-business-parabon-bode ("Since May, [Parabon Nanolabs] has identified suspects in 36 cold cases, according to its lead genealogist, CeCe Moore."); Heather Murphy, How an Unlikely Family History Website Transformed Cold Case Investigations, N.Y. Times (Oct. 15, 2018), https://www.nytimes.com/2018/10/15/science/gedmatch-genealogy-cold-cases.html (noting at least fifteen cases in which a GEDmatch DNA match "provided essential clues leading to a suspect in a murder or sexual assault case"); Emily Shapiro, She Was Sexually Assaulted and Killed in 1973. Now Genetic Genealogy Identified a Suspect., ABC News (Feb. 28, 2020), https://abcnews.go.com/US/sexually-assaulted-killed-1973-now-genetic-genealogy-identified/story?id=69281238 (reporting that, since April 2018, "over 100 suspects have been identified through the technology, according to Parabon NanoLabs Chief Genetic Genealogist CeCe Moore").

3 See Heather Murphy, Genealogists Turn to Cousins' DNA and Family Trees to Crack Five More Cold Cases, N.Y. Times (June 27, 2018), https://www.nytimes.com/2018/06/27/science/dna-family-trees-cold-cases.html (identifying five cases in which arrests were made or identities revealed using a "path from cousins to suspect" or "to identity"); Laurel Wamsley, In Hunt For Golden State Killer, Investigators Uploaded His DNA To Genealogy Site, NPR (Apr. 27, 2018, 7:31 PM), https://www.npr.org/sections/thetwo-way/2018/04/27/606624218/in-hunt-for-golden-state-killer-investigators-uploaded-his-dna-to-genealogy-site.

suspects for investigation and, in some instances, arrest, prosecution, and conviction.[4]

Law enforcement interest in using consumer genetics platforms to solve more crimes rapidly materialized and continues to grow. Parabon Nanolabs, the first private company to capitalize on law enforcement interest in genetic genealogy, claims that it has already identified more than one hundred suspects since the Golden State Killer arrest.[5] Meanwhile, America's largest forensic DNA testing company, Bode Technology, announced in February 2019 that it would also begin selling an investigative genetic genealogy service to law enforcement.[6]

On the database front, law enforcement has extended its reach as well. GEDmatch, the first consumer genetic platform utilized for law enforcement investigations,[7] has, by now, largely converted from a hobbyist's genealogy site to a law enforcement partner. In December 2019, GEDmatch announced its sale to Verogen, a private for-profit company with ties to the FBI.[8] By that time, two other consumer genetics platforms had already joined GEDmatch in cooperating with law enforcement to facilitate criminal investigations. In January 2019, FamilyTreeDNA acknowledged that it had quietly been working with the FBI for nearly a year to sequence and compare crime scene DNA evidence to the genetic profiles in its own database.[9] FamilyTreeDNA has since formalized and expanded its law enforcement program. And, in October 2019, Othram, a forensic genetics

[4] See Justin Jouvenal, To Find Alleged Golden State Killer, Investigators First Found His Great-Great-Great-Grandparents, Wash. Post (Apr. 30, 2018, 6:22 PM), https://www.washingtonpost.com/local/public-safety/to-find-alleged-golden-state-killer-investigators-first-found-his-great-great-great-grandparents/2018/04/30/3c865fe7-dfcc-4a0e-b6b2-0bec548d501f_story.html; Heather Murphy, Genealogy Sites Have Helped Identify Suspects. Now They've Helped Convict One, N.Y. Times, July 2, 2019, https://www.nytimes.com/2019/07/01/us/dna-genetic-genealogy-trial.html.

[5] See Shapiro, supra note 2; Natalie Ram, The U.S. May Soon Have a De Facto National DNA Database, Slate (Mar, 19, 2019, 7:30 AM), https://slate.com/technology/2019/03/national-dna-database-law-enforcement-genetic-genealogy.html. Although Parabon is a private entity, its conduct is properly attributable to the government. Law enforcement agencies pay Parabon for its genealogical genetic sleuthing and make DNA extracted from crime scene evidence available for its analysis and use. See also Frequently Asked Questions (FAQs) about Snapshot, Parabon Nanolabs, https://snapshot.parabon-nanolabs.com/faq (last visited Feb. 22, 2020).

[6] See Aldhous, supra note 2.

[7] Id.

[8] See Nila Bala, We're Entering a New Phase in Law Enforcement's Use of Consumer Genetic Data, Slate (Dec. 19, 2019, 7:30 AM), https://slate.com/technology/2019/12/gedmatch-verogen-genetic-genealogy-law-enforcement.html; Ed Cara, A Controversial DNA Database Used to Solve Crimes Has Gone Commercial, Gizmodo (Dec. 10, 2019, 1:50 PM), https://gizmodo.com/a-controversial-dna-database-used-to-solve-crimes-has-g-1840341074.

[9] See Salvador Hernandez, One of the Biggest At-Home DNA Testing Companies Is Working with the FBI, Buzzfeed (Jan. 31, 2019, 8:52 PM), https://www.buzzfeednews.com/article/salvadorhernandez/family-tree-dna-fbi-investigative-genealogy-privacy; Letter from Bennett Greenspan, President, FamilyTreeDNA.com, to Customers (Feb. 3, 2019), https://mailchi.mp/familytreedna/letter-to-customers?e=[UNIQID].

firm, launched DNASolves, a database to which individuals can contribute their genetic profiles explicitly, and solely, for law enforcement use.[10]

Proponents of using consumer genetics platforms to investigate and solve crimes have argued that the genetic data on which those investigations rely has been voluntarily uploaded and shared. The CEO of Parabon Nanolabs has emphasized that investigative use of consumer genetics platforms uses only "voluntary data,"[11] while the Parabon website explains that its genetic genealogy service "compar[es] a DNA sample to a database of DNA from volunteer participants."[12] In a recently issued interim policy governing federal use of investigative genetic genealogy, the US Department of Justice has similarly explained that this technique compares crime scene DNA profiles "against the genetic profiles of individuals who have voluntarily submitted their biological samples or entered their genetic profiles into" genetic genealogy services.[13] Meanwhile, both GEDmatch and FamilyTreeDNA have made the voluntary sharing of genetic data with law enforcement an explicit part of their platforms, adopting law enforcement matching options that users can opt out of, or into, should they wish to do so.[14]

Yet, in nearly every case thus far announced, the individual ultimately arrested did not himself upload his identifiable genetic information to a consumer genetics platform. Rather, he was identified through a match between crime scene DNA and the profile of a genetic relative.[15] In many instances, including in the case of the

10 See DNASolves, https://dnasolves.com (last visited Apr. 22, 2020).

11 Hearing on H.B. 30 before the H. Comm. on the Judiciary, 2019 Leg., 440th Sess. (Md. 2019) (statement of Dr. Steven Armentrout, CEO, Parabon Nanolabs), http://mgahouse.maryland.gov/mga/play/03249de3-3b03-4ed5-b4c9-3f25d8f87267/?catalog/03e481c7-8a42-4438-a7da-93ff74bdaa4c%20.

12 Snapshot Genetic Genealogy, Parabon Nanolabs (emphasis added), https://snapshot.parabon-nanolabs.com/intro (last visited Feb. 22, 2020).

13 U.S. Dep't of Justice, Interim Policy, Forensic Genetic Genealogical DNA Analysis and Searching 3 (2019), https://www.justice.gov/olp/page/file/1204386/download.

14 See Natalie Ram, Genetic Privacy after *Carpenter*, 105 Va. L. Rev. 1357, 1362–63 (2019) (describing these law enforcement options), Natalie Ram & Jessica L. Roberts, Forensic Genealogy and the Power of Defaults, 37 Nature Biotechnology 707 (2019) (comparing law enforcement matching options and the voluntariness of opt-in, versus opt-out, controls).

15 See, e.g., Alex Horton, A Suspected Killer Eluded Capture for 25 Years. Then Investigators Got His Aunt's DNA, Wash. Post (Feb. 17, 2019, 12:09 PM), https://www.washingtonpost.com/crime-law/2019/02/16/suspected-killer-eluded-capture-years-then-investigators-got-his-aunts-dna/ ("A forensic genealogist prepared a report on Dec. 18, comparing the suspect's genetic material from the crime scene to likely relatives. A woman's DNA profile emerged in the search. Investigators found their link: She was an aunt of Downs's."); J. D. Capelouto & Zachary Hansen, 21 Years Later, Police Make Arrest in Shooting Death of Fulton County Woman, Atlanta J.-Const. (Nov. 1, 2018), https://www.ajc.com/news/years-later-police-make-arrest-shooting-death-fulton-county-woman/BDCqr2HASqidoaUhURqV1 J/ ("Detectives sent the evidence to a DNA testing company, Parabon NanoLabs, which found a similar strand of DNA in their system from someone who was trying to find out about their family ancestry. Investigators discovered it was one of Lee's relatives, the news station reported."); Jocelyn Kaiser, We Will Find You: DNA Search Used to Nab Golden State Killer Can Home in on about 60% of White Americans, Science (Oct. 11, 2018, 2:00 PM), https://www.sciencemag.org/news/2018/10/we-will-find-you-dna-search-used-nab-golden-state-killer-can-home-about-60-white (reporting that, in the Golden State Killer investigation, "[s]earching

Golden State Killer, the genetic relative whose DNA and identity was available to police was a distant one.[16] In other words, the individuals identified as suspects did not voluntarily upload their genetic data to a consumer genetics platform. Rather, sufficient genetic data to identify them was uploaded without their knowledge or consent by a genetic relative – one with whom the suspect might share little or no social relationship and over whom the suspect could exercise little, if any, control.

Indeed, voluntariness is a poor fit for genetic relationships. I have argued elsewhere that individuals may knowingly and voluntarily consent to law enforcement use of their DNA.[17] The use of genetic data to identify genetic relatives as targets for investigation, however, raises significant and varied ethical and legal questions – and such use ultimately should be rejected.

This chapter unpacks the disjunction between genetic relatedness and voluntariness, and the challenges that disjunction poses for law enforcement use of consumer genetics platforms. While resolving cold cases and bringing wrongdoers to justice is laudable, genetic genealogy's reliance on matches between genetic relatives should prompt serious questions about whose identifying genetic data is included in law enforcement searches and with what justification. Section II exposes how the assertion of voluntariness on which proponents have grounded law enforcement use of consumer genetics platforms is mistaken on both intrinsic and practical grounds when it comes to genetic relatives, and how the rise of genetic genealogy compounds this involuntariness by dramatically expanding the web of genetic identifiability. Section III argues that this disjunction is both ethically and legally problematic. Section IV then offers a path forward, permitting law enforcement in some instances to use genetic data stored on consumer genetics platforms – but only to seek direct identifications.

II THE MISMATCH BETWEEN VOLUNTARINESS AND FAMILIAL DNA

Genetic data that can be used to identify and learn about an individual is shared in involuntary, immutable, and unmanageable ways. This makes assertions of voluntary conduct inapposite when law enforcement seeks to investigate genetic relatives of those who have shared their DNA on a consumer genetics platform. Section A explains that identifiable genetic data is nearly always shared among genetic relatives in ways we both do not choose and cannot change. Section B explores how the ever-widening web of genetic genealogy makes an individual's ability to control her genetic privacy a practical impossibility.

GEDmatch's nearly 1 million profiles revealed several relatives who were the equivalent to third cousins to the crime scene DNA linked to the Golden State Killer"); Murphy, supra note 3 (identifying five additional cases in which arrests were made or identities revealed using a "path from cousins to suspect" or "to identity").

16 See Kaiser, supra note 15 (third cousin); Murphy, supra note 3 (first cousin once removed; "two second cousins and two third cousins once removed;" and second cousins).

17 See Ram, supra note 14.

A *Intrinsic Constraints on Voluntariness*

All human beings are more than 99 percent genetically identical, with even unrelated individuals differing by only hundredths of a percent at the genomic level.[18] Yet that small proportion of differentiating DNA encodes a wide range of variability in human phenotype, health risks, and other information. Most salient for present purposes, the small proportion of human genetic variability is nonetheless sufficient to identify a particular individual.[19]

Individually identifying genetic variations do not, however, spring forth from the ether. Rather, they are inherited in predictable patterns. Children inherit 50 percent of their genetic material – and hence roughly 50 percent of their genetic variations – from each of their genetic parents.[20] Siblings who share the same parents are statistically likely to share about fifty percent of their genetic variations as well, though the particular mixture of parental DNA that each sibling inherits will be distinct.[21] More distant relatives will be statistically likely to have smaller proportions of genetic variations in common. Half-siblings are likely to share roughly 25 percent of their genetic variations, as are genetically related grandparents and grandchildren. First cousins are expected to share 12.5 percent of their genetic variations due to relatedness, while first cousins once-removed will be roughly 6.25 percent genetically similar. Genetic relatedness in second cousins drops to 3.125 percent and to less than 1 percent for third cousins.[22]

But, much of this sharing of identifying or identifiable genetic variation occurs without any voluntary conduct or choice. Genetic similarity arises as a product of biology. As Erin Murphy has put it: "[W]e all well know that we do not choose the families into which we are born."[23] Parents might, in some sense, be said to "volunteer" to share their genetic data with another by choosing to procreate. Children, however, cannot be said to have chosen their genetic parents. Nor do individuals in any real sense "choose" how many siblings their parents give them, or whether they have aunts, uncles, or cousins – or how many and what arrangement of each.

18 See Genetics vs. Genomics Fact Sheet, Nat'l Human Genome Res. Inst., https://www.genome.gov/19016904/faq-about-genetic-and-genomic-science/ (last visited Feb. 22, 2020).

19 See Natalie Ram, Fortuity and Familial Forensic Identification, 63 Stan. L. Rev. 751, 757 (2011).

20 See Bruce R. Korf, Human Genetics and Genomics 36 (3d ed. 2007). Moreover, "the vast majority of the differences . . . within an individual are inherited, rather than resulting from de novo mutation." T. Strachan & Andrew P. Read, Human Molecular Genetics 316 (3d ed. 2004).

21 See Korf, supra note 20, at 36. The exception here, of course, is identical twins, who are expected to inherit the same parental genetic mixture. See Daniel L. Hartl, Essential Genetics: A Genomics Perspective 477 (6th ed. 2014) (noting identical twins are genetically identical because they arise from splitting of single fertilized egg). Identical twins may, however, differ in a small number of genetic variations arising from de novo mutations occurring early in fetal development. See Carl Zimmer, One Twin Committed the Crime – but Which One? A New DNA Test Can Finger the Culprit, N.Y. Times (Mar. 1, 2019), https://www.nytimes.com/2019/03/01/science/twins-dna-crime-paternity.html.

22 See Natalie Ram, DNA by the Entirety, 115 Colum. L. Rev. 873, 901–02 (2015).

23 Erin Murphy, Relative Doubt: Familial Searches of DNA Databases, 109 Mich. L. Rev. 291, 336 (2010).

Moreover, these genetic ties are immutable. Large-scale gene therapy remains, for now, in the realm of science fiction. Accordingly, the identifying DNA an individual inherits from her parents is the identifying DNA that she will have for life.[24] This means that individuals cannot sever their ties to genetic relatives, no matter how limited their social relationship may be. The ability to cut ties is a crucial tool for mediating relationships within organizations and groups.[25] Yet it is simply unavailable in the context of genetic relatedness.[26]

These features – of intrinsic involuntariness and immutability – render genetic relatedness unlike most other relationships of data sharing in which individuals find themselves. Genetic relatedness is stickier even than the social relationships we have with our family members. Although minors may be limited in their ability to sever social relationships with their parents and siblings, adults are capable of keeping family members at arm's-length. Estrangement may exact a significant social or psychological toll on an individual, yet it is apparently not uncommon. One recent study of undergraduate students reported that more than 40 percent of participants reported experiencing an estrangement from either immediate or more distant family members.[27] In an estrangement, a family member might well not know about one's new girlfriend, one's comings and goings, and the like. And yet, that family member could still serve as reliable as ever a genetic "informant" for the estranged individual.

Similarly, social media sharing typically provides greater opportunity for choice and exit than genetic relatedness, though the quality of online social ties may be less robust than social familial relationships. Consider Facebook. Relationships on this large social media platform depend on a voluntary decision by a user to become "friends" or otherwise connected with another user. Should a lack of trust subsequently develop, moreover, such relationships can be severed through "unfriending." Thus, some measure of meaningful voluntary conduct can be attributed to an individual identified by police as a target for investigation through social or social media ties.

But the same cannot be said of genetic relatedness. These ties are a product of biology, not choice, and they offer no ready means of escape. Accordingly, even if an individual whose cells have been sequenced and shared on a consumer genetics platform like GEDmatch can be said to have volunteered for forensic identification, no voluntariness can be attributed to the genetic relatives who may ultimately be investigated or arrested by means of that genetic tie.[28]

24 See Ram, supra note 22, at 903.

25 See Albert O. Hirschman, Exit, Voice, and Loyalty (1970).

26 See Natalie Ram, Assigning Rights and Protecting Interests: Constructing Ethical and Efficient Legal Rights in Human Tissue Research, 23 Harv. J.L. & Tech. 119, 129 (2009).

27 See Richard P. Conti, Family Estrangement: Establishing a Prevalence Rate, 3 J. Psychol. & Behav. Sci. 28, 28 (2015).

28 That a criminal wrongdoer may leave his DNA at the crime scene does not resolve the problem of involuntariness. After all, "a usable forensic identification requires two matching parts: a crime scene sample and a database profile that matches it. Suspects identified through familial searches cannot be said to have voluntarily shared their genetic profile in a database of known individuals, even if

B *Practical Constraints on Voluntariness*

Assertions of voluntariness are misplaced with respect to genetic relatedness not merely on intrinsic, biological grounds; voluntariness is also a practical impossibility in light of the reach of current genetic genealogical methods. That is, even for a person who is not actively involved in an estrangement, it is impracticable to expect that person to know about, monitor, and influence the ways in which each of her relatives shares genetic information that may be used to identify or learn about her.

Traditionally, familial forensic identification – law enforcement efforts to exploit familial genetic similarity to identify targets for investigation – was limited in scope. These efforts utilized genetic profiles housed in the nationally administered Combined DNA Index System (CODIS).[29] Pursuant to federal law, local, state, and federal DNA laboratories may enter lawfully obtained genetic profiles into the central CODIS database. CODIS profiles consist of genetic data drawn from thirteen to twenty loci in highly variable portions of noncoding DNA.[30] A complete match between crime scene DNA and an offender profile in the database is probative evidence that the matching offender committed the crime.[31]

But CODIS loci are not selected with familial identification in mind, and they are not well-suited to that use.[32] Indeed, courts have repeatedly emphasized the limited informational content of CODIS profiles.[33] As a result, although some states permit law enforcement use of a partial CODIS DNA match for purposes of familial investigation,[34] these identifications have focused almost exclusively on first-degree relatives: parents, children, and full siblings.[35] This does not make familial searching in CODIS unproblematic – after all, genetic relatedness remains involuntary in the intrinsic ways set out above. But familial forensic identification using

a genetic relative has." Natalie Ram et al., Genealogy Databases and the Future of Criminal Investigation, 360 Science 1078, 1079 (2018).

29 See Ram, supra note 22, at 881–83 (describing "familial searching" in official law enforcement-related DNA profiles).

30 See id.

31 See id. at 881.

32 See id. at 883.

33 See, e.g., Maryland v. King, 569 U.S. 435, 436 (2013) ("[T]he only difference between DNA analysis and the accepted use of fingerprint databases is the unparalleled accuracy DNA provides."); United States v. Weikert, 504 F.3d 1, 3–4 (1st Cir. 2007) ("Profiling ... [uses] only so-called 'junk DNA,'" which "differs from one individual to the next and ... can be used for ... identification but which was 'purposely selected because [it is] not associated with any known physical or medical characteristics' and 'do[es] not control or influence the expression of any trait.'" (quoting H.R. Rep. No. 106-900(I), at 27 (2000)); Nicholas v. Goord, 430 F.3d 652, 670 (2d Cir. 2005) ("The junk DNA that is extracted has, at present, no known function, except to accurately and uniquely establish identity.").

34 See Ram, supra note 19 at 767.

35 See Ram, supra note 22 at 902; see Snapshot Kinship Inference, Parabon Nanolabs, https://snapshot.parabon-nanolabs.com/#kinship ("Traditional STR-based kinship analysis is limited to distinguishing parent/offspring relationships, often yielding inconclusive results for siblings or other second-degree relatives.").

CODIS loci is significantly limited in the scope of individuals it may indirectly implicate through a partial DNA match.

Genetic data generated or housed on consumer genetics platforms, by contrast, sweeps much more broadly. Consumer genetics platforms typically use wide ranging genetic sequence data, drawn from hundreds of thousands of DNA data points.[36] Companies like 23andMe, as well as platforms like GEDmatch that make secondary use of their data, typically examine "600,000 variations of individual DNA letters, known as SNPs (pronounced 'snips') for single nucleotide polymorphisms."[37] As one advocate of using genealogical DNA data to help reidentify crime victims explained, "[t]he statistics you can do on 600,000 SNPs are so much more powerful than statistics you can do on 20 [CODIS loci]."[38]

These genetic profiles yield an extensive web of genetic relatives through whom an individual may potentially be identified. Parabon Nanolabs advertises that it can "detect relatedness out to 9th-degree relatives (fourth cousins)," while determining "the precise degree of the relationship ... out to 6th-degree relatives (second cousins once removed)."[39]

Such broad identifiability makes large swaths of American residents genetically identifiable to law enforcement, whether or not they have themselves participated in a consumer genetics platform. According to one recent study, at least 60 percent of Americans of European descent are already within investigative reach.[40] With access to consumer genetics data for as little as 2 percent of the US population, as many as 90 percent of Americans of European descent would be identifiable through a third cousin or closer.[41] As law enforcement has already gained the cooperation of at least two consumer genetics platforms, GEDmatch and FamilyTreeDNA, that

36 See Tina Hesman Saey, New Genetic Sleuthing Tools Helped Track Down the Golden State Killer Suspect, Sci. News (Apr. 29, 2018, 9:49 AM), https://www.sciencenews.org/article/golden-state-killer-suspect-dna-genetic-genealogys.

37 Id.

38 Id.

39 Snapshot Kinship Inference, supra note 35.

40 See Yaniv Erlich et al., Re-Identification of Genomic Data Using Long Range Familial Searches, 362 Science 690 (2018) (demonstrating through statistical modeling that more than 60 percent of individuals of European-descent may be findable through a genealogical genetic database of as few as 1.3 million people). Consumer genetics platforms are disproportionately composed of individuals of European descent. See Natalie Ram et al., Genealogy Databases and the Future of Criminal Investigation, 360 Science 1078 (2018). But this does not limit the reach of law enforcement use of these platforms to white Americans. In light of America's history of slavery, and the sexual violence that often accompanied it, many African American individuals may also be implicitly implicated by law enforcement use of consumer genetics platforms. Moreover, as Elizabeth Warren's experience with claims of Native American ancestry demonstrate, mixture between European and Native American populations in the United States may expose many Native Americans to identification through genetic genealogy as well. See G. F., The Controversies over Claims to Native American Ancestry, Economist (Oct. 25, 2018), https://www.economist.com/the-economist-explains/2018/10/25/the-controversies-over-claims-to-native-american-ancestry.

41 See Erlich et al., supra note 40, at 690.

two percent figure is rapidly coming to fruition. Together, these platforms house genetic profiles from at least two million individuals,[42] while more than twenty-six million people have already made use of some consumer genetic service.[43]

The voluntary sharing of genetic data by a single individual acts as "a beacon who illuminates 300 people around you."[44] The web of identifiability may be even broader. According to 23andMe, "[u]nder a simple model where a family has 2–3 children, you would have 190 third cousins, 940 fourth cousins and a whopping 4,700 fifth cousins."[45]

Whether the correct number of genetic relatives whose DNA may enable law enforcement to infer the identity of an unknown individual is 300 or 940, in many instances, an individual will not know the identity of each of these many distant genetic relatives. 23andMe has a term for this concept as well: "cryptic (or non-obvious) relatives."[46] Attributing voluntariness to an individual's implicit identifiability in a consumer genetics database due to her failure to prevent genetic relatives' participation is fallacious. It is simply unmanageable for an individual to know of, monitor, and persuade each of those relatives to protect her genetic privacy, if that is what she desires.

III EXPLOITING INVOLUNTARY GENETIC TIES IS PROBLEMATIC

It is ethically and legally problematic for law enforcement to make use of genetic data that is not, in any sense, voluntarily shared. Section A unpacks the ethical dimensions of accepting involuntary relatedness as a basis for genetic identification by law enforcement.

Section B explains that the absence of any meaningful voluntary action by implicitly identifiable genetic relatives raises significant constitutional concerns about law enforcement use of genetic genealogy.

A *Ethical Concerns*

As set forth above, proponents of law enforcement use of genetic genealogy to investigate crimes have argued that such use is appropriate because the genetic data housed in consumer genetics databases is voluntarily placed there by knowing users.[47]

42 See Ram, supra note 14, at 1364.

43 See Antonio Regalado, More than 26 Million People Have Taken an At-Home Ancestry Test, MIT Tech. Rev. (Feb. 11, 2019), https://www.technologyreview.com/s/612880/more-than-26-million-people-have-taken-an-at-home-ancestry-test/.

44 See Oreskes et al., supra note 1 (quoting Yaniv Erlich, Chief Science Officer of MyHeritage.com and Assistant Professor at Columbia University).

45 The Method Behind the Relative Finder Tool, 23andMe: Blog (Apr. 19, 2012), https://blog.23andme.com/news/announcements/how-many-relatives-do-you-have/.

46 Id.

47 See supra notes 11–14 and accompanying text.

Voluntary sharing of data, in other words, is the rule for inclusion – the basis for appropriate law enforcement access to data.

But identification of genetic relatives whose profiles are not directly in a consumer genetics database of known users flunks this rule for inclusion. Genetic relatedness is involuntary, immutable, and unmanageable for purposes of genetic privacy. Genetic relatives are findable through consumer genetics platforms despite a lack of voluntary sharing of their genetic data on the platform.

This suggests that the involuntary inclusion of genetic relatives in law enforcement searches of consumer genetics databases is without justification. If the rule undergirding law enforcement use is voluntariness, and implicitly included genetic relatives are included involuntarily, then they do not fit the rule. Their inclusion in law enforcement efforts is therefore inappropriate.

Moreover, the result of familial inclusion in genetic genealogy for law enforcement use amounts to a de facto national DNA database – or something rapidly approaching one. Twenty-six million people have already made use of some consumer genetic service, and consumer genetics platforms continue to grow.[48] By one estimate, "[i]f the pace continues, the gene troves could hold data on the genetic makeup of more than 100 million people within 24 months."[49] Yet law enforcement access to as little as four million consumer genetics profiles could make 90 percent of Americans of European descent identifiable through a third cousin or closer.[50] A de facto national DNA database is on the horizon, if it is not already here.

This, too, is ethically problematic as no US jurisdiction has indicated that a comprehensive DNA database of residents would be appropriate.[51] Every state and the federal government has enacted legislation identifying whose DNA is subject to routine government search for crime detection purposes, and each has limited its database to some subset of individuals arrested or convicted of crimes.[52] While these databases have grown in size and scope over time, no jurisdiction to date has proposed using DNA from most or all of its residents for law enforcement purposes.[53]

Indeed, there is good reason to believe that states and citizens would not be willing to authorize a comprehensive DNA database for law enforcement use. Americans

48 See Regalado, supra note 43.

49 Id. Both 23andMe and AncestryDNA experienced declines in growth in 2019, perhaps in part due to growing law enforcement use of consumer genetics platforms and corresponding consumer concern. See Nicole Wetsman, Layoffs at Genetic Testing Companies Reflect the Changing Market, Verge (Feb. 6, 2020), https://www.theverge.com/2020/2/6/21126360/23andme-ancestry-layoffs-genetics-dna-market-privacy.

50 See Erlich et al., supra note 40, at 690; see also Ram, supra note 5.

51 Some scholars have advocated for an official comprehensive DNA database, arguing that this would be preferable to a de facto database of substantially similar reach. See J. W. Hazel et al., Is It Time for a Universal Genetic Forensic Database?, 362 Science 6417 (2018).

52 See Ram, supra note 14, at 1375–77.

53 See id. at 1377.

remain concerned about genetic privacy,[54] despite apparent public support for investigations like the one in the Golden State Killer case.[55] That concern was apparent in recent opposition to a proposed Arizona bill that would have drastically expanded the scope of the state's official DNA database to include "anyone who has to be fingerprinted by the state for a job, to volunteer in certain positions or for a myriad of other reasons."[56] The bill ignited widespread opposition, including from the Arizona Police Association,[57] and it was quickly amended twice and replaced with largely unrelated content.[58]

If an authorized comprehensive DNA database would be inappropriate as a matter of policy, the de facto accomplishment of the same end by involuntary genetic associations should be similarly inappropriate.[59] No existing rule for database inclusion justifies sweeping involuntarily associated genetic relatives into law enforcement searches. And the presence of more limited rules for database inclusion implies that individuals not fitting those rules are or ought to be excluded.[60] Involuntary genetic relatedness upsets that maxim. Familial forensic identification utilizing consumer genetics platforms is therefore unjustified.

B *Legal Concerns*

The implicit and involuntary inclusion of genetic relatives in law enforcement searches of consumer genetics platforms may also be legally problematic. As set forth above, such use is arguably inconsistent with established legislative frameworks about whose genetic data ought to be available to law enforcement for routine database search.[61] Existing state statutory schemes establishing and regulating official law enforcement DNA databases might impliedly preempt law enforcement aggregation of or access to other DNA repositories, particularly where such access cannot independently be justified.[62]

54 See David J. Kaufman et al., Public Opinion about the Importance of Privacy in Biobank Research, 85 Am. J. Human Genetics 643 (2009); see also Benjamin Berkman, You Share Your Genetic Data at Your Own Risk, Slate (Mar. 15, 2019, 1:28 PM), https://slate.com/technology/2019/03/consumer-dna-testing-disclosure-risks.html.

55 See Christi J. Guerrini et al., Should Police Have Access to Genetic Genealogy Databases? Capturing the Golden State Killer and Other Criminals Using a Controversial New Forensic Technique, 16 PLos Biology e2006906 (2018).

56 Bree Burkitt, You May Soon Have to Give Your DNA to the State and Pay $250 for the Privilege, Republic (Feb. 19, 2019, 5:00 AM), https://www.azcentral.com/story/news/politics/arizona/2019/02/19/arizona-bill-would-create-massive-statewide-dna-database/2873930002/.

57 See id.

58 See Bree Burkitt, Unrecognizable Version of DNA Bill Advances, Focuses on Rape Kits, Republic (Feb. 20, 2019, 6:16 PM), https://www.azcentral.com/story/news/politics/legislature/2019/02/20/arizona-dna-database-legislation-new-version-senate-bill-advances-rape-kit/2918578002/.

59 See David M. Jaros, Preempting the Police, 55 B.C.L. Rev. 1149 (2014).

60 See Clifton Williams, "Expressio Unius Est Exclusio Alterius," 15 Marq. L. Rev. 191 (1931).

61 See supra notes 51–58 and accompanying text (describing statutes).

62 See Jaros, supra note 59, at 1182–87.

Moreover, law enforcement's use of consumer genetics data to identify genetic relatives as targets for investigation begs a more fundamental constitutional question. The Supreme Court has interpreted the Fourth Amendment of the US Constitution to protect individuals against unreasonable government intrusion upon an "expectation of privacy ... that society is prepared to recognize as reasonable."[63] In applying this test, the Court has typically excluded from constitutional concern information that an individual knowingly or voluntarily shared with a third party – a rule known as the third-party doctrine.[64]

Courts have already held or implied that genetic data is information in which an individual may have a reasonable expectation of privacy.[65] The voluntariness rationale that proponents of law enforcement use of genetic genealogy have advanced similarly implies that, but for that voluntary sharing, it would be inappropriate for law enforcement to coerce or compel access to an individual's identifiable genetic data. That is, it would intrude on an individual's otherwise reasonable expectation of privacy regarding her genetic data.

But assumptions of either knowing or voluntary sharing of data are inapposite when applied to patterns of shared genetic data arising from relatedness. In the Supreme Court's recent *Carpenter* case, the court recognized that individuals maintain a reasonable expectation of privacy in their location information as revealed by cell-site location data, even though cell phone providers collect that data.[66] The court concluded that, among other things, the sharing of location data with one's cell phone provider was not really knowing or voluntary, given the ubiquity and necessity of the modern cell phone.[67] That same conclusion is even more warranted where genetic relatedness is at issue. Even if an individual may typically have a "reduced expectation of privacy in information knowingly shared with another,"[68] it is a practical impossibility for an individual to know of or monitor each of the hundreds of other individuals whose genetic data may illuminate her own.[69] "Neither does the second rationale underlying the third-party doctrine – voluntary exposure – hold up when it comes to" shared

63 Carpenter v. United States, 138 S. Ct. 2206, 2213 (2018) (internal quotation marks omitted); see also Katz v. United States, 389 U.S. 347, 361 (1967) (Harlan, J., concurring). This standard is frequently shortened to a "reasonable expectations of privacy" inquiry. See, e.g., Orin S. Kerr, An Equilibrium-Adjustment Theory of the Fourth Amendment, 125 Harv. L. Rev. 476, 533–34 (2011) (describing this as "the 'reasonable expectation of privacy' test").

64 See Smith v. Maryland, 442 U.S. 735, 744 (1979); United States v. Miller, 425 U.S. 435, 442 (1976). But see Carpenter 138 S. Ct. 2206 (holding that individuals retain an expectation of privacy in their cell-site location information, despite the collection of that data by their cell phone providers, because that collection is not really knowing or voluntary on the part of cell phone users).

65 See Maryland v. King, 569 U.S. 435 (2013); Ram, supra note 14, at 1380–91 (arguing that individuals have an expectation of privacy in their genetic data and that that expectation of privacy persists even if genetic data is shared with a third-party service provider, like a consumer genetics platform).

66 See Carpenter, 138 S. Ct. 2206.

67 Id. at 2219–20.

68 Id. at 2219.

69 See supra Section I.B.

identifiable genetic data.[70] As set forth above, identifiable genetic data among genetic relatives is shared involuntarily nearly all the time and always immutably.[71] In the absence of either knowing or voluntary sharing of data, the court has instead held that law enforcement access to private, sensitive data may run afoul of the Fourth Amendment.[72] That conclusion is warranted here too.

More broadly, voluntariness shapes Fourth Amendment doctrine in other ways. For instance, the doctrine of abandonment, which courts have held similarly negates an expectation of privacy, turns on some notion of volition – the "knowing exposure" of material or information to the public.[73] And the concept of third-party consent to search – as where a roommate consents to the search of a home[74] – similarly rests on the premise that co-occupants have "assumed the risk that one of their number might permit the common area to be searched."[75] But a genetic relative has not volunteered for anything and has "assumed" no such risk.

Accordingly, law enforcement's use of consumer genetics data to identify indirectly included genetic relatives as targets for investigation raises significant constitutional concerns.

IV A WAY FORWARD

In light of the ethical and legal challenges of familial forensic identification in the genetic genealogy sphere, courts, legislatures, and law enforcement must adapt and adopt a new way forward. In so doing, these legal actors would do well to consider how the law has adapted, and adapted around, another type of interdependent interests, that of tenancy by the entirety.

In earlier work, I have argued that the law of tenancy by the entirety offers a useful lens for thinking about the interdependent interests inherent in identifying genetic data.[76] Interests in tenancy by the entirety and in shared identifying genetic data

70 Carpenter, 138 S. Ct. at 2220.

71 See supra Section I.A.

72 See Carpenter, 138 S Ct. 2206; Ram, supra note 14, at 1372–75, 1380–91.

73 See Ram, supra note 22, at 905–06 (discussing abandonment); Elizabeth E. Joh, Reclaiming "Abandoned" DNA: The Fourth Amendment and Genetic Privacy, 100 Nw. U.L. Rev. 857, 865 (2006) (noting that the Fourth Amendment does not apply in cases where DNA is recovered from abandoned objects "'knowingly exposed' to the public"); *see also* United States v. Colbert, 474 F.2d 174, 176 (5th Cir. 1973) ("The issue is not abandonment in the strict property-right sense, but whether the person prejudiced by the search had voluntarily discarded, left behind, or otherwise relinquished his interest in the property in question so that he could no longer retain a reasonable expectation of privacy with regard to it ").

74 See Fernandez v. California, 571 U.S. 292 (2014) (holding that a co-occupant's consent to a search of shared premises prevails over an objecting co-occupant's refusal so long as the objector is not physically present at the time consent is given); Georgia v. Randolph, 547 U.S. 103, 106 (2006) (holding that "a physically present co-occupant's stated refusal to permit entry prevails" over another co-occupant's consent to a search of the shared premises).

75 Randolph, 547 U.S. at 110 (internal quotation marks omitted).

76 See Ram, supra note 22, at 906–38.

share foundational, structural, and historical kinship.[77] At the foundational level, both types of interests require conceptualizing two (or more) persons "as though they were one."[78] These (at least partial) unities of identity stem from different sources – one from legal fiction, the other from biological fact – but in both cases inextricable sharing is an essential component.[79] As a structural matter, modern tenancy by the entirety resolves the difficult task of "think[ing] about two persons as though they were one"[80] in favor of shared governance, rendering a unilateral encumbrance of the entireties property void.[81] If legal institutions hope to take seriously individuals' privacy interests in their identifiable genetic information, then they too should resolve conflicts about access to (involuntarily) shared identifiable genetic data in favor of shared governance and greater privacy.

Finally, the historical development of tenancy by the entirety commends it as a model for modernizing and expanding legal understandings of whose cells house "my" DNA. Tenancy by the entirety has experienced an arduous and ongoing process of ameliorating the role of women as entireties owners. For centuries, the law gave women no role in controlling entireties property in order to resolve the difficulty of "think[ing] about two persons as though they were one."[82] Under the modern majority rule, by contrast, both marital partners are equal, and a unilateral conveyance by either is void.[83]

To be sure, the tenancy by the entirety model is not a perfect fit for genetic relatedness in general, much less the sprawling family trees encountered in genetic genealogy. While involuntariness and immutability are key features that distinguish genetic relatedness, tenancy by the entirety is voluntarily undertaken, often only with substantial effort.[84] Tenancies by the entirety may also be severed, though this too requires substantial effort.[85] In addition, "tenancy by the entirety only ever requires mutual consent among two individuals, while those with interests in shared identifiable genetic information will inevitably be more numerous."[86] Where genetic genealogy is at issue, hundreds of individuals may be implicated by a single person's participation on a consumer genetics platform, and many of those individuals may be unknown to one another.[87]

77 See id. at 910, 910–18.

78 See John V. Orth, Tenancy by the Entirety: The Strange Career of the Common-Law Marital Estate, 1997 BYU L. Rev. 35, 40; Ram, supra note 22, at 914.

79 See Ram, supra note 22, at 910–11.

80 Orth, supra note 78, at 40.

81 See Ram, supra note 22, at 912.

82 Orth, supra note 78, at 40.

83 See Ram, supra note 22, at 917–18.

84 See id. at 914 (observing that "tenancies by the entirety may be burdensome to create, as they require five 'unities': time, title, interest, possession, and marriage").

85 See id. at 912 ("Tenancy by the entirety considers neither spouse to 'own any individual interest in the estate; rather it belong[s] to the couple', and therefore the estate may be severed only by divorce, joint conveyance, or conveyance from one co-owner to the other.").

86 Id. at 914.

87 See supra Section I.B.

Despite these shortcomings, however, utilizing the lens of tenancy by the entirety offers a principled way for thinking about complex interdependent interests, particularly with respect to the government's law enforcement mission. For instance, the government's forfeiture of a wrongdoer's interest in an entireties property must leave undisturbed the interest owned by an innocent spouse.[88] In the context of a criminal forfeiture of property involved in criminal activities, one court has explained that, because "entireties property may not be attached to satisfy the personal tax liability of a single spouse,"[89] "the government could not execute on a defendant's interest in a tenancy by the entireties while the interest was still intact, even if such interest was subject to forfeiture. To do so would burden the interests of . . . third party owners in the criminal forfeiture context."[90] Courts have reached similar results in civil forfeitures.[91] Moreover, the Supreme Court has implied that the civil forfeiture of property used in criminal activity without any voluntary action by an innocent owner would raise constitutional concerns.[92] Courts have reached these conclusions despite the fact that doing so may deprive the government of a valuable resource and may be more administratively difficult to realize.

Looking to tenancy by the entirety as a model for resolving privacy claims surrounding familial forensic identification suggests that government access to genetic data from a voluntary source need not – and should not – entail government access to involuntarily implicated genetic relatives. Although the government may be permitted to "forfeit" or use data properly surrendered by a known individual, that forfeiture ought not reach involuntarily implicated others, who are the equivalent of uninvolved third-party owners or innocent spouses in the forfeiture doctrine. On this understanding, a law enforcement search of a consumer genetics platform for a direct match between a crime scene profile and user genetic data might be appropriate, but a search for partial, indirect matches would not.

88 See Ram, supra note 22, at 920–25 (discussing judicial treatment of criminal and forfeitures of entireties properties).

89 United States v. 2525 Leroy Lane, 910 F.2d 343, 350 (6th Cir. 1990).

90 United States v. Kennedy, 201 F.3d 1324, 1332 (11th Cir. 2000) (describing 2525 Leroy Lane); see also United States v. Jimerson, 5 F.3d 1453, 1454 (11th Cir. 1993) (explaining forfeiture against guilty husband did not affect his wife's interest in their property owned by tenancy by the entirety because she "continues to hold an indivisible one-half interest in the entire residence property").

91 See 2525 Leroy Lane, 910 F.2d at 350–51; Kennedy, 201 F.3d at 1332 (describing 2525 Leroy Lane as concluding that executing on entireties property "would burden the interests of 'innocent owners' in the civil forfeiture context, and of third party owners in the criminal forfeiture context" (internal citation omitted)); United States v. 1500 Lincoln Avenue, 949 F.2d 73, 78 (3d Cir. 1991) (holding that an innocent spouse who owns otherwise forfeitable property as a tenant by the entirety is entitled to retain the "right to full and exclusive use and possession of the property during her life, her protection against conveyance of or execution by third parties upon her husband's former interest, and her survivorship right").

92 See Calero-Toledo v. Pearson Yacht Leasing Co., 416 U.S. 663, 689 (1974) (reiterating that the Court's prior cases have "implied that it would be difficult to reject the constitutional claim of an owner whose property subjected to forfeiture had been taken from him without his privity or consent").

Such an approach finds support in the Supreme Court's recent *Carpenter* decision. As described above, *Carpenter* held that the government engages in a Fourth Amendment "search" when it seeks to access location information about an individual that is held by that individual's cell phone carrier.[93] Crucially, in so doing, *Carpenter* recognized that an individual can have an expectation of privacy in information that is deeply revealing about her, even if she has no formal property interest in the information itself. The Court emphasized that "property rights are not the sole measure of Fourth Amendment violations."[94] And it explained that, although cell-site location records "are generated for commercial purposes," and thus are most typically the property of the cell phone company, "that distinction does not negate Carpenter's anticipation of privacy in his physical location."[95] The principal dissent in *Carpenter*, in turn, most harshly criticized the majority for "unhing[ing] Fourth Amendment doctrine from the property-based concepts that have long grounded the analytic framework that pertains in these cases."[96]

Carpenter allows for the reality that individuals may have legitimate expectations of privacy in information that carries weighty privacy implications for them, even if that information is under another's control. That is true for cell-site location information, which creates a detailed record of an individual's movements and is maintained and controlled by one's cell phone company. It is equally true for identifiable genetic data, which is an involuntary record of one's identity and genetic relationships, as well as a wealth of potentially medically relevant information, yet is maintained and controlled at least in part by one's genetic relatives.[97] Moreover, *Carpenter* invites broader elaboration of constitutionally relevant expectations of privacy than ordinary property concepts might otherwise embrace. In so doing, *Carpenter* opens the door to the quasi-property concepts described under the tenancy by the entirety model. After all, that model advocates for recognizing that individuals may have a Fourth Amendment interest in genetic data that can be used to identify them – even if that data resides in another person's cells.[98] In this way, *Carpenter* too breathes new life into arguments about the privacy wrongs of familial forensic identification.

93 Carpenter v. United States, 138 S. Ct. 2206 (2018).

94 Id. at 2213 (internal quotation marks omitted).

95 Id. at 2217.

96 Id. at 2224 (Kennedy, J., dissenting); see also id. at 2226–27 (Kennedy, J., dissenting) ("individuals lack any protected Fourth Amendment interests in records that are possessed, owned, and controlled only by a third party"); id. at 2227–28 (Kennedy, J., dissenting) (criticizing the majority for failing to adhere to the principle that "the absence of property law analogues can be dispositive of privacy expectations").

97 See Ram, supra note 14, at 1377–80; Ram, supra note 22, at 920–29.

98 See Ram, supra note 22, at 920–29.

V CONCLUSION

Law enforcement has eagerly embraced the use of consumer genetics platforms to solve crimes, arguing that the data available on those platforms has been "voluntarily shared" and is therefore fair game.[99] But notions of voluntariness are misplaced where familial forensic identification is at issue. Identifiable genetic data is shared in intrinsically involuntary and immutable ways, and the reach of consumer genetics platforms in identifying individuals whose genetic data is not directly in the database of known users makes genetic relatedness unmanageable too.

That is a problem, as every individual thus far arrested based on law enforcement use of genetic genealogy methods has been the relative of a consumer genetics user, rather than a user himself. The disjunction between the voluntary sharing of genetic data on consumer genetics platforms and the involuntary sharing of genetic data among genetic relatives is both ethically and legally problematic. Yet an appropriate way forward may not at first appear apparent.

Turning to a tenancy-by-the-entirety framework, undergirded by renewed elaboration of appropriate Fourth Amendment expectations of privacy in shared data, suggests one possible response. Courts should recognize that individuals have meaningful interests in genetic data that can be used to learn about and identify them, even where that data resides in another person's cells. Familial forensic identification defies available justifications for database inclusion – whether based on voluntary sharing or criminal history.[100] The repurposing of powerful genetic genealogy methods for law enforcement use should not render those justifications meaningless. Even if a law enforcement search of a consumer genetics platform for a direct match between a crime scene profile and known user genetic data is appropriate – because such data really is "voluntarily shared" – a familial forensic search and identification should not be.

99 See supra notes 11–14 and accompanying text.

100 See supra Section II.A.

PART V

The Impact of Genetic Information

Introduction to Part V

Melissa Uveges

The chapters in Part V of this volume, "The Impact of Genetic Information," highlight the implications of genetic testing for individuals, families, and health care providers. Each chapter addresses unique challenges posed by genetic tests and offers ways of thinking about these challenges. In some cases, the authors use an ethics-based approach to address questions raised by genetic testing information. Other chapters concentrate on regulatory mechanisms, which could ensure greater oversight of genetic testing implementation. Overall, Part V focuses the reader on the responsible use of genetic and genomic testing.

In the first chapter, *An Ethical Framework for Genetic Counseling in the Genomic Era*, Leila Jamal presents a novel framework designed to guide genetic counselors in making recommendations to patients who undergo genetic testing. The development of this framework is in response to the ever-broadening scope of the genetic counselors' role, against a backdrop of an historical emphasis within the genetic counseling (GC) profession on nondirectiveness. With her framework, Jamal suggests that genetic counselors have ethical license to offer more directive recommendations to patients in certain circumstances, especially when recommendations are based on clinical expertise; informed by patients' emotions, preferences, and values; and when relevant, their family members' input. Jamal's work offers the GC profession one useful path forward when faced with real-world problems, whether occurring in the clinical, research, or industry setting.

Emily Qian's chapter, *Physician-Mediated Elective Whole Genome Sequencing Tests: Impacts on Informed Consent* narrows in on the impact of genomic testing for consumers in a preventive medicine context. Qian first presents findings from a study examining characteristics of health care providers involved in authorizing physician-mediated consumer driven (PMCD) elective whole genome sequencing (WGS) through Veritas Genetics, a consumer genetic testing laboratory. From the study results, which revealed that mostly primary care-affiliated providers were involved in authorizing elective WGS for consumers, Qian highlights potential implications for both providers and consumers. Implications include a concern that informed consent for consumers seeking PMCD testing may not be adequate, given the limited genetics training of providers who authorized tests. Qian's piece raises questions of how, in an age where PMCD testing is on the rise, consumer companies can implement practices that ensure not only robust informed consent, but also accurate interpretation of WGS results for consumers. Qian offers an example of initial efforts taken at Veritas Genetics toward this end.

James Hazel's *Privacy Best Practices for Direct-to-Consumer Genetic Testing Services: Are Industry Efforts at Self-Regulation Sufficient?* transitions the reader's attention to regulating DTC testing. Hazel begins by evaluating a newly created set of guidelines, called "Privacy Best Practices for Consumer Genetic Testing Services." While he acknowledges the importance of these guidelines in advancing the dialogue about privacy in the direct-to-consumer testing realm, he also notes the limitations of these guidelines. He then offers an assessment of the degree to which industry leaders have assimilated these guidelines into practice. He notes that of eight companies evaluated, each offers more information and choice to consumers than the DTC industry as a whole, but none of these companies are in full compliance of the Privacy Best Practice guidelines. Hazel questions whether the broader consumer industry will voluntarily adopt these guidelines, and he concludes by recommending that greater involvement by the Federal Trade Commission could be a way to offer further oversight and industry self-regulation.

In *Regulatory and Medical Aspects of DTC Genetic Testing*, Catherine Sharkey offers the reader a second perspective. She makes the case for involving the FDA in regulating DTC genetic tests, opining that the FDA's potential role in regulating DTC genetic tests could be even more compelling than its current role in regulating conventional drugs and devices. This argument is based on the fact that the agency has traditionally served as a regulator of both safety (as a protector of patients and consumers), and health information. For Sharkey, the implications of the FDA's role in DTC testing regulation includes not only its ability to leverage its regulatory authority in order to coordinate the production of genomic information, but also the use of this information.

As the World Health Organization has noted, genetic testing has increasingly gained recognition for its contributions to prevention, treatment, and management of disease. Not only is genetic testing commonly implemented in formalized health care settings, but it is also now frequently accessed at the consumer level, with the growth of direct-to-consumer companies. Now, more than ever, the process of how we implement genetic testing and return results matters, as we consider implications for patients, families, and society, more broadly. Each of the chapters in this section directs us to consider either ways in which genetic testing can be conducted more safely and accurately, or how results can be returned in ways that best promote our patients' needs. Taken together, these authors move us forward in our thinking about how genetic testing and information ought to be handled.

17

An Ethical Framework for Genetic Counseling in the Genomic Era

Leila Jamal, Will Schupmann, and Benjamin E. Berkman

I INTRODUCTION

Since the inception of their profession, genetic counselors have helped patients and families make decisions influenced by powerful emotions and varied circumstances. In doing so, they have had to reconcile ethical principles with the value pluralism of their patients. While this challenge is not unique in medicine, it has preoccupied genetic counselors disproportionately because such a large share of genetic counseling work involves nuanced discussions about reproductive choices and the impact of difference and disability on people's lives.

Historically, the profession of genetic counseling has relied heavily on the method of "nondirectiveness" to guide practice. Nondirectiveness is generally understood to mean refraining from providing recommendations or advice to patients, in an effort to provide value-neutral counseling. The original ethical justification for practicing nondirectively was to respect individual patient autonomy.[1] This ethos grew out of a genuine respect for persons, particularly concerning abortion and disability rights.

As the field of genetics and genomics has diversified and commercialized over the past decade, the concept of nondirectiveness has come under increasing pressure.[2] This is in large part because as the profession has evolved, the complexity and number of ethical considerations relevant to genetic counseling has increased. In light of recent advances in genomics and the corresponding expansion of the genetic counseling profession, we believe it is time to revisit how ethical principles should be used to guide genetic counseling.

In this chapter, we argue that in today's wide-ranging terrain of genetic counseling work, there is a need for counselors to take a more expansive view of the ethical principles and relational considerations that impact their practice. While we

1 Alexandra M. Stern, A Quiet Revolution: The Birth of the Genetic Counselor at Sarah Lawrence College, 18 J. Genetic Counseling 1 (2009).

2 Michael Arribas-Ayllon & Srikant Sarangi, Counselling Uncertainty: Genetics Professionals' Accounts of (Non)Directiveness and Trust/Distrust, 16 Health Risk Soc. 171 (2014); Christoph Rehmann-Sutter, Why Non-Directiveness is Insufficient: Ethics of Genetic Decision Making and a Model of Agency, 1 Med. Stud. 113 (2009).

acknowledge that sophisticated new models of genetic counseling practice are emerging, they continue to emphasize patient autonomy (construed largely as freedom from interference in decision-making) as the core value guiding the profession. To challenge this stance, this chapter makes the case that genetic counselors should de-emphasize a narrow concept of individual autonomy in favor of a more explicit commitment to the principles of individual and familial beneficence and nonmaleficence, as well as a broader and more positive understanding of individual autonomy. To translate our arguments into practice, we present a framework of six considerations that can help genetic counselors determine whether it might be acceptable, or even desirable, to provide active recommendations to patients. These considerations are: (1) focus of counseling; (2) clinical relevance of genetic information; (3) informational burden of test options or results; (4) relational considerations; (5) role-based considerations; and (6) familial considerations.

II GENETIC COUNSELING: AN EVOLVING PROFESSION

Genetic counseling is a relatively young field. Since the 1990s, several of its leaders have called for the abandonment of nondirectiveness as a guiding concept for the profession.[3] Arguments against nondirectiveness include that it limits a counselor's engagement with the recipients of counseling, that it precludes counselors from discussing evidence-based medical recommendations, that it is not practically attainable, and that it reflects the profession's Western cultural bias.[4]

Recent scholarship has produced some promising but insufficient alternatives. Veach et al. have proposed a Reciprocal Engagement Model (REM), which incorporates both the teaching and education functions of genetic counseling while recognizing that patients' emotions, experiences, and characteristics bring about different decisions and outcomes in light of similar facts.[5] Austin et al. argue that genetic counseling ought to embrace an approach built from psychotherapeutic goals and techniques.[6] Ryan et al. highlight the profession's roots in feminist ethics and endorse a relational form of autonomy in which individuals' interests, motivations, and decisions derive meaning from family dynamics and social relationships.[7] While these conceptual models describe useful ideas, they are

[3] Barbara B. Biesecker & Kathryn F. Peters, Process Studies in Genetic Counseling: Peering into the Black Box, 106 Am. J. Med. Genetics 191 (2002).

[4] Jon Weil et al., The Relationship of Nondirectiveness to Genetic Counseling: Report of a Workshop at the 2003 NSGC Annual Education Conference, 15 J. Genetic Counseling 85 (2006).

[5] Patricia M. Veach et al., Coming Full Circle: A Reciprocal-Engagement Model of Genetic Counseling Practice, 16 J. Genetic Counseling 713 (2007).

[6] Jehannine Austin et al., Conceptualizing Genetic Counseling as Psychotherapy in the Era of Genomic Medicine, 23 J. Genetic Counseling 903 (2014).

[7] Jane Ryan et al., Ethical Issues Associated with Genetic Counseling in the Context of Adolescent Psychiatry, 5 Applied Translational Genomics 23 (2015).

relatively silent about whether genetic counselors are ever justified in making professional recommendations in specific aspects of their practice.

We do not dispute that there are compelling reasons for genetic counselors to promote individual patient autonomy, particularly in contexts where there are equally convincing, yet qualitatively different, conceptions of a good outcome of genetic counseling and/or testing. In bioethics, recognition of an individual's right to define her own conception of what is good (for her) is a response to a long history of medical paternalism. In genetic counseling specifically, an emphasis on autonomy acknowledges that women continue to face interference with their private decisions about reproduction and pregnancy, including decisions about whether to electively terminate or continue a pregnancy following the detection of a fetal anomaly. In some cases, the testing intended to inform these decisions is as likely to generate emotional strain and uncertainty as it is to aid decision-making.[8] In practice, there is evidence that women's autonomy is being eroded by the routinization of noninvasive prenatal testing, a trend that makes it more important than ever for counselors to actively help women and their partners to engage in reflective, decision-making about childbearing.[9]

That individual autonomy still has *value* in genetic counseling does not preclude us from questioning its outsized role in relation to other values that might move genetic counselors to make more active recommendations in some areas of their practice, as some evidence suggests they have been for some time.[10] In a recent survey of pregnant women, a majority wanted some direction about their options, preferring clear recommendations about which prenatal genome sequencing results to receive.[11] That these women wanted advice about their prenatal test results does not imply that a counselor should override a woman's right to make autonomous choices about her pregnancy. Rather, it suggests that the field may be misguided in assuming that all prenatal patients always want complete decisional independence regarding all aspects of pregnancy risk assessment.[12]

Revisiting the balance of ethical principles applied to genetic counseling is also necessary because today's genetic counselors work in some settings that differ in fundamental ways from the prenatal and pediatric clinics where the profession originated. Whereas most genetic counselors used to be concerned with diagnosing rare, life-altering conditions in the prenatal or pediatric periods, they now assess

8 Cecile Muller & Linda D. Cameron, It's Complicated – Factors Predicting Decisional Conflict in Prenatal Diagnostic Testing, 19 Health Expectations 388 (2016).

9 Celine Lewis et al., Offering Non-invasive Prenatal Testing as Part of Routine Clinical Service: Can High Levels of Informed Choice Be Maintained?, 37 Prenatal Diagnosis 1130 (2017).

10 Dianne M. Bartels et al., Nondirectiveness in Genetic Counseling: A Survey of Practitioners, 72 Am. J. Med. Genetics 172 (1997).

11 Haley K. Sullivan et al., Noninvasive Prenatal Whole Genome Sequencing: Pregnant Women's Views and Preferences, 133 Obstetrics Gynecology 525 (2019).

12 Shoshana Shiloh, Decision-making in the Context of Genetic Risk, in The Troubled Helix: Social and Psychological Implications of the New Human Genetics 82, 82–103 (T. Marteau & M. Richards, eds., 1996).

health risks and facilitate decision-making in medical subspecialties where genetic information can point to improved medical management or a reduction of disease risk through targeted surveillance. The expanded purview of genetic counseling has brought with it a longer and more varied list of ethical issues for genetic counselors to help patients understand and make decisions about. In a growing number of cases, considerations of benefit maximization or harm avoidance may counterbalance, if not outweigh, patient autonomy.

Our core claim is that owing to the expanded scope and complexity of genetic counseling work, the profession should favor a more explicitly normative framework that gives genetic counselors broader license to make recommendations operating within a well-defined scope of practice.

III AN ADAPTED ETHICAL FRAMEWORK FOR GENETIC COUNSELING PRACTICE

Thus far, we have acknowledged that while respect for individual autonomy will always be an important value in medicine, the profession of genetic counseling has emphasized individual autonomy at the expense of beneficence and nonmaleficence, two principles that have growing relevance as the profession expands. Beneficence, a welfarist principle, demands that genetic counselors use professional judgment and evidence to assess whether genetic testing might *benefit* a patient irrespective of her views about it. Nonmaleficence, a principle of harm minimization, demands that genetic counselors use expertise and evidence to prevent genetic testing and information from being used *harmfully*, where possible. Our framework further acknowledges that genetic counselors are bound to consider the *family* as a unit of significance. This requires them to reconcile their patients' individual autonomy interests with more nuanced concerns about benefits and harms to families. Where we do give deference to individual autonomy in our framework, we insist on a broad conception of autonomy that demands more of a clinician than noninterference in patient decision-making.[13] Our fuller notion of autonomy asks genetic counselors to use their unique skillset to help patients incorporate genetic information into truly informed, confident, and voluntary decision-making.

In what follows, we propose six considerations that can help a genetic counselor determine whether and why it might be ethically acceptable to provide normative recommendations to a patient or family: (1) focus of counseling; (2) clinical relevance of genetic information; (3) informational burden of test options or results; (4) relational considerations; (5) role-based considerations; and (6) familial considerations. The first three considerations pertain to the nature of the content being

[13] J. Hodgson and M. Spriggs, A Practical Account of Autonomy: Why Genetic Counseling is Especially Well Suited to the Facilitation of Informed Autonomous Decision Making, 14 J. Genet. Couns. 89–97 (2005).

discussed in a counseling session; the last three pertain to relational aspects of genetic counseling work that affect a counselor's purview to be directive.

These six domains do not constitute a code of ethics or a prescriptive set of universal rules. Rather, they offer general guidance about areas of genetic counseling practice where a directive approach may serve a patient or family's best interests.

A *Focus of Counseling*

Genetic counseling is a versatile profession. The genetic counseling process may include providing information about test options, helping patients and families communicate about genetic risk, facilitating adaptation to grief and loss, interpreting results, assisting with decision-making and referrals, or some combination of these things.[14] Genomic testing can also be used to answer qualitatively different questions, many of which raise equally valid yet distinct emotions and points of view.

Across the many contexts where genetic risk assessment is used, some counseling issues generate more moral consensus than others. For example, women have wide-ranging views about the desirability of diagnosing an intellectual disability syndrome prenatally, and the issue of abortion is perennially divisive.[15] However, most people value genetic test results and related interventions that can minimize disease-associated morbidity and mortality in a child.[16]

It follows from this that genetic counselors have more purview to provide recommendations to their patients when genetic information has the potential to facilitate an outcome that is widely understood to be good, such as the minimization of a patient's physical or emotional pain. In areas of practice that touch on differing conceptions of what is good, a counselor may have less purview to counsel directively. While the degree of moral consensus about a counseling issue is not the sole source of information that counselors should use to determine the acceptability of counseling directively (and might even obscure issues about which there is morally justified value pluralism) public attitudes can provide useful information about the range of values and interests that matter to patients in relation to a given counseling issue.

This is not to say that information about public attitudes can substitute for a patient's articulation of her own values and interests; it is merely one consideration among many that should be taken into account.

14 National Society of Genetic Counselors' Definition Task Force et al., A New Definition of Genetic Counseling: National Society of Genetic Counselors' Task Force Report, 15 J. Genetic Counseling 77 (2006).

15 Julie C. Sapp et al., Ambivalence toward Undergoing Invasive Prenatal Testing: An Exploration of Its Origins, 30 Prenatal Diagnosis 77 (2010); Rachel V. van Schendel et al., What Do Parents of Children with Down Syndrome Think about Non-Invasive Prenatal Testing (NIPT)?, 26 J. Genetic Counseling 522 (2017).

16 Qishan Lim et al., Parents' Attitudes toward Genetic Testing of Children for Health Conditions: A Systematic Review, 92 Clinical Genetics 569 (2017).

B *Clinical Utility of Genetic Information*

Genomic testing can provide information about diseases that vary with respect to prevention and treatment options. Ongoing research is generating evidence about which genetic findings are considered "actionable" according to criteria that take into account the severity and likelihood of a clinical outcome and the effectiveness of available interventions associated with findings in different genes.[17] The concept of "actionable genetic information" can be interpreted broadly, to include results that impact patients' financial, family planning, and lifestyle decisions or it can be interpreted narrowly, as a subset of results that point to effective medical interventions. Interview data show that patients' perceptions of actionability are highly context-dependent and that patients endorse a broader conception of actionability than medical professionals do.[18]

A key part of the person-centered genetic counseling process is to help patients explore what might change for them in light of a positive test result. When the consequences of a genetic test result are contingent upon personal and contextual variables, we acknowledge that patient choice plays a critical role in determining whether to pursue and how to act upon genetic information. However, when genetic information quite clearly has the potential to improve a patient's health through accessible, effective medical intervention, we agree with others that clinicians are bound by duties of beneficence to encourage patients to pursue an evidence-based course of action.[19] In the face of information that could potentially improve survival or quality of life, there is less of a compelling reason to treat genetic information differently than other medical information that may be undesirable to learn yet clinically useful.

C *Informational Burden of Test Options or Results*

Genetic testing and results vary in terms of their complexity and corresponding informational burden. The genomic tests that are commonly used today interrogate dozens or even hundreds of genes at once and have different sensitivities and specificities for each condition tested. Many of the conditions tested for are rare, with poorly understood natural histories, making it challenging for the average person to comprehensively understand the range and limits of the information

17 Elizabeth M. Webber et al., Evidence-Based Assessments of Clinical Actionability in the Context of Secondary Findings: Updates from ClinGen's Actionability Working Group, 39 Human Mutation 1677 (2018).

18 Leila Jamal et al., When Bins Blur: Patient Perspectives on Categories of Results from Clinical Whole Genome Sequencing, 8 AJOB Empirical Bioethics 82 (2017).

19 Collen Caleshu et al., Use and Interpretation of Genetic Tests in Cardiovascular Genetics, 96 Heart 1669 (2010); Heather Hampel, Genetic Counseling and Cascade Genetic Testing in Lynch Syndrome, 15 Familial Cancer 423 (2016); Amy McGuire et al., Point-Counterpoint. Ethics and Genomic Incidental Findings, 340 Sci. 1074 (2013).

a test might provide.[20] Genomic testing is also interpreted using a series of inferences and analytical steps that rely on information in the scientific literature and in public and private databases. Tests have varied technical specifications and may detect variants with unclear clinical significance.

The complexity and uncertainty associated with genetic information can be difficult to discuss in a concise and impartial manner that is accessible to patients.[21] This is particularly true when a test detects a variant of uncertain clinical significance (VUS).[22] There is evidence that health care providers, including physicians, may over-interpret the clinical significance of VUSes, using them to guide medical management when this is at best wasteful and at worst harmful.[23] Because of their unique expertise and duty to minimize harms to patients, genetic counselors are ethically bound to point out when genetic test results do not have clear-cut medical implications or when it may be premature to act upon them. This is not to imply that genetic counselors should make *all* the decisions about the use of genetic information in a patient's medical management. Rather, as a health professional who is trained in genetics and genomics, a genetic counselor should recommend an evidence-based course of action to patients and colleagues who might otherwise allow patient care to be influenced by a test result with an unclear association to disease.

D *Relational Considerations*

Thus far, we have focused on the role genetic counselors play as medical providers who educate patients about diagnostic or risk information. This belies the reality that some of the most meaningful aspects of the genetic counseling process are relational and have little to do with technical information. In general, the closer the relationship between a genetic counselor and patient or family, the more purview she has to be directive in counseling them.

Two aspects of a counseling relationship are ethically salient. The first is the degree to which empathy has been established between counselor and patient. Patients consistently report higher satisfaction with genetic counseling when it resembles a therapeutic relationship characterized by genuine empathy and low verbal dominance.[24] Evidence also suggests that genetic counseling is more effective

20 Iris Schrijver et al., Opportunities and Challenges Associated with Clinical Diagnostic Genome Sequencing, 14 J. Molecular Diagnostics 525 (2012).

21 Paul K.J. Han, A Taxonomy of Medical Uncertainties in Clinical Genome Sequencing, 19 Genetics Med. 918 (2017); Debra Skinner et al., The Nuanced Negative: Meanings of a Negative Diagnostic Result in Clinical Exome Sequencing, 38 Soc. Health & Illness 1303 (2016).

22 Julie O. Culver et al., Variants of Uncertain Significance in BRCA Testing: Evaluation of Surgical Decisions, Risk Perception, and Cancer Distress, 84 Clinical Genetics 464 (2013).

23 Sharon E. Plon et al., Genetic Testing and Cancer Risk Management Recommendations by Physicians for At-Risk Relatives, 13 Genetics Med. 148 (2011).

24 Debra Roter et al., The Genetic Counseling Video Project (GCVP): Models of Practice, 142 C Am. J. Med. Genetics 209 (2006).

at promoting positive health behavior change and minimizing decisional regret when genetic counselors establish genuine empathy with a patient or family.[25] This is not surprising; the very information genetic counselors need to know about their patients comes through listening and dialogue.

Fundamentally, the goal of psychotherapeutic genetic counseling is to establish "a helping relationship in which one person has the knowledge and skills relevant to helping another person address a problem through conversation."[26] This model does not preclude counselors from tailoring information based on patients' needs or from using crisis intervention skills, grief counseling techniques, and behavior change interventions to benefit patients. In fact, veteran genetic counselors have long argued that a psychotherapeutic model of genetic counseling is more effective at achieving desired outcomes through purposeful intervention than purely didactic counseling methods.[27]

The second relevant feature of a counseling relationship is the degree of shared cultural understanding between patient and counselor. While genetic counselors practice in increasingly diverse societies and have a rapidly growing international presence, the profession remains overwhelmingly white, female, young, and primarily English-speaking.[28] Evidence demonstrates that systemic, cultural, and linguistic barriers pose challenges to effective communication and counseling about genetic risk.[29] In many societies, the unit of decisional significance is the household or community,[30] challenging an individual autonomy-focused model of genetic counseling. Even within the same society, there may be socioeconomic and cultural differences affecting the rapport between a patient and counselor, many of which are exacerbated in a medical environment that fosters power asymmetries between

25 Henriëtta Dijkstra, Nonverbal Communication and Conversational Contribution in Breast Cancer Genetic Counseling: Are Counselors' Nonverbal Communication and Conversational Contribution Associated with Counselees' Satisfaction, Needs Fulfillment and State Anxiety in Breast Cancer Genetic Counseling?, 93 Patient Educ. and Counseling 216 (2013); Vlatka Duric et al., Reducing Psychological Distress in a Genetic Counseling Consultation for Breast Cancer Reducing Psychological Distress in a Genetic Counseling Consultation for Breast Cancer, 12 J. Genetic Counseling 243 (2003).

26 Jehannine Austin et al., Conceptualizing Genetic Counseling as Psychotherapy in the Era of Genomic Medicine, 23 J. Genetic Counseling 903 (2014).

27 Biesecker & Peters, supra note 3.

28 MaryAnn Abacan et al., The Global State of the Genetic Counseling Profession, 27 Eur. J. of Hum. Genetics 183 (2019).

29 Amanda M. Gutierrez et al., Portero versus Portador: Spanish Interpretation of Genomic Terminology during Whole Exome Sequencing Results Disclosure, 14 Personalized Med. 503 (2017); Charles Muller et al., Low Referral Rate for Genetic Testing in Racially and Ethnically Diverse Patients Despite Universal Colorectal Cancer Screening, 16 Clinical Gastroenterology & Hepatology 1911 (2018); Rayna Rapp et al., Sociocultural Differences in the Impact of Amniocentesis: An Anthropological Research Report, 8 Fetal Diagnosis & Therapy 90 (1993); Kendra L. Schaa et al., Genetic Counselors' Implicit Racial Attitudes and Their Relationship to Communication, 34 Health Psychol. 111 (2015).

30 Charles Rotimi et al., Community Engagement and Informed Consent in the International HapMap Project, Community Genetics 186 (2007).

patients and providers.[31] Sociocultural or linguistic differences may undermine a patient's ability to make informed decisions; power differentials may undermine truly voluntary decision-making. As such, both are ethical concerns for a genetic counselor.

Owing to practical constraints of modern genetic counseling practice, genetic counselors may not always be able to establish a truly therapeutic relationship with a patient or family. Nor does it seem routinely feasible to ask that genetic counselors always communicate in a culturally competent fashion and be fully aware of the power asymmetries that matter to their patients. Yet, genetic counselors can and should practice with self-awareness about their own cultural biases and the nature of their relationships with patients. The closer and more therapeutic a relationship a counselor has with a patient or family, the more likely it is that she truly understands a patient or family's preferences, decision-making style, and appetite for information. Similarly, the more culturally synchronized a counselor and patient are, the more likely they are to operate based on a shared ethical frame of reference. It is in the context of these deeper and more therapeutic relationships that counselors may use what they know about a patient or family to tailor recommendations for them.

E *Role-Based Considerations*

The institutional vantage point (that is, clinical, research, industry) of a genetic counselor also affects her ethical responsibilities. While all genetic counselors have a professional responsibility to provide compassionate and accurate counseling to their patients, counselors who work in direct patient care settings have the strongest and most explicit duties to maximize the benefits and minimize the harms of genetic counseling and testing. Motivated by beneficence and nonmaleficence, genetic counselors practicing in clinical roles should recommend the genetic and genomic tests with highest sensitivity and specificity, fewest limitations, and which are priced most reasonably given a patient or family's needs.

Genetic counselors who work in research may also assume duties of care to patients. This is especially true when they see research participants and families with rare diseases, who may not have access to care outside of a study or clinical trial. That said, research studies have limited resources to clinically confirm research results, return them to patients, and provide responsible follow-up. When counseling a research participant, a genetic counselor has a primary responsibility to convey the purpose of the research study and the limits of what information and services the

[31] Chanita H. Halbert, Low Rates of African American Participation in Genetic Counseling and Testing for BRCA1/2 Mutations: Racial Disparities or Just a Difference?, 21 J. Genetic Counseling 676 (2012); Ilana S. Mittman et al., Exploring the Discourse between Genetic Counselors and Orthodox Jewish Community Members Related to Reproductive Genetic Technology, 65 Patient Educ. & Counseling 230 (2007).

study can provide. If the research participant's medical needs would be better served elsewhere, a research-based genetic counselor should make this clear and if possible, *recommend* other avenues for obtaining necessary care.

Since the 1990s, a growing number of genetic counselors have taken jobs in industry, where many of them provide direct patient care via telemedicine.[32] These new kinds of counseling relationships have raised questions about conflicts of interest. In addition, a new class of so-called consumer-initiated testing has become available, granting access to genetic testing with indirect or minimal involvement of a health care provider. These developments place new responsibilities on genetic counselors to serve as intermediaries between the commercial interests of for-profit laboratories and patients seeking testing.

Genetic counselors working in commercial settings must acknowledge that conflicts of interest exist and have the potential to undermine trust in the profession. In addition to being transparent about conflicts of interest, where possible, genetic counselors should base their practice on guidelines, evidence, and the goals of maximizing benefits and minimizing harms. By incorporating the values of transparency, beneficence, and nonmaleficence into their practice, industry genetic counselors have a crucial role to play in bolstering the legitimacy and integrity of their field as new genomic products and markets emerge. They should work to mitigate the role of commercial interests in making genetic testing available to patients, and at times, this may require them to be directive. To practice "nondirectively" from an industry vantage point would risk diverting patients to other sources of recommendations about genomics, such as commercial advertising or mainstream media. These sources of information have been found to be incomplete (at best) and misleading (at worst), making it highly irresponsible for genetic counselors to wholly defer to them.

F *Familial Considerations*

The sixth ethically salient consideration we highlight is that much genetic and genomic information is shared by family members. Broadly speaking, there are two rationales for involving a patient's relatives in the genomic testing process. The first is to benefit a patient's *relatives* by identifying whether they are at increased risk of developing a preventable or treatable disease. The second is to benefit a *patient*, either by identifying the most informative family member to test, exploring how a variant segregates with disease in a family, or determining whether a variant occurred de novo in a patient. Contacting a patient's relatives is not a peripheral matter in genetic counseling; it is an essential step in maximizing the accuracy, precision, and utility of genetic testing. In addition, sharing genetic information

[32] National Society of Genetic Counselors, Professional Status Survey (2018).

among family members can be a way to help a family adapt to and provide mutual support when faced with a genetic disease or risk.

Concerning the first reason for involving relatives (that is, to benefit them) the bioethics literature is divided about the extent of genetic counselors' responsibilities. The issue arises most frequently in discussions about whether genetic counselors ever have "duties to warn" at-risk relatives about an inherited disease risk when doing so goes against a patient's expressed preference. Some argue that a genetic counselor's primary duty is to her patient. Under this view, she must never breech the sanctity of patient confidentiality.[33] Others have pointed out that in practice, it is rare for patients to insist strongly on nondisclosure of genetic test results to relatives.[34] Instead of using confidentiality to the individual patient as the default priority, they suggest that genetic information should be conceptualized as familial. Under this so-called joint account model, the disclosure of medically useful genetic information to relatives is the default practice unless there are strong reasons to privilege individual patient confidentiality.[35]

Concerning the second reason for involving relatives (that is, to benefit the patient) it is now clear that familial testing is a valuable method of understanding the penetrance and pathogenicity of a genetic variant. As guidelines show, familial testing can provide critical information needed to classify a genetic variant according to best practices.[36] While it is never the place of a genetic counselor to force a patient to disclose information against his or her will, we feel that duties of care and group beneficence should motivate genetic counselors to recommend familial testing, sometimes strongly, when it is medically indicated or will add clarity to a genetics evaluation. In many instances, failure to collect familial samples for testing means that a patient is left with an inconclusive or uninformative result that cannot be used to inform his or her care.

We agree with others that an individual-focused analysis of the direct benefits and harms to an individual excludes important ethical considerations that should factor into genetic counseling. Although the details of specific cases will vary, in general, we see a need for genetic counselors to consider the risks and benefits that might accrue to a patient in a wider family context. A child diagnosed with an inherited cancer syndrome is unlikely to do well if his mother develops an advanced, undetected cancer because she was unaware of her own elevated cancer risk.

33 Mark A. Rothstein, Reconsidering the Duty to Warn Genetically At-Risk Relatives, 20 Nature Pub. Group 285 (2018).

34 Sandi Dheensa et al., "Is This Knowledge Mine and Nobody Else's? I Don't Feel That." Patient Views about Consent, Confidentiality and Information-Sharing in Genetic Medicine, 42 J. Med. Ethics 174 (2016).

35 Id.; see also Sandi Dheensa et al., Approaching Confidentiality at a Familial Level in Genomic Medicine: A Focus Group Study with Healthcare Professionals, 7 BMJ Open e012443 (2017).

36 S. Richards et al., Standards and guidelines for the interpretation of sequence variants: a joint consensus recommendation of the American College of Medical Genetics and Genomics and the Association for Molecular Pathology, 17 Genet. Med 405–24 (2015).

We also acknowledge that some think relatives have a "right not to know" genetic information about themselves. However, we find it ethically untenable to make defending a strong interpretation of the "right not to know" the default goal of genetic counseling practice, because it is based on largely hypothetical worries about the psychological harms of genetic information, which have not yet been borne out by evidence.[37] In addition, a default practice of withholding health information from a patient's relatives does not give due ethical weight to the benefits of targeted health interventions that genetic information can lead to, such as cancer and cardiovascular screening or avoidance of life-threatening anesthesia. Genetic counselors have training and skills that can help families manage the disclosure of genetic risk information, even when it is practically and emotionally challenging to do so.

IV CONCLUSION

In this chapter, we have argued that genetic counselors have more reason than ever to consider the benefits and harms of genetic testing (to both patients and families) when providing counseling, and that considerations related to beneficence and nonmaleficence give them ethical license to provide recommendations to patients in at least some circumstances. As the field of genetic counseling diversifies, we have also suggested that genetic counselors should reflect on the nature of their relationships with patients and families, their roles in the health care system, and the ethical implications of these variables. While individual patient autonomy always matters in health care, we believe autonomous decision-making is best served by providers who make carefully chosen, relevant recommendations to patients based on clinical expertise and informed by the expressed preferences, emotions, and values of patients and, where relevant, their family members. Critically, our assertion that genetic counselors should feel *licensed* to make evidence-based recommendations does not *preclude* counselors from deferring to patient preferences in situations where countervailing personal, familial, emotional, or cultural values also matter.

Some have argued that ethical frameworks are little more than checklists of values that lack coherence or normative force because they are divorced from the comprehensive, overarching theories they originated from.[38] Responses to this rest on at least three assertions: (1) that there may be reasonable disagreement about the right outcome of a real-life ethical dilemma; (2) that the interpretation and specification of principles are desirable and necessary steps in applied ethics; and (3) that practicability is an important criterion for judging the adequacy of an applied ethical framework.[39]

37 Benjamin E. Berkman, Refuting the Right Not to Know, 19 J. Health Care L. & Pol'y 1 (2017); Anya E. R. Prince & Benjamin E. Berkman , Reconceptualizing Harms and Benefits in the Genomic Age, 15 Personalized Med. 419 (2018).

38 K. Danner Clouser & Bernard Gert , A Critique of Principlism, 15 J. Med. & Phil. 219 (1990).

39 Tom L. Beuchamp & James F. Childress, Principles of Biomedical Ethics (1989); Tom L. Beuchamp, Principlism and Its Alleged Competitors, 5 Kennedy Inst. Ethics J. 181 (1995).

These three assertions map well onto preoccupations about ethics that have been raised in the field of genetic counseling. Genetic counselors have always been concerned with respecting pluralism, recognizing that two different patients with the same genetic test result may arrive at different, equally justifiable responses to the same information. They also strive to incorporate particular facts of a case, including aspects of context and specific patient preferences, into their counseling. As clinicians, genetic counselors are predominantly concerned with norms that can be put into practice, as we have tried to do in this chapter.

The goal of modern bioethics is not to provide a single, unifying theory of right or wrong behavior. Rather, it is to provide a stable yet flexible method of identifying values that may be in conflict or traded off when decisions are made in real life. In this tradition, our framework is meant to be a point of departure for additional interpretation, specification, and balancing. To say that an updated ethical framework for genetic counseling practice might be *useful* is not to claim that there is a universal system of ethics that applies to all problems that genetic counselors are faced with, nor that ethics is a sufficient lens to base all of genetic counseling practice upon. We merely assert that genetic counselors should not eschew a range of established ethical principles that may be readily adapted to add clarity to difficult problems that arise in their work.

18

Physician-Mediated Elective Whole Genome Sequencing Tests

Impacts on Informed Consent

Emily Qian, Magalie Leduc, Rebecca Hodges, Bryan Cosca, Ryan Durigan, Laurie McCright, Doug Flood, and Birgit Funke

I INTRODUCTION

Veritas Genetics is a commercial genetic testing laboratory that has been offering a whole genome sequencing (WGS) test to consumers since 2016 at the price of $999 USD. This test is offered to generally healthy adults and is designed to provide a broad range of genetic information that can be used for disease prevention as well as "recreational" (non-health related) genetic information. Clinical reports contain information regarding risk of developing common genetic conditions such as inherited cancer syndromes and cardiovascular disease, reproductive risks, pharmacogenomics, genetic influences on certain traits, and ancestry information. The test order can be initiated by consumers themselves, but requires authorization from a health care provider before proceeding. The authors are employees of Veritas, in various capacities, and, in this chapter, we provide information about its relatively new service delivery model, and data characterizing the population of providers that have authorized 500 of our consumer-driven WGS tests. We start, though, by describing the history and evolution of genetic testing service delivery models; spanning medical genetics in the clinic to recreational genetics at home.

II BACKGROUND ON GENETIC TESTING

Genetic testing has been available since the 1950s and is increasingly incorporated in medical management decision-making. Clinical geneticists and genetic counselors who assess patients presenting with symptoms order testing to clarify underlying etiologies and elucidate disease risks for the patients and their relatives. In recent years, the genomic testing landscape in the USA is beginning to shift with increased accessibility and an increasing interest of individuals to drive their own health care. This paradigm shift has also brought a change of terminology from "patients" to "consumers." "Patients" implies that the individual is ill or presenting with symptoms while "consumers" is a broader term referring to individuals regardless of disease status, which includes predictive applications. All references made to "genetic testing" hereinafter refer to germline DNA testing, which describes testing the DNA inherited from a parent and transmitted through generations. This distinction is made to differentiate from tumor testing, which analyzes somatic, or acquired DNA mutations.

Commercialization, competition, and the development of new technologies has helped to foster the development of cost-efficient genetic analyses, as well as expand applications.[1] Genetic tests are now applied to various areas including preventive medicine and non-health care purposes. With consumers increasingly driving their health care, the traditional path of a clinic visit with genetic counseling prior to ordering a test (also known as pre-test counseling) is no longer the only option. Alternate models are "consumer initiated, physician approved genetic testing," and "direct to consumer (DTC)" testing, the latter being decoupled from physician interactions. The scope of DTC testing is usually limited to non-health care related testing. However, companies may be able to perform certain DTC tests and report health-related information under the condition that they obtain FDA pre-market approval. One such example is 23andMe, who obtained FDA-approval for certain sensitive results, such as the three common Ashkenazi Jewish variants associated with Hereditary Breast and Ovarian Cancer syndrome in the *BRCA1* and *BRCA2* genes. This example is rare and clinical laboratories without this approval reporting health-related information are required to receive pre-test authorization from a health care provider.

Clinical laboratories are regulated by the Center for Medicare and Medicaid Services (CMS), which administers the Clinical Laboratory Improvement Amendments (CLIA). Pre-test authorization by health care providers are required for some genetic tests and are regulated by CLIA, which only specifies that tests can only proceed "at the request of an authorized person."[2] The definition of an "authorized person" then refers to "an individual allowed by State law or rule to order tests or receive test results."[3] Scope-of-practice laws for nonphysician health care providers vary from state to state and are ever-changing[4] and few state legislatures for nongenetic professionals mention genetic tests specifically. Several other organizations (including the College of American Pathologists (CAP)) have been granted "deemed status" by CMS to accredit laboratories and typically have more stringent requirements and guidance. However, the CAP also does not offer additional guidance on this topic. The growing administration of genetic testing outside

1 Kathryn A. Phillips et al., Genetic Test Availability and Spending: Where Are We Now? Where Are We Going?, 37 Health Affs. 710 (2018).

2 42 C.F.R. § 493.1241 (2011).

3 42 C.F.R. § 493.2 (2010).

4 Catherine Dower, Jean Moore, & Margaret Langelier, It Is Time to Restructure Health Professions Scope-of-Practice Regulations to Remove Barriers to Care, 32 Health Affs. 1971 (2013).

traditional expert environments exposes a need to clarify legislative guidance. Furthermore, ordering a genetic test goes far beyond simply providing authorization of a test.

In the medical setting, an individual normally seeks a trained health care provider who collects disease information and family history to assist in the selection of an appropriate genetic test, if any. A critical aspect of this pre-test consultation is obtaining "informed consent," which is a matter of state tort law. Informed consent as defined by the American Medical Association (AMA) is the process where communication between a patient and physician results in the patient's authorization or agreement to undergo a specific medical intervention. The AMA recommends that physicians assess the patient's ability to understand relevant medical information and implications of treatment alternatives and to make an independent, voluntary decision.[5] For genetic testing, informed consent typically covers the following main elements: test purpose, procedure, benefits, risks, and limitations.[6]

The following is an example of the informed consent process in a medical genetics clinic based on the authors' experiences in providing genetic testing, which incorporates concepts previously described in the literature.[7]

A patient with hypertrophic cardiomyopathy (HCM) presents in the genetics clinic. After collecting personal and family history information, a genetic counselor or other trained health care provider explains to the patient that genetic testing may help to identify the cause of HCM and influence the patient's medical and lifestyle decisions, as well as inform relatives. These are the benefits of testing. It is also explained to the patient that the test is voluntary, and there may be risks involved. If the patient expresses interest in genetic testing to better understand why they developed HCM, the provider would then explain that there are many types of tests available, but not all may be used for the intended purpose. For example, a cardiovascular wellness DTC test is inappropriate and unlikely to be useful for identifying the underlying cause of HCM.

The provider then goes on to explain the available clinical tests, ranging from sequencing of single genes related to HCM to Whole Exome Sequencing (WES). The likelihood and consequences of receiving a positive, negative, or inconclusive result and the complexities are reviewed. A positive result may impact the patient's medical management and their lifestyle. It can also affect their relationship with relatives as providers typically encourage patients to share such results so relatives may consider predictive testing. On the other hand, a negative finding (no variant identified explaining the patient's disease) or inconclusive result (variant(s)

[5] Frank A. Riddick Jr., The Code of Medical Ethics of the American Medical Association, 5 Ochsner J. 6 (2003).

[6] Gail Geller et al., Genetic Testing for Susceptibility to Adult-Onset Cancer the Process and Content of Informed Consent, 277 J. Am. Med. Ass'n 1467 (1997).

[7] Jason Cowan et al., Genetic Testing and Genetic Counseling in Cardiovascular Genetic Medicine: Overview and Preliminary Recommendations, 14 Congestive Heart Failure 97 (2008).

identified for which the available evidence is insufficient to determine whether it explains the disease) would not change the patient's current medical management. Due to the limitations of the test and current medical knowledge, negative results do not necessarily indicate that there is no underlying genetic etiology as our knowledge of the genetic architecture of most diseases is still nascent and most available tests are not yet able to provide this resolution. Some reasons for a test's inability to detect causal variants are their location (most tests today cannot interpret intronic variants) or a technical limitation of the assay (for example, next generation sequencing is suboptimal with regard to deletion/duplication analysis). Inconclusive results may sometimes be clarified by testing of additional relatives, but may also cause undue anxiety. The potential psychological impacts of testing are also explored during this process.

Other information discussed includes the risk of unexpected results (nonpaternity, secondary findings outside of HCM for exome/genome-based testing), genetic discrimination and the limits of legal protection against it, and data or leftover sample retention and usage policies. Out-of-pocket cost and insurance coverage differences are reviewed for each type of test.

As demonstrated above, many of the nuances and considerations of genetic testing are complex and require highly specialized knowledge to communicate accurately to a consumer, as well as psychosocial concerns that a clinician would elicit during a pre-test consultation. These central themes are applicable across all genetic tests, regardless of the test purpose. Physician-led test ordering and guided informed consent has traditionally been a part of medical care in a genetic clinic setting. However, the paradigm shift in genetic testing has led to test models where the classic patient–physician interaction is changing. Even with physician-mediated consumer-driven (PMCD) testing, traditional office visits with well-established consenting procedures may not happen and, in the case of DTC testing, consenting is always reduced to an online exercise without health care provider guidance.

For DTC-GT, the American College of Obstetricians and Gynecologists (ACOG) committee opinion has advised against pursuing testing without the involvement of a knowledgeable health care provider, although they do not specify how a consumer can identify a "knowledgeable" provider.[8] A recent study found that consumers often do not consider the potential risks prior to purchasing,[9] suggesting a need for providing adequate education prior to testing. The American College of Medical Genetics (ACMG) position statement regarding DTC genetic tests recommends that board-certified genetics professional involvement should be utilized during the testing process to reduce a number of risks.[10] The Association for

8 American College of Obstetricians and Gynecologists, Committee Opinion No. 724: Consumer Testing for Disease Risk, 130 Obstetrics & Gynecology e270 (2017).

9 J. Scott Roberts et al., Direct-to-Consumer Genetic Testing: User Motivations, Decision Making, and Perceived Utility of Results, 20 Pub. Health Genomics 36 (2017).

10 ACMG Board of Directors, Direct-to-Consumer Genetic Testing: A Revised Position Statement of the American College of Medical Genetics and Genomics, 18 Genetics Med. 207 (2016).

Molecular Pathology (AMP) position statement is in strong support of consumers seeking genetic counseling and recommend laboratories encourage their consumers to pursue genetic counseling for further education.[11]

Another consideration of PMCD genetic testing is the novel challenge that the consumer can drive the process but may not have access to a qualified, genetics literate provider as they traditionally work in highly specialized academic medical centers. In contrast, those physicians who see individuals in a screening setting (primary care) are often ill equipped to handle genetic testing and informed consent. It is evident that there is a shortage of certified genetic professionals, who can assist with the informed consent process.[12] Over half the medical geneticists report new patient wait times of over one month.[13] Elective genomic screening tests are expected to be delivered mainly in a primary care setting as that is the setting in which most asymptomatic screening tests are performed. Many screening tests are ordered in the primary care setting for preventive measures to identify individuals at higher risk for disease, before the disease manifests.[14] However, many physicians without formal genetics training do not feel comfortable interpreting and explaining genetic tests.[15] Furthermore, studies suggest that physicians who are not genetic professionals may not follow guideline-based genetics procedures for intake and informed consent[16] and it is unclear how appropriate consenting can be ensured for these preventive medicine genetic tests.[17]

Veritas is not the only PMCD genetic testing company, many clinical laboratories have also adopted this model for certain genetic tests such as Invitae and Color Genomics.[18] With this comes the need for finding health care providers willing to

11 Position Statements & Letters, Association for Molecular Pathology, https://www.amp.org/advocacy/position-statements-letters/ (last visited Aug. 15, 2019).

12 Jennifer M. Hoskovec et al., Projecting the Supply and Demand for Certified Genetic Counselors: A Workforce Study, 27 J. Genetic Counseling 16 (2018).

13 Deborah R. Maiese et al., Current Conditions in Medical Genetics Practice, 21 Genetics Med. 1874 (2019).

14 Published Recommendations. U.S. Preventive Services Task Force, https://www.uspreventiveservicestaskforce.org/BrowseRec/Index (last visited May 10, 2020).

15 Susanne B. Haga et al., Primary Care Physicians' Knowledge of and Experience with Pharmacogenetic Testing, 82 Clinical Genetics 388 (2012); Robert Klitzman et al., Attitudes and Practices among Internists Concerning Genetic Testing, 22 J. Genetic Counseling 90 (2013); Amanda L. Laedtke et al., Family Physicians' Awareness and Knowledge of the Genetic Information Non-Discrimination Act (GINA), 21 J. Genetic Counseling 345 (2012); Sarah Macklin et al., Physician Interpretation of Variants of Uncertain Significance, 18 Familial Cancer 121 (2019); Louise Wideroff et al., Hereditary Breast/Ovarian and Colorectal Cancer Genetics Knowledge in a National Sample of US Physicians, 42 J. Med. Genetics 749 (2005).

16 Susan T. Vadaparampil et al., Pretest Genetic Counseling Services for Hereditary Breast and Ovarian Cancer Delivered by Non-Genetics Professionals in the State of Florida, 87 Clinical Genetics 473 (2014).

17 Kayte Spector-Bagdady, Reconceptualizing Consent for Direct-to-Consumer Health Services, 41 Am. J.L. & Med. 568 (2015).

18 Proactive Test Selection, Invitae, https://www.invitae.com/pio/order/proactive(last visited Aug. 8, 2019); Purchase Your Color Test, Color, https://www.color.com/purchase/ordering-physician?sku=combo%203 (last visited Aug. 8, 2019).

offer test authorization services, ideally coupled with interactions with the consumer ensuring proper informed consent. The emergence of telemedicine, independent physician networks such as Genome Medical, InformedDNA, and PWN Health are offering test authorization and genetic counseling services to cover this need. Studies investigating practices and consequences of the PMCD genetic testing model are needed[19] as it becomes more widely adopted and the evidence presented in this study provides a look into the backgrounds of the health care providers authorizing the Veritas elective WGS test.

III PHYSICIANS INVOLVED IN VERITAS GENETICS' TESTING

A *Approaches Used by Veritas Genetics*

Consumers initiate testing online from the Veritas Genetics website and self-report their residence mailing address for kit delivery, first and last name. This includes accepting the terms of service and an attestation that the informed consent document available during the ordering process has been reviewed. At the time of online order, the informed consent form available in English included the following topics: voluntary participation, test purpose, WGS information, screening of adults only, reporting, types of results, incomplete medical knowledge, medical care, risks (unperceived, sample collection, genetic discrimination, electronic security), implications for family, genetic counseling, test information and limitations, sample requirements, disclosure to health care provider, and additional use of sample. The consumer is required to scroll through the form in order to reach the checkbox indicating the above information was reviewed. The form is also available as a downloadable and printable PDF.

Additional online resources for identifying local genetic counselors are also included in the document. During the ordering process, consumers are asked to specify their qualified health care provider, who is then contacted by Veritas to obtain authorization.

Veritas Genetics then contacts the listed provider via either secure fax or email and asks the provider to approve the test order requested by the consumer. A myGenome requisition form is sent to the provider with the requesting patient's first and last name and other demographic identifiers. The fields the provider is asked to provide includes first and last name, NPI (National Provider Identifier)

19 Carmen Ayuso et al., Informed Consent for Whole-Genome Sequencing Studies in the Clinical Setting. Proposed Recommendations on Essential Content and Process, 21 Eur. J. Hum. Genetics 1054 (2013); Eline M. Bunnik, A. Cecile J.W. Janssens, & Maartje H. N. Schermer, Informed Consent in Direct-to-Consumer Personal Genome Testing: The Outline of A Model between Specific and Generic Consent, 28 Bioethics 343 (2014); Eline M. Bunnik, A. Cecile J. W. Janssens, & Maartje H. N. Schermer, A Tiered-Layered-Staged Model for Informed Consent in Personal Genome Testing, 21 Eur. J. Hum. Genetics 596 (2013); Heidi C. Howard & Pascal Borry, Is There a Doctor in the House?, 3 J. Community Genetics 105 (2012).

number, a method for receiving the report (fax or email), date of signature, and signature attesting that they are the referring physician or authorized health care professional and that the patient voluntarily decided to have the Veritas myGenome test performed. Other nonrequired fields included practice name, practice address, email address, phone number, fax number, and indication of preferred methods of receiving a report. Accepted orders included valid payment for the test and provider approval. Orders with residences in New York state are not accepted, regardless of payment or provider approval status as the laboratory does not hold a New York State Department of Health clinical laboratory permit.

B *Study Cohort and Data Analysis*

We selected 500 Veritas Genetics' myGenome orders placed between May 2016 and November 2018 as follows. We excluded international orders from this analysis and orders that declined to participate in research for publication. Business to business myGenome orders (that is, concierge clinics or pilot programs) were also excluded, as these were physician-initiated and did not fit the scope of this analysis.

All remaining orders that were complete with regard to the required information were sorted to select the first 500 for further analysis. Information utilized for analyses included consumer US state, consumer last name, and ordering provider NPI number. The ordering providers' NPI numbers were used to extract ordering provider information from the NPI database's downloadable .csv file provided by the National Plan and Provider Enumeration System (NPPES) (last updated on December 9, 2018). A Python script was used to extract the following information from the NPI database .csv file: ordering providers' last name, provider credential text, business practice location address state name, provider license number state code_1, provider license number state code_2, health care provider taxonomy code_1, and health care provider taxonomy code_2. Ordering provider taxonomies were mapped to the corresponding Level I, Level II, and Level III (if applicable) classifications as provided by Version 19.0 of the code set, last updated on January 1, 2019 (maintained by the National Uniform Claim Committee (NUCC); http://nucc.org/). A reviewer then confirmed accuracy by manually entering the NPI number into the NPI registry (https://npiregistry.cms.hhs.gov/). A file was created for analyses (see Figure 18.1) where the last names of the consumers and ordering providers were removed and simply stated as "match" if identical (not case sensitive), and "no match" if not identical, in addition to the ordering providers' primary and secondary reported taxonomy codes, provider primary and secondary states of licensure, provider primary business location state, and consumer state.

If a consumer's state did not match their ordering provider's practice location state or their primary or secondary states of licensure, the reviewer performed a search in the consumer's state's board of registry of medical providers for the ordering provider

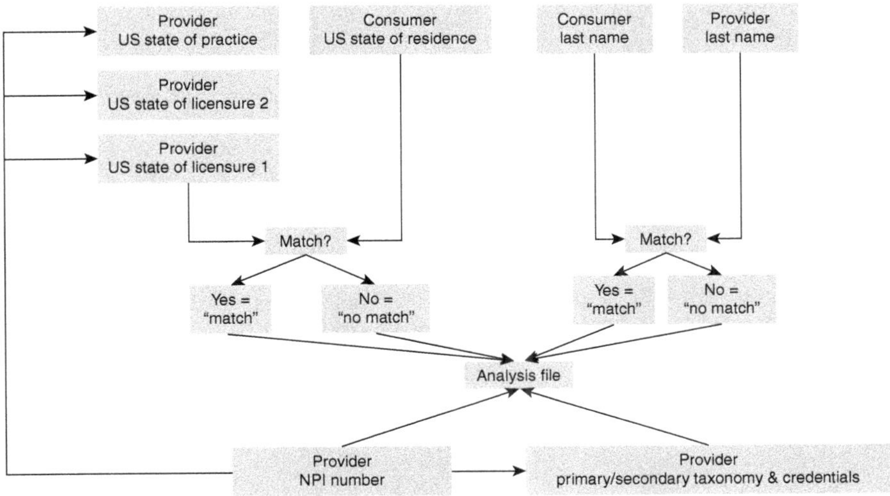

FIGURE 18.1 Diagram of analysis file creation

in question. If the provider was listed as an actively licensed health care provider, then it was recorded as "match." If not, it was recorded as "no match."

All data were collected and analyzed in a de-identified aggregate format with Institutional Review Board (IRB) approval or were available in publicly available datasets. Demographic characteristics were analyzed in Microsoft Excel (2018). Descriptive statistics of the demographic characteristics consisted of counts and percentages for categorical variables.

C *Results*

Ordering provider specialties ("taxonomies") were grouped into "expected" and "unexpected" areas of practice (Figure 18.2 and Table 18.1). These groupings were based on the expected ability of the ordering provider to interpret genetic results or the health status of the patient. Areas of practice categorized as "expected" reflect primary care or genetic specialties and included: family medicine (no level III specialty), geriatric medicine, general practice, internal medicine (no level III specialty), preventive medicine, and medical genetics. Nurse practitioners and physician assistants were all in primary care-like specialties and were grouped under "expected." Overall, genetics providers were not utilized often (1.6 percent, n=8), which is unsurprising given that these providers typically serve individuals with genetic disease and are therefore inaccessible to healthy consumers. Because the test is intended for generally healthy individuals, physicians with disease specializations were counted as "unexpected" providers. Additionally, n=10 (2.0 percent) of ordering providers reported a taxonomy of "174400000X" which corresponds to a level II classification

TABLE 18.1 *Top five specialty areas categorized as "unexpected" ordering providers*

Level II taxonomy	n	% of total orders (N=500)
Internal medicine* *(with level III specialty)*	40	8.0%
Psychiatry & neurology	22	4.4%
Ophthalmology	10	2.0%
Pediatrics	10	2.0%
Obstetrics & gynecology	9	1.8%

* *Level III specialties included the following: advanced heart failure and transplant cardiology; cardiovascular disease/medicine; clinical cardiac electrophysiology; critical care medicine; endocrinology, diabetes and metabolism; gastroenterology; hematology and oncology; infectious disease; interventional cardiology; nephrology; pulmonary disease; rheumatology; sleep medicine.*

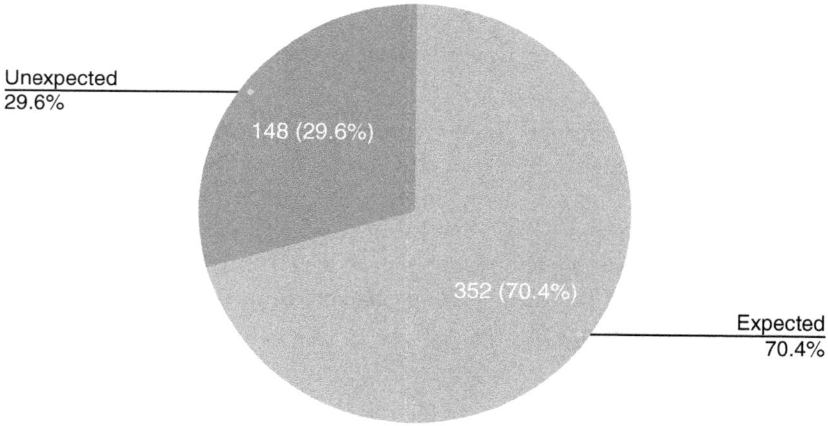

FIGURE 18.2 Ordering provider areas of practice

of "Specialist," which was grouped into "unexpected." Because there was no specific disease area, it was excluded from Table 18.1. While pediatrics is also considered primary care, we categorized it as "unexpected" for this analysis as the test order required individuals to be at least eighteen years of age, and therefore most consumers are expected to have transitioned out of the pediatrician's care by that point.

Most orders were approved by medical doctors and doctors of osteopathic medicine (MDs, DOs: n=464; 92.8 percent). The remaining ordering providers are displayed in Table 18.2.

Additional analyses revealed that n=53 (10.6 percent) of the orders were from providers who did not appear to provide medical care in the consumer's state of residence (as judged by their office address and state licensures). Finally, we observed that n=31 (6.2 percent) of providers had a last name identical with the

TABLE 18.2 *Non-MD/DO ordering provider credentials (degree)*

Credentials (Degree)	*n*	% of total orders (N=500)
Nurse Practitioner (NP)	17	3.4%
Physician's Assistant (PA)	9	1.8%
Doctor of Naturopathy/Doctor of Naturopathic Medicine (ND, NMD)	5	1.0%
Doctor of Dental Surgery (DDS)	2	1.0%
Doctor of Chiropractic (DC)	2*	0.4%*

* *Note:* one provider had both DC & ND credentials. For this table, we categorized it as DC.

consumer's last name they were providing test authorization for, raising the possibility that these are physicians who ordered for family members.

IV DISCUSSION

Our analysis of Veritas' myGenome orders provides insight to the characteristics of providers who are willing to provide approval for physician-mediated WGS.

Our analysis showed that contrary to the medical setting, genetic providers are rarely included in the initial ordering process of elective WGS (1.6 percent, n=8) and that primary-care-like providers are providing a majority of test authorizations. Anecdotally, Veritas' genetic counselors had spoken to many consumers who had ordered genetic testing for diagnostic purposes (to reveal a genetic etiology for symptoms) using their specialty provider. Nearly a third of the orders were from specialists (29.6 percent, n=148; see Table 18.1), therefore we suspect that a portion may have been involved in the care of a consumer searching for a genetic diagnosis. While genetic testing may have been indicated, the myGenome test itself is not designed to search for and report putative causes for disease, and therefore is not the correct test for the scenario. Board-certified genetic professionals have the expertise to differentiate between the genetic tests and would have selected a different genetic test for these consumers, however, their services were either inaccessible or were not sought after. This may be due to current wait times in genetics clinics acting as a barrier preventing consumers obtaining a test order through a genetic professional. There is an active effort in the community to increase accessibility by increasing the number of trained professionals, in addition to adopting alternative service delivery models for pre- and post-test counseling.[20] These alternative services could be expanded to PMCD genetic testing.

[20] Hoskovec et al., supra note 12; Stephanie Cohen et al., Analysis of Advantages, Limitations, and Barriers of Genetic Counseling Service Delivery Models, 25 J. Genetic Counseling 1010 (2016).

Because of the nature of the test (elective, consumer-driven), we expected primary care-like providers to provide the majority of test authorizations and indeed found that the majority of providers appear to be in a primary care-like specialty (n=344; 68.8 percent). However, primary care providers often lack adequate genetic training to provide pre-test information, which likely impacts the informed consent process. The concept of genomic screening at a population level has been under discussion since the availability of large-scale genetic testing. Primary care providers are expected to be involved in the process if such screening is to be implemented and it has been shown even recently that many feel unprepared. A recent review of genomic education initiatives found that there has been an effort to utilize creative approaches through immersive and experiential learning, interdisciplinary and interprofessional education, and electronic and web-based methods.[21] There are also third party physician networks that are offering test authorization services, who can also play a role in informed consent. This provides a basis for targeted education efforts regarding population WGS screening tests and reviewing of the genetic test ordering process as a whole.

Another potential area of improvement is the informed consent procedure for consumers. Veritas' in-house genetic counselors providing post-test counseling have anecdotally encountered several consumers that had not been adequately informed of the test limitations, which were expected to be reviewed and outlined during the informed consent process before pursuing testing. Educational videos and resources have been developed and are available on the website where the order is placed, however, they are underutilized. For example, the education video explaining possible risks of genetic testing was only viewed 541 times from June 2017 through August 2019.[22] While alternative consenting models have been proposed, it is unknown how or if these models are used for PMCD genetic testing.[23] It is clear that the commercialization of genetic testing has added a twist to the traditional process of ordering a medical test. As genetic tests become more widespread and consumers gain increased access, it is an important area needing monitoring for all stakeholders including health care providers, laboratories, and consumers.

To further complicate the ethical and legal considerations of health care providers authorizing PMCD genetic testing, our data have revealed that there are a small number of ordering providers in chiropractic or naturopathic medicine (n=7; 1.42 percent). Veritas does not actively market its genomic screening test to physicians outside of primary care specialties. In fact, inquiries from providers or

[21] Caryn Kseniya Rubanovich et al., Physician Preparedness for Big Genomic Data: A Review of Genomic Medicine Education Initiatives in the United States, 27 Hum. Molecular Genetics R250 (2018).

[22] Veritas FAQ: What are the possible risks of genetic testing?, YouTube (Jun. 14, 2017), https://youtu.be/pPokp3mDN4g.

[23] Bunnik et al., Informed Consent, supra note 19; Gail E. Henderson et al., The Challenge of Informed Consent and Return of Results in Translational Genomics: Empirical Analysis and Recommendations, 42 J.L. Med. & Ethics 344 (2014).

consumers with intent to use the test for purposes outside of preventive screening purposes are heavily discouraged from ordering the test. These data, along with the anecdotal inquiry experiences of the clinical and customer service teams at Veritas, suggest that there is a need for re-education regarding genetic tests for health care providers in complementary and alternative medicine. While these health care providers are a minority of the orders represented here, they may also cause the greatest amount of harm regarding result misinterpretation.

Naturopaths utilizing genetic testing in the context of recommending nutritional supplements to consumers have been scrutinized in the media.[24] The Association of Professors of Human and Molecular Genetics has developed curricula for medical doctors, which were updated in 2013,[25] however, other nongenetic professionals have largely been ignored regarding education efforts. According to the National Board of Chiropractic Examiners, 4 percent of the certification exam includes is devoted to chromosomal disorders, inborn errors of metabolism, and congenital disorders.[26] However, it does not assess the understanding of the rationale for ordering genetic tests, result interpretation, or any other forms of medical genetics. While the Council on Naturopathic Medical Education handbook of accreditation states that accredited schools and programs must include coursework on genetics, there is no information as to what aspects of genetics are needed in the curricula.[27] Furthermore, the chiropractic and naturopathic scope of practices highly differ between state licensures.[28] This evidence suggests that this is an area in need of further discussion and regulation.

Our study also showed that nearly one third of providers were either MDs or DOs in highly specialized disease areas, or were non-physicians without formal genetic training (Table 18.2, n=148; 29.6 percent). Reasons may include consumers pursuing testing for diagnostic purposes, such as uncovering etiologies of existing conditions. It is also possible that these ordering providers were not intending to use this test for diagnostic purposes, and were simply satisfying the wishes of their patients. For example, if an oncologist was ordering the test for a patient with breast cancer and was suspicious of a pathogenic *BRCA1/2* variant being the cause, the Veritas' elective WGS test would have a residual risk of >10 percent due to the limitations of the

24 Britt Marie Hermes, How Your Genetic Sequence Can Be Exploited By the Supplement Industry, Forbes (Nov. 14, 2016), https://www.forbes.com/sites/brittmariehermes/2016/11/14/genetic-sequence-exploited-supplement-industry/#1e79011a2e67.

25 Association of Professors of Human and Molecular Genetics, Medical school core curriculum in genetics 2013, https://adebf24d-d0c7-4842-b28b-a002a216f521.filesusr.com/ugd/3a7b87_e338afb6862747c7b6c6f9183d086a7b.pdf.

26 Part I Test Plan, Nat'l Board of Chiropractic Examiners, https://mynbce.org/prepare/part-i/part-i-test-plan/ (last visited Nov 1, 2020).

27 Council on Naturopathic Medical Education, https://cnme.org/ (last visited Mar. 1, 2019).

28 Mabel Chang, The Chiropractic Scope of Practice in the United States: A Cross-Sectional Survey, 37 J. Manipulative & Physiological Therapeutics 363 (2014); Sara A. Fleming & Nancy C. Gutknecht, Naturopathy and the Primary Care Practice, 37 Primary Care 119 (2010).

technology and filtering criteria. Meanwhile, comprehensive tests for *BRCA1/2* variants are available at the fraction of the cost of Veritas' elective WGS test.

We also speculate that there are providers who authorized tests for their friends and family, as approximated by the last name analysis which revealed that 6.2 percent (n=31) of all orders had identical provider and consumer last names. While providers are promoting access to genetic tests by being available for their friends and family, it may not be ethically responsible, as the AMA recommends against the treatment of friends and family because health care providers may struggle with objectivity and preserving patient autonomy when providing care for their friends and family.[29] The informed consent process typically includes discussion about familial relation implications which has potential to be severely impacted if it is a family member explaining these intricacies. It may also be difficult for providers to be objective when explaining the benefits and risks of genetic testing to a family member, as it inherently also provides benefits and risks for the provider themselves and their relatives. It is unclear whether the ordering providers who are relatives of the consumer were aware of the possible implications on familial relations, or if the consumers were unaware as well. Further studies may investigate physician opinions on consumer-initiated genetic testing and the considerations of authorizing genetic tests for friends and family.

V LIMITATIONS

The consumer and ordering provider last name identical match was used as an approximation for determining the number of orders approved by consumers' relatives. This may be influenced by common names, in addition to inaccurate spellings and typos during the ordering process. Additionally, there may also be consumer relatives acting as ordering providers with different or alternate last names.

Another limitation is that we only pulled the ordering providers' primary and secondary health care taxonomies. As these taxonomies are self-reported by the ordering providers while applying for an NPI number, it is possible that the taxonomies were not updated, or the ordering provider did not provide a taxonomy that was most relevant to their primary area of practice.[30]

We acknowledge that the data presented is not representative of the general population, due to the product being commercially priced at $999 out-of-pocket cost for consumers. Furthermore, consumers needed to have access to the internet in order to place the order and to have valid card payment. We did not collect the socioeconomic status (SES) data of the consumers, and are therefore unable to assess the SES of the consumers. Therefore, health care providers authorizing

29 Code of Medical Ethics Opinion 1.2.1, https://www.ama-assn.org/delivering-care/ethics/treating-self-or-family (last visited Nov. 1, 2020).

30 Taxonomy, Centers for Medicare & Medicaid Services (Feb. 11, 2020), https://www.cms.gov/medicare/provider-enrollment-and-certification/medicareprovidersupenroll/taxonomy.html.

PMCD genetic testing may vary depending on the cost of the test and the scope of the test ordered, and these results may not apply to all consumer-driven tests. Additionally, consumers with primary residences in New York state were unable to order the test.

Finally, our analyses are only able to provide insight to the demographics of health care providers authorizing PMCD genetic testing. We are unable to provide data regarding the providers who are returning results to consumers, or if the ordering providers are the consumer's true primary care provider. While the state concordance rates may provide a general estimation, it is under the assumption that a primary care provider practices or holds licensure in the same state as the consumer. However, we understand that consumers may utilize practitioners in neighboring states (for example, a consumer in New Jersey may obtain health care in New York). We were also unable to measure direct impact on informed consent.

VI CONCLUSION

This study provides data that is useful for policy-making decisions surrounding PMCD genetic testing. We have identified areas of concern that could impact proper informed consent for genetic tests, such as the practice of ordering medical tests for relatives and the prevalence of providers lacking formal genetic training ordering PMCD genetic testing. WGS is one of the most complex commercially available tests at this time, and therefore the presented data should be interpreted in this context. Based upon these initial findings and concerns, Veritas now provides a physician-of-record service through a third-party network of genetic professionals as an alternative. Utilizing this network alleviates the worries of result misinterpretation, however, it does not solve the issue of informed consent. Although pre-test counseling has been available, the uptake rate has been quite low. It remains to be determined whether these services prove to be of benefit to consumers. We encourage other laboratories, in particular, those utilizing the PMCD model, to consider review of "authorized requestor" demographics to evaluate whether interventions are beneficial for obtaining proper informed consent from consumers, and whether there should be concerns regarding inadequate genetic literacy for correct result interpretation. This characterization of health care professionals offering PMCD genetic testing provides a basis for evidence-based recommendations regarding the ethics of genetic testing, in particular, the regulations surrounding authorized requestors of such tests.

19

Privacy Best Practices for Direct-to-Consumer Genetic Testing Services

Are Industry Efforts at Self-Regulation Sufficient?

James W. Hazel[*]

I INTRODUCTION

In 2008, 23andMe was awarded *Time* magazine's "Invention of the Year" for a direct-to-consumer genetic test that provided consumers with insights into their "predisposition for more than 90 traits and conditions ranging from baldness to blindness."[1] In the decade that followed, dramatic advances in the sophistication and affordability of genetic testing and analysis resulted in proliferation of the direct-to-consumer genetic testing (DTC-GT) industry. Today, hundreds of companies offer a wide range of genetic testing services directly to consumers without the involvement of a health care provider.[2] More than twenty-six million consumers have flocked to these companies in an attempt to translate their genetic data into insights into their health, ancestry, physical traits, and lifestyle choices.[3]

The vast amount of genetic data generated by these services is becoming an increasingly valuable resource not only for DTC-GT companies, which are beginning to monetize that data through commercial partnerships, but also to academic researchers, citizen scientists, and law enforcement. These developments give rise to unique ethical, legal, and privacy issues. However, despite numerous potential

[*] The author would like to thank Ellen Wright Clayton and Christopher Slobogin for their support and constructive feedback on the manuscript. This work was sponsored by GetPreCiSe through a grant from the National Human Genome Research Institute, National Institutes of Health (#RM1HG009034).

[1] Anita Hamilton, Best Inventions of 2008, Time (Oct. 29, 2008), http://content.time.com/time/specials/packages/article/0,28804,1852747_1854493_1854113,00.html.

[2] See James W. Hazel & Christopher Slobogin, Who Knows What, and When?: A Survey of the Privacy Policies Proffered by U.S. Direct-to-Consumer Genetic Testing Companies, 28 Cornell J. L. & Pub. Pol'y 35, 47 (2018); Andelka M. Phillips, Only a Click Away—DTC Genetics for Ancestry, Health, Love . . . and More: A View of the Business and Regulatory Landscape, 8 Applied & Translational Genomics 16, 16–19 (2016).

[3] Antonio Regalado, More than 26 million people have taken an at-home ancestry test, MIT Technology Review (Feb. 11, 2019), https://www.technologyreview.com/s/612880/more-than-26-million-people-have-taken-an-at-home-ancestry-test/.

uses of these data and the wide variety of actors who might wish to exploit them, federal and state laws are often ambiguous about the types of disclosures that companies must make to consumers about how the genetic information they obtain is collected, used, and with whom it is shared. Indeed, recent studies reveal tremendous variability in the quantity and quality of information provided to consumers in the privacy policies and terms of service documents utilized by DTC-GT companies.[4]

In the summer of 2018, leading DTC-GT companies partnered with the Future of Privacy Forum (FPF) to develop *Privacy Best Practices for Consumer Genetic Testing Services*,[5] nonbinding guidelines for the collection, use, and sharing of consumer genetic data. The FPF is a Washington-based think-tank that "brings together industry, academics, consumer advocates, and other thought leaders to explore the challenges posed by technological innovation and develop privacy protections, ethical norms, and workable business practices."[6] In drafting the guidelines, the "FPF and privacy leaders at the companies incorporated input from the FTC, a wide variety of genetics experts, and privacy and consumer advocates."[7]

This article provides an in-depth analysis of the FPF's Best Practices and reports on a systematic assessment of whether, and to what extent, industry leaders have implemented the nonbinding guidelines. It explores the implications and potential shortcomings of this self-regulatory effort, including issues surrounding the use and sharing of de-identified genetic data (whether aggregated or at individual-level), ownership of genetic data, and the lack of robust enforcement mechanisms or avenues for consumer redress. Finally, the article proposes the FTC as a potential source of government oversight. The agency is perhaps the best positioned to achieve the right balance between oversight and industry self-regulation, such that consumer privacy can be protected without unduly inhibiting the personal, commercial, and research benefits that come from the flow of genetic information.

4 See, e.g., Hazel & Slobogin, supra note 2. See also Linnea I. Laestadius et al., All Your Data (Effectively) Belong to Us: Data Practices Among Direct-to-Consumer Genetic Testing Firms, 19 Genetics Medicine 513, (2017); Andelka M. Phillips, Reading the Fine Print When Buying Your Genetic Self Online: Direct-to-Consumer Genetic Testing Terms and Conditions, 36 New Genetics Soc. 273 (2017).

5 Privacy Best Practices for Consumer Genetic Testing Services, Future of Privacy Forum (July 31, 2018), https://fpf.org/wp-content/uploads/2018/07/Privacy-Best-Practices-for-Consumer-Genetic-Testing-Services-FINAL.pdf [hereinafter "Privacy Best Practices"].

6 Future of Privacy Forum, https://www.fpf.org/about/ (last visited Nov. 1, 2020).

7 Future of Privacy Forum and Leading Genetic Testing Companies Announce Best Practices to Protect Privacy of Consumer Genetic Data, Future of Privacy Forum (July 31, 2018), https://fpf.org/2018/07/31/future-of-privacy-forum-and-leading-genetic-testing-companies-announce-best-practices-to-protect-privacy-of-consumer-genetic-data/.

II THE FUTURE OF PRIVACY FORUM'S BEST PRACTICES

The following discussion is based on an analysis[8] of the privacy documents of the eight DTC-GT companies that were either involved in drafting the FPF's *Privacy Best Practices for Consumer Genetic Testing Services* (Ancestry,[9] 23andMe,[10] Helix,[11] MyHeritage,[12] and Habit[13]) or subsequently expressed public support for the guidelines as of January 2019 (African Ancestry,[14] FamilyTreeDNA,[15] and Living DNA).[16,17]

The Best Practices consist of eight principles designed to "promote transparency," "provide choices," and "enhance protections":

A. *Transparency*: Provide clear and complete information regarding the Company's policies and procedures for the management of personal data (personally identifiable information, Genetic Data, and protected health information) and de-identified information.[18]
B. *Consent*: Obtain express consent for collection, analysis, sharing, or reporting of Genetic Data.[19]
C. *Use and Onward Transfer*: Commit to collecting, using, and sharing Genetic Data in ways that are compatible with reasonable Consumer expectations for the context in which the data was collected.[20]
D. *Access, Integrity, Retention, and Deletion*: Provide the Consumer with access to their Genetic Data and inform the Consumer of what rights they have to correct or amend the record, how to report security concerns, and how long their Genetic Data and the original Biological Sample will be maintained.[21]
E. *Accountability*: Designate a responsible office or official who is accountable for the organization's compliance with the Privacy Principles.[22]

8 Company websites were reviewed for policy documents that described the company's practices with respect to the collection, use, and sharing of genetic information (for example, privacy policies or statements, terms or conditions of use, terms or conditions of service, and platform or research consent documents). All readily accessible policy documents were collected from company websites in January 2019 and analyzed using a grading rubric created using the FPF Best Practices as a guide.
9 Ancestry, https://www.ancestry.com/dna/ (last visited Nov. 1, 2020).
10 23andMe, https://www.23andme.com/ (last visited Nov. 1, 2020).
11 Helix, https://www.helix.com/ (last visited Nov. 1, 2020).
12 MyHeritage, https://www.myheritage.com/dna/ (last visited Nov. 1, 2020).
13 Habit, https://www.habit.com/ (last visited Nov. 1, 2020).
14 African Ancestry, https://www.africanancestry.com/ (last visited Nov. 1, 2020).
15 FamilyTreeDNA, https://www.familytreedna.com/ (last visited Nov. 1, 2020).
16 Living DNA, https://www.livingdna.com/ (last visited Nov. 1, 2020).
17 Privacy Best Practices, supra note 5.
18 Id. at 3.
19 Id. at 4.
20 Id. at 7.
21 Id.
22 Id. at 9.

F. *Security*: Maintain a comprehensive security program that is reasonably designed to protect the security, privacy, confidentiality, and integrity of Genetic Data against risks – such as unauthorized access or use, or unintended or inappropriate disclosure or breach – through the use of administrative, technological, and physical safeguards appropriate to the sensitivity of the information.[23]

G. *Privacy by Design*: Implement technological controls that support or enforce compliance with these principles in addition to policy, legal, and administrative measures.[24]

III ANALYSIS OF THE FPF'S BEST PRACTICES AND COMPLIANCE WITH THE GUIDELINES

Recent efforts by the FPF and leading DTC-GT companies to define best practices for their industry are a positive development. In the current environment, which relies so heavily on self-regulation, efforts such as these are important to advance the dialogue on privacy issues surrounding the use of these services. Overall, the drafters and early signatories to the Best Practices have adopted privacy policies that provide substantially more information and choice to consumers regarding the collection, use, and sharing of their genetic data than those currently used by the industry as a whole.[25] Yet, as the following analysis indicates, not only do the Best Practices have several limitations and shortcomings, but none of the eight companies examined appeared to be in full compliance with the guidelines.

It is also worth noting the limited scope of the Best Practices: the guidelines do not place any restrictions on the use and sharing of aggregated, de-identified information. Nearly every company had policies that permitted the broad use and sharing of aggregated data with third parties (for example, sharing with third parties for "any purpose" or for internal, business, and research purposes). The Best Practices do place restrictions on individual-level de-identified data.[26]

23 Id.

24 Id.

25 See Hazel & Slobogin, supra note 2 (surveying the privacy policies of ninety US-based DTC-GT companies in 2017).

26 The Best Practices do not place restrictions on de-identified information, "provided that the deidentification measures taken establish strong assurance that the data is not identifiable." Privacy Best Practices, supra note 5, at 3. The guidelines note that "currently, Genetic Data held at the individual-level that has been de-identified cannot be represented as strongly protecting individuals from re-identification, based upon existing deidentification tools and standards." Id. at 3.

A *Transparency*

A central tenet of the Best Practices is transparency. The guidelines call on companies to "[p]rovide clear and complete information regarding the Company's policies and procedures for the management of personal data (personally identifiable information, Genetic Data, and protected health information) and de-identified information."[27] All eight companies had prominent, publicly accessible privacy policies and terms of service documents that were fairly comprehensive and explicitly referenced the companies' genetic data practices, a marked improvement when compared to the industry as whole.[28]

But despite calling on companies to be transparent and adopt policies that are "clear" and "easy to read,"[29] the Best Practices do not define these terms or set specific guidelines such as readability requirements. As a result, early adoptees of the Best Practices continued to use lengthy privacy policies and terms of service documents that likely required a college reading level or above for full comprehension.[30] In addition, information relevant to compliance with the Best Practices was often spread across multiple policy documents and only three companies – Ancestry, 23andMe, and Helix – provided the recommended high-level overview preceding their full policy that contained the "basic, essential information about the Company's collection, use, and sharing of Genetic Data."[31]

1 Policy Changes and Transfer of Ownership

Each company reserved the right to change its privacy policies and terms of service documents at any time, but they differed with respect to the level of notice that would be provided to consumers. Notably, the Best Practices do not define "prominent notice" of changes or specify what constitutes adequate consumer consent to changes,[32] a shortcoming that raises serious concerns about the extent to which consumers are informed, and consent to, potentially

27 Id. at 3.

28 See Hazel & Slobogin, supra note 2, at 48–49 (finding that nearly 40 percent of the companies surveyed had either no posted privacy policy or no policy document that explicitly referenced genetic information).

29 The Best Practices state that "[p]rivacy policies should be prominent, publicly accessible, and easy to read. They should specify the Company's data collection, consent, use, onward transfer, access, security, and retention/deletion practices." Privacy Best Practices, supra note 5, at 3.

30 Privacy policies varied widely in length (from 900 to 9,705 words, with an average of 5,072 words) and had Flesch-Kinkaid Grade Levels ranging from 11.5–5 (corresponding to a college reading level. Terms of Service documents were generally longer (2,206 to 10,459 words, with an average of 6,598) and had Flesch-Kinkaid Grade Levels ranging from 12–7 (corresponding to a college or college-graduate reading level).

31 FPF Best Practices, supra note 5, at 3.

32 The Best Practices simply state that "[p]olicies should indicate that material changes will not be made without first providing prominent notice and obtaining Consumer consent before data is used in any manner inconsistent with terms initially provided." See id. at 3.

new and unanticipated uses of their genetic data. Changes to policies were generally said to become effective immediately or after a specified period of time (for example, thirty days), and continued use of the services by a consumer was typically sufficient to constitute consent to the changes. Less than half of the companies examined explicitly stated that consumers would be individually notified of material changes and/or given the opportunity to review any changes and choose whether to continue to use the services. And while all eight companies had policy provisions governing a transfer of ownership,[33] only six explicitly stated that a successor entity would be subject to the same commitments for genetic data and biological samples that were made under the preexisting privacy policy or terms of service (as called for by the Best Practices).

2 Transparency Reporting

Given the recent, intense interest surrounding law enforcement access to genetic information, it is applaudable that the Best Practices call on companies to regularly release transparency reports that describe law enforcement requests for genetic data or other personal information.[34] Yet only three of the eight companies examined in this study publicly released such reports (23andMe, Ancestry, and FamilyTreeDNA). An analysis of these reports indicates that to date, law enforcement requests appear to have been relatively limited and have focused predominately on nongenetic information (generally in the context of credit card misuse, fraud, and identity theft).[35] However, the accuracy of such reports has recently been called into question; during the course of this study, FamilyTreeDNA removed its most recent transparency report from its website after the *New York Times* revealed its cooperation agreement with the FBI. It is in the process of revising it to include details of that agreement, which was not initially disclosed to consumers in its transparency report.

B *Consent*

Another central tenant of the Best Practices is informed consent from consumers, which calls on companies to "[o]btain express consent for collection, analysis, sharing, or

33 See id. at 4.

34 The Best Practices call on "[c]ompanies [to] provide a public report describing requests from law enforcement for Genetic Data. Such reports should be made on at least an annual basis." See id. at 4.

35 The only evidence of compelled disclosure of genetic data to law enforcement comes from Ancestry's 2015 transparency report, which states that it provided such information in response to "a 2014 search warrant ordering [Ancestry] to provide the identity of a person based on a DNA sample that had previously been made public for which the police had a match. [Ancestry] disclosed information in response to that valid warrant." Ancestry 2015 Transparency Report, Ancestry, https://www.ancestry.com/cs/transparency-2015 (last visited Nov. 1, 2020).

reporting of Genetic Data"[36] and provide guidelines surrounding what information should be included in seeking the initial consent to utilize the services. The Best Practices also specify activities that require "separate express consent." The term is not clearly defined but appears to indicate consent separate from the initial consent to utilize the services.

1 Initial Express Consent

The Best Practices state that in obtaining initial express consent, companies must "clearly specify the uses of Genetic Data, who will have access to test results, and how that data will be shared."[37] Companies must also describe "inherent contextual uses" of data, such as "providing the specific genetic analysis product or service, data use for product and service review and improvement, or new product development."[38] Each company examined provided at least some information about each of these aspects of their data practices, although the level of detail provided about these activities varied significantly.

One key area surrounding initial consent where the Best Practices do not provide any guidance is the ownership of biological samples or the resulting genetic data or the appropriate scope of a company's rights and licenses to utilize such information. Although half of the companies explicitly stated that consumers retained ownership of both their submitted biological sample as well as the resulting genetic data, nearly every policy examined required consumers to grant the company broad rights and/or licenses that appeared to go beyond that which would be required to simply the deliver the services (for example, product development and commercialization).

2 Separate Express Consent

As noted above, a major area of ambiguity in the Best Practices is the ill-defined concept of "separate express consent," which the guidelines require for the onward transfer of individual-level information to third parties other than vendors and service providers (except when such disclosures are required by law). Although not clearly defined, the term appears to contemplate consent separate from the initial consent to utilize the services.[39] Under this definition, all eight companies appeared to require separate express consent for the requisite activities; companies generally explicitly stated that personal information, including genetic information, would not be shared

36 FPF Best Practices, supra note 5, at 4.

37 Id.

38 Id.

39 The Best Practices state that separate express consent will be required for: (1) "onward transfer of individual-level information … to third parties for any reason, excluding vendors and service providers"; (2) "incompatible uses of Genetic Data"; and (3) "Consumers or organizations that submit biological samples or Genetic Data on behalf of other individuals." See id. at 4–5.

with third parties without consent, followed by a list of exceptions (for example, service providers, commonly owned entities, and disclosures required by law).

But companies varied with respect to their policies governing the submission of samples on behalf of other individuals, a scenario that also requires separate express consent under the Best Practices. Several companies permitted individuals to submit samples from other people if the submitters had legal authority, including children. However, the Best Practices do not define what would constitute the recommended "reasonable steps" by a company to ensure that an individual is either the owner of a sample or has authorization to submit it on behalf of another person. Instead, companies appeared to rely on consumers to certify that they were abiding by the company's terms and conditions with respect to the submission of samples on behalf of others (that is, none appeared to require verification).

3 Informed Consent for Research

The Best Practices are particularly ambiguous with respect to the level of consent required for transfer of consumer genetic data to third-parties for research activities.[40] Although the Best Practices state that separate express consent is required for transfer of individual-level genetic data "to third parties for any reason," the guidelines subsequently indicate that such data can be shared with third-party researchers with either "specific separate express consent or informed consent from the Consumer" (presumably as part of the initial consent to services).[41] The Best Practices also permit research use of genetic data without separate or informed consent if (1) such research is done under control of the company for purposes other than publication or generalizable knowledge[42] or (2) where such research has been "otherwise approved by an institutional review board (IRB) or internal ethical review process."[43] This limited definition of research, coupled with a lack of clarity surrounding what level of corporate ethical review would be sufficient to override consent, represents a significant shortcoming in the Best Practices.

Each company (with the exception of African Ancestry) had policies that provided for sharing of genetic data and other self-reported information with third parties for research purposes, generally described in a separate informed consent for research document. But despite the lack of clarity in the Best Practices, each of these companies, with the

40 The Best Practices require informed consent when "Genetic Data is transferred to third parties for research purposes" and when "research is done under the control of the company . . . for the purpose of publication or generalizable knowledge" (a definition that explicitly "excludes product development, quality control, or data processing to support inherent contextual uses)". Id. at 5.

41 Id. at 7.

42 Such as "product development, quality control, or data processing to support inherent contextual uses." Id. at 5.

43 The Best Practices note that an internal ethical review process might take the form of "corporate IRB, Consumer subject review board, or corporate ethics board[]" but do not provide specific details nor elaborate on what level of internal review would be adequate. See id. at 5–6.

exception of Habit (which had an unclear policy), required *separate* express consent from consumers before this sharing would occur (that is, consumers were provided the opportunity to opt-in before such sharing would take place).

4 Marketing

One of the more forward-looking aspects of the Best Practices is its restrictions on marketing based on genetic information in the absence of separate or initial consent and the ability to opt-out. However, the guidelines narrowly define marketing to exclude "provision of customized content or offers by the Company on its own websites and services." With the exception of African Ancestry, each company provided consumers with the ability to opt-out of certain marketing or "optional" communications from the company, although the extent to which consumers could do so or the underlying basis for marketing activities was often unclear.[44] Only Helix explicitly stated that it would not utilize a consumer's genetic data to promote its services or those of its partners.

5 Minors' (Under 18) Genetic Data

Scholars, medical professionals, and professional organizations have raised concerns surrounding genetic testing of children and adolescents.[45] The Best Practices prohibit marketing or offering services to anyone under the age of eighteen but allow parents/guardians to consent on a child's behalf. All but two companies allowed a parent/guardian to submit a sample or utilize the services on behalf of a minor or allowed minors to participate with the permission of a parent/guardian (and only one stated that parents should first obtain assent from the child). 23andMe and MyHeritage were the only companies that explicitly permitted a parent or guardian to consent to research use of a minor's data, both of which informed parents/guardians that they should first obtain assent from the child. Minors were generally defined as anyone under the age of eighteen, although a subset of companies indicated that parents could not submit a sample on behalf of a child under thirteen. And despite the Best Practices' call to provide a prominent method for minors to access their account once they reached the age of eighteen, only Living DNA did so.

C *Use and Onward Transfer*

The Best Practices call on companies to "[c]ommit to collecting, using, and sharing Genetic Data in ways that are compatible with reasonable Consumer

44 See id. at 6.

45 See, e.g., Jeffrey R. Botkin et al., Points to Consider: Ethical, Legal, and Psychosocial Implications of Genetic Testing in Children and Adolescents, 97 Am. J. Hum. Genetics 6 (2015).

expectations for the context in which the data was collected."[46] The guidelines specifically define third parties to which genetic information should not be disclosed, impose requirements on sharing with service providers and vendors, and specify the level of consent required for onward transfer to researchers (sharing with third parties and researchers, which is discussed in greater detail in the context of Consent).

The majority of companies explicitly stated that genetic data would not be disclosed to third parties prohibited by the Best Practices, such as employers and/ or insurance companies.[47] Interestingly, Living DNA noted that while it "do[es] not routinely share genetic information with [its] professional advisers," it reserved the right to share genetic or other personal information with its own insurer or insurance advisers. And while it is difficult to assess a company's actual practices with respect to service providers and vendors, all eight companies stated that vendors or service providers were bound by the same privacy policies and/or contractual agreements designed to ensure confidentiality of data.[48]

D *Access, Integrity, Retention, and Deletion*

Another important aspect of the Best Practices is guidelines surrounding the rights and choices that should be afforded to consumers regarding access, retention, and deletion of their biospecimens or the resulting genetic data. For example, the guidelines call on companies to "[p]rovide the Consumer with access to their Genetic Data and inform the Consumer of what rights they have to correct or amend the record, how to report security concerns, and how long their Genetic Data and the original Biological Sample will be maintained."[49]

1 Access

Each company, with the exception of African Ancestry, informed consumers of the ability to correct or amend personal information (that is, registration and self-reported information but sometimes explicitly defined to include genetic

46 FPF Best Practices, supra note 5, at 7.

47 The Best Practices state that "Genetic Data, by definition linked to an identifiable person, should not be disclosed or made accessible to third parties, in particular, employers, insurance companies, educational institutions, or government agencies, except as required by law or with the separate express consent of the person concerned." Id.

48 The Best Practices call on companies "to ensure that any vendors and service providers are bound to the same level as the Company's privacy commitments [and] policies" and "have no independent rights to use Genetic Data or other personal information outside the scope of their role in providing the primary product or service." Id. The guidelines also state that "[i]n the case of a Company ending or selling its business, it should either dispose of Consumers' Genetic Data and Biological Samples securely, or ensure recipient third-party commitments consistent with the original notices provided to the Consumer." Id.

49 Id.

information) and most allowed consumers to download their raw genetic data.[50] However, less than half of the companies lived up to the Best Practices requirement that companies should either provide consumers with the ability to assign a beneficiary to their account in the event they became incapacitated or deceased and/or implement a process for a successor to request access.

2 Integrity

The Best Practices state that "Genetic Data should be maintained at an industry standard of accuracy."[51] However, it is difficult or impossible to assess a company's actual practices with respect to the accuracy of retained genetic data based solely on an analysis of policy documents. Notably, all companies, with the exception of Living DNA, had policies that contained broad disclaimers about the accuracy/reliability of their services (often coupled with broad waivers of liability). The Best Practices do not speak to the acceptability of such waivers.

3 Retention

Company policies varied widely with respect to their retention practices for biological samples and the resulting genetic data.[52] Half of the companies analyzed – Ancestry, MyHeritage, FamilyTreeDNA, and Living DNA – stated that physical samples (for example, buccal swabs, saliva, or blood samples) would be retained unless the consumer requested destruction of the sample. Only 23andMe and African Ancestry had a default policy to destroy physical samples after analysis was completed, although 23andMe provided consumers with the opportunity to opt-in for storage of their physical samples by consenting to an optional Biobanking Agreement. Retention practices for the resulting genetic data were often much less clearly defined and also varied by company.

4 Deletion

All companies, with the exception of African Ancestry, described a process by which consumers could request deletion of their account, physical sample (for example,

50 The Best Practices state that "[c]ompanies should provide a method for Consumers to access their Genetic Data through the services." Id. The guidelines also call on companies to "[p]rovide a process for Consumers to indicate the handling of their account, such as granting access, deletion, and/or transferring account control, in case of death or if a Consumer becomes incapacitated; and/or . . . [i]mplement a process for a successor to request the transfer of an account." Id. at 7–8.

51 Id. at 8.

52 The Best Practices state that "[c]ompanies should set reasonable practices for Genetic Data retention and data minimization, taking into account the existence of active Consumer accounts, inherent contextual uses, and regulatory retention requirements Retention practices should address both the Biological Sample provided and Genetic Data." Id. at 8.

buccal swab, saliva, or blood), and/or the resulting genetic data.[53] The process varied by company and often differed depending on whether the consumer wanted the company to destroy their physical sample or the resulting genetic data. All seven companies with provisions regarding deletion of data and/or the destruction of physical samples informed consumers, with varying degrees of specificity, of potentially relevant limitations, such as retention pursuant to legal or regulatory requirements.

5 Law Enforcement Access

The Best Practices prohibit disclosure of genetic information to law enforcement without consent or valid legal process.[54] All eight companies informed consumers of the possibility of disclosure of personal information to law enforcement and indicated that they would do so only in response to a valid legal process (for example, a court order, subpoena, warrant or pursuant to a regulation). However, policies varied widely in the amount of detail provided about the process for dealing with such requests. Only 23andMe definitively stated that it had obtained a Certificate of Confidentiality from the NIH, which may shield certain research data from compelled disclosure to law enforcement.[55]

But the Best Practices are silent regarding a key emerging trend surrounding law enforcement access to genetic datasets: the submission of genetic information derived from crime scene samples to public and private resources, such as GEDmatch or FamilyTreeDNA, in an attempt to locate possible relatives of a suspect or to gain additional information about an individual.[56] Only three companies – 23andMe, MyHeritage, and FamilyTreeDNA – expressly addressed utilization of their services for such purposes: 23andMe expressly prohibited forensic uses in their terms of service, while MyHeritage permitted such uses with a court order and prior consent from the company. FamilyTreeDNA permitted the submission of samples "obtained and authorized by law enforcement," apparently without a court order, in order to identify

53 The Best Practices state that "[u]nless otherwise required by law, Companies should provide Consumers clear and prominent methods to delete their account and Genetic Data and destroy their Biological Sample, and describe any relevant limitations." Id. at 8.

54 In addition, the Best Practices state that "[w]hen possible, companies will attempt to notify Consumers on the occurrence of personal information releases to law enforcement requests [and] consider the feasibility of applying for certificates of confidentiality for relevant research." Id. at 8–9.

55 Certificates of Confidentiality, issued by the National Institutes of Health, may limit the ability of law enforcement to compel disclosure of personal information, including genetic information, that is collected and used in the context of certain research activities. See Certificates of Confidentiality (CoC) – Human Subjects, Nat'l Insts. Health, https://grants.nih.gov/policy/humansubjects/coc.htm (last visited Jan. 1, 2019); see 21st Century Cures Act, Pub. L. No. 114-255, 102 Stat. 1033 (2016).

56 Ellen M. Greytak, CeCe Moore & Steven L. Armentrout, Genetic Genealogy for Cold Case and Active Investigations, 299 Forensic Sci. Int. 103 (2019).

human remains as well as suspects in murder or sexual assault cases.[57] During the course of this study, FamilyTreeDNA revealed a cooperation agreement with the FBI and was subsequently removed from the list of supporters of the Best Practices by the FPF. The company has since modified its policies to allow consumers to opt-out of law enforcement matching but has not yet been reinstated as a signatory by the FPF.[58]

E *Accountability*

One of the key limitations of voluntary guidelines such as the Best Practices is the lack of a robust enforcement mechanism necessary to ensure that companies are held accountable for their privacy practices. Although the Best Practices outline a number of measures that companies can take to increase accountability[59] and encourage companies to "[p]rovide public/consumer facing commitments that are enforceable by the FTC, State Attorneys General, or other authorities,"[60] the guidelines do not specify best practices with respect to the avenues of redress that should be available to consumers nor do they speak to the widespread use of extensive waivers of liability or forced arbitration clauses. For example, each company, with the exception of Living DNA, had policies with broad clauses limiting the company's potential liability: five companies limited consumers to binding arbitration and both 23andMe and Helix stated that consumers may be responsible for attorney's fees and/or the cost of arbitration. This raises serious concerns about the extent to which consumers would have any remedy in the event of a dispute.

Furthermore, it is unclear whether companies will voluntarily adopt policies that could undermine their business models. For example, the Best Practices place restrictions on the analysis of samples submitted without the consent of the owner of the biological material, a guideline antithetical to the business models of the large number of companies that appear to permit or encourage individuals to submit the samples of others.[61] It is also unclear whether companies will be willing to make commitments that are not currently mandated under existing laws and regulations, especially ones that could potentially expose a company to unnecessary liability.[62]

57 FamilyTreeDNA, Terms of Service, https://www.familytreedna.com/legal/terms-of-service (last visited Nov. 1, 2020).

58 Connecting Families and Saving Lives, FamilyTreeDNA (Feb. 1, 2019), https://blog.familytreedna.com/press-release-connecting-families-and-saving-lives/; see also Matthew Haag, FamilyTreeDNA Admits to Sharing Genetic Data with F.B.I., N.Y. Times (Feb. 4, 2019), https://www.nytimes.com/2019/02/04/business/family-tree-dna-fbi.html.

59 FPF Best Practices, supra note 5, at 9.

60 Id.

61 See Hazel & Slobogin, supra note 2, at 48 (describing the prevalence of US-based companies offering surreptitious genetic testing services).

62 See Complaint, In re GeneLink, Inc. & Foru Int'l Corp., No. 112-3095 at 12 (F.T.C. Jan. 7, 2014), https://www.ftc.gov/system/files/documents/cases/140512genelinkcmpt.pdf.

F & G *Security and Privacy by Design*

It is difficult or impossible to assess compliance with Principles Six and Seven of the Best Practices – Security[63] and Privacy by Design[64] – based solely on a review of a company's privacy documents. Although all eight companies contained a "security" section or subsection in their policy documents, the amount of information provided ranged from detailed descriptions of security measures and protocols to broad assurances of security and confidentiality of data.

H *Consumer Education*

Finally, the Best Practices call on companies to "[m]ake available to Consumers resources that advise about the implications and consequences of genetic testing, research, and data sharing."[65] Yet policies varied widely in terms of both the quantity and quality of such information and in how it was conveyed to consumers. For example, 23andMe and Helix placed much of this information directly in their privacy policies and terms of service documents in addition to providing more detailed information on their websites. Others relied more heavily on consumers to seek out this information on their websites (from customer support pages, "FAQs," or other web-based resources).

IV DISCUSSION

Recent efforts by the FPF and leading DTC-GT companies to define best practices for their industry represent a positive development that advances the dialogue on important privacy issues surrounding the use of these services. The findings described in this article indicate that the drafters and early signatories to the Best Practices have adopted privacy policies that provide substantially more information and choice to consumers regarding the collection, use, and sharing of their genetic data than those currently used by the industry as a whole. However, as the preceding analysis indicates, none of the eight companies examined appeared to be in full compliance with all aspects of the Best Practices guidelines, which themselves have serious limitations.

A *Greater Role for the Federal Trade Commission*

In the absence of comprehensive federal privacy legislation in the United States,[66] the FTC is currently the agency best positioned to address the deficiencies in

63 See FPF Best Practices, supra note 5, at 9.

64 See id. at 9–10.

65 Id. at 10.

66 It is worth noting that state governments may also exert regulation on the industry in the form of specific restrictions on DTC-GT services. See Helen C. Dick, Risk and Responsibility: State Regulation and Enforcement of the Direct-to-Consumer Genetic Testing Industry, 6 St. Louis

ongoing industry efforts at self-regulation, such as the FPF's Best Practices, and to exercise additional oversight where these efforts fall short. Under the Federal Trade Commission Act,[67] the FTC has broad authority to regulate the privacy practices of companies offering DTC-GT, including the associated research activities involving DTC data.[68]

Despite calls by numerous advisory committees[69] and prominent politicians[70] for the FTC to exercise additional oversight of the DTC-GT industry, the agency has taken a relatively hands-off approach, instead relying on industry self-regulation. Although the FPF states that the FTC provided input during the development of the Best Practices, the agency has thus far declined to release its own guidance or best practices for companies that offer DTC-GT services, despite having done so in the context of similar industries (for example, mobile apps that provide health information directly to consumers).[71] Instead, the agency has chosen to release only consumer- facing educational resources about the potential privacy implications of DTC-GT and a short business blog post targeted at companies offering DTC-GT services.[72]

The FTC has the ability to shape the debate surrounding best practices for DTC-GT through its authority to generate reports and recommendations for Congress and the public. The FTC should use this authority to conduct, in coordination with

U. J. Health L. & Pol'y 167, 174–84 (2012). In addition, state data privacy laws, such as the California Online Privacy Protection Act (CalOPPA) of 2004 or the recently enacted Consumer Privacy Act of 2018, may also implicate companies offering DTC-GT Services. See, e.g., Cal. Bus. & Prof. Code §§ 22575–22579 (2004); Mark G. McCreary, The California Consumer Privacy Act: What You Need to Know, Law.com (Dec. 1, 2018), https://www.law.com/njlawjournal/2018/12/01/the-california-consumer-privacy-act-what-you-need-to-know/?slreturn=20190214145708.

67 15 U.S.C. §§ 45, 52–5.

68 15 U.S.C. § 45.

69 Sec'y's Advisory Comm. on Genetics, Health, & Soc'y, U.S. Dep't of Health & Hum. Servs., U.S. System of Oversight of Genetic Testing: A Response to the Charge of the Secretary Health and Human Services, 70 Fed. Reg. 17085 (2005), https://www.federalregister.gov/documents/2005/04/04/05-6614/secretarys-advisory-committee-on-genetics-health-and-society-office-of-the-secretary-hhs-request-for; Sec'y's Advisory Comm. on Genetics, Health, & Soc'y, U.S. Dep't of Health & Hum. Servs., Direct-To-Consumer Genetic Testing (Apr. 2010), https://osp.od.nih.gov/wp-content/uploads/2013/11/SACGHS_DTC_Report_2010.pdf.

70 Press Release, Charles E. Schumer, United State Senator for New York, Schumer Reveals: Popular at Home DNA Test Kits Are Putting Consumer Privacy at Great Risk, as DNA Firms Could Sell Your Most Personal Info & Genetic Data to All-Comers; Senator Pushes Feds to Investigate & Ensure Fair Privacy Standards for All DNA Kits (Nov. 26, 2017), https://www.schumer.senate.gov/newsroom/press-releases/schumer-reveals-popular-at-home-dna-test-kits-are-putting-consumer-privacy-at-great-risk-as-dna-firms-could-sell-your-most-personal-info-and-genetic-data-to-all-comers-senator-pushes-feds-to-investigateensure-fair-privacy-standards-for-all-dna-kits.

71 U.S. Fed. Trade Comm'n, Mobile Health App Developers: FTC Best Practices, https://www.ftc.gov/tips-advice/business-center/guidance/mobile-health-app-developers-ftc-best-practices.

72 DNA Test Kits: Consider the Privacy Implications, FTC (Dec. 12, 2017), https://www.consumer.ftc.gov/blog/2017/12/dna-test-kits-consider-privacy-implications; Direct-to-Consumer Genetic Tests, FTC (Feb. 2018), https://www.consumer.ftc.gov/articles/0166-direct-consumer-genetic-tests; Selling Genetic Testing Kits? Read On., FTC (Mar. 21, 2019), https://www.ftc.gov/news-events/blogs/business-blog/2019/03/selling-genetic-testing-kits-read.

other relevant government agencies (for example, the FDA and CMS), a systematic assessment of whether ongoing self-regulatory efforts and the existing regulatory framework afford sufficient protection to consumers of DTC-GT services. These efforts should incorporate feedback from a wide variety of stakeholders, including consumer and industry advocacy groups, science and technology experts, DTC-GT companies, and the public.

Given the limitations and shortcomings of the voluntary Best Practices, the FTC should develop additional regulations and establish binding requirements for the DTC-GT sector. Where appropriate, the Commission should utilize its authority to promulgate and enforce rules that "defin[e] with specificity acts or practices that are unfair or deceptive, and establish[] requirements designed to prevent such acts or practices."[73] Such rules might impose readability and comprehension requirements for the privacy documents governing DTC-GT services and/or establish mandatory disclosures about the risks, limitations, and consequences of genetic testing, data sharing, and research. Regulations might also clarify the requisite level of consent required for internal and external research activities, as well as address best practices with regard to ownership of biological samples and the resulting genetic data.

In the interim, the FTC should be more aggressive in bringing enforcement actions against DTC-GT companies that engage in unfair and deceptive business practices. To date, the FTC has been reluctant to bring enforcement actions except in cases of particularly egregious conduct.[74] Interestingly, reporting in the summer of 2018 (just prior to the release of the Best Practices) appears to suggest that "[p]opular DNA testing companies like 23andMe and Ancestry.com are being investigated by the FTC over their policies for handling personal info and genetic data, and how they share that info with third parties."[75] It remains to be seen whether these reports, apparently based solely on the agency's cryptic response to a Freedom of Information Act (FOIA) request, are accurate and whether the agency will take a formal stance on the adequacy of the industry-developed Best Practices.

It also remains to be seen what impact state-level data privacy legislation will have on the DTC-GT industry. While Congress debates national legislation, state governments are enacting sweeping data privacy laws with potentially significant implications for genetic data. For example, the California Consumer Privacy Act of 2018 (CCPA),[76] which took effect on January 1, 2020, places restrictions on the collection,

73 See Federal Trade Commission Act, FTC, https://www.ftc.gov/enforcement/statutes/federal-trade-commission-act (summarizing the responsibilities of the FTC under the Federal Trade Commission Act).

74 See, e.g., Complaint, In re GeneLink, Inc. & Foru Int'l Corp., No. 112-3095 (F.T.C. Jan. 7, 2014), https://www.ftc.gov/system/files/documents/cases/140512genelinkcmpt.pdf; see also Hazel & Slobogin, supra note 2, at 42–43 (describing the Genelink complaint in detail).

75 Marcus Baram, The FTC Is Investigating DNA Firms Like 23andMe and Ancestry over Privacy, Fast Company (June 5, 2018), https://www.fastcompany.com/40580364/the-ftc-is-investigating-dna-firms-like-23andme-and-ancestry-over-privacy.

76 California Consumer Privacy Act of 2018 (CCPA), Cal. Civ. Code §§ 1798.100–.199 (West 2018), available at https://leginfo.legislature.ca.gov/faces/billTextClient.xhtml?bill_id=201720180SB1121.

use, and sharing of personal information, including biometric data. The law defines biometric data as "an individual's physiological, biological or behavioral characteristics, including an individual's deoxyribonucleic acid (DNA), that can be used, singly or in combination with each other or with other identifying data, to establish individual identity."[77] New York is currently considering similar, even more stringent legislation in the New York Privacy Act[78] and other states seem posed to follow.[79]

V CONCLUSION

The FPF's "Best Practices for Consumer Genetic Testing Services" represents an important step forward in terms of self-regulation by the DTC-GT industry. However, it remains to be seen whether the nonbinding guidelines will be widely adopted across the diverse DTC-GT industry. Although the industry leaders involved in producing this document certainly occupy a large market share, they represent only a small fraction of the many companies offering these services. It is unclear whether companies will be willing to adopt policies that could undermine their business models or make commitments that are not currently mandated under existing laws and regulations, especially disclosures that could potentially expose them to liability. Therefore, it is likely that self-regulatory efforts such as the Best Practices will need to be coupled with appropriate government oversight. The FTC appears to be the agency best positioned to achieve the right balance between oversight and industry self-regulation so that consumer privacy can be protected without unduly inhibiting the personal, commercial, and research benefits that come from the flow of genetic information.

77 Id. at § 1798.140(b).

78 New York Privacy Act, S. B. 5642, 2019 Leg., Reg. Sess. (N.Y. 2019), available at https://legislation.nysenate.gov/pdf/bills/2019/S5642.

79 See, e.g., The International Association of Privacy Professionals, US state comprehensive privacy law comparison, https://iapp.org/news/a/us-state-comprehensive-privacy-law-comparison/.

20

Regulatory and Medical Aspects of DTC Genetic Testing

Catherine M. Sharkey, Xiaohan Wu, Michael F. Walsh, and Kenneth Offit

I INTRODUCTION

The recent Food and Drug Administration (FDA) marketing authorizations granted for testing mutations associated with hereditary breast and colon cancer,[1] as well as pharmacogenomic susceptibilities,[2] provide an opportunity to reexamine the medical as well as regulatory underpinnings of DTC-GT. In this chapter, we make the case for federal regulation of DTC-GT at two levels: protecting consumers/patients who access particular tests and building an informational environment for genetic testing that supports innovation in the aggregate.

II THE RISE OF DTC GENETIC TESTING

The rise of DTC-GT has been the result of a confluence of events, including increased Internet access to health-related information, the removal of intellectual property barriers governing germline DNA sequencing, minimally regulated entrepreneurism and consumer "empowerment," and – most significantly – technological advances in sequencing human DNA.[3] As the costs of genetic testing continue to drop,[4] DTC-GT is estimated to have

1 See FDA, DEN170046, Evaluation of Automatic Class III Designation for the 23andMe Personal Genome Service (PGS) Genetic Health Risk Report for BRCA1/BRCA2 (Selected Variants) Decision Summary (2018), https://www.accessdata.fda.gov/cdrh_docs/reviews/DEN170046.pdf [hereinafter FDA BRCA1/BRCA2 Decision Summary]; FDA, 510(k) Substantial Equivalence Determination Decision Summary (2019), https://www.accessdata.fda.gov/cdrh_docs/reviews/K182784.pdf.

2 See FDA, DEN180028, Evaluation of Automatic Class III Designation for the 23andMe Personal Genome Service (PGS) Pharmacogenetic Reports Decision Summary 17 (2018), https://www.accessdata.fda.gov/cdrh_docs/reviews/DEN180028.pdf [hereinafter FDA Pharmacogenetic Decision Summary].

3 See Kenneth Offit, The Future of Clinical Cancer Genomics, 43 Seminar Oncology 615 (2016).

4 See, e.g., Megan A. Allyse et al., Direct-to-Consumer Testing 2.0: Emerging Models of Direct-to-Consumer Genetic Testing, 93 Mayo Clinic Proceedings 113, 114 (2018).

reached millions of people.[5] More than 200 companies "offer some form of DNA test online."[6]

Nearly twenty years after mapping the human genome, next generation sequencing (NGS) provides a less costly means to accurately sequence inherited alterations associated with a number of diseases, including cancer.[7] As a result, geneticists are poised to decipher more efficiently the meaning of genomic alterations found from individuals' genomes.[8] Elucidating the significance of disease-causing mutations from normal variations, however, remains a work in progress.[9] While the costs of DNA sequencing have declined, because of the complexity of the human genome and of the biologic mechanism of diseases, the field remains in the era of "the $1,000 genome and the $100,000 interpretation."[10] Thus, while a DTC DNA sequence test may be inexpensive to perform, it may also be indiscernible and of unclear clinical significance.

Along with these technological developments, a landmark US Supreme Court decision, *Association for Molecular Pathology v. Myriad Genetics Inc.*,[11] facilitated the commercial embrace of cancer predisposition testing, with implications for other genetic tests. Whereas Myriad followed a "medical" model and developed educational materials for care providers as well as consumers,[12] the same is not true of all DTC-GT companies.

III MEDICAL BENEFITS AND RISKS OF DTC GENETIC TESTING

While DTC-GT products were initially developed to detect single nucleotide variations with little clinical significance offered under the rubric of "recreational" genomics, testing menus grew to include genetic health risks, carrier status, ancestry, wellness, and general traits, further challenging health care providers

5 See Antonio Regalado, 2017 Was the Year Consumer DNA Testing Blew Up, MIT Tech. Rev. (Feb. 12, 2018), https://www.technologyreview.com/s/610233/2017-was-the-yearconsumer-dna-testing-blew-up/; Our Story, Ancestry, https://www.ancestry.com/corporate/about-ancestry/our-story ("over 10 million people in its consumer DNA network"); 23andMe, https://mediacenter.23andme.com/company/about-us/ ("more than 10,000,000 customers").

6 Andelka M. Philips, Only a Click Away – DTC Genetics for Ancestry, Health, Love . . . and More: A View of the Business and Regulatory Landscape, 8 Applied & Translational Genomics 16, 17 tbl. 1 (2016).

7 See F. J. Couch, K. L. Nathanson & K. Offit, Two Decades after BRCA: Setting Paradigms in Personalized Cancer Care and Prevention, 343 Science 1466 (2014).

8 See, e.g., D. Mandelker et al., Mutation Detection in Patients with Advanced Cancer by Universal Sequencing of Cancer-Related Genes in Tumor and Normal DNA vs Guideline-Based Germline Testing, 318 J. Am. Med. Ass'n 825 (2017).

9 See, e.g., M. S. Cline et al., BRCA Challenge: BRCA Exchange as a Global Resource for Variants in BRCA1 and BRCA2, 14 PLoS Genetics e1007752 (2018).

10 See E. R. Mardis, The $1,000 Genome, the $100,000 Analysis?, 2 Genome Med.84 (2010).

11 569 U.S. 576 (2013).

12 See K. Offit et al., Gene Patents and Personalized Cancer Care: Impact of the Myriad Case on Clinical Oncology, 31 J. Clinical Oncology 2743 (2013).

to interpret findings provided to them by self-directed patients.[13] This has also spawned companies geared to interpret raw data for consumers,[14] with little or no regulation.

A *Benefits*

Testing for medical risks may be viewed as analogous to testing for "recreational" purposes, such as ancestry or specific traits like ear hair. Individuals seeking DTC medical and recreational genetic testing may perceive the benefits in similar ways.[15] Clinically significant results may be generated from DTC testing, allowing individuals to gain knowledge of risks pertaining to various diseases, and interfacing with a web portal provides ready access and a means for communication.

B *Risks*

The business model of DTC companies, which is based on testing as many individuals as inexpensively as possible, regardless of their actual risk for a disease in question, increases the risk for false reassurances. First, less expensive testing methodologies may miss genomic rearrangements or structural alterations that may only be detected by more complex tests. Second, there may be other genetic disease markers not included in the DTC test being offered. In a medical model, these concerns are addressed by regulation of test quality at the laboratory level, as well as by mandated provision of counseling services to interpret results, point out limitations, and recommend additional tests as needed.

The most recent FDA DTC genetic test market authorizations did not fully address false reassurances. Without undergoing traditional pre-test/post-test counseling, DTC-GT consumers may be falsely reassured they are not predisposed if the analytical validity[16] of the assay performed is insufficient.[17] With respect to the *BRCA1/2* test, individuals tested for Ashkenazi Jewish mutations may still be at risk for other breast cancer risk mutations not covered by the test. Similarly, individuals tested for *MUTYH* mutations, a very rare form of recessive colon cancer, may still be

13 See D.B. Pet et al., Physicians' Perspectives on Receiving Unsolicited Genomic Results, 21 Genetics Med. 311 (2019).

14 For example, for as little as $12, consumers can use Promethease to generate personal DNA reports based on their DTC test results. See Promethease, https://www.promethease.com/.

15 See, e.g., B. F. Darst et al., Characteristics of Genomic Test Consumers Who Spontaneously Share Results with Their Health Care Provider, 29 Health Comm. 105 (2014).

16 How Can Consumers Be Sure a Genetic Test Is Valid and Useful?, Genetics Home Reference (Mar. 17, 2020), https://ghr.nlm.nih.gov/primer/testing/validtest ("Analytical validity refers to how well the test predicts the presence or absence of a particular gene or genetic change. In other words, can the test accurately detect whether a specific genetic variant is present or absent?").

17 See Stephany Tandy-Connor et al., Advocating for the Consumer: Clinical Confirmation of All Direct-to-Consumer Raw Data Alterations Remains Critical, 21 Genetics Med. 760 (2019).

at risk for the more common forms of hereditary colon cancer caused by mutations in *MLH1*, *MSH2*, *MSH6*, *PMS2*, and other genes.[18]

Not all genomic variations in *BRCA1/2* from the human reference genome is cancer predisposing, and many variants of uncertain significance exist. Individuals undergoing DTC genetic tests may be unaware of these nuances,[19] and may interpret results falsely or inappropriately.[20] In the case of *MUTYH* testing, current medical opinion is that detection of one copy of this mutated gene does not increase colon cancer risk to the threshold of clinical actionability.[21] Thus, the FDA-authorized *MUTYH* DTC test may be analytically valid, but of no clinical validity[22] or clinical utility,[23] other than as recessive carrier screening for purposes of future reproduction.

C *Initial Clinical Impact Assessment*

Studies on the clinical impact of DTC-GT contain mixed results, but there are some concerning findings. One large study quantified the effect on consumer risk perception of cancer genetic testing information returned directly to consumers without clinician involvement.[24] Observations included a modest impact without extreme changes in perceived risk and a trend of diminishing impact with time, suggesting the ability of DTC-GT as it pertains to personal genomics to effect changes to cancer screening and prevention behaviors is limited by relatively small change in perceived risk. A later prospective longitudinal cohort study demonstrated that 27 percent of patients shared their genetic results with health care providers, 40 percent did not feel their results were important enough to share, and 37 percent reported not having time.[25] A meta-analysis failed to support DTC-GT as a means to motivate risk-reducing behavior.[26]

18 See Katerina Wells & Paul E. Wise, Hereditary Colorectal Cancer Syndromes, 97 Surgical Clinics N. Am. 605 (2017).

19 See Jenny E. Higgs et al., The BRCA2 Polymorphic Stop Codon: Stuff or Nonsense?, 52 J. Med. Genetics 642 (2015).

20 Direct to Consumer Genetic Testing and the Consequences to the Public: Hearing Before the S. Comm. on Oversight and Investigations, 111th Cong. 70–99 (2010) (statement of Jeffrey Shuren).

21 See Samir Gupta et al., NCCN Guidelines Insights: Genetic/Familial High-Risk Assessment: Colorectal, Version 3.2017, 15 J. Nat'l Comprehensive Cancer Network 1465 (2017).

22 Genetics Home Reference, supra note 16 ("Clinical validity refers to how well the genetic variant being analyzed is related to the presence, absence, or risk of a specific disease.").

23 Id. ("Clinical utility refers to whether the test can provide information about diagnosis, treatment, management, or prevention of a disease that will be helpful to a consumer.")

24 See Deanna Alexis Carere et al., The Impact of Direct-to-Consumer Personal Genomic Testing on Perceived Risk of Breast, Prostate, Colorectal, and Lung Cancer: Findings from the PGen Study, 8 BMC Med. Genomics 63 (2015).

25 See Cathelijne H van der Wouden et al., Consumer Perceptions of Interactions with Primary Care Providers after Direct-to-Consumer Personal Genomic Testing, 164 Annals Internal Med. 513 (2016).

26 See Gareth J Hollands et al., The Impact of Communicating Genetic Risks of Disease on Risk-Reducing Health Behaviour: Systematic Review with Meta-Analysis, 352 BMJ i1102 (2016).

IV CURRENT AND PROPOSED REGULATORY SCHEMES

Historically, the FDA has taken divergent approaches to regulate the DTC-GT industry.[27] In the early days of the industry, there were no clear regulatory mechanisms to assess the benefits and risks of specific DTC genetic tests, partially due to the FDA's decision to absent itself from oversight of laboratory developed tests (LDTs).[28] In the face of mounting public concern regarding the quality and reliability of DTC-GT, however, the FDA ordered several companies to stop marketing their health-related genetic testing services.[29] This shutdown led to criticism that the FDA was being overly cautious and stifling innovation.[30] Beginning in February 2015, the FDA granted 23andMe (the dominant health-related DTC-GT company) authorization to market a number of DTC genetic tests as Class II medical devices.[31] Recognizing the deficiencies of the traditional review process,[32] and perhaps conforming to the current deregulatory climate, the FDA seems to be embracing more flexible regulatory paradigms.

A *Traditional Premarket Approval or Clearance Processes for Medical Devices*

Under the 1976 Medical Device Amendments to the Food, Drug, and Cosmetic Act, the FDA has authority to regulate all medical devices. The FDA classifies devices into three categories based on the health risks associated with their use: Class I, low-risk devices subject to general controls; Class II, medium-risk devices subject to special controls; and Class III, high-risk devices subject to the premarket approval process.[33]

In Vitro Diagnostics (IVDs)[34] are regulated like traditional medical devices.[35] Certain IVDs categorized as LDTs, on the other hand, traditionally have been

27 See generally Catherine M. Sharkey, Direct-to-Consumer Genetic Testing: The FDA's Dual Role as Safety and Health Information Regulator, 68 DePaul L. Rev. 343 (2019).

28 See, e.g., Kayte Spector-Bagdady & Elizabeth R. Pike, Consuming Genomics: Regulating Direct-to-Consumer Genetic and Genomic Information, 92 Neb. L. Rev. 677, 727 (2014).

29 See, e.g., FDA, Doc. No. GEN1300666, FDA Warning Letter to 23andMe, Inc., http://www.fda.gov/iceci/enforcementactions/warningletters/2013/ucm376296.htm.

30 See, e.g., Robert C. Green & Nita A. Farahany, Regulation: The FDA Is Overcautious on Consumer Genomics, 505 Nature 286, (2014).

31 See Lists of Direct-to-Consumer Tests with Marketing Authorization, FDA (Dec. 20, 2019), https://www.fda.gov/MedicalDevices/ProductsandMedicalProcedures/InVitroDiagnostics/ucm624726.htm#list.

32 FDA Should Facilitate Lab Test Innovation, Craft Long-Term Regulatory Overhaul, Gottlieb Says at ACLA, GenomeWeb (Mar. 8, 2018), https://www.genomeweb.com/regulatory-news/fda-should-facilitate-lab-testinnovation-craft-long-term-regulatory-overhaul.

33 21 U.S.C. § 360c(a).

34 IVDs are defined in 21 C.F.R. § 809.3 as: "[T]hose reagents, instruments, and systems intended for use in diagnosis of disease or other conditions, including a determination of the state of health, in order to cure, mitigate, treat, or prevent disease or its sequelae. Such products are intended for use in the collection, preparation, and examination of specimens taken from the human body."

35 See Overview of IVD Regulation, FDA (Sept. 16, 2019), https://www.fda.gov/MedicalDevices/DeviceRegulationandGuidance/IVDRegulatoryAssistance/ucm123682.htm.

excluded from FDA regulation because they were viewed as "relatively simple lab tests and generally available on a limited basis."[36] Although it is not unequivocal whether all genetic tests are IVDs subject to FDA regulation (as opposed to LDTs subject to the FDA's traditional "homebrew" exception), the FDA has made clear that its LDT enforcement discretion policy does not apply to DTC genetic tests.[37]

B *Expedited* De Novo *Process*

The FDA's *de novo* review process, which opened a shortcut for DTC genetic tests, is somewhat in flux. The "direct *de novo*" process allows medical device sponsors to submit a *de novo* application in the first instance without a prior 510(k) "substantial equivalent" application.[38] Manufacturers of low-to-moderate-risk (that is, Class I or II) devices for which there is no existing predicate on the market can use this pathway to obtain preclearance.

Moreover, future 510(k) submissions may use devices authorized through the *de novo* process as the predicate.[39] Regulatory expectations for DTC-GT companies are patterned after the FDA's April 2017 market authorization of 23andMe's Genetic Health Risk (GHR) tests, which were submitted and authorized through the direct *de novo* process.[40]

C *Precertification Model*

In November 2017, the FDA announced that, seeking to adapt its regulatory scheme to the challenges of new DTC-GT technologies without sacrificing safety, it intended to provide a new review pathway for DTC GHR tests that would resemble its proposed precertification program designed for digital health products.[41] The precertification model would allow "manufacturers . . . to come to FDA for a one-time review to ensure that they meet the FDA's requirements, after which they may enter the market with new GHR tests without further review."[42] Under this firm-

[36] Laboratory Developed Tests, FDA (Sept. 27, 2018), https://www.fda.gov/MedicalDevices/ProductsandMedicalProcedures/InVitroDiagnostics/LaboratoryDevelopedTests/default.htm.

[37] See, e.g., Sidley Austin, FDA Challenges Direct-to-Consumer Genetic Tests, Law360 (2016), https://www.law360.com/articles/772679/fda-challenges-direct-to-consumer-genetic-tests.

[38] See, e.g., FDA, De Novo Classification Process (Evaluation of Automatic Class III Designation): Guidance for Industry and Food and Drug Administration Staff 4 (Oct. 30, 2017), https://www.fda.gov/downloads/MedicalDevices/DeviceRegulationandGuidance/GuidanceDocuments/ucm080197.pdf.

[39] See Evaluation of Automatic Class III Designation (De Novo) Summaries, FDA (Feb. 26, 2020), https://www.fda.gov/AboutFDA/CentersOffices/OfficeofMedicalProductsandTobacco/CDRH/CDRHTransparency/ucm232269.htm.

[40] See id.

[41] See Press Release, Statement from FDA Commissioner Scott Gottlieb, M.D., on Implementation of Agency's Streamlined Development and Review Pathway for Consumer Tests that Evaluate Genetic Health Risk, FDA (Nov. 6, 2017), https://www.fda.gov/NewsEvents/Newsroom/PressAnnouncements/ucm583885.htm.

[42] Id.

based approach, the FDA would review whether the manufacturer of DTC GHR tests meets FDA expectations for identifying genetic variants with accuracy, assessing clinical evidence to support claims of safety and effectiveness, and conducting user comprehension studies.[43]

It is unclear what specific measures will be used in such a precertification review for DTC-GT companies, but the current digital health precertification program might provide some insight into the FDA's thinking. The pilot precertification program for digital health products listed "product safety," "product quality," "clinical responsibility," "cybersecurity responsibility," and "proactive culture" as the five "culture of quality and organizational excellence principles" based on which companies would be evaluated.[44]

D *Third-Party Accreditation*

Former FDA Commissioner Scott Gottlieb touted third-party accreditation as "designed to reduce the burden on test developers and streamline the regulatory assessment of eligible innovative products."[45] The FDA recently accredited the New York State Department of Health (NYSDOH) as a third-party reviewer of certain IVDs.[46] Laboratories with such IVDs that have obtained NYSDOH approval do not need to separately file a 510(k) application with the FDA.[47] While the third-party accreditation programs do not currently include genetic tests,[48] it seems that they could be expanded. The NYSDOH, for example, is accredited to review submissions of NGS-based tumor profiling tests, which are used to detect mutations in genes obtained from tumor specimens.[49] NYSDOH determinations of analytical and clinical validity of inherited genetic markers, such as those promulgated by DTC companies, however, apply only to tests ordered on those living in New York. Nor, as of yet, has NYSDOH certification been used by the FDA as a model for other states or municipalities.

43 See Jeffrey Shuren, Remarks at the Fostering Digital Health Innovation: Developing the Software Precertification Program Public Workshop 19 (Jan. 30, 2018), https://www.fda.gov/downloads/MedicalDevices/NewsEvents/WorkshopsConferences/UCM600093.pdf.

44 See Digital Health Software Precertification (PreCert) Program, FDA (July 18, 2019), https://www.fda.gov/medical-devices/digital-health/digital-health-software-precertification-pre-cert-program.

45 Scott Gottlieb, Remarks by Dr. Gottlieb at the American Clinical Laboratory Association Annual Meeting, FDA (Mar. 6, 2018), https://www.fda.gov/NewsEvents/Speeches/ucm599551.

46 Press Release, FDA Unveils a Streamlined Path for the Authorization of Tumor Profiling Tests Alongside Its Latest Product Action, FDA (Nov. 15, 2017), https://www.fda.gov/newsevents/newsroom/pressannouncements/ucm585347.htm.

47 See id.

48 No class of devices under the "molecular genetics" category is eligible for third party review. See List of Devices for Third Party Review, FDA (Feb. 7, 2002), https://www.accessdata.fda.gov/scripts/cdrh/cfdocs/cfThirdParty/current.cfm?.

49 See Product Classification, FDA (Mar. 16, 2020), https://www.accessdata.fda.gov/scripts/cdrh/cfdocs/cfPCD/classification.cfm?id=5060.

E *The DAIA and the VALID Act*

Industry and the FDA concur that, rather than regulating diagnostic tests as traditional medical devices, the FDA should adopt regulatory frameworks specifically designed for diagnostics.[50] In March 2017, a bipartisan discussion draft of the Diagnostic Accuracy and Innovation Act (DAIA), covering all ICVTs and LDTs, was released.[51] Under the Act, IVCTs would become a new regulatory category, separate from drugs, biologics, or medical devices; the FDA would be required to establish a new center devoted to IVCTs; and test development and manufacturing activities would be under the FDA's exclusive jurisdiction, while CMS would have exclusive jurisdiction over laboratory operations, and the states would exclusively oversee medical use and interpretation.[52]

While the FDA conceded that "it is necessary to create pathways that are efficient and achieve reasonable assurance of analytical and clinical validity, without imposing unnecessary burdens,"[53] it put forth its own proposal. The FDA's proposal defined IVCTs more broadly to cover "test protocol," "test platform," and "software" used for the same purposes;[54] included its precertification model;[55] and replaced the "predicate device" concept that has been used in the medical device 510(k) clearance process with the new "test group" concept.[56]

The draft Verifying Accurate, Leading-edge IVCT Development (VALID) Act incorporates some of the FDA's proposals.[57] It makes explicit the FDA's authority to regulate IVCTs, including LDTs over which the FDA has historically exercised enforcement discretion.[58] While the VALID Act enjoys bi-partisan support in

50 See, e.g., FDA Should Facilitate Lab Test Innovation, Craft Long-Term Regulatory Overhaul, Gottlieb Says at ACLA, GenomeWeb (Mar. 8, 2018), https://www.genomeweb.com/regulatory-news/fda-should-facilitate-lab-testinnovation-craft-long-term-regulatory-overhaul.

51 Summary of the Diagnostic Accuracy and Innovation Act, U.S. Congressman Larry Buchson, M.D., https://bucshon.house.gov/sites/bucshon.house.gov/files/documents/daia%20summary.pdf; Turna Ray, FDA Recommends Precertification Program to Legislators as They Consider Dx Regulatory Reform, GenomeWeb (May 4, 2018), https://www.genomeweb.com/molecular-diagnostics/fda-recommends-precertification-program-legislators-they-consider-dx.

52 Id.

53 FDA's Views on the Diagnostic Accuracy and Innovation Act (DAIA) 1, available at http://www.fdalawblog.net/wp-content/uploads/2018/08/FDA-LDT-Draft-Leg.pdf.

54 Id. at 2.

55 See id. at 26–32.

56 Jeffrey N. Gibbs, FDA's IVD TA: It's Not Just Technical Assistance, FDA Law Blog (Aug. 14, 2018), http://www.fdalawblog.net/2018/08/fdas-ivd-ta-its-not-just-technical-assistance.

57 Available at https://www.genomeweb.com/sites/default/files/valid_act_discussion_draft_12.6.18.pdf.

58 See Legislators Release New Draft Bill Incorporating FDA Ideas for Diagnostics Regulation, GenomeWeb (Dec. 10, 2018), https://www.genomeweb.com/molecular-diagnostics/legislators-release-new-draft-bill-incorporating-fda-ideas-diagnostics.XnghHYhKi0o.

Congress, it has been criticized for increasing regulatory burdens and creating ambiguities.[59]

V EVALUATING THE FDA'S ROLES IN REGULATING DTC GENETIC TESTING

A *The FDA as Safety Regulator*

Even as the FDA signals a policy shift away from the protective model for regulating traditional medical devices, it has insisted on keeping its regulatory hand in oversight of DTC genetic tests. Concerned with the risks of "provid[ing] consumers with incorrect or misleading information that may be used to make health choices without the advice of a medical professional," "the FDA seeks to strike a balance that provides for an efficient pathway to bring these tests to consumers, without sacrificing the assurances offered by FDA oversight."[60]

One of the FDA's chief concerns regarding DTC genetic tests is that, without physicians as learned intermediaries, consumers may act on incorrect or misleading information to the detriment of their health and safety. With that consideration in mind, the FDA embraces direct consumer access to some types of health-related genetic information while maintaining stricter regulatory oversight over diagnostic and other more clearly medical results. While the FDA has not been clear on what constitutes a diagnostic test, in its April 2017 authorization of 23andMe's GHR tests, it suggested that "[d]iagnostic tests are often used as the sole basis for major treatment decisions, such as a genetic test for BRCA, for which a positive result may lead to prophylactic (preventative) surgical removal of breasts or ovaries."[61] However, this is somewhat perplexing in light of the FDA's March 2018 authorization of 23andMe's cancer health risk test that provides information on three out of more than one thousand known *BRCA1/2* mutations.[62] The FDA did nonetheless impose a "special condition for use statement(s)" to specify that "[t]he test does not

59 See, e.g., Allyson B. Mullen & Jeffrey N. Gibbs, A Summary of the Verifying Accurate Leading-Edge IVCT Development (VALID) Act of 2018 at 1, available at http://www.fdalawblog.net/wp-content/uploads/2019/01/VALID-Act-Summary.docx; Comments of Personalized Medicine Coalition on the Verifying Accurate Leading-Edge IVCT Development (VALID) Act of 2018, available at http://www.personalizedmedicinecoalition.org/Userfiles/PMC-Corporate/file/PMC_Comments_VALID_Act.pdf.

60 FDA, supra note 41.

61 Press Release, FDA Allows Marketing of First Direct-to-Consumer Tests that provide Genetic Risk Information for Certain Conditions, FDA (Apr. 6, 2017), https://www.fda.gov/NewsEvents/Newsroom/PressAnnouncements/ucm551185.htm.

62 See, e.g., American College of Medical Genetics and Genomics, AMCG Responds to FDA's Approval of Direct-to-Consumer Testing for Three BRCA Gene Mutations, http://www.acmg.net/docs/2018/ACMGRespondstoFDAsApprovalforDirect-to-ConsumerTestingforThreeBRCAGeneMutations.pdf; Turna Ray, Oncology Community Sees Potential for Patient Harm in FDA OK of 23andMe BRCA Test, GenomeWeb (Mar. 7, 2018), https://www.genomeweb.com/molecular-diagnostics/oncology-community-sees-potential-patient-harm-fda-ok-23andme-brca-test.

diagnose cancer or any other health condition and should not be used to make medical decisions."[63]

As an alternative to maintaining the diagnostic boundary line, the FDA could emphasize the risk-based classification for specific genetic associations. The FDA's regulatory framework for analyte-specific reagents (ASRs) could provide guidance. ASRs are used in certain IVDs and one of a handful of devices designated "restricted" by regulation.[64] The majority of ASRs were classified as Class I medical devices and exempted from the 510(k) premarket notification requirement. But the FDA classified a small number of ASRs as Class II or Class III devices because it determined that additional requirements were necessary for their safe and effective use,[65] even though, at the time, genetic tests using ASRs were "homebrew" LDTs not subject to FDA regulation.

The FDA's practice to date with respect to the authorized DTC genetic tests could be considered a rough attempt to do just that. Along with each authorization, the FDA established special controls to assure the test's accuracy, clinical performance, and labeling. For example, as part of its authorization for 23andMe's Pharmacogenetic Reports, the FDA set up six special controls, including a requirement that the labeling must warn the consumer not to "use the test results to stop or change any medication."[66] These controls serve as "risk management strategies" central to the FDA's assessment of the benefits and risks of the DTC test.[67] The FDA also took a further step to warn consumers more broadly about DTC genetic tests "that claim to predict how a patient will respond to specific medications."[68]

B *The FDA as Health Information Regulator*

1 The FDA's Traditional Role in Information Production

The FDA has long served an information production function. Rebecca Eisenberg pioneered the view that some of the FDA's drug regulation is best understood not only as safety regulation but also as incentivizing the production of data and information, and innovation policy more generally.[69] For example, the regulation prohibiting drug manufacturers from marketing off-label use, separate from any

[63] FDA BRCA1/BRCA2 Decision Summary, supra note 1.

[64] See Eric Richardson, FDA Small Business Regulatory Education for Industry: Medical Device Labeling 9, FDA (Sept. 29, 2015), https://www.fda.gov/downloads/Drugs/DevelopmentApprovalProcess/SmallBusinessAssistance/UCM466479.pdf.

[65] 62 Fed. Reg. 62243, 2244 (Nov. 21, 1997).

[66] FDA Pharmacogenetic Decision Summary, supra note 2, at 17.

[67] See id. at 15–16.

[68] See FDA Statement on Agency's Warning to Consumers About Genetic Tests That Claim to Predict Patients' Responses to Specific Medications (Nov. 1, 2018).

[69] Rebecca S. Eisenberg, The Role of the FDA in Innovation Policy, 13 Mich. Telecomm. & Tech. L. Rev. 345 (2007).

safety rationale per se, incentivizes manufacturers to submit additional clinical trial evidence to the FDA to obtain approval of the additional indicated use.

The FDA's information production function persists as well in the emerging regulatory framework for DTC genetic tests. In its 2017 final guidance on the *de novo* process, the FDA required manufacturers to "[p]rovide a summary of all non-clinical and clinical testing (if applicable) that provide a reasonable assurance of safety and effectiveness "[70] Indeed, the data requirements in the *de novo* process are more stringent than those required for the 510(k) review and "more closely resemble those for PMAs."[71] The FDA's authorization decisions regarding DTC genetic tests further attest to this information production function. As part of its authorization of 23andMe's pharmacogenetic tests, the FDA imposed special controls requiring "[d]ata appropriate to demonstrate the analytical accuracy and reliability of the device in intended use specimens, including but not limited to precision, reproducibility, accuracy, limits of detection, and interferences."[72]

Without the specter of FDA oversight, DTC-GT companies are not forced to provide, and therefore might not produce, underlying scientific data and information. The FDA, in its comments pushing back against the DAIA draft bill, voiced concern that the legislation would restrict the FDA's ability "to ask for raw data to further evaluate the analytical and clinical validity of these tests," even though it "could require pre- and post-market clinical trial data for high-risk IVCTs."[73]

2 The FDA's Enhanced Role in the Era of Big Data

Information production may be even more critical for DTC-GT than for drugs given the reliance of DTC genetic tests on the "robustness of genetic variant data aggregation."[74] 23andMe's practice illustrates the force of private market incentives in the development of DTC genetic tests and the accumulation of aggregate databases. 23andMe encourages its users to opt in to research studies in which users volunteer to answer questions about their personal and medical histories.[75] These companies either use the data in their

70 FDA, De Novo Classification Process (Evaluation of Automatic Class III Designation): Guidance for Industry and Food and Drug Administration Staff 16, https://www.fda.gov/downloads/MedicalDevices/DeviceRegulationandGuidance/GuidanceDocuments/UCM080197.pdf.

71 Michele L. Buenafe, Factors to Consider before Submitting a *de novo* Request, FDLI Update 11 (March/April 2017), https://www.fdli.org/2017/04/factors-consider-submitting-de-novo-request.

72 FDA Pharmacogenetic Decision Summary, supra note 2, at 16.

73 Turna Ray, FDA Recommends Precertification Program to Legislators as They Consider Dx Regulatory Reform, GenomeWeb (May 4, 2018), https://www.genomeweb.com/molecular-diagnostics/fda-recommends-precertification-program-legislators-they-consider-dx.

74 See Arti Rai, Risk Regulation and Innovation: The Case of Rights-Encumbered Biomedical Data Silos, 92 Notre Dame L. Rev. 1641, 1664 (2017).

75 See, e.g., Research, 23andMe, https://www.23andme.com/research (last visited Nov. 1, 2020)

own additional analyses or farm out the data to drug and biomedical companies.[76]

The accumulation of immense private genetic datasets by companies such as 23andMe poses a peculiar regulatory challenge for the FDA. The FDA may nonetheless be uniquely well suited to serve as a model for an experimentalist approach to health information regulation, especially in light of some nascent initiatives at the frontier of data aggregation and advanced analytics. The FDA launched the Sentinel Initiative, a national electronic system for monitoring safety problems with drugs, vaccines, biologics, and medical devices, relying on data from electronic health records, insurance claims, and other sources.[77] As the FDA noted, "the ability to share information in a public forum about why products fail, without compromising proprietary information, presents the potential to save companies millions of dollars by preventing duplication of failure."[78] More ambitiously, as part of its global product safety and quality strategy, the FDA articulated its intent "to develop a global data information system and network in which regulators worldwide can regularly and proactively share real-time information and resources across markets."[79]

In the genetic testing area, the FDA can leverage its regulatory authority to coordinate both the production and use of genomic information. Existing law does not provide any regulatory data exclusively for FDA-approved diagnostic tests – or for medical devices more generally. In this way, the policy environment differs sharply from that governing pharmaceutical drug trial data disclosure. In the absence of Congressional action, the FDA should consider stepping in to provide incentives to DTC genetic test companies like those contained in the Hatch-Waxman Act.[80] Scholars have proposed mandatory disclosure of proprietary information coupled with FDA-administered data and market exclusivities like those that are available for innovative drugs.[81]

VI CONCLUSION

A *The Necessity of the FDA's Oversight for Safety Reasons*

The FDA's traditional role as safety regulator should extend to the oversight of the DTC-GT industry. The varying levels of analytical and clinical validity in

76 See e.g., Kayte Spector-Bagdady, "The Google of Healthcare": Enabling the Privatization of Genetic Bio/Databanking, 26 Ann. Epidemiology 515, 516 (2016).

77 See FDA's Sentinel Initiative, FDA (Oct. 18, 2019), https://www.fda.gov/safety/fdas-sentinel-initiative.

78 See FDA, Driving Biomedical Innovation: Initiatives to Improve Products for Patients (2011), https://www.fda.gov/downloads/aboutfda/reportsmanualsforms/reports/ucm274464.pdf.

79 See Dara Katcher Levy, Pathway to Global Product Safety and Quality – FDA's Report Regarding Improving the Quality of Imports (June 23, 2011), http://www.fdalawblog.net/2011/06/pathway-to-global-product-safety-and-quality-fdas-report-regardingimproving-the-quality-of-imports.

80 See Anna B. Laakmann, The New Genomic Semicommons, 5 U.C. Irvine L. Rev. 1001, 1036 (2015).

81 See, e.g., Rebecca S. Eisenberg, Data Secrecy in the Age of Regulatory Exclusivity, in The Law and Theory of Trade Secrecy: A Handbook of Contemporary Research 467, 472–73 (Rochelle C. Dreyfus & Katherine J. Strandburg, eds., 2011).

health-related DTC genetic tests raise concerns about consumer safety. The risk-based classification approach is more suited than the precertification model to address risks inherent in DTC genetic tests.

Different genetic tests can pose unique risks to consumers, and the FDA is in an advantageous position to mitigate those risks through regulation. Risk-based classification gives the FDA precise tools such as special controls to customize its regulatory oversight. A firm-level precertification model, on the other hand, would not enable the FDA to directly address novel or unique risks associated with particular DTC tests.

B *FDA Authorization of Third Parties in Regulatory Practices*

One way to address concerns about the scarcity of resources within the FDA and the regulatory burdens on DTC manufacturers is to expand the third-party accreditation program to engage trusted organizations in the review process for DTC genetic tests. This would allow the FDA to structure the division of labor between itself and the accredited third-party reviewers more flexibly. An important step in this direction was the formal recognition by the FDA in December 2018 of the genetic variant information in the Clinical Genome Resource (ClinGen) consortium's ClinGen Expert Curated Human Genetic Data, which is funded by the National Institutes of Health (NIH), as a source of scientific evidence that can be used to support clinical validity in premarket submissions.[82] Such recognition acts to increase safety by increasing availability of information on clinical validity as well as pathogenicity of individual genomic variants, as vetted by over 700 geneticists and medical genetic stakeholder groups aiming to standardize clinical annotation and interpretation of genetic data.[83]

ClinGen and its variant database partner ClinVar play a vital role in curating genomic information in order to support genomic medicine and research.[84] However, these databases rely on voluntary contribution of data by academic and commercial laboratories, posing an additional challenge as laboratories vary substantially in their procedures for variant classification.[85] At least one laboratory which has attained FDA approval of a gene-based test as a companion diagnostic to identify patients newly diagnosed with ovarian and breast cancers has thus far not

82 FDA News Release: FDA Takes New Action to Advance the Development of Reliable and Beneficial Genetic Tests That Can Improve Patient Care, FDA (Dec. 4, 2018), https://www.fda.gov/news-events/press-announcements/fda-takes-new-action-advance-development-reliable-and-beneficial-genetic-tests-can-improve-patient.

83 See FDA Recognizes ClinGen Assertions in ClinVar, ClinGen (Feb. 1, 2019), https://www.clinicalgenome.org/docs/fda-recognizes-clingen-assertions-in-clinvar-frequently-asked-questions/.

84 See Heidi L. Rehm et al., ClinGen—The Clinical Genome Resource, 372 New Eng. J. Med. 2235 (2015).

85 See Julianne M. O'Daniel et al., A Survey of Current Practices for Genomic Sequencing Test Interpretation and Reporting Processes in US Laboratories, 19 Genetics Med. 575 (2017).

contributed data to unrestricted federally maintained genomic databases.[86] This laboratory has cited evidence that their proprietary databases are superior to the federally supported open access databases.[87] The FDA's role in mediating these disputes that bear on the public health is imperative to motivate DTC laboratories to carry out additional laboratory studies that may be required, for example, to inform and improve variant classification.

C FDA Participation in International Genomic Initiatives as Information Aggregator

Another initiative that addresses safety considerations in genetic testing calls for international cooperation in compiling genomic variant information.[88] For example, the BRCA Challenge is a long-term data-sharing project initiated within the Global Alliance for Genomics and Health to aggregate *BRCA1/2* data to support collaborative research activities.[89] The data set is based on shared information from existing clinical and population databases linked to a single point of access, with input from the international Evidence-based Network for the Interpretation of Germline Mutant Alleles.[90] The FDA is one of the founding sponsors of the BRCA Challenge. Continued – and more vigorous – FDA leadership of such efforts would serve a forward-looking role for the FDA as an aggregator of genomic databases to provide an alternative to the amassed datasets of private companies.

Such actions would also be consistent with previous initiatives of the FDA and HHS, which have previously contemplated a more prominent role for the FDA in coordinating public genomic databases. The idea of a Comprehensive Test Information System (CTIS) appeared in both the FDA's Technical Assistance to the DAIA[91] and HHS's Technical Assistance to the VALID Act.[92] HHS envisioned that CTIS would function as a centralized platform for IVCT information – it would amass data on analytical and clinical validity of "all tests being offered in the United

86 See Myriad Will Seek FDA Approval of BRAC Analysis CDx® as a Companion Diagnostic for Lynparza® (olaparib) in Men with Metastatic Castrate-Resistant Prostate Cancer, Myriad (Aug. 7, 2019), https://investor.myriad.com/news-releases/news-release-details/myriad-will-seek-fda-approval-bracanalysis-cdxr-companion.

87 See William Gradishar et al., Clinical Variant Classification: A Comparison of Public Databases and a Commercial Testing Laboratory, 22 The Oncologist 797 (2017).

88 See Juli M. Bollinger et al., BRCA1/2 Variant Data-Sharing Practices, 47 J. L. Med. & Ethics 88 (2019).

89 See Melissa S. Cline et al., BRCA Challenge: BRCA Exchange as a Global Resource for Variants in BRCA1 and BRCA2, 14 PLoS Genetics e1007752 (2018).

90 See id.

91 See FDA's views on the Diagnostic Accuracy and Innovation Act (DAIA) 4 (Aug. 3, 2018), http://www.fdalawblog.net/wp-content/uploads/2018/08/FDA-LDT-Draft-Leg.pdf.

92 See Department of Health and Human Resources, Technical Assistance on VALID Act of 2018 at 1 (Apr. 5, 2019).

States" and make the data publicly available to benefit patients, health care providers, and test manufacturers.[93]

D *Final Conclusion*

The FDA's dual regulatory purpose is even more compelling for genetic testing than for conventional drugs and devices. Genetic testing is inherently informational, such that the value of a given product (and the ability to assure its safety and effectiveness) is closely tied to the amount and reliability of background genetic information. While the FDA's role in overseeing information production is a necessary and required first step, genomic information that is incorrectly interpreted or applied may not improve (or may damage) the public health. In the case of pharmacogenomic testing for cancer therapy, for example, clinical utility must be assessed by medical professional guidelines and scholarly analyses, which have thus far shown uncertain efficacy for the clinical application of many common pharmacogenomic tests to predict treatment outcome.[94]

Moreover, "as the big data industry matures, the companies that traffic in health-related big data will face competitive pressures to make more aggressive claims regarding what their analytics can predict."[95] DTC-GT has medical as well as non-medical applications and consequences. As DTC testing is increasingly offered outside the context of an established, physician-led health care system, it is even more critical to consider protections in place against the long-term effects of genetic entrepreneurship.

93 Id. at 1–2.
94 Daniel L. Hertz & James Rae, Pharmacogenetics of Cancer Drugs, 66 Ann. Rev. Med. 65 (2015).
95 Nathan Cortez, Substantiating Big Data in Health Care, 14 ISJLP 61, 62 (2017).